A History of Byzantium

Blackwell History of the Ancient World

This series provides a new narrative history of the ancient world, from the beginnings of civilization in the ancient Near East and Egypt to the fall of Constantinople. Written by experts in their fields, the books in the series offer authoritative accessible surveys for students and general readers alike.

Published

A History of Byzantium
Timothy E. Gregory

A History of the Ancient Near East
Marc Van De Mieroop

In Preparation

A History of Ancient Egypt
David O'Connor

A History of the Persian Empire
Christopher Tuplin

A History of the Archaic Greek World
Jonathan Hall

A History of the Classical Greek World
P. J. Rhodes

A History of the Hellenistic World
Malcolm Errington

A History of the Roman Republic
John Rich

A History of the Roman Empire
Michael Peachin

A History of the Later Roman Empire, AD 284–622
Stephen Mitchell

A History of Byzantium

Timothy E. Gregory

Blackwell
Publishing

© 2005 by Timothy E. Gregory

BLACKWELL PUBLISHING
350 Main Street, Malden, MA 02148-5020, USA
9600 Garsington Road, Oxford OX4 2DQ, UK
550 Swanston Street, Carlton, Victoria 3053, Australia

First published 2005 by Blackwell Publishing Ltd

5   2007

Library of Congress Cataloging in Publication Data

Gregory, Timothy E.
   A history of Byzantium / Timothy E. Gregory.
      p. cm. — (Blackwell history of the ancient world)
   Includes bibliographical references.
   ISBN 978-0-631-23512-5 (hardback : alk. paper)—ISBN 978-0-631-23513-2 (pbk. : alk. paper)
1. Byzantine Empire—History.   I. Title.   II. Series.

DF552.G68 2005
949.5′02—dc22

2004012925

A catalogue record for this title is available from the British Library.

Set in 10½/12½ pt Plantin
by Graphicraft Ltd, Hong Kong
Printed and bound in India
by Replika Press Pvt. Ltd

The publisher's policy is to use permanent paper from mills that operate a sustainable forestry policy, and which has been manufactured from pulp processed using acid-free and elementary chlorine-free practices. Furthermore, the publisher ensures that the text paper and cover board used have met acceptable environmental accreditation standards.

For further information on
Blackwell Publishing, visit our website:
www.blackwellpublishing.com

Contents

Figures

Maps

Boxes

Preface

This is a book on the history of the Byzantine Empire, one of the longest-lived and most important cultures in Western civilization, but also one of the least understood. The book is meant to be both concise and comprehensive, and as such it has been necessary to make a variety of decisions and sacrifices. The history of Byzantium is well over a thousand years in duration and any reasonable book on the subject must prepare the ground with consideration of the institutions and the issues of what came before; it must also consider the aftermath of the empire and the ways in which its culture has continued to affect our lives over the past 500 years. Given all that, serious thought had to be devoted to organization and to questions of inclusion and focus.

In recent years it has become fashionable to write introductory histories that focus primarily on social, economic, and cultural topics, with heavy doses of everyday life and the *mentalité* of the societies being studied. While I appreciate such an approach and most of my own research and writing has been concerned with such issues, I feel that this is not appropriate for a book that seeks to provide an introduction to a civilization such as that of Byzantium. Rather, I believe that a "traditional" political narrative is essential, especially for the vast majority of readers who will know little or nothing about Byzantium at the outset. This chronological frame is designed to portray the enormous geographical, chronological, and topical sweep of Byzantine history and to allow readers to see the vast cultural changes that occurred within this same civilization over time. Some readers may criticize such an approach or feel that it is "old-fashioned," and I can certainly understand such a view. Nonetheless, this is the basis of the organization of the book, and I hope that some readers will find it satisfactory and be encouraged to go on to more specialized texts that treat the art, society, and culture of Byzantium in greater detail.

This organization is not meant to imply that imperial policy and the personalities of the individual emperors were necessarily the driving forces in the

Byzantine period, although the centralized nature of the Byzantine state certainly gave them an importance we might not find in all other states. Rather, as an approach to understanding Byzantine history, these individual reigns form convenient blocks of time against which to view broader developments.

This is not to say, then, that this book is essentially about politics and the military: important as these are in their own right, I hope that the reader will see these primarily as a means to "situate" Byzantine history and to allow us to experience something of what life was like for Byzantines of all classes and of both genders. The narrative will, by necessity, focus more on emperors and on men in general, since our written sources tell us more about them. But we shall try throughout to connect the events of war and politics with the lives of all people, and to invite the reader to a personal encounter with the inhabitants of the Byzantine Empire.

Weaving a narrative that includes culture, daily life, and religion around a basically chronological frame poses serious challenges, not least of which is the reality that not all phenomena change and develop at the same rate. Thus, although the present book uses the reigns of individual emperors as a means of organization, religious issues, philosophical movements, architectural change, and economic trends do not always move in time with changes on the imperial throne. I have, however, tried to discuss these broader issues within the frame of the chronologically based chapters, rather than providing chapters on each of these that would stand alone, essentially outside of time. The result, therefore, may at times seem a little choppy, as we move from the politics of succession to military policy, to religion, society, and the economy. And at times, we have to stand back and look at certain developments that stretch across a broader time frame and thus escape, temporarily at least, from the rigid confines of the chronological organization. I hope the reader will be able to bear with me in these cases, and maintain the basic flow of the book and the broader themes it seeks to address.

On many occasions it seemed to me that specific examples – of persons and/or issues – might be useful to illustrate individual phenomena, but these examples do not easily fit into the chronological frame. For this reason we have made use of what we here call "boxes." These sometimes focus on the life and/or work of an individual person or event or they are devoted to the insight provided by specific primary sources. I hope that they will be useful in bringing a little more "life" to the sometimes dry facts of historical narrative. In any case, they are meant to be a kind of "snapshot" into historical questions and aspects of Byzantine life that certainly deserve greater depth of treatment but which the confines of space do not easily allow.

Every book on Byzantium must say a word about systems of transliteration, since such a book must constantly refer to names of individuals, places, and institutions that were not originally written in the Latin alphabet. No single system of transliteration is universally acceptable, but for Greek I have generally followed a system that renders the Greek literally, as it would be pronounced today, without Latinization: thus *vestiarios* and Palaiologos, rather than *bestiarius* and Palaeologus. Exceptions are cases in which names are reasonably enough known in English to make substitution awkward: one thinks of Constantinople (not *Konstantinoupolis*), Athens (not *Athenai* or *Athena*), and (normally) Basil (not Vasileios or Vasili). For Arabic, Slavic, and other non-Greek or non-Latin words, the transliterations of the *Oxford Dictionary of Byzantium* have been preferred. Some inconsistencies inevitably remain, such as 'Cappadocian Fathers" and "John the Kappadokian."

I would like to take this opportunity to thank various individuals and institutions who have assisted me with this book. The Alexander Onassis Foundation provided me with a fellowship in 2001–2, and much of the first phase of writing was accomplished during that time. The Department of History at Ohio State University has been a good place to work on the book and a succession of Chairs has allowed me considerable flexibility in arranging my teaching schedule. Many years of teaching Byzantine history at Ohio State gave me the incentive to write this book, and the students who have passed through my classes asked the questions I have sought to answer here. Various people kindly helped me locate suitable illustrations for the book; Natalia Teteriatnikov and Brooke Schilling of Dumbarton Oaks deserve special thanks. Angela Cohen and Sandra Raphael patiently provided invaluable editorial help and saved me from many errors. Finally, my wife Lita and our sons Yianni and Panayioti have been understanding and supportive in every way, and they have provided me, probably unbeknownst to themselves, with significant insight into the Byzantine tradition as it continues to live today.

Ancient Korinth,
24 May 2004.

Introduction

250	500	750	1000	1250	1500

306   Constantine I emperor

330   Foundation of Constantinople

1204 Fourth Crusade sacks Constantinople

Medieval and Modern Attitudes toward Byzantium

Byzantium was a place of paradox. The inhabitants of the Byzantine Empire called themselves "Romans" and they would not have known themselves as "Byzantines," a term used by modern historians to distinguish them from the earlier Romans. The Byzantine Empire was a crucial link between the ancient and the modern worlds, but it is far less studied than most other cultures of the Middle Ages and there is very little understanding of Byzantium among the general public. The Byzantine Empire flourished at a time when Western Europe had sunk to a level of barbarism, but the very term "Byzantine" is used in English to denote a system of bizarre and sinister complexity. Byzantium is regarded as a place of mystery, yet its people were Christians and the Byzantine theologians and bishops created the teachings and organizational structure that characterize Christianity today. In a religious context the designation "Byzantine Catholics" is used to describe Christians who acknowledge the supremacy of the pope, while the Orthodox Christians loyal to the Byzantine tradition have generally been regarded in the West as schismatics or even heretics.

The Byzantine Empire was, in fact, the Roman Empire as it continued to exist for a thousand years after the old Rome had fallen to the barbarians. Even more, it was regarded by its people as an eternal empire, established by God to rule mankind from the coming of Christ until the end of time. It was multi-ethnic and multicultural, although Greek culture and the Greek language were seen as normative; Christianity was the dominant, the "official" religion of the state, although Judaism and Islam were generally tolerated (Christian heretics were not!). The Byzantine Empire was centered on the "new" capital of Constantinople, the city known as Byzantium in antiquity (and hence the term "Byzantine") and as Istanbul today.

Overall, it is fair to say that there is "prejudice" against Byzantium in the West (Western Europe, North America, Australia, etc.), and especially in the English-speaking world. While the culture and history of the western Middle Ages are taken seriously and regarded positively (one thinks of King Arthur, "knights in shining armor," Robin Hood, and Magna Carta), Byzantium is considered negatively – if at all. Orthodox Christians (mainly Greeks, Slavs, and other Eastern European peoples, in Europe and throughout the world) generally know the names of Byzantine emperors and many saints, but others would hardly recognize a person or an event from Byzantine history, even though these (in fact) played important roles in making the world the way it is today. This attitude toward Byzantium is not something new, but is, rather, derived from ways that westerners viewed Byzantines and the Byzantine Empire in the Middle Ages. These, as we shall see, were characterized by suspicion, distrust, and a tendency to regard the Byzantines as haughty, dishonest, and not exactly "proper" Christians. Western Europeans could not understand why the Byzantines were so different from themselves, since they were Christians and their own culture was also derived from Greek and Roman antiquity. It is certainly a truism that individuals and cultures generally dislike and go out of their way to distinguish themselves from those whom they most resemble, and this is probably the case with the relations between Byzantium and the West. Although the West has generally admired the cultures of China, India, and places more remote and "exotic," it has rarely had the same interest in Byzantium, which has commonly been viewed as a "decadent poor relative" to the West.

In part this attitude derived from the undeniable tendency of the Byzantines to regard themselves as superior to others – since they saw their culture as more advanced, and they looked upon themselves as the true chosen people of God. In addition, both the Byzantines and medieval westerners regarded their version of Christianity as "correct" and that of their opponents as flawed; both thought that the other's bishops, priests, and lay people looked and acted strangely and their means of conducting the liturgy seemed foreign and in-appropriate. Such attitudes are probably encouraged by an exclusive religion such as Christianity, which regards itself as correct and any deviation as wrong by definition. To be sure, Christianity considers other religions as inherently false, but their adherents can be forgiven since they may not "know better." Christians who disagree, however, have presumably been exposed to the truth and they cannot be excused so easily; this attitude presumably carries over into areas beyond theological belief.

Other than the differences in religion, easterners and westerners were, and remain, divided by the historical experience of the Crusades. This phenomenon, of course, had important religious connections, but the Byzantines were never able fully to understand the religious basis of the westerners' desire to conquer the Holy Land. The Byzantines, as we shall see, always felt that they continued to "own" territories that had once been a part of the empire and, as a result, they believed that the Holy Land rightfully belonged to them and that the Crusades were an intrusion into Byzantine affairs. Thus, when the Crusaders arrived – uninvited – in Byzantine territory, they expected a warm and friendly welcome and full cooperation, but they were greeted with suspicion, a lukewarm reception, and occasional opposition. The westerners regarded this as hostility to the good intentions of the Crusaders, and the mistrust became mutual. Byzantine hostility to the westerners, of course, hardened as a result of the conquest of Constantinople and the partition of the empire by the Fourth Crusade (1204), while westerners regarded the unwillingness of "the Greeks" to accept their rule and religion as perverse and wrongheaded. These attitudes, on both sides, remained for the whole of the Middle Ages and into the modern period.

The ideas of the Enlightenment, which were hostile to the Middle Ages in general and to the medieval church in particular, were naturally not well disposed to the Byzantine Empire, where monasticism, miracles, and the organized church played such a large role. Edward Gibbon, one of the foremost historians of the period, devoted much of his multi-volume *The Decline and Fall of the Roman Empire* to Byzantium, and his scathing denunciation of the Byzantines and their culture has influenced historical thinking up to the present.

In more modern times the Byzantine tradition has been associated with poor peoples who were under Turkish rule and later inhabitants of Balkan countries notorious for murderous divisiveness and political intrigue. The only major power directly associated with Byzantium was Russia, which was regarded as a notorious autocracy on the fringes of Europe and, for most of the twentieth century – in the guise of the Soviet Union – the main enemy of the West.

In this book I have tried to move beyond these cultural prejudices against Byzantium and many readers will probably even detect a hint of admiration in the author's tone. This is not because I think that the Byzantine Empire and Byzantine culture were any "better" than other civilizations, but rather because I think the study of Byzantium has intrinsic interest and that our society loses a great deal by not knowing more about it.

The Institutions of the Roman Empire

Since the Byzantine Empire was the continuation of the Roman Empire, it is crucial that the reader be familiar with the basic political institutions of the Roman state. By the time of Constantine the Great, the old Roman Republic

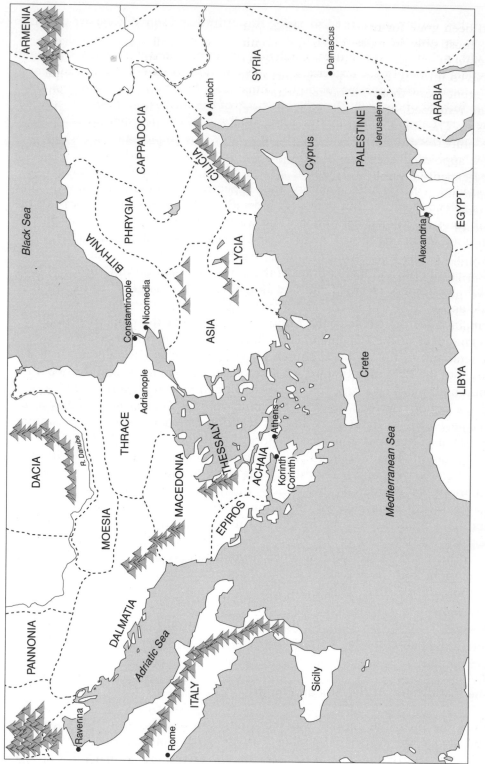

Map 0.1 The Eastern Mediterranean, showing geographical divisions, ca. 300 AD

had been gone for nearly half a millennium, but some of its institutions lived on, most only in name but a few continuing to fulfill something like their original functions. Many of the old offices of the Roman state (the magistracies) survived into the Byzantine era, most of them with tasks that were completely different from those of the past, and alongside the autocracy of Byzantium there remained, at least among some intellectuals, an admiration of republicanism. The *consul* continued to exist, appointed now by the emperor (when the emperor did not hold the office himself) and frequently more than two were appointed each year since the *consuls* were expected to provide lavish, very expensive public entertainments. The *quaestor* had emerged as the most important legal adviser of the emperor and he continued to fulfill that task at least through the seventh century. The old Roman Senate, which by the time of the early empire had lost its political power, continued to exist, in Rome until the fall of the West, and in Constantinople until the end of the empire. Members of the Senate (the senatorial order) in Constantinople were, generally speaking, men who had risen in the imperial service, and they were normally the "emperor's men," rather than members of a traditional aristocracy.

The most important political office of both the Roman and the Byzantine Empires was, of course, the emperor. By the second century AD, if not before, the emperor had essentially become a monarch, and his word was law. There were still expectations that the emperor would rule fairly and wisely, and philosophical considerations, especially from Stoicism, argued that the emperor had to rule for the benefit of his subjects. These considerations minimized autocratic and arbitrary behavior on the part of the emperor, as did, increasingly as time went by, the moral authority of the Christian church, which could appeal to specific expectations based on Biblical texts and the development of canon law. In addition, the real power behind the throne always was the army, and no emperor could succeed if he did not have a successful military career and the support of the senior officer corps.

Despite the enormous power the emperors held, it is interesting that the Romans never developed a consistent "constitutional" means to arrange the succession. Commonly, the reigning emperor would choose his successor, and the election of a new emperor by this means rarely encountered any opposition. Normally, the elder emperor would make his choice of a successor publicly known, and he would "associate" the new ruler with him on public occasions to make the situation clear and give subjects the opportunity to get used to the new emperor. Furthermore, there always existed a tendency for the development of dynasties, with son succeeding father on the throne: undoubtedly this had some connection with Roman culture in general, which seems to have seen such transfers of power in a positive light.

There was, nevertheless, no coronation ceremony in the Roman Empire, nor any one moment when it could be said that a private citizen actually came to be emperor. When the succession wasn't clear and there was no obvious candidate for the imperial throne, the outcome almost always depended on the peculiarities of the individual situation and the mix of personalities and power that could be brought to bear at the time.

Among the individuals who might have a say in the choice of a new emperor were the administrators, advisers, and personal servants who made up the imperial court. These persons often had direct access to the emperor, his papers, and the instruments of state (such as seals and various symbols) and these could all be useful in the issue of succession. The weakness of the court was that its members were not always individuals of high social standing and their point of view could be simply swept aside by the use of violence.

Potentially more important were members of the Senate, who sometimes were also members of the court, but who normally possessed independent wealth and bases of power. There also was a tradition, not always respected, that the Senate as a body might act in cases where the succession to the throne was not clear. The weaknesses of senatorial power were that members of that body did not always agree, nor did they normally act quickly, and a decision at court or elsewhere might catch the senators napping.

The third base of power in the choice of an emperor was the army, and this was frequently the most important of the three, especially in cases where an emperor was overthrown. A military revolt was one of the more frequent means for the removal of an unsuccessful emperor and, in such cases, the army might be expected to promote a new candidate for the job. Most favorably placed for such intervention were the Praetorian Guard, theoretically the body-guard of the emperor, who played the role of "emperor-maker" on many occasions. The legionary troops also could play a role, although the danger here was the threat of civil war, as well as the logistical difficulties involved in bringing troops to a place where they could have an effect.

Aside from the lack of provision for the succession, the Roman political system had one other characteristic that distinguished it from most other imperial systems. This was the small size of the staff of provincial governors and the generally low level of governmental involvement in local affairs. The Roman Empire has often been called an "alliance of cities," and the description is not totally inappropriate. Most of the functions one might normally associate with provincial government – such as police and fire protection, public works, the maintenance of food supplies, and public amenities – were commonly not provided by the Roman state, but rather by the local councils (*curiae*) of the cities of the empire. Naturally, this allowed Rome to administer the empire at a remarkably low cost.

Over the history of the Roman Empire, from Augustus (27 BC–AD 14) onward, the machinery of the state did grow and a central administration (as opposed to provincial government) slowly emerged to assist the emperor with the job of running the state. This bureaucracy was to develop considerably in the Byzantine period and became one of the most characteristic features of the Byzantine state.

In general, the Roman central government could be broken into three broad areas: the military, the administrative, and the fiscal, although there was naturally considerable overlap. One need say little about the military organization, since to a large degree the commanders of the armies were the governors of provinces along the frontier, and military affairs were naturally controlled tightly by the emperor himself. Administrative and fiscal concerns were closely linked and in the first century AD they tended to be managed by individuals of low standing (sometimes former slaves) who were directly dependent on the emperor. As time went on, into the second and third centuries, emperors came to rely on administrators of higher status, some of them from the senatorial order itself. Legal issues were naturally of primary importance and lawyers came to play an increasingly important role as advisers to the emperor.

There was no clear division between the emperor as an individual and the emperor as ruler of the Roman world: the emperor's private and public wealth were frequently one and the same (at least in practice) and his personal advisers were the most important political figures. No constitutional "council of ministers" emerged, but naturally these advisers frequently met, at the emperor's pleasure, to help him determine matters of state policy.

In social and economic terms the Roman Empire was an interesting contrast. On the one hand, a powerful aristocracy of landowners dominated society at all levels, especially in provincial cities. Trade and the merchants who engaged in it were looked down upon and landowning was thought to be the only "profession" for a gentlemen. There was nothing like a middle class in the Roman Empire and the vast majority of individuals were poor farmers, either engaged in subsistence agriculture or tenant farmers who worked the fields of the large landowners. Slavery was, of course, common and new supplies of slaves were provided by wars and piracy. Some slaves were condemned to especially difficult lives, in the mines or the large farms and ranches of the extraordinarily rich, and few of these survived very long. One should be careful, however, not to overestimate the numbers of slaves, which certainly declined as time went by, or their importance in the overall economy, which continued to be dominated by the poor but free farmer.

Thus, on the one hand, society and economy were dominated by age-old systems that had not changed for centuries and in which the majority could not hope for advancement in their position. On the other hand, the power of the emperor, his desire for administrators who could serve him well, and the lack of racial or legal restraints meant that many individuals did, in fact, rise in Roman society, and the phenomenon of the slave who came to be the emperor's most trusted associate or a wealthy trader in Rome was not at all uncommon. Probably even more important, the army provided a remarkably effective means of social and economic change. New recruits were, not surprisingly, mainly enlisted from the more backward parts of the empire (Spain, the Balkans, the northern frontiers), and cleverness, strength, and bravery often brought rapid advancement. The higher commands in the army were generally reserved for members of the aristocracy, but as time went on soldiers from the lowest ranks were promoted even to these and there was, thus, at the

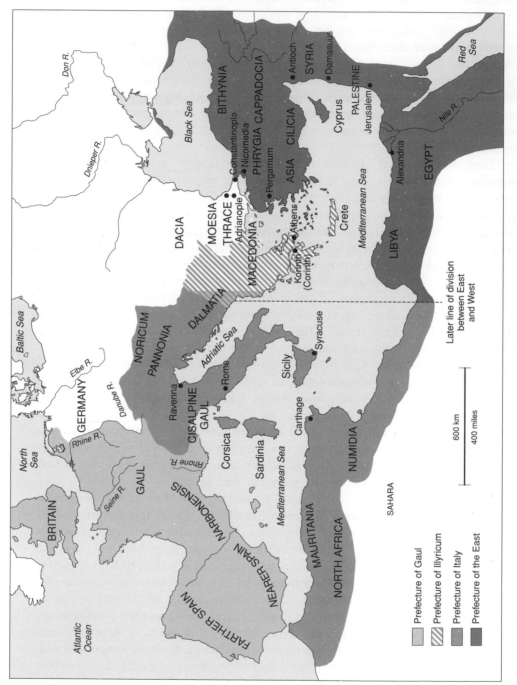

Map 0.2 The restored Roman Empire, ca. 300 AD. After Jackson J. Spielvogel, *Western Civilizations*, fifth edition (Wadsworth, 2003), map 6.4, p. 153

very highest level of society remarkable mobility and change, not all of it naturally to the liking of the traditional aristocracy.

Christianity and the Christian Church

The Byzantine Empire was a thoroughly Christian society and the institutions and teachings of the Christian church influenced it in all its aspects. Most readers of this book will be familiar with the Gospel stories and the origins of Christianity, on the one hand, and, on the other, the basic ideas of Christianity as they are accepted today. Most readers will not, however, be fully aware of Christianity as it was practiced for the thousand years of the Byzantine Empire, a period representing more than half of the religion's existence up to today.

This book will naturally not attempt to present all the details of Byzantine theology, nor will it take any position about the validity of various ways of interpreting the Christian message. We should, however, point out that readers of this book should not expect the Christianity of the Byzantines to be identical to that practiced in the West today. In fact, it might be suggested that readers approach the study of Byzantine Christianity with an open mind and a willingness to explore it in the same way one might examine the religion of ancient Greece or China. There will be times when Byzantine Christianity will seem very familiar to most readers, but there will also be times when it will seem very new.

By the time of Constantine (AD 306–37), when this book begins, Christianity had already moved into a phase characterized by a reasonably complex institutional structure. Although not yet universally accepted, bishops had come generally to dominate the church in an essentially monarchical fashion: each bishop ruled his city (and its hinterland) as a supposedly unquestionable figure who had acquired his authority in a direct line going back to the Apostles of Christ (the idea of apostolic succession). The bishops were essentially independent of all other authority, although a rough ranking of bishops, based largely on the importance of their cities, had emerged. Bishops controlled the increasingly significant wealth of the local churches and they determined the nature of public worship, the disbursement of charity, and the regulation of the increasingly large number of clergy (priests, deacons, and minor clerics) under their control. The bishop was thus emerging as a major figure in society as a whole.

By the time of Constantine there was a general agreement among Christians about which books should be considered part of the Bible. There was also a basic agreement that God was a Trinity, made up of the Father, Son, and Holy Spirit. In addition, it was agreed that Christians should lead a certain kind of life and worship together and in private according to standards that were still set at the local level. Christian authors of the post-apostolic age had begun the development of the principles of Christian theology and it was generally agreed that this could, and should, make use of the logic and tools of contemporary (pagan) philosophical discourse.

The Christian church had experienced increasingly severe bouts of persecution, primarily at the local level but occasionally at the level of the empire, and we will discuss this in some detail in the next chapter. The phenomenon of persecution – along with resistance to it, as well as the crystallization of institutional and belief structures – were the main characteristics of Christianity at the beginning of the Byzantine period. These two latter were to be considerably developed under Byzantium, while the former continued to provide a historical backdrop against which contemporary religious conflicts were to be fought out.

The Geographical Background of Byzantine History

A basic understanding of geography is essential for a consideration of the history of the Byzantine Empire. This is obvious for any period in the past, but the Byzantine Empire encompassed a remarkably varied geographical frame that played an especially important role in the history of Byzantine civilization.

The Byzantine Empire was, first of all, a state built around the Mediterranean Sea, and the core of the empire was heavily influenced by that fact. Throughout its history the Byzantine Empire was closely focused on that central sea, and its communication, trade, industry, and climate were all determined largely by the characteristics of the Mediterranean.

Conditions along the Mediterranean littoral, from west to east, do not vary much in climate, soil, natural resources, vegetation, and the potential to support life. That littoral is always very narrow, rarely extending more than a hundred kilometers from the coast. Beyond the littoral, conditions change drastically and they vary considerably from one area to another, but nearer the sea, where many of the great cities of the empire were once located, the situation is much the same throughout. The climate is mild and reasonably consistent, with cool, wet winters and hot, dry summers, winds that blow from the west and northwest in the winter and the west and southwest in the summer. The winter winds thus bring the colder air from northern Europe down into the Mediterranean, while the summer winds can, at one moment, be hot and bring the sands of the Sahara into these areas, while at the next, they can bear down strongly for hours from the north. Overall the seasonal winds can be predicted to allow traditional sailing vessels to travel both east and west in the Mediterranean by selecting the proper time for departures and appropriate destinations. Local winds, however, can be violently changeable, especially among the islands, and shipping can be adversely affected by the winds in any season.

The coasts of the Mediterranean are very uneven, filled with numerous bays and coves in the east, more regular in the west, but still with many places for safe anchorage. These physical conditions have always encouraged transport and trade around the Mediterranean and contributed to contact among the people living along its shore.

Rainfall along the Mediterranean littoral is generally low and concentrated in the winter months, meaning that the growing of dry-farming crops (such as cereals) usually follows a cycle of winter sowing and spring harvest. The soils are generally thin and poor, meaning that agricultural yields are rarely high and can vary considerably from year to year; in addition, wind and water can easily carry off the soil and ruin agricultural productivity altogether. Mountains frequently form the interior border of the Mediterranean littoral, and streams normally rush down from them to the sea, but these are often mere seasonal torrents that run heavily in the winter and early spring but dry up in early summer. They are generally not useful for transport.

Behind the Mediterranean littoral lay much larger land masses, each of which has its own characteristics. (Note that this introduction will not attempt to describe the inland areas of the West, since they essentially lay outside the areas controlled by the Byzantine Empire.) In the early Byzantine period (i.e., down to the seventh century) two of these major areas were Syria and Egypt, both of which were lost to the empire in the Arab invasions. They were exceedingly productive agricultural areas, much more than one would think, given their relatively poor conditions today. Both, of course, have large desert areas, but there are also vast regions that can support a rich agricultural production: the valley of the Nile in Egypt and the interior plains of Syria, Lebanon, and Jordan. The Nile Valley was undoubtedly the richest agricultural area in the ancient world, because of its favorable climate, the plentiful water for irrigation, and the regular replacement of fertile soils in the annual floods. The most productive part of the Syrian interior in the Byzantine period seems to have been the upland plateaus of the north, between the Orontes River on the west and the Euphrates on the east, which seems to have been especially densely populated, with large cities and many apparently wealthy villages.

Asia Minor was both politically and geographically the center of the Byzantine Empire, its true heartland up to the end of the eleventh century. Its coasts, on the Aegean, Black, and Mediterranean Seas, belong to the category of the littoral, while the vast interior was marked off by its mountain ranges. In the east these are high and difficult to cross, with especially treacherous passes, toward Armenia and the Caucasus to the north and Mesopotamia and Syria to the south. On the north and the south the interior of the peninsula is shut off from the sea by chains of mountains, while in the center is the great Anatolian plateau, dry and harsh, hot in summer and bitterly cold in winter. To the west a series of mountain chains run roughly east–west down from the plateau to the Aegean Sea, and several broad rivers run among the mountains, following their general course to the Aegean. The valleys between these western mountains, in Caria, Lydia, Bithynia, and (to a certain degree) Phrygia are the richest parts of Asia Minor. Roads ran across the whole of the peninsula, and even in the interior, especially in Galatia and Kappadokia, there were many small plains, large cities, and villages. Many parts of Asia Minor, especially in the center and east, were especially suited for grazing, rather than agriculture, and population there was always thin and scattered.

After Asia Minor, the second most important region of the Byzantine Empire was the Balkans, a far poorer area but significant nonetheless, especially in the early Byzantine period and from the ninth century onward, when Byzantine power began to reassert itself in the area. The Balkans are defined in the north by the Danube River, flowing west to east from the Pannonian plain (modern Austria) to the Black Sea, with fertile plains on both sides. To the south is the Aegean Sea and to the west the Adriatic Sea. To the northeast there is a narrow passage between the Black Sea (on the east) and the Carpathian Mountains (on the northwest), in the area of modern Romania and Moldavia, where passage is easy between the southern Russian plain (the Ukraine) and the Balkan interior. Historically this was the western terminus of the "steppe corridor" that provided easy access to Europe for the nomadic warriors who periodically swept across it from Central Asia.

The Balkans are mountainous, with the Dinaric Alps to the west, the Balkan Mountains in the center/east, and the Pindus chain running north–south through the Greek peninsula. Aside from the Danube, which provides admirable east–west transport, most of the rivers of the peninsula run from north to south toward the Aegean Sea: the Vardar (to Thessaloniki), the Struma, and the Nesta. These river routes provided the main means of access from the central Balkans to the cities along the sea.

Within the Balkan peninsula the mountains break the land into very small parcels that tend not to communicate with each other easily or well. This has certainly contributed to the cultural isolation of many of these sub-units at various times in the past and produced a significant difference between the culture of the coast and that of the interior, leading to disagreements, political fragmentation, and war among the peoples of the Balkans. The nomenclature and boundaries of the regions of the Balkans have, we should note, changed over time, largely as a result of political change. Thus, for example, in the tenth century Bulgaria extended far west of the modern state of the same name, and Serbia once controlled the Greek peninsula as far south as Thessaly.

Greece itself is geographically distinct from the rest of the Balkans, in part because it is surrounded on three sides by water and includes thousands of islands. Thus, on the one hand, all of Greece might belong to the category of the littoral, but the inland parts, especially in the Taygetos and Pindos ranges, have more in common with the mountainous areas of the rest of the Balkans.

All of the factors briefly discussed above the geography of the Byzantine Empire, along with its natural resources and barriers to communication, the preconditions of the Roman political state, the basic belief-system and administration of the Christian church – played their roles in the historical development of Byzantium. The people, however, in their endless variety and remarkable ability to change and adapt over a period of a millennium, were the major players and the shapers of the history of Byzantium.

Sources for Byzantine History

The historical sources for any culture naturally form and shape our knowledge of that society. The written sources for Byzantine history are, at first sight, very similar to those for ancient history, and significantly different from those for the history of the medieval West. Thus, one important class of Byzantine sources are historical works that consciously continued the tradition of classical historiography, especially the works of Herodotus, Xenophon, and most notably Thucydides. In the early Byzantine period some histories were written in Latin, most famously the work of Ammianus Marcellinus, but from the fifth century onward most were written in Greek, mainly in a highly artificial language that imitated the Greek written in Athens in the fifth and fourth centuries BC and that would have been difficult for most Byzantines to understand. Prokopios (sixth century) is the outstanding classicizing historian of the early Byzantine period, but this tradition revived in the eleventh and even more the twelfth centuries in the works of Constantine Porphyrogenitos and his school (tenth century), Psellos (eleventh century), Anna Komnena, and Nikitas Choniates (both twelfth century). This style of historical writing, which made use of either an annalistic or a biographical approach, continued in the later Byzantine period in the works of historians such as Akropolites, Pachymeres (thirteenth century), and Gregoras (fourteenth century). The last century of the Byzantine Empire produced a remarkable number of quite competent classicizing historians who were able to chronicle the decline and fall of Constantinople: among them Sphrantzes, Chalkokondyles, Doukas, and Kritoboulos, some writing well after the Ottoman conquest.

Alongside this tradition the genre of ecclesiastical history (history of the church) was essentially created by Eusebios of Caesarea (fourth century) and continued by Philostorgios, Socrates, Sozomen, Theodoret (mostly fifth century) and Theodore Lector (sixth century). After this time ecclesiastical history merged with that of more general history, but it was resurrected by Xanthopoulos in the fourteenth century.

In addition, a slightly different type of historical work was the Byzantine chronicle (*chronikon*), whose origins can be traced to the Chronicle of Eusebios of Caesarea and the short histories written in both Greek and Latin in the fourth and fifth centuries. These chronicles were sometimes only lists of events, often of a miraculous or memorable character (birth of two-headed calves, earthquakes, eclipses, etc.) along with the main acts of the great rulers, but they often also contained commentary by the author, frequently of a moralizing or theological nature, explaining the "meaning" of the historical events to readers. In most cases the authors of chronicles sought to use historical events to demonstrate theological truth or the penalties paid by rulers or others who failed to heed the will of God or the teaching of the church. These chronicles were commonly written in a somewhat simpler and less pretentious language than the classicizing histories and they were frequently composed by monks.

At one time it was customary to describe these works as monastic chronicles, but it is now clear that they represented many of the same ideas and concerns as the classicizing historians and the line of division should not be taken too strictly.

Malalas (sixth century) was the author of the first fully developed chronicle of this type. His work was concerned to unite secular and divine history, beginning with the Creation of the world, retelling the basic Biblical histories in their broader context, and continuing up through the reign of Justinian. The most important of the Byzantine chronicles is that of Theophanes (the "Confessor") who wrote in the early ninth century and whose work provides most of the information we have for the history of the seventh and the eighth centuries. Theophanes was a monk and a devoted Iconophile who saw all of world history through the lens of the struggle over the veneration of ikons. Theophanes' work was continued by an unknown author and a series of other writers of the tenth century who brought his chronicle up to their own time. John Skylitzes (eleventh century) and John Zonaras (twelfth century) wrote important chronicles, with much independent information; after that time the chronicle continued to be a major form of historical writing and many chronicles focused on local affairs and short periods of time, right up to the Ottoman conquest and beyond.

These products of varying historical traditions allow us to piece together the basic political and military history of the Byzantine Empire and provide considerable information about isolated events. But they are all significantly biased in favor of or against different rulers and dynasties, and they do not provide much information about the economy, society, ordinary people (including women), and daily life. They also almost all had a linear view of history in which Christian ideas of salvation played a dominant role and the Byzantine Empire was the central player.

Hagiography (the biographies of saints) provides a significantly different insight into Byzantine life. Saints' lives were once shunned and ridiculed by modern historians since they seemed to be comprised almost solely of pious stories and miracles that may not have had much grounding in historical reality. It is clear that the genre of hagiography lends itself to repetition, and the formulaic nature of saints' lives means that we cannot believe all the details of each life. Nonetheless, most of the lives contain a wealth of information about daily life, the economy, and local conditions that, although incidental to the main purposes of the author, are nevertheless of considerable interest to the historian. They also portray, often in a striking way, the beliefs, hopes, and aspirations of ordinary people, and they provide an essential source for the study of Byzantine spirituality and religious practice. One should also note that, although most Byzantine saints' lives were written in Greek, many were also written in (or translated into) Slavonic, Arabic, Coptic, and – especially – Syriac. These non-Greek biographies often provide a very different view of things from those written in the Byzantine heartland and provide a contrast of considerable importance.

Literature, such as poetry, the novel, and epistolography (letter-writing), tended to be dominated by classical models and traditions, and it is difficult to use them to reconstruct much of the life of the Byzantine period, in part because they valued rhetorical virtuosity rather than realism and the "timeless" rather than the contemporary. Nevertheless, changing values and even insights into personal feelings can sometimes be seen in a number of works, such as those of Photios, Psellos, and Niketas Choniates. An important development was the slow emergence of vernacular literature, particularly from the twelfth century onward, and the influence of Western ideas (and the reactions to them) in the same period.

The law codes, of course, provide a rich source of information, especially for the early Byzantine period, with the wealth of data in the Codex Theodosianus and the Justinianic Corpus. Subsequent law codes, such as the so-called Farmer's Law, the Ekloga, the Basilika, and the Book of the Eparch, are mines of information for social, economic, and (of course) legal issues. Some very few governmental documentary sources survive, such as the idiosyncratic works of the emperor Constantine VII Porphyrogenitos: the so-called *De Administrando Imperio* (a handbook of foreign relations, with many historical reports from earlier ages apparently copied verbatim), the *De Thematibus* (on the administration of the provinces), and the *De Ceremoniis* (on palace ceremonial). Many military manuals also survive, including the *Strategikon* of the emperor Maurice, the *Taktika* of Leo VI, and a number of works that come from the circle of Nikephoros II Phokas. These, of course, were based on ancient models, but they were apparently considered of real practical value and they therefore contained much information that was new and important for Byzantine commanders.

Historians of thought, especially science, mathematics, medicine, and philosophy produced enormous numbers of works, most of them still not translated into modern languages and many not even properly edited. Nonetheless, the works of Arethas of Caesarea, Photios, Psellos, Metochites, Gennadios Scholarios, and Plethon, as well as numerous treatises on astronomy, mathematics, physics, astrology, and alchemy, provide information about how Byzantine thinkers looked at the world.

Not surprisingly, sermons, Biblical commentaries and studies, and theological treatises make up a very large proportion of surviving Byzantine literature. Much of this is a little difficult for the modern reader to master, but nearly every theological work provides information of historical importance, whether this is insight into the theological disputes or incidental detail of daily life included in the thousands of surviving Byzantine sermons and theological works.

Unfortunately, very little survives of the documentary sources that have done so much to enliven the history of the medieval West. Even though the Byzantine state was enormously bureaucratic in nature and vast records were kept concerning the operation of the government, taxes, land-holding, and personal information, most of this is now lost, casualties of the final collapse and destruction of the apparatus of the Byzantine state. Some such records do survive, e.g., those preserved in the work of Constantine Porphyrogenitos (mentioned above), the *Cadaster of Thebes*, numerous papyri of the early period, and the voluminous records of the monasteries of Mount Athos. The latter are particularly important, especially since the monasteries were large landowners and they kept detailed records of their holdings throughout Macedonia, allowing the reconstruction of society there in the late Byzantine period in a way that simply cannot be done in other parts of the empire. In the fourteenth and fifteenth centuries copies of treaties, account-books, and personal letters survive in greater numbers than those from previous years.

The Byzantine written sources, of course, provide the historian with the most significant information, but sources written by "outsiders" are also very significant, especially in terms of shedding light on Byzantine foreign and military activities, but also by filling in significant gaps on many internal issues and giving us a glimpse of how others viewed the Byzantines. Perhaps most important in this regard are the Arabic historians, such as al-Baladhuri, Tabari, and Jahja of Antioch, and geographers, such as al-Masudi and al-Idrisi. These, and other sources written in Armenian, Georgian, and Persian, provide us with significant information and a salutary corrective to the Byzantine texts.

Western sources such as Liudprand of Cremona and the Lives of the popes provide a western view of Byzantium, very different from that of the Byzantines themselves. From the twelfth century onward, and especially in the era of the Crusades, Western sources become especially important, and the so-called *Chronicle of the Morea* is the most significant source for the history of Greece under Latin occupation. Venetian, Genoese, and other Italian sources (including many documentary records) provide invaluable information, not only about Italians and other westerners in the East, but also concerning economic history and the various attempts by a succession of Byzantine rulers to secure help from the Italian republics.

Also of special importance are the Slavic sources, from the *Russian Primary Chronicle* to the Slavonic translations of various Byzantine works, and chronicles and other works from Serbia, Bulgaria, and elsewhere in the Slavic world.

Beyond the written sources there are many important materials useful for the study of Byzantine history. These include such material as the voluminous Byzantine coinage. The coins provide an especially vivid record of the basic lines of imperial propaganda (since they were one of the best ways for the emperor to speak directly to his subjects), concerning military affairs and, even more, dynastic policies: coins were one of the commonest ways to announce the elevation of a new emperor and/or the choice of an individual as heir to the throne. In addition, the coins provide direct evidence about the economy of the state, including phenomena such as the stability of the coinage, debasement, and the size and circulation of the money supply across time. The discovery of coin hoards, in addition, allows us to measure possible periods of disturbance and/or foreign threat, to examine the coins that circulated together, and to trace the export of Byzantine coins, which was carried out in large volume, either as the result of trade or imperial largesse.

Similar to the coins are the seals (most of them lead) that were used to close important documents and insure their integrity and authenticity. These seals, missing of course the documents that once accompanied them, survive by the thousands. They preserve the names of individuals and the offices they held. The evidence of the seals helps enormously in understanding the administrative history and the economy of the empire and its institutions and occasionally the official careers of otherwise anonymous individuals.

The archaeological evidence for the history of Byzantium is abundant and informative, although it has not been used as fully as it ought to be. As a result of the many excavations in the Mediterranean region over the past 150 years, many sites of Byzantine date are known. Unfortunately, since the interest of earlier excavators was the classical or prehistoric period, the Byzantine (and later) remains of these sites were frequently ignored or, even worse, completely destroyed in the rush to uncover earlier levels. Happily, this situation has been generally righted in recent years, but much of the damage has already been done and precious data have been lost forever. Probably more seriously in the short run, the Byzantine material in many excavations has not been intensively studied, meaning that it is frequently difficult to integrate into synthetic studies. Furthermore, there have been few major excavations in Constantinople – for fairly obvious reasons: modern Istanbul is a major city with a thickly packed population and the modern Turkish state has (perhaps naturally) not always been especially concerned about the remains of Byzantine date. The archaeological evidence that now exists, however, provides considerable opportunity for younger scholars to make a significant contribution to our understanding of Byzantine history.

Even in the present situation some observations can be made about the nature of the archaeological evidence and its contribution to understanding Byzantine history today. In the first place, since most of the major Mediterranean excavations have focused on the cities of the Greek and Roman worlds, we now already have significant evidence about how the cities of the Roman Empire changed in the early Byzantine period. We can see the construction of huge ecclesiastical complexes in most cities and the decay and abandonment of many of the religious sanctuaries that had been major centers of polytheism and classical culture. What happened to the urban core, the open spaces and secular public buildings, is still a matter of debate, but the archaeological evidence is certainly the major source for understanding the period of transition at the end of the ancient world and the "Dark Ages" of the seventh and eighth centuries.

In fact, attempts to identify the remains of various "barbarian" raids and settlements in the Byzantine Empire have been a key interest of archaeologists and historians of the Dark Ages, but recent research has suggested this question is especially complicated and many past conclusions cannot be trusted, especially since these often have been significantly influenced by modern political and ethnic considerations. In the eastern provinces of the Empire, for example, especially in Syria, archaeological research now seems to suggest considerable continuity through the period of the Arab invasions; prosperity continued in the city and countryside and the momentous events of the period (wars and the spread of Islam) seem not to have affected local society nearly as much as we would think.

After the Dark Ages (ninth century onward), the archaeological evidence for Byzantium again becomes more plentiful and we have evidence of city life resuming and monumental architecture again being built, but certainly not on the vast scale that characterized the early Byzantine period. The cities, as far as we can tell, were significantly constricted, and many may have been confined, either fully or in part, within fortification walls. Overall, the archaeological evidence seems to show a steady growth in prosperity and complexity from the ninth century onward, with an apparent "explosion" of material in the twelfth and thirteenth centuries. The ramifications and problems with this evidence will be discussed in the chapters that follow, but it would seem that there are problems in correlating the archaeological and the "historical" evidence derived from texts for this period. The apparent wealth of the archaeological record seems to continue into the fourteenth century, but during that period there seems to have been a collapse and our evidence dwindles to very little.

Archaeological survey, the examination of vast stretches of countryside, including villages and remote areas, has in recent years significantly expanded our archaeological view beyond the confines of the cities that have been excavated. Archaeological survey can often be irritatingly imprecise and its methods and conclusions have often been questioned, even by other archaeologists. Nonetheless, especially as more data are collected from surveys in different parts of the empire, survey archaeology will shed important light on the villages and farms that formed the basis of Byzantine life.

Naturally, the study of the architecture of the Byzantine period provides evidence of its own, and the examination of standing buildings has long played an important role in Byzantine studies. Most of the surviving buildings are churches, and this has biased our study of the architectural wealth of Byzantium, but some secular structures and the remains of many fortifications help to redress the balance somewhat. The study of Byzantine churches provides us with insight, not only into the wealth and the building techniques of the period, but also into the cultural and spiritual values of the era. It does so in an especially "concrete" way, allowing us to see the same things that the Byzantines saw and putting us into "direct contact" with them in a way that the texts do not always allow. We, of course, look at these buildings with the benefit of our own experiences and expectations, but as we see them (either in person or through photographs) we can also imagine the ideas that lay behind the structures and how the city-dwellers, villagers, monks, women, and men might have felt as they saw these buildings in their daily lives and as they gathered together to worship, transact business, or enjoy social interaction.

The early Byzantine (early Christian) churches were often enormous structures, some of them designed to hold thousands of worshippers and overawe them with their splendor and richness. The Middle Byzantine buildings (ninth–twelfth centuries), by contrast, were normally much smaller and they emphasized a much more "internalized" experience. These sometimes tiny churches, often described as "jewel-like," were commonly domed and their interiors symbolized the entire universe, with the Pantokrator (Christ, as Ruler of All) depicted in the dome and scenes from the Bible and regiments of individual saints painted or depicted in mosaic on the surfaces of architecturally important parts of the building. The worshipers stood in this sacred space, on the lowest level but still part of the elaborate and ongoing relationship between heaven and earth.

The churches of the Later Byzantine era (thirteenth–fifteenth centuries) continued the tradition established in the earlier centuries, but with considerably greater regional variation, an indication that the empire itself was beginning to evolve into different cultural, and sometimes political, regions. The central plan and the intimate nature of the Byzantine church was maintained, but there was greater emphasis on verticality and height and on the surface decoration of the exterior. Western influences naturally came to play a greater role, as they did in the politics, economy, and thought of this era.

Painting, especially the production of ikons, manuscript illuminations, fresco, and mosaic, also provides important clues to the historian of the Byzantine Empire. These include the formal development of representational art and regional and external influences, the break presented by the Iconoclastic Controversy, and the ways in which individuals and scenes from daily life were depicted in painting. Byzantine painting is, generally speaking, two-dimensional, formalized, and symbolic (rather than realistic). Interestingly enough, although this painting was influential in the development of art in the Italian Renaissance, it was afterwards disdained as "religious" and "unrealistic." It was, however, "rediscovered" in the early part of the twentieth century, when art critics noted the apparent similarity with some aspects of "modern art." Byzantine art, therefore (and especially ikons), has come to be admired among connoisseurs, and the unfortunate result is the despoiling of churches of their ikons, paintings, and mosaics and a high-priced following for things Byzantine in the art market.

Byzantine painting, like literature, tended to be somewhat formulaic and to focus on similar Biblical stories, making use of techniques and means of depiction inherited from the ancient world. Art historians, however, have discerned the rise and decline of different styles and schools of painting over the thousand-year history of Byzantium, with special diversity in the Late Byzantine period. The same themes we have noted in literature, the influence of classicism versus "vernacular" tradition and the emergence of individuality and diversity, can be seen in the history of painting. Byzantine painting likewise sometimes rises to a high level of inspiration, and some of the truly great examples of this art are on a par with any in the world. In addition, painting often depicts scenes of daily life and the activities of women and children, as well as scenes from nature and the agricultural cycle. Painting also preserves a picture of the world that presumably represents at least one way it was seen by the Byzantines themselves; historians can use such a "window into the Byzantine mind" as an opportunity to explore Byzantine society and its people in a more intimate way.

The "minor arts," such as jewelry, enamel, and ivories, display the abilities of Byzantine craftsmen and the liveliness of the workshop tradition in Byzantium. These objects, often made of precious metals and provided as gifts by emperors to high Byzantine officials and to kings, emperors, and chieftains in other parts of the world, have been prized from the moment of their manufacture. In part because they are easily portable, such objects are found in museums throughout the world, where they readily attest to the wealth and splendor often associated with Byzantium.

Overall, there is no dearth of source material for the study of the Byzantine Empire. The difficulty for the beginning student is that, although the written sources are vast in number and diversity, relatively few have been translated into modern languages, and the great majority have still not been properly edited. There is no proper handbook in English for Byzantine history or literature and no guide to the historical sources. Although the situation is better for Byzantine art and architecture, where several solid introductions exist, the material is still diverse and not published in any single series to which a student can go for a broad overview.

FURTHER READING

H.-G. Beck, *Kirche und theologische Literatur im byzantinischen Reich*. Munich, 1959.

H.-G. Beck, *Geschichte der byzantinischen Volksliteratur*. Munich, 1971.

F. W. Carter, ed., *An Historical Geography of the Balkans*. London, 1977.

R. Cormack, *Writing in Gold. Byzantine Society and its Icons*. Oxford, 1985.

F. W. Deichmann, *Einführen in die christliche Archäologie*. Darmstadt, 1983.

S. Hackel, ed., *The Byzantine Saint*. London, 1981.

P. Horden and N. Purcell, *The Corrupting Sea*. Oxford, 2000.

H. Hunger, *Die hochsprachliche profane Literatur der Byzantiner*, 2 vols. Munich, 1978.

J. Karyannopoulos and G. Weiss, *Quellenkunde zur Geschichte von Byzanz (324–1453)*. Wiesbaden, 1982.

A. Kazhdan and G. Constable, *People and Power in Byzantium*. Washington, 1982.

R. Krautheimer, *Early Christian and Byzantine Architecture*, 4th edn. Harmondsworth, 1986.

A. Laiou-Thomadakis, *Peasant Society in the Late Byzantine Empire: A Social and Demographic Study*. Princeton, 1977.

C. Mango, *Byzantine Architecture*. New York, 1970.

N. Oikonomides, *A Collection of Dated Byzantine Lead Seals*. Washington, 1986.

N. J. G. Pounds, *An Historical Geography of Europe, 450 BC–AD 1330*. Cambridge, 1973.

J. M. Wagstaff, *The Evolution of the Middle Eastern Landscapes*. Canterbury, 1984.

J. M. Wagstaff, ed., *Landscape and Culture: Geographical and Archaeological Perspectives*. Oxford, 1987.

1
The Crisis of the
Third Century

250	500	750	1000	1250	1500

253–268   Gallienus

The Byzantine Empire does not have a proper "beginning" since it was, in fact, the continuation of the Roman state, which had begun (according to tradition) in 753 BC. A convenient starting date is the reign of Constantine, but the events of his reign cannot be understood without a consideration of the events and problems of the third century after Christ, since those set the scene for the restructuring and "revival" of Rome in the years that followed. We begin our survey, therefore, with the crisis that affected the Roman world in the middle years of the third century.

The 50 years between the death of Severus Alexander and the accession of Diocletian (235–284) witnessed the near collapse of the whole Roman way of life, from the government and military structure to the economy and the thought-system that had characterized the ancient world until then. In political terms, no emperor during this entire period was secure, and nearly every one of them died a violent death at the hands of rebels. The frontiers of the empire gave way, the enemies of the state, especially in the north and the east, came flooding in, and various parts of the empire became essentially independent. Meanwhile, the economy collapsed, inflation drove prices up, and the coinage became virtually worthless. Not surprisingly, amid these difficulties there developed what we may call a cultural crisis, characterized by changes of style in art, literature, and religion. Historians often describe this period as one of "military anarchy," since few of the emperors reigned long enough to establish dynasties or even firm policies; most of these ephemeral rulers were rough soldiers without much in the way of education or preparation for ruling the empire.

It is not entirely clear what precipitated this crisis. It has been customary to blame the emperors of this period, but it is difficult to know what could have been done, given the nearly complete collapse of the fabric of the empire. Some have pointed to a "constitutional" problem, in the sense that the Roman Empire never developed a clear means to provide for the succession – despite the fact that the empire had become essentially an autocracy. In this situation there were no clear-cut ways for an emperor to establish legitimacy, except, of course, for the "normal" situation in which an emperor selected his successor during his reign. In the first century and after AD 180 this tended to be along family lines, especially with son succeeding father, although in the second century, the "Five Good Emperors" had no sons and they arranged the succession through the choice of the "best man." When the emperor died without naming an heir, however, no clear mechanism existed for the selection of a new emperor, although this was normally achieved either by members of the civil administration (the court, the bureaucracy, and the Senate) or by the army (especially the Praetorian Guard and, rarely, the frontier troops).

On a number of occasions in the first two centuries the change of emperor was accomplished by a palace or military coup or, occasionally, through a civil war. In the period after AD 235, however, civil war became endemic and no emperor was on the throne long enough to establish his own legitimacy.

Some historians have cited other political problems to help explain the difficulties of the third century. One particularly interesting approach is to point out that the Roman Empire had never developed sophisticated or entirely adequate institutions for provincial government: instead the early Roman Empire was essentially a "federation of cities," in which the cities of the empire provided local government, while the Roman governor and the army looked after the collection of taxes, the administration of Roman justice, and defense. The local council (curia) was administered, and local expenses provided, by the local aristocracy, the so-called curiales, who had come to identify Roman interests with their own and who competed among themselves in giving gifts to the cities and providing most of the maintenance the cities required.

In the course of the second century AD, however, it became clear that the local councils were having difficulties, especially in terms of meeting the necessities of proper urban life. The ultimate cause of this phenomenon is difficult to ascertain, but it may have to do with the tendency for aristocratic families either to die out or to rise to the higher level of the imperial service and thus leave local responsibilities to the poorer families who were less able to bear the financial burden.

In this situation, the central administration had little choice except to step in – always unwillingly – to fill the void and to expend money to provide essential services and local government. All of this, of course, came at a price. The imperial administration and the imperial treasury were now required to provide resources which they had never been set up to supply and – like the "unfunded mandates" of modern governments – these became an enormous burden for the central government. As a result, the government had to place a greater tax burden on its citizens to pay for increased administration at the same time as increased resources were needed to meet the military problems of the age. Regardless of the cause, the state became ever more demanding of its citizens and ruthless in the means of tax collection, while the fabric of Roman society essentially came unstuck.

End of the Severan Dynasty and the Beginning of Anarchy

Until the early third century, a series of family-based dynasties ruled the Roman world, frequently with a son succeeding a father. The last of these dynasties was that of the Severi, who reigned from 196 to 235. The last member of the dynasty was Severus Alexander, who attempted some significant reforms, in part to restore the ancient Roman Senate to a semblance of power. Severus, however, encountered difficulty when he sought personally to command a joint force, made up of troops from both east and west against the Alamanni (a Germanic people) on the Rhine frontier. The emperor constructed a bridge over the river, but he then hesitated and sought a negotiated settlement. The troops rebelled against Severus, proclaimed their commander Maximinus as emperor, and murdered the old emperor. C. Julius Verus Maximinus, usually known as Maximinus Thrax (Maximinus the Thracian) was an obscure provincial, the son of a peasant who had risen in the army partly thanks to his physical strength and size. He was the first of the so-called "Barracks Emperors," rulers, commonly from the more "backward" areas of the empire, who rose from the ranks of the army to seize power by force.

The Senate, although certainly upset at the loss of Severus, could do nothing other than accept the *fait accompli* and recognize Maximinus. The new emperor stabilized the military situation, which had been left in confusion at Severus' death, and he carried out a difficult but successful campaign against the Germans, after which he had his son elevated as co-emperor. Nevertheless, opposition developed against Maximinus, especially on the part of former supporters of Severus and those who looked back with longing to the rule of a civilian emperor. There was at least one serious conspiracy, and Maximinus responded by removing most senators from positions of military command and by punishing those he thought were disloyal to him.

The ancient sources are almost universally hostile toward Maximinus, in part because of the contrast he posed with the last of the Severan emperors. They accuse him of avarice and of collecting taxes using harsh and unjust measures. We may doubt that Maximinus was personally avaricious, but the needs of the state, especially military requirements, made necessary the infusion of considerable amounts of cash, and Maximinus probably could have done little else. These methods led to a revolt in the province of Africa in 238, which was supported by Gordian, the proconsul of Africa, who was a member of an old senatorial family and an educated man who had been appointed by Severus Alexander. Despite the support of the Senate, the revolt of Gordian I (and his son Gordian II) failed, and both were killed. The Senate sought to maintain control in its own name, but the situation deteriorated after the appointment of Gordian's grandson as emperor (Gordian III), and a three-way civil war ensued, resulting in the death of Maximinus and the elevation of Gordian III by the Praetorian Guard.

The new emperor was only 13 years old, and the Senate seems to have continued to be very influential at the outset of his reign. The new government sought to curb abuses and limit the insolence and political power of the soldiers. The German frontier was at first stable, thanks to the successes of Maximinus, but the growing power of Sassanid Persia – Rome's great rival in the East – began to press on Roman territory in that direction.

In 241 Gordian appointed the equestrian Timistheus as praetorian prefect. An eloquent and well-educated man, he had served the empire in a wide variety of offices and his daughter was married to the young emperor. For three years Timistheus was the real power behind the throne and he wielded this carefully and wisely. The appearance of Timistheus came at an especially fortunate time, for in 241 Shapur I acceded to the throne of Persia and undertook an ambitious campaign against Roman territory, pushing far into Syria and threatening Antioch itself. In 243 Timistheus arrived in the East, accompanied by the young emperor, and the tide of battle turned. The Romans were successful and the whole of Mesopotamia fell again into Roman hands. A campaign against the Persian capital of Ctesiphon was contemplated, but Timistheus suddenly died, and the situation changed completely.

M. Julius Philippus, usually known as Philip the Arab, was appointed to succeed the loyal Timistheus. Philip was the son of an Arab sheik and he had already attained a high position in Rome. He seems to have begun plotting against the emperor almost immediately. Food shortages among the army gave him an opportunity and, when Gordian III was assassinated by the troops in March of 244, Philip became emperor.

Philip wished most of all to have his position confirmed by the Senate, so he made a hasty peace with the Persians and returned quickly to Rome. He honored the memory of his predecessor, and the Senate had no alternative but to recognize the new emperor. Contemporaries hoped for a revival of a liberal regime under Philip and, at first, they were not disappointed. He attempted to control the troops and to reform the administration in the direction of greater fairness. Philip also sought to promote the interests of his family, and he had his young son crowned first as Caesar and then as Augustus. He was able to wage successful campaigns against the Carpi across the Danube and in 248 he presided over the celebration of the thousandth anniversary of the founding of Rome. He proclaimed the beginning of a new *saeculum* (a new millennium or a new era), and some observers might have felt optimism about the future.

Nevertheless, there was considerable dissatisfaction among various parts of the army, and revolts broke out in the Danube regions and in the East. Philip offered to resign his office, but he was persuaded to stay on. In this difficult situation he appointed the City Prefect, Decius, as commander in the Danube area. Decius distinguished himself in this command and he was therefore proclaimed by the troops in June of 249. Even though both sides might have been willing to compromise, a civil war ensued, and Philip was defeated and killed.

Decius (249–251)

Decius wished to secure his claim to the throne, so he withdrew toward Italy, essentially abandoning Dacia to its fate. By so doing he left the frontier open to Germanic peoples, primarily Goths, who were being pushed against Roman territory by the Alans, a nomadic people from the steppes of Asia. The Goths thus ravaged the whole of the Balkans as far south as Thrace. Decius sought to drive the invaders out, but he was twice defeated by a Gothic leader named Cniva in the Dobrudja (the Danube delta in modern Romania). The Roman defeat was facilitated by the disloyalty of some of the Roman commanders, and Decius was killed in the second battle (251).

Decius is perhaps best known as one of the fiercest persecutors of the Christians. He began his persecution almost immediately after his accession and he may have been the first Roman emperor who sought actively to destroy Christianity. The clergy were singled out for special attention, and the bishop of Rome was one of the first to be executed. But the persecution was widened, and ordinary citizens were questioned about their religious affiliation. In some parts of the empire the emperor required everyone to obtain a certificate saying they had sacrificed to the gods (the Romans knew that the Christians would by no means agree to this), and many of these certificates have been found, especially in Egypt. Nevertheless, despite its initial ferocity, the persecution faltered when the emperor's attention turned to the invasions, and it ceased upon his death. Further, many local officials were hesitant to carry out the imperial order and many Christians escaped with their lives.

Valerian (253–260)

The death of Decius led to civil war among the surviving commanders, and no one was able to gain a secure hold on the throne until 253. At that time P. Licinius Valerianus was nominated by the troops. He was the last representative of the old Republican aristocracy to hold the imperial office, and he sought to rule by cooperating with the Senate and by controlling the worst excesses of the soldiery. Unfortunately, the military chaos of the past 20 years had led to the complete collapse of the empire's frontier. Goths and Alamanni crossed over the Danube, while the Franks first appeared in 256 and quickly overran the Rhine frontier; in the far northwest the Saxons began to attack the British coast. Meanwhile Shapur and the Persians attacked in the East. The Sassanids overran Syria and seized Antioch in 256. Valerian hastened to the East and recovered the city. He sought a negotiated settlement with the Persians in 259, but at the critical moment the Persians broke their faith and seized the unfortunate emperor, who ended his life in captivity. As if this were not enough, in the midst of the difficulties a great plague spread over the empire.

Valerian had appointed his son Gallienus as Augustus and as his co-ruler; he had left him in Rome during the eastern campaign, and during this time Gallienus had to put down at least nine usurpers.

Secessionist states

Odenathus was the King of Palmyra, an important desert city on the empire's eastern frontier. His small state depended almost entirely upon trade, and it had developed a friendly, if dependent, relationship with Rome. Besides his economic power, however, Odenathus had assembled a considerable military force, dominated by mobile archers and heavy mailed cavalry similar to those that were the mainstay of the Persian army. Odenathus had assisted Valerian in the war against Shapur, and he received high honors from him. Gallienus then sought to make Palmyra the focus of Roman military policy in the East. Gallianus encouraged Odenathus to adopt Roman titles; the king styled himself *imperator* and *corrector totius Orientis* ("supervisor of the whole East") and he was allowed to wear the laurel crown of the emperor. Palmyra defeated the Persians twice, but then Odenathus suddenly fell victim to the knife of an assassin, who may have been acting in the interests of Rome, since the king's ambitions had begun to overshadow his usefulness to Rome. Odenathus was then succeeded by his widow Zenobia, a woman every bit his equal, who ruled in the name of her young sons.

While this was going on in the East, similar developments took place in the West. Postumus, one of Valerian's best generals in the struggle against the Germans, sought the throne after the emperor's death. Civil war broke out between Gallienus and Postumus, without either side being able to defeat the other. Vast resources were directed to the civil war, at the expense of defense against the barbarians. Postumus declared himself as emperor, even though he held only the northwestern provinces; he struck his own coins, had his primary residence at Trier, and set up an administration and court that paralleled that of Gallienus. This independent "Gallic Empire" was to outlast Postumus himself and to provide a dangerous precedent for the division of the empire.

Gallienus (253–268)

Gallienus has earned the reputation of an emperor who presided over the virtual dismemberment of the empire. In part this reputation is the result of his general disregard for the Senate. He took most military commands from the senators and gave them to the *equites* (members of the Roman wealthy class that was below the senators in prestige); henceforth it was unusual for senators to command the army. Gallienus developed new cavalry troops, designed essentially to counter the heavily armored cavalry of the Persians, and for the first time the Roman army began to turn away from the system based on the legionary foot soldier.

Unlike most of the soldier-emperors of the third century, Gallienus was an educated man, and a "Gallienic Renaissance" has been identified under his reign. Gallienus found a brief respite from usurpations and invasions (even though the Gallic Empire still remained unreduced), and he gathered around his court the Neoplatonic followers of Plotinus. Gallienus also wanted a religious revival and hoped to satisfy the need of the people for intimate religion by reviving the Eleusinian mysteries, one of the ancient religions that offered its members a hope of immortality and thus could perhaps compete with Christianity. He realized that the persecution of Christianity had failed to secure its desired aims, so he called a halt to the policy and returned to a position of general toleration.

In many ways the reign of Gallienus set the stage for the recovery that was ultimately to come. Yet that event was still some time off. The emperor had expended considerable energy attempting to rebuild the defenses of the empire, both by constructing military fortifications and by rebuilding the effectiveness of the army and the navy. Nonetheless, in 267 the Goths and the Heruli broke into the Balkans. They got as far as the Aegean, sacked Athens, and even attacked the cities of the western coast of Asia Minor. Gallienus won a victory over them at Naissus, but he was called back suddenly to Italy, where a revolt had broken out. As Gallienus was occupied in the reduction of the enemy, his general staff conspired against him, and the emperor was murdered (268). The Senate and the people of Rome turned their wrath against Gallienus' family members in the city, and they were massacred. The army, however, revered the murdered emperor's memory, and even his assassins continued to follow the policies set by Gallienus.

Claudius Gothicus (268–270)

One of the murderers of Gallienus, an Illyrian officer named Claudius, seized imperial power. In marked distinction to the attitude of his predecessor, Claudius openly courted the support of the Senate. He briefly contemplated an attack on the Gallic Empire, but he realized that many of the Rhine legions were of doubtful loyalty, and the Goths were still at large in the Balkans. In a brilliant military maneuver Claudius intercepted the Gothic invaders and dealt them a crushing defeat, securing the Danube frontier for years to come. From this achievement Claudius accepted the epithet Gothicus, by which he is usually known. Yet, in 270, at this moment of success, the emperor died of the plague.

Aurelian (270–275)

Upon the death of Claudius the Senate proposed the election of his brother Quintillus as emperor. Quintillus, however, had no following among the soldiers and could never make his power secure. Thus, another of Gallienus' murderers, the commander of the cavalry, Aurelian, rose in revolt, spreading the rumor that Claudius had designated him, and not Quintillus, as his successor.

If Gallienus laid the foundations for ultimate restoration, Aurelian was the first to begin to revive the power of the Roman Empire. He was, like many of the other emperors of the period, an Illyrian soldier of humble origins. Lacking in tact and refinement, his major virtues were strength and determination, and his nickname *manu ad ferrum* ("with hand on hilt") says a good deal about how he appeared to contemporaries. At his succession the military situation was critical: the barbarians had not been driven out of the Balkans and the Juthungi invaded Italy itself. Aurelian caught up with the latter as they moved back toward the Danube and soundly defeated them; they returned later to plunder northern Italy and the emperor again dealt them a serious blow. He drove the Vandals from Pannonia and completed the control of the frontier. Yet he realized how serious the danger had been to Rome itself, and in 271 he ordered the refortification of the city. The capital that had long been protected only by the valor of the legions was once again dependent on defenses of bricks and mortar.

In 271 Aurelian made a major policy decision that has been seen by some historians as the beginning of the dismemberment of the empire. Feeling that he could no longer afford the military expenditure required to defend Dacia (the area of modern Romania), he withdrew Roman troops and citizens from the province, and re-established the Roman frontier along the Danube.

Meanwhile Zenobia, the queen of Palmyra, had conquered almost all the East; she controlled Egypt and was moving troops into Asia Minor. Aurelian set out boldly against her in 271 and in a daring campaign moved quickly across Asia Minor, taking everything before him. Most cities opened their doors to the emperor and Egypt returned to allegiance, as Zenobia's supporters deserted her. At Antioch he first met organized resistance, including two Roman legions that had gone over to the Palmyrenes and the heavily armed cavalry that formed the core of Zenobia's army. But Aurelian countered the enemy with

light-armed Moorish and Dalmatian cavalry, whom he ordered to feign with-
drawal in order to tire out their opponents. This victory won, Aurelian moved
to Emesa, where he narrowly won again, ascribing his success to the support of
the sun-god. The emperor then besieged Palmyra itself and, when hoped-for
relief did not come from the Persians, Zenobia lost her nerve and attempted
flight. She was captured, the city surrendered, and the war was at an end (272).
Aurelian returned to the Danube, but there he received word that Palmyra had
again revolted. He quickly marched back again, reduced the city, allowed it to
be sacked, and had its walls dismantled. The city was henceforth deserted.

Aurelian was then able to turn his attention to the Gallic Empire. The
usurper Postumus had died in 268. He was succeeded by Victorinus and then
by Tetricus. In 274 Aurelian marched to Gaul and defeated Tetricus' army
after the would-be emperor had already surrendered. Aurelian returned to
Rome to be honored by one of the greatest triumphal processions the Roman
world had ever known: the captives included Zenobia (bound in golden chains)
and both Tetricus and his son. Yet Aurelian was magnanimous in victory and
he settled Zenobia in Italy and married her to a senator, while he rewarded
Tetricus with a significant administrative post. Aurelian could rightfully claim
the title of *restitutor orbis* ("restorer of the world").

Freed from the immediate need of military emergency, Aurelian also
attempted some internal reform. He sought to restore confidence in the Roman
coinage, and he severely punished evil-doers in both the civil and the military
service of the state. He carried out significant public works programs, especially in Rome, and he actively promoted the cult of the sun-god, which he
apparently hoped to use as a basis for political loyalty to himself. Nonetheless,
a conspiracy at court, probably formed for insubstantial reasons, led to the
assassination of the emperor in 275. The next nine years were characterized by
instability, with one emperor succeeding the other with unfortunate regularity.
Various emperors in this period made attempts to change the governmental
system and allow stability, but none was on the throne long enough to implement institutional reforms.

Political, Economic, and Social Problems

It is obvious that, in one way, the crisis of the third century was essentially
military and political in nature. The political and military crisis of the third
century, however, was accompanied by significant changes in economic and
social life. Indeed all these phenomena were clearly interrelated and they had
an impact on the intellectual and spiritual fabric of the empire (to be discussed
in the next section of this chapter).

The most notable phenomenon of the third century was the nearly continuous state of civil war and the uncertainty about who was, in fact, the emperor.
Thus, it is indeed remarkable that the empire survived at all. The reasons
behind that survival probably have to do with the continuities within the

imperial bureaucracy, where the business of government probably went on more or less as usual.

The political and military crisis certainly exacerbated the economic problem. We have already suggested, at the beginning of this chapter, that the state had a chronic fiscal problem, not so much because income declined, but because the demands on government increased and the state was required to do much more, hence requiring greater expenditure. At the same time, the demands of the military grew, not only because of the barbarian threat but because all claimants to the throne realized that their success or failure would depend almost entirely on the loyalty of the troops. It was therefore imperative not only to make sure the soldiers were paid but that they were paid handsome gifts of coins: to celebrate the elevation of an emperor, every anniversary of that event, and on the occasion of victories or any other success that could possibly be celebrated.

In antiquity it was generally believed that coins had intrinsic value – the value of the amount of metal they contained (gold, silver, or copper). The head of the emperor and other state-based symbols were of course important instruments of propaganda, but they were also simply marks by the state guaranteeing that the weight and the purity of the metal were standardized. In the economic difficulties of the third century the temptation to devalue the coinage was simply too great. Thus, emperors took coins that were, for example, essentially silver (although they were always an alloy and pure silver was never used) and they diminished the quantity of silver per coin. In the short run this produced a windfall for the state, since undebased coins were taken in (mainly as taxes) and then larger numbers of coins were turned out, using the same total weight of precious metal. Debasement thus proceeded apace and by the 270s the silver *denarius*, for example, had gone from a coin with 35 percent silver content to one that was only dipped quickly in silver to produce the appearance of a silver coin.

This phenomenon was naturally noticed by the moneychangers; the new, devalued coins were not accepted at "face value" and prices accordingly went up quickly. It is difficult to be certain about the meaning of this, but one estimate is that prices between 235 and 284 rose approximately 700 percent. The result of this is easy to predict: the unwillingness of consumers and merchants alike to use coins and the reversion of much of the economy to a barter system. This happened not only in the ordinary marketplace, but also in the taxes themselves, where the state didn't want to be paid in its own devalued coins, but instead collected taxes in kind (wheat, oil, wine, etc.) which could then relatively easily be transferred to the soldiers in the field and other places where they were needed.

As we have already seen, the difficulties of this period seem to have fallen especially hard on the local aristocracy, the *curiales*. A few curial families rose into the senatorial ranks, but many more lost their fortunes and fell from the curial lists for that reason. Not surprisingly, no one was willing to rush in to fill their role on the local city council.

Philosophy and Religion in the Third Century

The third century witnessed important changes and developments in intellectual and religious life. These included serious persecution of the Christians as well as the growth of Neoplatonism and Gnosticism, movements that had a philosophical base but were essentially much more religious in character.

NEOPLATONISM

Neoplatonism, as its name suggests, was based loosely on the teachings of Plato, but we should remember that "Neoplatonism" is a modern term that is in some ways misleading. The "founder" of Neoplatonism was Plotinus (205–70), who studied in Alexandria and then set up a philosophical school in Rome. He had many followers among the senatorial class and was a friend of the emperor Gallienus. Like Plato, he emphasized the existence and importance of an immaterial world beyond that which we can see, a world that has ultimately greater importance. His greatest student was Porphyry (233–ca. 306), whose original name was Malchos. He studied philosophy at Athens under Longinus and then at Rome under Plotinus. Porphyry edited the works of Plotinus and wrote a biography of his teacher. Porphyry was very prolific, he had many students (such as Iamblichos), and he was author of some 78 works on a wide variety of topics, from vegetarianism to science. His book "Against the Christians" earned him the enmity of the church, despite his influence on Christian teaching, and the book was ordered to be destroyed. Porphyry's work is largely derivative, but it had considerable influence.

One of the basic teachings of Neoplatonism is the theory of "emanation," involving the way in which God (the One) reaches down to material creation: from the One through its *hypostases* (Intellect and Soul) to matter. In this regard it was possible to understand some manner of connection between the world of perfection and that of everyday human existence. Clearly important is the soul's search for salvation; in general it was felt that the individual soul could not easily be united to the universal Soul (God), but through the phenomenon of *epistrophe* (return) to God, through thinking, faith, truth, etc., there was hope of such unification. Salvation was seen as "ascent" and was viewed as essentially an intellectual operation. Especially in its later forms, Neoplatonism was frequently connected with magic and theurgy. *white magic*

GNOSTICISM

Gnosticism (from the word *gnosis*, "knowledge") is a modern term for a number of related approaches to religion and religious experience, from the Hellenistic period onward. Gnosticism is poorly understood, in part because it is not a single phenomenon and in part because most of the books in which it was expounded were destroyed by the Christians. The discovery of the so-called Nag Hammadi Library in Egypt, with many Gnostic texts, has increased our knowledge of this complex phenomenon. One branch of Gnosticism was associated with Hermes Trismegistos (Hermes Thrice-Greatest), the Greek name of the Egyptian Thoth, the god of wisdom. The texts described as the *Hermetica* contain this group's teachings. They are concerned with magic, alchemy, philosophy, and astrology, and are considered the revelations of the god Hermes. The texts were the basis of many later magical compilations.

A basic tenet of Gnosticism is "dualism," the concept that there is a primary force of good and a primary force of evil (essentially two diametrically opposed gods). Gnostics associated the God of the Old Testament with Satan and taught that everything material was evil; this led some Gnostic sects to abolish marriage and even encourage suicide. Gnostic teaching was not unified, but varied widely, from decidedly non-Christian traditions to beliefs that combined Christian and pagan ideas (e.g., the Christian heretic Marcion). In the second century Gnosticism was a serious rival to Christianity, but by the third century it had begun to be absorbed into other traditions. Much of early Christian theology developed as a reaction to Gnosticism, and as Christian theologians sought to maintain belief in a single (good) God and the reality of Christ's Incarnation. Both Neoplatonism and Gnosticism, however, influenced the development of Christian thought, especially in the so-called "school" of Alexandria.

Overall, the crisis of the third century had ramifications in all areas of life, as a relatively stable political, economic, and cultural system was shaken to its very core. To a contemporary it must have seemed that the world was literally coming apart. As a reaction, some individuals sought stability in new ideas, institutions, and ways of looking at the world. Out of that attempt arose the world of medieval Byzantium.

FURTHER READING

Garth Fowden, *The Egyptian Hermes: A Historical Approach to the Late Pagan Mind.* Cambridge, 1986.

Ramsay MacMullen, *Roman Government's Response to Crisis, A.D. 235–337.* New Haven, 1976.

David S. Potter, *Prophecy and History in the Crisis of the Roman Empire.* Oxford, 1990.

Susan Wood, *Roman Portrait Sculpture, A.D. 217–260: The Transformation of an Artistic Tradition.* Leiden, 1986.

2
The Revival under Diocletian

The Rise of Diocletian (284–305)

After the death of the emperor Carus (282–4) the army in the East chose Diocletian, one of their officers, as emperor. In the West, Carinus (the son of Carus) refused to accept this proclamation and prepared for battle. The two armies met (285) in Moesia, and the forces of Carinus had the upper hand, but just at that moment Carinus fell to an assassin, and Diocletian was proclaimed by both armies.

Diocletian was, like most of his predecessors, a military officer from the Balkan peninsula. Unlike them, however, he was able to implement his reforms, and his rule marks the end of the crisis of the third century and the beginning of a new period of greater stability, as well as a new direction in imperial policy. He was not an innovator, and most of his policies had been anticipated by one or other of his predecessors. Nonetheless, Diocletian was a hard-working and talented administrator and he was able to build on the failures of previous emperors.

Diocletian's first task was to stabilize his own power and provide firm military leadership for the whole of the empire. Experience had shown that the army (and probably the empire as a whole) was simply too large for a single person to administer effectively, and Diocletian sought a colleague to work with him in this task. For this he chose Maximian, an old comrade in arms, whom he named as Caesar and sent to Gaul to deal with the rebellion of the Bagaudae (bands of robbers) and the incursions of the Germans in Gaul. Maximian was successful in both of these and Diocletian rewarded him with promotion to the rank of Augustus. Diocletian, meanwhile, was active in the East, restoring Roman power on the Danube, in Armenia and Mesopotamia, and in Egypt.

The Tetrarchy

In Britain and northwest Gaul, however, the rebel Carausius had established himself, and he resisted all attempts to oust him. Perhaps for this reason, Diocletian decided to expand the concept of collegial rule and he appointed two Caesars (*Caesares*, junior emperors) as assistants to the two *Augusti* (senior emperors). Thus, he named a Danubian officer, Galerius, as his own Caesar, and Constantius Chlorus, yet another Danubian, as the Caesar of Maximian. This system, called the Tetrarchy (or "rule of four men") was designed to preserve the integrity of imperial power while broadening the exercise of that authority. Thus, in theory there was no division of the empire: laws issued by each emperor were valid throughout the empire, and each ruler was to consult with and cooperate with the others. In fact, the superior authority of Diocletian served to keep the system together, and each emperor was responsible for governmental functions in a given part of the state: Constantius in the northwest (Gaul and Britain), Maximian in Italy and North Africa, Diocletian in the Balkans and Asia Minor, and Galerius in the East. Each of them had his own court, military and administrative organization, and style of governing. Nevertheless, especially under the watchful eye of Diocletian, the senior Augustus, all imperial propaganda stressed the cooperation among the emperors and their solidarity in the face of potential enemies, domestic and foreign. Furthermore, the Tetrarchy was designed to solve one of the foremost political problems of the Roman state: the issue of the succession. Thus, the Caesars were promised that they would, in time, succeed their respective *Augusti* and then choose new Caesars to perpetuate the dynasties. Diocletian emphasized his connection with divine power and his place as senior emperor by taking the name *Jovius* (Jupiter-like) for himself and Galerius, while the name *Herculius* (Hercules-like) was assigned to Maximian and Constantius.

Military Successes

Freed from the constant threat of civil war, Diocletian and his colleagues were able to turn their attention to matters of military concern and domestic reform. Constantius was given the task of subduing the usurper Carausius. He

Figure 2.1 The Tetrarchs. Porphyry group, San Marco, Venice. This sculpture depicts the Tetrarchs the way they wanted to be viewed: strong, determined, tough, and – most of all – united. They are shown in the typical style of the day, with stubbly beards, short, thick necks, and simplified features; they hold each other by the shoulders, while one hand is placed firmly on their swords. This group was taken from Constantinople at the time of the sack of the city in 1204 and brought to Venice. Photo: Timothy E. Gregory

first defeated the usurper's barbarian allies; Carausius was assassinated in 293, and in 296 Constantius invaded Britain and restored Roman power in the whole of the island south of Hadrian's Wall. He then returned to the mainland and thoroughly defeated the Alamanni in 298, bringing many years of peace and quiet to Gaul. In 296 there was a revolt in Egypt that Diocletian had to put down, and, while he was thus occupied, Narses, the King of Persia, took advantage of the situation and invaded Armenia and Syria. Galerius was put in charge of operations against the Persians. He was at first defeated, in 297, but the next year he was able to win an overwhelming victory, including the capture of the king's harem. He followed this by reconquering Mesopotamia and then forced the Persians into a peace which recognized Roman dominance throughout the East.

The Position of the Emperor and his Court

The reforms carried out by Diocletian and his successor Constantine departed notably from the system of government established by Augustus and modified over time by his successors. Obviously, many of the elements of these reforms had been introduced by one or more of the third-century emperors, and we can see these changes as evolutionary rather than revolutionary, yet their cumulative effect – and the luxury of a period without disruptive civil or foreign wars – gave them a new character. It is also not always possible to distinguish the measures introduced by Diocletian from those of Constantine. Thus, we will discuss the reforms of Diocletian and Constantine together at this point in our narrative, but it should be borne in mind that we cannot always tell who was the author of an individual measure, let alone what his motives were. In the troubled situation of the time, governmental changes may have been more a matter of expedience than of policy, and we can only wonder that the system worked as well as it did.

At the heart of the Diocletianic system was the elevated position of the emperor. The empire of Augustus is often described as the "principate" (rule of the "first citizen") while that of Diocletian is known as the "dominate" (rule of the *dominus* or "lord"). The emperor was secluded from the general public in an elaborate palace and surrounded by a court that was involved in a ceaseless round of ceremonial. Much of this was copied, quite directly, from the court of the Sassanid Persians. Thus, everything about the emperor was "sacred": his bed-chamber was the *sacrum cubiculum* and his council of state the *sacrum consistorium*. The emperor wore distinctive clothes: richly embroidered garments studded with precious stones and a jewel-encrusted diadem. His clothes were colored with a purple dye that commoners were forbidden ever to use. The emperor was no longer to be seen as an ordinary human being who went about his business like other people; instead, he moved about the city in elaborate processions and appeared to his people and to ambassadors from abroad in carefully orchestrated audiences and manifestations. He acted, in other words, like a god, and his divinity – or connection with god – was stressed wherever possible. As we have seen, the members of the Tetrarchy were closely connected with the gods Jupiter and Hercules, and in this new system the power of the emperor was seen as descending directly from the gods, rather than ascending from the will of the people, as had generally been the case under the earlier empire. Thus, Diocletian and his colleagues followed the lead of emperors such as Aurelian, who had stressed the divine aspect of their rule. Of course, in many ways this was nothing other than a new twist on the old idea of the emperor cult that stretched back to the days of the principate, but the emphasis placed on the divine origin of imperial power was something new at this time.

As the emperor withdrew into the narrow confines of palace and court, those who were close to him naturally gained considerable real power, though not always the prestige that went with it. Thus, the members of the emperor's family, especially his wife and mother, and the chamberlains and other domestic servants (who were often eunuchs) gained appreciably in power. They frequently controlled access to the emperor, and individuals who wished to present petitions or seek the ear of the emperor often had first to secure the favor of these influential people.

Administrative Reforms

The purposes of the reforms of Diocletian and Constantine were two-fold: to provide effective government and to avoid usurpation. The latter goal is easy to understand, and it is often cited as the primary purpose of the reforms, an effort to spread power broadly throughout the political system so as to prevent the rise of the "over-powerful subject" who might rise to a position that would threaten that of the emperor. Nonetheless, it is clear that the broader goal of providing good and effective government throughout the empire was just as important. In many ways the task of governing the empire had grown too large for the relatively simple administrative structure established by Augustus and developed by his successors. Both because the empire was large in size and varied in almost all its aspects, and because more and more tasks of government were being shifted to the central administration, the imperial government often simply did not have the resources to deal with the problems that it faced without considerable reorganization. The reforms of Diocletian and Constantine were designed to resolve these problems.

In the first place, there was henceforth a strict division between civil and military aspects of government. Distinct hierarchies existed, and individuals in one "branch" of government normally did not cross over to the other. Civil officials no longer had any troops at their disposal or any military responsibilities, while military commanders had no direct access to the civil administration. Most important, there was a strict separation of the tax-collecting system from the military, and military commanders had to seek supplies and payment for their troops from the appropriate civilian officials.

The civil bureaucracy was vastly increased at this time, in order to handle the increased task of governing the empire, and the number of administrative subdivisions was likewise made greater, with each of them smaller in size than they had been previously. The basic organizational structure of the state remained the individual city (Greek *polis*, Latin *civitas*) with its surrounding territory; each city was administered locally by a city council (Greek *boule*, Latin *curia*) made up of wealthy individuals. In the reforms of Diocletian and Constantine, however, the provinces were subdivided and made smaller, increasing the number from about 50 to around 100, and each province was included in a new administrative district called a diocese. There were twelve of these dioceses, each of them administered by a vicar (*vicarius*). The dioceses, in turn, were grouped into four praetorian prefectures, each of them controlled by a praetorian prefect, who was the chief administrative official and right-hand man of one of the emperors. The civil administrative structure, therefore, looked something like this:

```
Empire (or part of Empire)
        Emperor

      Prefectures
   Praetorian Prefects

        Dioceses
      Vicars (vicarii)

         Cities
   City Councils (curiae)
```

Within the central government there were numerous bureaus to deal with civil affairs, especially financial ones. The heads of those departments, along with the chief military officers, were members of the *comitatus* (imperial court). Among these were the following:

- *magister officiorum* (Master of Offices): responsible for court ceremonial, transport, the secret police;
- *comes sacrarum largitionum* (Count of the Sacred Largesse): responsible for mines, mints, collection of certain taxes, and payment of special bonuses to the troops;
- *comes rei privatae* (Count of the Emperor's Private Account): responsible for management of the emperor's vast personal wealth, especially large tracts of rental land; .
- *praepositus sacri cubiculi*: chamberlain, chief eunuch, who often controlled access to the emperor.

Military Reform

As we have seen, the military chain of command was separated from that of the civil administration and military service became more of a career unto itself. In addition, there were changes in the organization of the army. The old border troops of the empire, stationed in permanent camps along the border, were called the *limitanei*. These became essentially a local militia, poor in training and martial spirit and made up of peasants who were willing to defend their own territory but who might not be anxious to fight farther away. The *limitanei* were allowed to exist, but their importance declined considerably.

Much more important were the mobile field armies, the *comitatenses*. These were stationed in the interior of the empire in large concentrations, but they were never located in fixed permanent quarters; they were always ready to move, at a moment's notice, to meet a threat to the empire. The *comitatenses* were primarily infantry, but the cavalry, especially the heavily armed soldiers, were increasingly important. Finally, there were various kinds of imperial guards: the old praetorian guards existed until they were abolished by Constantine. After that the *scholae* and other guards' units protected the emperor; they were picked troops, impressive for their physical appearance, and they came to play an increasingly ceremonial function, although they could still act to protect (or overthrow) an emperor, and the emperor could bring the guards directly to the battlefield to take part in a war effort.

At the top of the military hierarchy, in a position similar to that of the praetorian prefect, was the *magister militum* (or *magistri militum*, since there was normally more than one) who frequently acted as commander of the army, unless the emperor sought to fulfill this task himself. Below the *magister militum* were the *comites* (singular *comes*) and below the *comites* were the *duces* (singular *dux*). The military "chain of command" thus strongly reflected that of the civil administration, although the latter may, in fact, have been developed on the basis of the military structure.

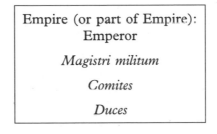

Empire (or part of Empire): Emperor

Magistri militum

Comites

Duces

Economic Policies

A primary duty of the civil administration was the preparation of a state budget and the collection of the taxes necessary to pay for it. The primary tax was the *annona*, a land-tax that was, at the time, payable largely in kind: that is, payment was normally made in grain, oil, and other foodstuffs. These goods were taken by the state and distributed to state officials and the military. Such payment in kind was necessary because of the nearly complete collapse of the monetary economy in the third century and the concern of the state that it receive income that was not devalued as a result of the economic crisis.

Collection of the *annona* was based on a system called *capitatio-iugatio*. This system called for a regular census (*indictio*) on land, at first every five years, later every 15. At the time of the *indictio* the property of every landowner was evaluated, both for quantity and quality, with higher figures assigned for better-quality land than for poorer land. In addition, this evaluation was modified by a consideration of the amount of labor available to work the land. Thus, a man counted for more than a woman and a woman more than a child, although all were recorded; and the number and the kind of animals, both those used for draft and those used for food, affected the tax liability. In the end, a base number was assigned to the taxpayer, but this was not the final tax, merely an index that would be used to calculate the family's tax liability. The praetorian prefect, in consultation with the emperor and other members of the court, would determine an amount of income the state would need in a given year. This total figure was then divided among all the available landowners, on the basis of the figures that had been obtained at the time of the *indictio*. The duty of actually collecting the taxes was passed on to the individual provincial governors and, from them, on to each city. The councils (*curiae*) of each city were then made collectively responsible for the collection of the taxes; in the case of a shortfall the members of the council, the *curiales*, were personally responsible for payment of the amount owed to the state, and there can be no doubt that some such local officials were driven to destruction as a result. The system, however, was designed to be fair to the landowners, and to tax them, not on the basis of what they actually produced but on their potential ability to produce, so that a landowner would be encouraged to produce goods in greater quantity, since the tax would in any case remain the same and excess produce would lead to immediate profit for the landowner.

In AD 301 Diocletian attempted to put a stop to inflation by issuing a detailed imperial order, fixing the maximum prices allowed for various goods and services. Copies of this order, with lists of the maximum prices, were prepared and dispatched to major cities throughout the empire. The tone of this so-called "Price Edict" was harsh and threatening, an indication of the severity of the issue and the approach by which Diocletian hoped to address it. The edict may have had some initial effect, but in the end it was a failure.

At the same time Diocletian sought to reform imperial coinage, which had become nearly worthless over the past 50 years. The value of the coins, it will be remembered, was based on the purity of the metal used and the weight of the individual coins. Diocletian issued a coin made of good-quality gold, called the *aureus*; each coin was 1/60th of a pound in weight. He hoped to retain this standard, despite inflationary pressures and the continuing demands put upon the state. The income of the government, however, was not sufficient for this and the attempt failed, although it was an indication that Diocletian was aware of the problem. Later on, his successor Constantine was to try a similar policy, issuing a gold coin, called the *solidus*, with each coin weighing 1/72nd of a pound. The *solidus* remained a stable currency for the empire, and much of the medieval world, until the middle of the eleventh century. The long-term stability of the *solidus* is an indication of the eventual success of these economic reforms and the strength of the Byzantine economy.

Box 2.1 *Diocletian's Attempt to Control Prices*

It is interesting that Diocletian's edict on maximum prices, issued in AD 301, assumed that the high prices of goods in the marketplace were due simply to the greed of suppliers and merchants. This edict was published in both Greek and Latin, and copies of it were carved into stone slabs and set up in most of the important cities of the empire. The inscription was prefaced by a long condemnation of the profiteering that was going on at the time, and it then provided a list of prices for goods and services that were set as the highest that could be charged. It is interesting to think how a government at the time believed that it could control prices in this manner, and it is clear that the attempt failed; but the document, along with other records that have survived, provides us with important information about the nature of the economy of that age.

It is difficult, if not impossible, to convert sums of money from the past into anything meaningful today, but a list of some of the maximum prices in Diocletian's edict may provide a useful idea. The prices in the edict were given in *denarii communes*, which were not real coins, but a standard of account used by the government that could be converted to real money, depending on various rates of exchange that prevailed at the time. Below is a sample of some of the items listed in the Price Edict:

1 day's wages for a baker: 50 d.c.
1 day's wages for a farm laborer: 25 d.c.
1 day's wages for a picture painter: 150 d.c.
1 Italian pound (about 325 grams) of pork: 12 d.c.
1 Italian pound of beef: 8 d.c.
1 Italian sextarius (about half a liter) of ordinary wine: 8 d.c.
1 modius of wheat (ca. 8 liters): 100 d.c.
1 pair fashionable shoes: 150 d.c.

The penalty for charging higher prices was death, but it is not difficult to imagine the real impact of the edict. As the historian Lactantius (who was a hostile contemporary of Diocletian) said, the result of the edict was that merchants were afraid to offer goods for sale, since their cost was higher than what they could charge, and the result was that prices rose even higher than they had been before!

Religion and Culture

Diocletian was a soldier and he saw things as a military commander. Thus, he approached reform in a logical, rational manner; he issued strict, detailed orders and he expected that they would be obeyed. In making appointments he preferred other military men and he almost completely overlooked the senatorial class, seeking out *equites* and soldiers instead.

Figure 2.2 Arch of Galerius. The Arch of Galerius was erected in Thessaloniki, where Galerius had his official residence. It was to honor the emperor's victory over the Persians in 298. This scene depicts Galerius, dressed as a general, offering sacrifice to the pagan gods for a successful outcome of the war. His hand is stretched out toward an altar, while priests and state officials stand by. Photo: Timothy E. Gregory

In broader cultural terms the age of the Tetrarchy preferred simple and straightforward representation: architecture, for example, was powerful and heavy, without sophistication or conceit. Sculpture is perhaps the clearest indication of the spirit of the age: somewhat abstract and simple, with figures presented in heavy, almost exaggerated realism – emperors who all look alike, with thick necks, close-cropped hair, and stubbly beards. The representation of the Tetrarchs, a porphyry group now in San Marco's in Venice, is perhaps the best example of this approach, as are the many coins and medallions of the emperors. The Arch of Galerius in Thessaloniki likewise proclaims the military power of the emperors, their defeat of the Persians, and the harmony between the gods and the rulers of Rome in simple and clear-cut statements.

Thus, authoritarianism, uniformity, rigidity, and appeals to strength were the primary characteristics of the age. And these were the obvious and perhaps necessary reactions to the collapse and instability of the period that came before. Furthermore, they probably best explain the emperor's reaction to the Christians and the outbreak of the so-called Great Persecution, which was to become the last attempt of the Roman state to suppress Christianity. During most of his reign Diocletian had ignored the Christians, while his colleague

Box 2.2 *The Great Persecution*

The persecution of the Christian church, initiated by Galerius and Diocletian in AD 302, had a powerful impact on later Byzantine Christianity. This persecution was unlike anything that had struck the church previously, in part because it was an official government-initiated attempt to stamp out the religion and in part because it resulted in the suffering and death of many Christians, particularly among the leaders. Most studies of the persecutions have focused on the reasons behind the phenomenon and the legal issues behind it. But it is clear that the persecution affected many aspects of later Christianity as well.

The Great Persecution was aimed directly at the organizational structure of the Christian church, the bishops, the Scriptures, and the church buildings themselves. Although some Christians betrayed their faith in the face of government action, many resisted and were killed. This provided Christians, both at the time of the persecutions and in later centuries, with a heroic set of oppositions: the evil persecutors and those who yielded on the one side and those saints who resisted the emperors' orders, even to the point of death, on the other.

Written accounts of heroic martyrdom were, of course, already known, beginning with that of the protomartyr Stephen (Acts 7.58) and the famous letter from the church of Smyrna on the martyrdom of St. Polycarp (ca. AD 155). But the accounts of the Great Persecution by Eusebios of Caesarea and Lactantius were written by eyewitnesses who described the victims as "countless" in number but – at the same time – essentially failed to present any of their names or the exact circumstances of their death (cf. Eusebios, *Ecclesiastical History* 8.6: "who could again at that time count the multitude of martyrs throughout each province . . .").

From the reign of Constantine, of course, the Christian church was triumphant and it could look back on the Great Persecution as a time of great trial just before the final victory. Those who directed the church in this phase had lived through the persecution and it affected the way they saw the relationship between the church and the emperor at that time. The broader phenomenon, and the sources associated with it, encouraged the development of hagiographic myth and the "discovery" of the identities and the heroic resistance of the martyrs: St. Pelagia of Tarsos (who spurned the amorous advances of Diocletian's son), the 10,000 Martyrs of Nicomedia, St. Demetrios (supposedly executed by Maximian), St. George (executed under Diocletian), and many others. These martyrs, then, served as the models for the Christian life in general, and of ascetics more particularly. The Byzantine church, therefore, looked back to a "heroic age," frequently placed in the reign of Diocletian, when the values of renunciation of the world were clearly spelled out in stark terms. In addition, the refusal of the martyrs to compromise their faith, even in the face of enticements and threats – indeed, their frequently mentioned search for martyrdom – became an inspiration for later Byzantines who felt they had to resist the erroneous ways of individual emperors, on either doctrinal or moral grounds. This is certainly one of the explanations for the apparent paradox that, although the Byzantine state was a Christian autocracy, the emperor was very frequently opposed by individuals who were quite willing to defy him openly on religious matters.

Galerius seems always to have been hostile toward them. Diocletian, perhaps inspired by Galerius and almost certainly irritated by the Christians' refusal to follow his order to sacrifice in the name of the emperor, finally began to persecute the Christians in 302 (the so-called Great Persecution). He ordered that the clergy be arrested and that Christian sacred books be confiscated and destroyed. There even was an attempt to ferret out individual Christians by requiring all citizens of the empire to sacrifice. The persecution was violent, but brief, and before his abdication in 305 Diocletian became aware that the policy was a failure and he began to relax its terms. The Great Persecution, however, shook the foundations of the Christian church, in part because a significant number of Christians apparently submitted to the imperial will and betrayed their faith. On the other hand, the steadfast resistance of the martyrs and their sometimes horrific deaths set a standard of behavior and resistance to imperial authority that the church was to carry into a new era in which Christianity was to become the dominant religion.

FURTHER READING

Simon J. J. Corcoran, *The Empire of the Tetrarchs: Imperial Pronouncements and Government, AD 284–324*. Oxford, 1996.

R. MacMullen, *Roman Government's Response to Crisis, A.D. 235–337*. New Haven, 1976.

S. Williams, *Diocletian and the Roman Recovery*. London, 1985.

3

The Age of Constantine the Great

250	500	750	1000	1250	1500

306	Constantine proclaimed emperor
312	Battle of the Milvian Bridge
325	Council of Nicaea
330	Founding of Constantinople

The age of Constantine the Great can reasonably be seen as the watershed between the old Roman Empire and the new Byzantine Empire. Such a division is, to some degree, artificial, dependent on historians' need to break the past up into comprehensible chunks: many elements of ancient civilization survived for centuries into the Byzantine period, and many historians regard Byzantium as, in fact, a survival of the ancient world. Indeed – as we have seen – the Byzantines themselves recognized their connection to the Roman Empire and, for the whole of the Byzantine Empire (and even after its fall!) they continued to refer to themselves as "Romans."

Nonetheless, it is clear that the early fourth century witnessed many new phenomena that were henceforth to characterize the Byzantine Empire, and what emerged from those changes was a society significantly different from what had come before. The most significant of these changes were the emergence of Christianity as the favored (and then the official) religion of the state and the creation of Constantinople as the new urban center of the empire on the shores of the Bosphoros, mid-way between all the empire's frontiers. The period was also marked by many other changes, some connected with these two overarching phenomena, others independent of them, and many with deep roots in the crises of the third century. These changes did not take place in a single moment and many of them took years, or even centuries, to work themselves out, one of the reasons that has led historians to view the Byzantine period, or at least its early years, as one of transformation, as a bridge between the ancient and the medieval worlds, or even between the ancient and the modern worlds.

The Rise of Constantine

In AD 305 the arrangement of the imperial college was as follows:

	East	**West**
Augustus	Diocletian	Maximian
Caesar	Galerius	Constantius Chlorus

On 1 May 305 Diocletian formally abdicated in the presence of his soldiers at Nikomedia, after a rule of over 20 years that put the Roman state on a new foundation. Diocletian pressured Maximian to abdicate at the same time, although it is clear that the latter was not really ready to do so.

By the arrangements already agreed upon, Galerius and Constantius Chlorus became *Augusti*. These changes of course required the nomination of new *Caesares*. Both Constantius and Maximian had capable sons (Constantine and Maxentius, respectively), who were eager to participate in the imperial college. Galerius, however, hated Maximian and his son, while Diocletian was always suspicious of Constantine, and he strongly opposed the nomination of sons to succeed their fathers, since this would introduce the principle of hereditary succession into the system. As a result, Maximinus Daia, Galerius' nephew, became Caesar in the East, while Flavius Valerius Severus became Caesar in the West – and the old *Augusti* withdrew into retirement, Diocletian to his monumental palace at Split on the Dalmatian coast.

The official arrangement from 305 to 308, then, was as follows:

	East	**West**
Augustus	Galerius	Constantius Chlorus
Caesar	Maximinus Daia	Severus

Galerius clearly was the strong man in this system, in part because both Maximinus Daia and Severus were his appointees and neither was strong enough to act against him. Constantine, the son of Constantius, was a virtual hostage at Galerius' court, in part to assure Constantius' cooperation in the new arrangement.

As one of his first actions, Constantius Chlorus undertook a military expedition in Britain. In 306 the Picts, a people native to what is now Scotland, invaded Roman Britain and Constantius wished to push them back. He sought Galerius' permission to have Constantine join him in his campaign and Galerius agreed, although he perhaps changed his mind and attempted to bring Constantine back.

Constantius and his son reached Britain, but Constantius unexpectedly died at York, on 25 July 306, throwing the new arrangement of the Tetrarchy into total confusion. Throughout Roman history, the military troops were normally loyal to the sons of their commanders, and the soldiers of Constantius were no exception. Immediately upon the death of the Augustus the troops proclaimed Constantine as emperor. Constantine wrote to Galerius, asking him to ratify the situation (i.e., to recognize Constantine as Augustus) and he then went to southern Gaul to await an answer from the senior emperor. Galerius agreed to a compromise: Constantine was to be recognized as Caesar, while Severus was to be Augustus. Constantine agreed, and for the time being the Diocletianic system remained intact.

In the meantime, however, in Rome the Praetorian Guard was discontented with its loss of power and prestige, along with the people of Rome, who were now being forced to pay taxes. They thus joined in proclaiming Maximian's son Maxentius as Caesar. Maxentius asked his father to return from retirement, and Maximian did so, resuming the title of *Augustus*. Galerius ordered Severus to attack Maxentius, but his troops mutinied and he fled to Ravenna, where he was killed in 307.

All parties agreed that only the prestige of Diocletian could save the situation, and Galerius organized a meeting at Carnuntum in 308, attended by Diocletian and Maximian. Galerius secured the support of the senior ex-emperors to appoint his old colleague Licinius as Augustus. Licinius had distinguished himself as a commander in Galerius' Persian campaign and was thus an experienced general. Constantine and Maximinus Daia were required to accept the rank of Caesars.

	East	West
Augustus	Galerius	Licinius
Caesar	Maximinus Daia	Constantine

The conference was therefore directed primarily against Maxentius and served to isolate him from the "legitimate" emperors. Maxentius, however, remained in effective control of Rome. Constantine, meanwhile, divorced his first wife (Minervina), the mother of his son Crispus, and married Fausta, the daughter of Maximian (and thus the sister of Maxentius). In 310, however, Constantine abandoned his adherence to the Herculian dynasty when Maximian attempted a coup against him and was subsequently murdered. Constantine then announced that he was descended from Claudius Gothicus and thus a member of the ancient Roman imperial family of the Flavians. At the same time he apparently selected Sol Invictus (the Unconquered Sun) as his patron deity, thus breaking with the religious patronage of both the ruling "families" of the

Tetrarchy, but reaching back to one of the gods favored by several of the military emperors of the third century. In addition, the sun-god was apparently popular in Gaul, Constantine's current base of power. During this period Constantine sought to strengthen his support in this area, while perhaps laying plans for an eventual attempt to control the whole of the empire.

While near death in 311 Galerius proclaimed the end of the persecution of the Christians and toleration for all religions throughout the empire. After his death cooperation among members of the Tetrarchy completely fell apart: Maximinus Daia attempted to seize the lands that had belonged to Galerius, but he was opposed by Licinius. In this situation Maximinus Daia sought an alliance with Maxentius, while Licinius and Constantine opposed them.

Battle of the Milvian Bridge, 312

Thus, in the West, the situation came down to a struggle between Constantine and Maxentius. The latter was in control of Rome, which had been powerfully fortified since the 270s, and he had a stronger military force. In the spring of 312 Constantine crossed the Alps and invaded Italy, bringing with him a force of perhaps 40,000 troops. Maxentius remained in Rome but sent a large cavalry detachment against Constantine. This was defeated near Turin and all the cities of northern Italy opened their doors to Constantine. As Constantine marched southward Maxentius prepared his defenses inside the city, destroying the old Milvian Bridge (across the Tiber on the Flaminian Way); in its place Maxentius constructed a narrow pontoon bridge, made up of two sections held together by a chain. Constantine, meanwhile, encamped just north of the city. Either there or somewhere earlier along his march, a remarkable event apparently happened to Constantine that was to have long-term effects on the history of the world. Lactantius and Eusebios present varying accounts of what actually happened, and we will probably never know the truth of the matter: according to later tradition, in Eusebios' *Life of Constantine,* the emperor witnessed a cross of light in the sky with the words "victory though this" written underneath. Constantine, regardless of how he understood it, used the cross (or some variant) as a symbol for his troops from this time onward.

As Constantine neared the city, Maxentius made a fatal mistake. Instead of remaining within the security of the walls of Rome, he decided to bring his troops outside the city to face Constantine. In this he may have been influenced by religious omens or by the danger of a popular revolt. Regardless, he placed his army in an untenable situation with the mountains to their left and the river to their right, and the forces of Constantine straight ahead. In this situation, Constantine attacked and won an overwhelming victory. Maxentius' troops were driven back against the narrow bridge and many of them – including Maxentius himself – were killed. The next day Constantine entered the city in victory, where he was greeted as a liberator by the Senate and the people of Rome.

The "Conversion" of Constantine

It is quite impossible to determine when, and how, Constantine was converted to Christianity. The real issue is one of definition: what it means to be a Christian and what one means by conversion. Certainly we should not assume that Constantine ever had the kind of personal experience and thorough change of attitude that one means by conversion in a modern Christian context. And Constantine was such a significant figure for later Christianity – as the first Christian emperor – that he is in many ways more a figure of myth than of history. Some of Constantine's Christian advisers, people such as Hosius of Cordoba, certainly played an important role in explaining to Constantine that he had won his victory over Maxentius through the power of Christ and that the miracle of the cross in the sky was God's sign to him. They also certainly pointed out to the emperor that he had specific duties as a result of his allegiance to Christianity.

There can be no doubt that, from 312 onward, Constantine favored the Christian church and that he offered it considerable wealth. He clearly became deeply involved in the religious controversies of the age (see below) and he favored Christians in the employ of the state. At the same time, Constantine continued to hold the office of *pontifex maximus* (chief priest of the state religion), and pagan symbols continued to appear on his coins, at least until 323. Constantine was finally baptized, but only on his deathbed in 337. This, however, was not an unusual situation, and many individuals who were firmly committed to Christianity delayed baptism until just before they died. All in all, then, it is very hard to gauge what Constantine's personal feelings and attitudes about religion really were. He was, after all, not a scholar or a particularly pious person but had lived all his life as a soldier. It seems very unlikely that he saw Christianity as offering him very much in a purely political sense and he probably did not understand, at least at first, the spiritual aspects of Christianity. We are, today, at a considerable disadvantage in trying to understand Constantine since we generally assume that people act for "spiritual" reasons that are essentially outside the experience of individuals at the time of Constantine, at least those who had not grown up in the Jewish or Christian tradition. On the other hand, Constantine must have been impressed by the apparent power of the Christian God, as demonstrated at the Battle of the Milvian Bridge and afterwards.

Lactantius, who was writing about a year after the battle, was aware that some religious event had been associated with that event, but his account is imprecise and unclear. At just about the same time the Roman Senate, wishing to endear itself to the new ruler of Rome and make up for its support of Maxentius, erected a triumphal arch that still stands between the forum and the Colosseum. The inscription, which the senators knew had to be acceptable to Constantine, says that the emperor's victory was due to the "greatness of his mind" and the "inspiration of the divinity." The use of the singular here and the lack of reference to the traditional gods of the Roman pantheon are suggestive of Constantine's movement toward Christianity, although the inscription obviously lacks the details that were to mark the fully developed myth of the miraculous cross that was apparently already circulating before Constantine's death.

In the aftermath of the defeat of Maxentius Constantine met Licinius in 313 at Milan, where Licinius married Constantia, Constantine's half-sister. At this time the two emperors published a series of documents, which apparently included an edict that Galerius had issued earlier, ending the persecution of Christians. This so-called Edict of Milan guaranteed religious toleration to all, promised freedom of action to the Christian church, and offered protection to the church under Roman law.

After the meeting in Milan, Constantine marched into Gaul to deal with a Frankish incursion, and Maximinus Daia used the opportunity to move into Licinius' territory in Thrace. Licinius defeated Maximinus in battle near Adrianople and Maximinus died shortly thereafter in Asia Minor.

Empire divided between Constantine and Licinius: 314–324

From this point the empire was divided between East and West. There were strains from the very beginning and war broke out in 316, but this resulted in a compromise when Licinius agreed to leave the whole of the West (with the exception of Thrace) to Constantine. The situation continued to deteriorate, however, made worse by Licinius' decision to resume persecution of the Christians. Constantine had become more and more open in his support of Christianity, and Licinius may have felt that the church in his territory was a force loyal to Constantine rather than to himself. Licinius' persecution gave Constantine the excuse he needed to initiate war. In addition, when the Goths invaded Moesia and Thrace in 323, Constantine repulsed them, crossing deliberately into Licinius' territory. There ensued a short war that ended with Licinius' defeat in 324. As a result of Constantia's intervention, Licinius' life was initially spared, but six months later he was killed. Constantine was ruler of an undivided empire.

The Undivided Reign of Constantine the Great

After 324 Constantine continued and modified the reforms that Diocletian had instituted and he brought to completion the governmental system that was to dominate the Byzantine world for centuries to come. Meanwhile, his alliance with the Christian church continued to grow more important – and more complex – in imperial policy. Constantine discovered at an early date that the benefits he gained from his support of Christianity carried with them real responsibilities.

Figure 3.1 *Solidus* of Constantine I. The *solidi* (gold coins) of Constantine were one of the emperor's most important economic achievements. They characteristically depict the emperor as clean-shaven and with a calm and confident appearance, normally in civilian dress. The reverse (back) of the coin, however, shows Roman military standards and reminds us of the importance of the military situation in Constantine's reign. Photo: Dumbarton Oaks

Heresy

One of the most important phenomena in this period is what we call "heresy." This term is somewhat misleading since it implies a judgment of who is "wrong" (the heretics) and who is "right" (the orthodox) in a religious dispute. The word is usually meant to indicate a teaching or a group that holds "incorrect" religious beliefs. What this means, of course, is to a degree a matter of opinion or a matter of definition: any group that disagrees with the "orthodox" church is "heretical," but heresies almost always arose in situations where no official position had yet been taken; thus, in practical terms, heresy meant the position that was eventually condemned by the official, or orthodox, church, often after considerable debate and disagreement. The concept of heresy is comprehensible only in an exclusivist religious tradition, where there is an assumption that one set of beliefs is correct and all others are wrong (thus the idea of heresy would not have come up in an earlier Roman context). In addition, it must be understood that in the Christianity of the time (and of many other periods as well) salvation was not seen simply as a matter of accepting God's plan for mankind or even of living a good life and avoiding sin; rather, salvation was possible only for those who accepted the "correct" teachings of Christianity, however those were ultimately defined.

Heresy literally means "choice" (what we might even call "freedom of thought") and this was something that contemporary Christianity could not tolerate, since it seemed to encourage people to make a choice that could prevent their salvation. What makes this concept more significant is the belief that Christians—and Christian leaders in particular—were obliged not only to hold correct religious beliefs themselves, but also to make sure that others held them as well (after all, heretics would be condemned to hell). And of course, as the first Christian emperor, Constantine believed (or at least was told by his Christian advisers) that he had a special responsibility from God to protect the church from heresy (as well as any other harm) and that his political and military successes were dependent directly on his ability to maintain the unity and the correct belief of the church.

Heresy had been a problem in Christianity from the very beginning, since it is clear that people often had differing understandings of the basic ideas of Christian belief. Nonetheless, from the time of Constantine the problem of heresy took on a new significance, in part because the state became deeply involved. Furthermore, as Christianity came to accept the traditions and the terminology of classical culture, Christian theology was expressed in terms derived from the schools of "pagan" (i.e., pre-Christian) philosophy. This was to have enormous ramifications, since it meant that Christian ideas were to make use of and thus preserve the traditions of classical thought, and that discussions about Christian truth would be put into the already age-old framework of the Greco-Roman world. At the same time, the academic differences among the various schools of classical philosophy would then come to characterize debates among Christian theologians, which would elevate the intellectual content of the debate while hardening the differences among the various sides, since each of them came to the controversy with significant intellectual preconceptions and approaches toward the definition of truth. Furthermore, these issues were not simply academic or theological disputes, since they involved questions of personal salvation and, although ordinary believers may not have been able to understand the subtle differences among the various theological positions, they clearly did understand that their own salvation depended not only on their acceptance of the "correct" position but also on the triumph of that position in society as a whole. Thus, theological debate, the attempt to determine theological "truth," and significant divisions among church leaders and their followers were important characteristics of the age. If Constantine had hoped that Christianity would bring unity to the Roman Empire, he must have been sadly disappointed.

Donatism

Almost immediately after the Battle of the Milvian Bridge Constantine encountered the religious controversy over Donatism, which had seriously split the church of Africa. Donatism arose in the aftermath of the persecutions under Diocletian, when many Christians apparently yielded to the persecutors and either denied their faith or handed over sacred books to the officials of the state. When these *traditores* (those who failed in the test of their faith) sought forgiveness and reinstatement in the church, some bishops were willing to forgive them, while others maintained a stricter standard and refused to do so, saying that their serious sin could not be forgiven. The leader of the latter movement was a priest of Carthage by the name of Donatus, who condemned the practice of allowing the *traditores* to resume their duties. In a sense, the Donatists, as they came to be called, had a different view of the nature of the church than did the orthodox. The Donatists thought the church was to be made up only of the "saints," who lived a holy life; the orthodox, on the other hand, felt that the church had the power to forgive all sins and that those who had sinned should be forgiven as long as they repented of their mistakes.

The dispute in Africa arose when the Donatists raised objections to Caecilian, the bishop of Carthage, who was willing to pardon the *traditores* and even welcome them back into the clergy. The bishop of Rome (the pope) had supported Caecilian, but the Donatists rejected this decision and elected Donatus himself as bishop of Carthage. In most ways Donatism can therefore be viewed as a schism (an administrative split within the church) rather than a heresy, since it dealt primarily with disciplinary and organizational matters within the church. Nonetheless, the denial that the church had the power to forgive certain sins and that the sacraments performed by sinful priests were invalid had important theological ramifications. Historians have long wondered at the power of Donatism in North Africa (it had virtually no supporters elsewhere) and its spread in the African countryside. W. H. C. Frend argued that Donatism was essentially a social or even a cultural movement, a means by which the "native" (pre-Roman) population of North Africa could express its opposition to Rome and forcible Romanization. Most authorities today do not agree with this view, and they see Donatism as a purely religious movement.

Constantine necessarily got involved in the Donatist controversy when he sought to restore the property of the African church to its rightful owners in 313: which of the two bishops was the rightful representative of the church? Constantine at first simply asked the two parties to solve their differences and live in peace – but this naturally did not work. Next he summoned two church councils, in 313 and 314, and these ruled against the Donatists. The Donatists then appealed directly to the emperor, who also finally decided that the "orthodox" were in the right. When they refused to submit, Constantine ordered the army to force the Donatists into submission – the first official persecution carried out in favor of Christianity. The Donatists suffered martyrdom with the same zeal as the early Christians, and Constantine finally gave up. Donatism thus remained a vital movement, the church was officially split, and Constantine's first experience with heresy was not at all a positive one.

Arianism

Meanwhile, in Alexandria another type of heresy grew up. Alexandria was the intellectual center of the eastern Mediterranean, if not of the whole empire, and the Christians of the city already had a reputation for heated debate about the nature of their religion. Already there were strong Christian intellectual traditions, based mainly on the philosophical schools of antiquity. The dominant view in Alexandria was one devised by Origen and based largely on the ideas of Neoplatonism. Among the main aspects of this teaching were an allegorical and spiritual (i.e., not necessarily literal) reading of the Scriptures and an emphasis on the absolute power and "otherness" of God.

Arius, a priest in Alexandria, disagreed with many of the teachings of this tradition and wished to stress the humanity of Christ, in distinction to the divinity of God the Father. Thus, the controversy that resulted was connected closely with the nature of the Trinity, especially the relationships among the members of the Trinity (Father, Son, and Holy Spirit). Arius taught that Christ (the Son) was not as fully God as the Father, and that he had been made in time by the Father. This teaching was condemned by Alexander, the bishop of Alexandria, and an enormous controversy ensued. This attracted the attention of Licinius, then ruler of the East, and in 320 he used the controversy as an excuse to resume the persecution of the Christians.

After he defeated Licinius in 324, Constantine had to deal with the problem of Arianism. As he had in the Donatist controversy, Constantine seems to have thought that a solution could be found if both sides simply looked for common ground, and he wrote letters calling for compromise and harmony. When this failed Constantine decided to call a council of all the bishops of the empire to decide the issue. In Byzantine parlance the empire was commonly seen as the *oikoumene* (the "universe" or what one might call the "civilized world"); hence such a council was called "empire-wide" or "ecumenical." The practice of discussing difficult issues at church councils already had a long history (going back, one might argue, to New Testament times), but these had always been local. Constantine probably saw the council as something similar to the Roman Senate, a forum for discussion among leaders that the emperor could dominate by a show of his own authority. In this regard he obviously misunderstood the depth of feeling on doctrinal matters and the importance they were given by church leaders and laity alike.

The first ecumenical council opened in Nicaea (in Bithynia) on 20 May 325. The emperor presided over the opening ceremony in person and he presented a speech in which he proclaimed his own faith and besought the fathers to restore the unity of the church. The politics of the council were complex and compromise was impossible. For one reason or another, the opponents of Arius decided that the important thing was that Arius be condemned, and they sought a statement that would divide the two sides clearly. Finally, a creed was developed (the so-called Nicene Creed) which the Arians would not accept. This said that Christ (the Son) was "begotten, not made, of the same substance (*homoousios*)" with the Father. This meant that the Father and the Son were declared to be equally God and that both had existed (along with the Holy Spirit) for all eternity. The Council of Nicaea also went on to define other issues, such as the date of Easter (as it is defined still today – the first Sunday after the first full moon after the vernal equinox) and 20 canons (rules) for the governing of the church.

The council, however, had unfortunate consequences, since the Arians did not simply give up and accept the orthodox decision. Rather, they maintained that they were right and that the orthodox were the heretics. This stalemate was disturbing to Constantine, since he hoped that the council would produce unity, and he believed that God had charged him with the duty of protecting the unity of the church and making sure that heretics were converted from their false beliefs. The continued dispute also raised the disturbing question of how God ultimately allowed heresy to exist and even flourish: if the Arians were wrong, why did God not destroy them? Future emperors, and even Constantine himself, asked this same question and could not come up with a good answer.

Secular Policies

As mentioned previously, Constantine largely continued the administrative and political policies of Diocletian, and it is frequently difficult to tell which emperor initiated a given reform. In economic policy, Constantine sought to succeed where Diocletian had failed. In part because he confiscated the treasures of the pagan temples, Constantine was able (as we mentioned above) to strike a gold coin, the *solidus*, at a fixed rate of 72 to the pound (i.e., each coin weighted 1/72nd of a pound). As a result of a stronger economic base, Constantine was able to collect some of the land taxes in cash, and he introduced a tax on businessmen, the so-called *collatio lustralis* or *chrysargyron*.

In 312 Constantine abolished the Praetorian Guard (in part because of its support of Maxentius) and replaced it with an elite guard of crack troops, many of whom were Germans: the so-called *scholae*. As under the Tetrarchy, the emperor was surrounded by his close associates and advisers, the *comitatus*, and the troops assigned directly to the emperor were the *comitatenses* and the elite corps of the *palatinae*.

Under Constantine Italy and Rome lost their special place of primacy in the empire (something Diocletian and Galerius had already sought to do) and they were now made part of the regular administrative structure of the state. Although the two consuls continued to be appointed, the political head of the city was the urban prefect (*praefectus urbi*), an imperial official, who also presided over the Senate. The Roman Senate became little more than the urban council of the city, and it lost some of its ancient prestige. Constantine abolished the distinction between senators and *equites*, and *equites* who held high office formally became senators, so that the number of senators rose to about 2,500. The prestige of the senators, however, did not decline, and many of them, especially in the West, enjoyed great wealth on their enormous landed estates. Constantine honored the senators by the revival of the title *patricius* (patrician), which was awarded to individual senators for meritorious service to the emperor.

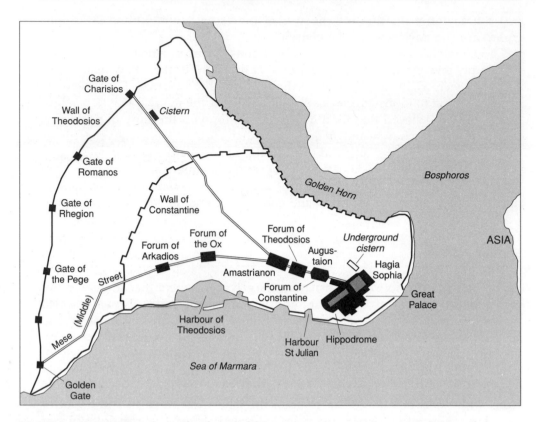

Map 3.1 Constantinople in the fourth-fifth century. From Jackson J. Spielvogel, *Western Civilizations*, fifth edition (Wadsworth, 2003), map 7.5, p. 182

The Founding of Constantinople (330)

During his wars with Licinius, Constantine was impressed with the natural location of Byzantium, on the easternmost tip of Europe, facing Asia across the narrow strait of the Bosphoros. After his victory, Constantine wanted to build a city as a monument to his military success, following a tradition of great commanders since the time of Alexander the Great. At first he considered refounding Troy, but settled on Byzantium, in part because he was impressed by its physical setting on the Bosphoros, surrounded on three sides by water. In addition, he cannot have been unaware of its location, almost exactly mid-way between the eastern and the western frontiers and on the natural crossroads of the whole of the empire. According to tradition, Constantine laid out the circuit of the city himself, guided personally by an angel: the city was indeed enormous, many times the size of the old Byzantium, and protected on its landward side by a powerful wall.

From 324 to the dedication of the city in 330 Constantine spared no expense in planning and decorating this new center, stripping many great monuments of the ancient world in order to create a beautiful city, worthy of himself and

Box 3.1   *The Founding of Constantinople*

The founding of Constantinople, on the site of the ancient Greek city of Byzantium (Byzantion), was – as it turned out – one of the most important achievements of Constantine the Great. At the time it probably was regarded as significant, but many emperors had previously founded "new" cities and named them after themselves. Thus, contemporaries probably could not know how important this new city would be in the future of the Byzantine Empire. Eusebios of Caesarea, in his biography of Constantine, hardly made reference to the event. Within a century, however, Constantinople had grown dramatically and had become the most important city of the Mediterranean world.

The church historian Sozomen, writing about the middle of the fifth century, paid special attention to the event. Notice that, according to this account, Constantine had thought of building his new city at the famous site of Troy, but that God himself intervened, causing Constantinople to go to the ancient city of Byzantium in Thrace:

> The emperor [Constantine], always intent on the advancement of religion, erected the most beautiful temples to God in every place, particularly in metropolises, such as Nicomedia in Bithynia, Antioch on the river Orontes, and Byzantium. He greatly improved this latter city, and constituted it the equal of Rome in power, and participation in the government; for, when he had settled the affairs of the empire according to his own mind, and had rectified foreign affairs by wars and treaties, he resolved upon founding a city which should be called by his own name, and should be equal in celebrity to Rome. With this intention, he repaired to a plain at the foot of Troy, near the Hellespont, above the tomb of Ajax, where, it is said, the Achaians had their naval stations and tents while besieging Troy; and here he laid the plan of a large and beautiful city, and built the gates on an elevated spot of ground, whence they are still visible from the sea to those sailing by. But when he had advanced thus far, God appeared to him by night, and commanded him to seek another spot. Led by the hand of God, he arrived at Byzantium in Thrace, beyond Chalcedon in Bithynia, and here he was desired to build his city and to render it worthy of the name of Constantine. In obedience to the words of God, he therefore enlarged the city formerly called Byzantium, and surrounded it with high walls. He also erected magnificent dwelling houses southward through the regions. Since he was aware that the former population was insufficient for so great a city, he peopled it with men of rank and their households, whom he summoned hither from the elder Rome and from other countries. He imposed taxes to cover the expenses of building and adorning the city, and of supplying its inhabitants with food, and providing the city with all the other requisites. He adorned it sumptuously with a hippodrome, fountains, porticos, and other structures. He named it New Rome and Constantinople, and constituted it the imperial capital for all the inhabitants of the North, the South, the East, and the shores of the Mediterranean, from the cities on the Ister and from Epidamnus and the Ionian gulf, to Cyrene and that part of Libya called Borium.

He constructed another council house which they call the senate; he ordered the same honors and festal days as those customary to the other Romans, and he did not fail studiously to make the city which bore his name equal in every respect to that of Rome in Italy; nor were his wishes thwarted; for by the assistance of God, it had to be confessed as great in population and wealth. I know of no cause to account for this extraordinary aggrandizement, unless it be the piety of the builder and of the inhabitants, and their compassion and liberality towards the poor. The zeal they manifested for the Christian faith was so great that many of the Jewish inhabitants and most of the Greeks were converted. As this city became the capital of the empire during the period of religious prosperity, it was not polluted by altars, Grecian temples, nor sacrifices; and although Julian authorized the introduction of idolatry for a short space of time, it soon afterwards became extinct. Constantine further honored this newly compacted city of Christ, named after himself, by adorning it with numerous and magnificent houses of prayer. And the Deity also co-operated with the spirit of the emperor, and by Divine manifestations persuaded men that these prayer houses in the city were holy and salvatory

As time went on and the fame of Constantinople grew, authors came to embellish the story of the city's founding, adding many legendary and fantastic details, showing particularly how God had a hand in the details. The famous British historian Edward Gibbon, writing at the end of the eighteenth century, summarized one of those stories, when the emperor, surrounded by his army and advisers, laid out the extent of what would become an enormous city:

[Constantine] was anxious to leave a deep impression of hope and respect on the minds of the spectators. On foot, with a lance in his hand, the emperor himself led the solemn procession, and directed the line which was traced as the boundary of the destined capital, till the growing circumference was observed with astonishment by the assistants, who, at length ventured to observe that he had already exceeded the most ample measure of a great city. "I shall still advance," replied Constantine, "till HE, the invisible guide who marches before me, thinks proper to stop."

Edward Gibbon, *The Decline and Fall of the Roman Empire*, ed. J. B. Bury (New York, 1946), vol. 1, p. 460.

the new order he sought to create. He deliberately wished to duplicate the features of ancient Rome, from the seven hills to the forum, and a population that was exempt from taxation and supplied with lavish entertainment and free food. The official name of the city always was Nea Romē (New Rome), although it was also called Constantinople, the city of Constantine.

Constantine laid the foundations for many of the great buildings that were to grace the new city: the Great Palace, the cathedral of Hagia Sophia, the

Figure 3.2 Column of Constantine, Constantinople. Roman emperors had commonly erected monumental columns to honor themselves and their military victories, several of these survive in Rome, including the column of the Byzantine emperor Phokas (602–10). Constantine erected this column in Constantinople and it became, in many ways, the center of the city. The column was surrounded by a round colonnade, creating thus the Forum of Constantine, and the main street of Constantinople (the Mese, or "Middle Street") passed through the monumental complex. Later emperors, when successful in war, passed from the Golden Gate, through the Forum of Constantine, to the palace complex. The column was surmounted by a statue of Constantine, which had been made by re-carving a statue of the god Apollo in order to give it the features of the emperor. According to one tradition, Constantine had the nails from the Crucifixion and the Palladium built into the column – the latter was the sacred cloak of Athena, which had been brought to Italy from Troy after the sack of the city and became the special protection of Rome. According to another tradition, Constantinople would never fall to any of its enemies as long as the sculpture remained in place. Photo: Timothy E. Gregory

university, hippodromes, baths, and numerous other churches, including his own burial-place, the church of the Holy Apostles. On 11 May 330 the city was dedicated, amid much celebration and fanfare.

Constantine certainly did not seek to build a new capital, nor to move the capital from Rome to the East. The very idea of a "capital" was, in fact, foreign to the Roman mind, but the location of Constantinople destined the city for greatness. The natural defense provided by the waters of the Bosphoros was also to help the city many times to resist the barbarian hordes that crashed against it over the centuries. Furthermore, most of Constantine's successors, for the rest of the century, remained mainly in Constantinople, and this had important ramifications in focusing emerging Byzantine institutions in the new imperial city. Thus, the founding of Constantinople, along with the linking of the Christian church with the Roman state, was certainly one of the most lasting accomplishments of the first Byzantine emperor.

Constantine's Building Program

Constantine was particularly concerned to build and decorate the new city of Constantinople, but he also built many lavish structures throughout the Mediterranean world. These were to have an enormous impact, not only because they were associated with Constantine, but also because, as in so many other areas, the decisions taken by Constantine (or taken in his name) were to have great significance for centuries to come. One of the main issues was the shape that Christian churches were to take, since there was not, apparently, a tradition of monumental church buildings when Constantine decided to help the Christian church build a series of truly spectacular structures.

The main form that these churches took was that of the *basilica*, a multipurpose rectangular structure, based ultimately on the earlier Greek *stoa*, which could be found in most of the great cities of the empire. Christianity, unlike classical polytheism, needed a large interior space for the celebration of its religious services, and the basilica aptly filled that need. We naturally do not know the degree to which the emperor was involved in the design of new churches, but it is tempting to connect this with the secular basilica that Constantine completed in the Roman forum (the so-called Basilica of Maxentius) and the one he probably built in Trier, in connection with his residence in the city at a time when he was still Caesar. This latter was 67 meters long, with a huge interior space not interrupted by interior supports. Two rows of tall windows ran along each of the long sides of the basilica and the building ended in a large apse, within which the emperor presumably sat in state. The Trier basilica, unlike most other secular basilicas, was apparently entered from the short side opposite the apse, providing a long vista toward the other end of the building and the seat of imperial power. This was a perfect setting for the worship of the Christian God, who was perceived in so many ways as similar to the emperor.

Shortly after the Battle of the Milvian Bridge, perhaps as early as 313, Constantine's architects began work on the basilica now known as San Giovanni in Laterano on the slopes of the Caelian Hill in the southeastern corner of Rome. The building was completed remarkably rapidly and by 318 it was ready for use. This was an enormous building of basilican type, with a central nave 100 meters long, terminating in an apse, with two side aisles on either side of the nave, and with a total width of over 53 meters. As with basilicas of similar types, the aisles were separated by colonnades and the wooden roof of the central nave was raised higher than the single-story roofs over the side aisle, this system allowing considerable light to enter the building through a series of windows at clerestory level. The interior decoration was colorful and lavish: the columns of the nave were of red granite, those of the aisles were of green stone; the floors were paved in marble and the half-dome of the apse was covered with an aniconic gold mosaic (that is, one without human figures). The Lateran Basilica, completed apparently within six years of the Battle of the Milvian Bridge, was to set the standard followed by most Christian churches, East and West, from that time until our own.

Box 3.2 *Eusebios of Caesarea's Opposition to Christian Images*

Eusebios of Caesarea was among those who was opposed to representational art in a Christian context. One should remember that up until the second or third century Christians in general hesitated to make pictures of the saints or of God himself, apparently regarding this an act of idolatry. From the time of Constantine onward, however, Christian representational art was increasingly common. Constantine himself seems to have promoted such displays and there is evidence that religious paintings were on display in the Forum of Constantine in Constantinople. Eusebios of Caesarea was aware of this practice and that the "men of old" had paintings of the Apostles and even Christ himself. Yet, Eusebios strongly disagreed with this practice. On one occasion, Constantina, the sister of Constantine, wrote to the bishop and asked him to send her an image of Christ. Eusebios responded in a letter that survives, in which he sets out the theological reasons why Christ should not be represented in art. In short, he says that Christ, as God, cannot possibly be "captured" in an image, while the Second Commandment (Exodus 20:4, Deuteronomy 5:8) prohibits the worship of "graven images":

> You also wrote me concerning some supposed image of Christ, which image you wished me to send you. Now what kind of thing is this that you call the image of Christ? I do not know what impelled you to request that an image of Our Saviour should be delineated. What sort of image of Christ are you seeking? Is it the true and unalterable one which bears His essential characteristics,

or the one which He took up for our sake when He assumed the form of a servant . . . Granted, He has two forms, even I do not think that your request has to do with His divine form . . . Surely then, you are seeking His image as a servant, that of the flesh which He put on for our sake. But that, too, we have been taught, was mingled with the glory of His divinity so that the mortal part was swallowed up by Life . . . Who, then, would be able to represent by means of dead colors and inanimate delineations (*skiagraphiai*) the glistening, flashing radiance of such dignity and glory, when even His superhuman disciples could not bear to behold Him in this guise and fell on their faces, thus admitting that they could not withstand the sight? . . .

But if you mean to ask of me the image, not of His form transformed into that of God, but that of the mortal flesh before its transformation, can it be that you have forgotten that passage in which God lays down the law that no likeness should be made either of what is in heaven or what is in the earth beneath? Have you ever heard anything of the kind either yourself in church or from another person? Are not such things banished and excluded from churches all over the world, and is it not common knowledge that such practices are not permitted to us alone?

Once – I do not know how – a woman brought me in her hands a picture of two men in the guise of philosophers and let fall the statement that they were Paul and the Saviour – I have no means of saying where she had this from or learned such a thing. With the view that neither she nor others might be given offense, I took it away from her and kept it in my house, as I thought it improper that such things ever be exhibited to others, lest we appear, like idol worshippers, to carry our God around in an image. I note that Paul instructs all of us not to cling any more to things of the flesh; for he says, though we have known Christ after the flesh, yet now henceforth know we Him no more.

Translation from C. Mango, *The Art of the Byzantine Empire, 312–1453: Sources and Documents* (Englewood Cliffs, NJ, 1972, reprint, Toronto, 1986), pp. 16–18.

Most scholars have argued that Constantine's use of the basilica for the dominant type of early Christian church was derived from a strong connection between the emperor and the Christian God: that the perception of God on the part of ordinary believers (including Constantine) was derived from the overwhelming figure of the emperor. Just as the emperor sat enthroned in the basilica, so Christ must sit enthroned in his church and in the Kingdom of Heaven. Recently T. F. Mathews has challenged this view and has argued that the inspirations for Christian art and architecture of this period are not to be found in Roman imperial art. It is perhaps too early to decide on this question, but there can be no doubt about the importance of early church foundations at this time and their influence in later centuries.

The emperor simultaneously undertook other building programs in Rome, including the Basilica of Maxentius already mentioned, a huge secular structure

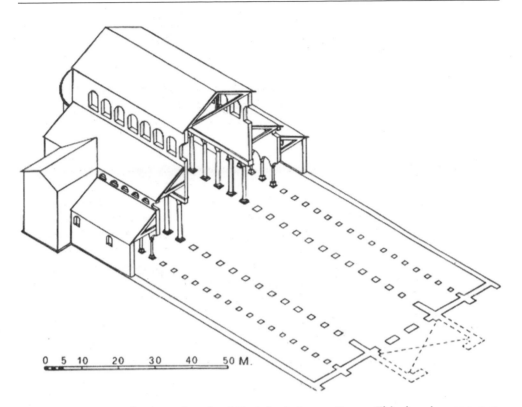

0 5 10   20   30   40   50 M.

Figure 3.3 Isometric view, church of St. John Lateran, Rome. This drawing conveys much of the structure of a basilica, used mainly for governmental services and imperial audiences in Roman times, but transformed by the Christians into the most common form of religious buildings. From Richard Krautheimer, *Three Christian Capitals* (Berkeley: University of California Press, 1963)

left unfinished at the time of the battle in 312. He likewise undertook and apparently quickly completed the Christian basilica of St. Peter's in the Vatican in Rome, a building that resembled the Lateran basilica in size and shape and that was to serve as one of the most important Christian centers until its reconstruction during the Renaissance. Even though the old St. Peter's was a basilica in plan, it also functioned as a *martyrion*, a building housing the tomb of a Christian martyr and designed to accommodate the pilgrims who came to worship there.

Constantine may also have been responsible for construction of the present church of Santa Costanza in Rome, originally built as a mausoleum for his half-sister Constantia, who had been married to his then colleague Licinius. This building, as many other mausolea of the time, is centrally planned, with a circular floor-plan. An exterior porch leads into a circular barrel-vaulted ambulatory surrounding the central domed space. The ambulatory is decorated with mosaics and the central space is separated from the ambulatory by 12

Box 3.3 *Arrangements for a Church*

Although there were originally no specific directions set forth for the arrangement of a Christian church, standard basic features began to arise already in the time of Constantine. These presumably differed from place to place. The *Apostolic Constitutions*, a work written about AD 375, lays down some of these:

First, let the church (*oikos*) be elongated (inasmuch as it resembles a ship), turned to the east, and let it have the *pastophoria* [seats for the priests] on either side, towards the east. The bishop's throne is to be placed in the middle, and on both sides of him the presbyters shall sit, while the deacons stand by, trimly dressed, without any superfluous clothing, since they are like seamen or boatswains. It shall be a concern of the latter that the laity is seated in the other part [of the church] in a quiet and orderly fashion, the women sitting apart and observing silence. The lector [reader] shall stand in the middle, on an eminence, and read the books of Moses and Joshua, son of Nun, of the Judges and the Kings . . .

Translation from C. Mango, *The Art of the Byzantine Empire, 312–1453: Sources and Documents* (Englewood Cliffs, NJ, 1972, reprint Toronto, 1986), p. 24.

pairs of coupled Corinthian columns with arches between them supporting the dome. Circular, square, and rectangular centrally planned buildings were also used for churches, and they provided an organization of space and an appearance different from those of the more common basilica.

Constantine was also especially concerned about the construction of Christian monuments in Jerusalem. Eusebios of Caesarea's *Life of Constantine* (3.25–8) presents the full story of how the tomb of Christ was supposedly found under a mass of debris from the pagan temple of Venus that had been constructed there. Constantine then ordered a magnificent five-aisled basilica to be built on the spot. This was later embellished by the construction of a rotunda directly over the place of the tomb, and the huge complex became the most important pilgrimage place in the Christian world.

The Death of Constantine (337)

Constantine's last years were marred by personal tragedy and doubt, brought on in part by the realization that his policy at Nicaea was a failure. God had certainly rewarded him for his "piety" by an unbroken string of military victories and stability within the empire, but Constantine must certainly have wondered why Arianism had continued to flourish, even after its condemnation in 325.

As a result Constantine began to consider whether the decision of Nicaea had, in fact, been a mistake, and he began to move toward an acceptance of Arian teachings. He surrounded himself with advisers who tended toward Arianism, bishops such as Eusebios of Nicomedia. A possible indication of God's judgment was the tragedy that struck Constantine's own family. In 326 Constantine's wife Fausta accused her stepson Crispus of raping her. In a rage, Constantine had his eldest son executed, despite his brilliant military reputation and the likelihood that he would have succeeded as emperor. Afterward, Constantine's mother Helena reported the dishonesty of Fausta, saying that she had committed adultery with a slave. Shortly thereafter Constantine had Fausta scalded to death in her bath.

In 337 Constantine marched against the Persians in retaliation for their attack on Arabia. On the way he suddenly fell ill and returned toward Constantinople. Reaching Nicomedia, he felt the end was near and he summoned the bishop Eusebios of Nicomedia and was baptized. Shortly thereafter he died and was buried in the church of the Holy Apostles, as he had wished. The legacy of Constantine is enormous and it is only unfortunate that the sources do not really allow us to approach him as a person, since he has merged so fully into a mythic figure which was already being created during his lifetime. Like individuals such as Achilles, Alexander the Great, and Augustus, Constantine's real personality and motives are probably beyond our ability to fully understand, but there can be no doubt about the powerful effect that his reign had on subsequent events.

FURTHER READING

J. Curran, *Pagan City and Christian Capital. Rome in the Fourth Century*. Oxford, 2000.
A. H. M. Jones, *Constantine and the Conversion of Europe*. London, 1948.
R. Krautheimer, *Three Christian Capitals*. Berkeley, CA, 1983.
Ramsay MacMullen, *Constantine*. New York, 1969.
T. F. Mathews, *The Clash of Gods: A Reinterpretation of Early Christian Art*. Princeton, NJ, 1993.
Margaret Visser, *The Geometry of Love: Space, Time, Mystery and Meaning in an Ordinary Church*. London, 2001.

4

The Fourth Century: Constantius II to Theodosios I

250	500	750	1000	1250	1500

361	Julian "the Apostate" emperor
378	Battle of Adrianople
381	Council of Constantinople

The achievements of Diocletian and Constantine were real and revolutionary in many ways. Nonetheless, there was no way to know whether the reforms would survive and continue to guide the empire into the future. The task of providing continuity, of solidifying the situation and bringing these reforms to fruition, was left to Constantine's successors. These would determine, for example, whether Christianity would remain the religion of the empire or whether there would be a return to classical polytheism.

The Sons of Constantine

Oddly enough, Constantine had not made secure arrangements for the succession. To be sure, his three surviving sons had all been made Caesars: Constantine II (in 316), Constantius II (in 326), and Constans (in 336). All three were the sons of Constantine and Fausta. But Constantine had also elevated his two nephews, Dalmatius and Hanibalianus, to the rank of Caesar. The Caesars were dispatched to various parts of the empire where they all gained experience by ruling in the name of Constantine. Hanibalianus, interestingly enough, was named king of Armenia.

After Constantine's death in 337 there was a period of remarkable indecision, lasting four months, when it was unclear who would actually seize power
and rule the empire. For one reason or another, rumors arose that Constantine's
half-brothers had poisoned him, and stories of conspiracies spread throughout
the empire. The troops, however, ultimately made their opinion known and
took an oath that they would support no one other than the sons of Constantine.
Accordingly, a massacre took place: Dalmatius and Hannibalianus were murdered, along with all the members of their families, with the exception of two
young sons of Constantine's half-brother Julius Constantius, Gallus and Julian.

The sons of Constantine were thus formally acknowledged as *Augusti*:
Constantine II was 21, Constantius II 20, and Constans I 17. The empire was
then divided: Constantine II received the western part of the empire, Constans
held Italy, Africa, and Illyricum, and Constantius II was to control the East. A
dispute soon broke out among the brothers. In 340 Constantine II attacked
Constans, but he was defeated and killed; Constans inherited his brother's
territory and controlled the entire West. While Constans was occupied in
defending the Roman frontier in Britain and Germany, Constantius II had to
deal with a revitalized Persia under the ambitious Shapur II (309–79). A long
and difficult war in Mesopotamia was terminated by a treaty in 350. In the
West Constans earned the displeasure of the troops because of his harshness,
and in 350 he was overthrown and killed in an insurrection led by the officer
Magnentius, who was of Germanic origin. Three claimants arose for the throne:
Magnentius, Vetranio (the *magister militum*), and Nepotianus, a nephew of
Constantine. Magnentius emerged from the struggle and gained control of the
West. Constantius refused to recognize him, marched westward, and engaged
him in a series of battles from 351 onward, which finally resulted in Magnentius'
defeat and death. By 353 Constantius II was ruler of an undivided empire.

Constantius II, however, realized the difficulty of ruling the whole empire by
himself and he sought a co-emperor. Turning naturally to the few remaining
members of his own family, he selected Gallus – one of the two of his nephews
to survive the massacre – and made him Caesar. Gallus was married to Constantius' sister Constantia and sent to deal with the Persian frontier. His success
against the Persians, however, as well as his temper, excited Constantius' jealousy
and suspicion. The emperor recalled Gallus and had him executed in 354.

Constantius next turned to Gallus' younger half-brother Julian, who was
named Caesar in 355 (at age 23). Although Julian had no previous military
experience, and had spent nearly all of his time in the study of literature and
philosophy, he soon became a popular and successful commander. He was
able to put down a military insurrection in Gaul and to secure the stability of
the frontier in Britain and along the Rhine, against the Alamanni and Franks
(357–9). Constantius, however, became suspicious of Julian's success and at
the beginning of 361 he ordered the bulk of the Caesar's troops to leave Gaul
and move to the eastern frontier. Unwilling to leave their homes in the West,
the armies revolted and proclaimed Julian as emperor, supposedly against his
will. Julian sought Constantius' approval for his new status as Augustus, but

the elder emperor refused. In 361 the two armies marched toward each other for a battle to decide the issue, but Constantius suddenly and unexpectedly became ill and died. He had no sons, and Julian became emperor of the whole empire.

Meanwhile, the Arian controversy continued to cause difficulties in the years after Constantine's death. In the West, the decisions of the Council of Nicaea were more or less accepted, but in the East opinion was divided. Athanasios, bishop of Alexandria, maintained a hard-line policy that people must accept the teaching of Nicaea that the Son was *homoousios* (of the same substance) with the Father (so the supporters of the council are called *homoousians*). The emperors Constantine II and Constans I generally supported Nicaea, while Constantius II supported Arianism. There were, however, many shades of Arianism: "Semi-Arians" emerged in part as a result of attempts to find a compromise on this difficult question. Constantius was a moderate Arian, but bishop Makedonios of Constantinople was more militant and he was quite willing to persecute the Nicaeans, something to which the emperor occasionally agreed and for which he was unfavorably remembered by the orthodox tradition. Generally speaking, Constantius II sought to find some formula for compromise and summoned several councils for that purpose, but they all failed. Not surprisingly, the bishops were at the center of the controversy and many of them took stands that did not allow for compromise. The most famous case in this regard was Athanasios of Alexandria, and Constantius had him exiled and reinstated several times.

Constantius II and his brothers, unlike their father, were raised as Christians and they accepted without question their responsibility, before God, to defend the church and, more specifically, to maintain the unity of the faith through the elimination of heresy. Despite the controversy over Arianism, there was relative political stability during the quarter-century after the death of Constantine, and this was certainly important in the triumph of Christianity in the empire.

Constantius II was influential in the development of Constantinople; he raised the prestige of the Senate there and granted eastern senators a rank equal to those of Rome. Constantius also constructed the first church of Hagia Sophia (Agia Sophia, Aya Sofia) in Constantinople, the church that was to become almost synonymous with the empire itself. Later literary sources glorify Constantine as the founder of the Byzantine "system," dominated by the emperor and the patriarch of Constantinople (as the bishop of Constantinople came to be called), but it is clear that much of the responsibility should be accorded to Constantius II, whose long reign regularized the new arrangement and made it the norm.

Julian the Apostate (361–363)

Julian the "Apostate" will always remain a mysterious and controversial figure, admired by some but feared and detested by others. His reign was a serious

---

Box 4.1 *Constantius II Visits Rome (AD 357)*

In 357 the emperor Constantius II came to Rome for the first time. Although he had been emperor then for 20 years, he had never visited the city, an indication of the way that Rome was no longer the center of empire. Constantius' entry into the city, however, as described by Ammianus Marcellinus, provides a good example of what was expected of an emperor at that time: he was no longer a mere mortal, but a figure who played a highly ceremonial role, not only in politics and in court, but also on the streets of the cities of the empire. He was, to a certain degree, like a statue, and he presented the idea of empire in visible form to his subjects. As such a figure, he was larger than life and, even though Ammianus says that Constantius was rather short, he nonetheless ducked his head when passing under arches and gates, to give the impression that he was of such godlike dimensions:

> Accordingly, being saluted as Augustus with favouring shouts, while hills and shores thundered out the roar, he never stirred, but showed himself as calm and imperturbable as he was commonly seen in the provinces. For he both stooped when passing through lofty gates (although he was very short), and as if his neck were in a vise, he kept the gaze of his eyes straight ahead and turned his face neither to right nor to left, but, just as though he were an ordinary person, neither did he nod when the wheel jolted nor was he ever seen to spit, or to wipe or rub his face or nose, or move his hands about.

Ammianus Marcellinus, 16.10.9–10, trans. (slightly modified) John C. Rolfe, Loeb Classical Library (Cambridge, MA, 1935), vol. 1, p. 247.

---

threat to the Constantinian system and to the dominance of Christianity, and one will never know what might have happened had his reign not been cut suddenly short.

Julian, like the other members of his family, had been raised as a Christian, and he had even taken lower clerical orders (as a "lector" – or "reader" – in the church). He had studied under bishop George of Kappadokia, but he was particularly attracted to Hellenic (i.e., classical, pagan) learning, literature, and philosophy. He studied rhetoric at Pergamum and philosophy in the famous schools of Athens. It is impossible to know exactly when Julian decided to make a break with Christianity and put his pagan leanings into practice, but shortly after the death of Constantius II he officially cancelled the laws issued against pagan practices. The bases of Julian's political policy were his philosophical and personal attraction to classical Hellenism and his hostility toward the policies of Constantine and his family. The latter probably arose as a reaction to the terrible massacre of his family in 337, but the former seems to have been a genuine personal preference, deeply seated in Julian's own experience and his education in the world of classical antiquity. Julian's paganism was a curious blend of intellectual preference for classical literature and a crude superstition, based apparently on the influence of some of the "sophists" who surrounded him. Some of these were genuine intellectuals, but others were theurgists, "holy men" loosely connected with Neoplatonism, who, at their best, e.g., Iamblichos and Proklos, sought union with God through religious ritual or prayer. At their worst, however, the theurgists were charlatans who used magic, fraud, and sleight of hand to fool the gullible. The theurgist Maximos, whom Julian apparently met at Pergamum, was one of the most notorious of these, and he had considerable influence on the young prince. Julian was initiated into the sacred mysteries at Ephesos and later at Eleusis (near Athens), and he invited Maximos to join him at court.

Julian did not openly persecute the Christians, but rather offered toleration to all, including heretics and Jews. He encouraged the latter to rebuild the Temple at Jerusalem (inviting all kinds of apocalyptic expectations of the end of the world), knowing that this would confound the Christians, who generally believed that the destruction of the Temple in AD 70 had fulfilled a prophecy of Christ and had demonstrated that God had abandoned the Jews. He also knew that toleration of heretics would quickly lead to infighting and even bloodshed among the Christians, and he was correct in this expectation. He believed in the superiority of polytheism and thought that if people were given a free choice, they would quickly abandon Christianity and revert to polytheism, and, of course, many did. But Julian also sought to reshape and reinvigorate polytheism, unifying and organizing it, and encouraging the priesthood to set a good example of charity and proper behavior. His religion was essentially monotheistic and philosophical, although, again, his ideas were also influenced by magic, emotionalism, and superstition. The one serious criticism of his policies, made by pagans and Christians alike, was that he forbade Christians to teach in the schools – saying they could retire and teach the Gospels! Many of these Christian teachers turned their talents to other tasks, including Apollinarios and his like-named son, who set about turning the Gospels into proper classical verse.

Julian also had political views that he thought harked back to the "great" days of the earlier Roman Empire. Thus, he wished to avoid the trappings of imperial power that had been used since the reign of Diocletian, and he even wished to see himself, as the emperor Augustus had done, as a "first citizen" rather than as a despot. Instead of imperial regalia, Julian wore simple clothes and a beard, showing himself to be a "philosopher" as much as an emperor. He realized that the cities of the empire had been the core of the Roman political structure and he wished to see them revived, along with the local urban aristocracy, the *curiales*. He restored to the cities the properties that Constantine had confiscated and encouraged the local aristocrats to resume their places as the leaders of society.

Julian quickly turned his attention to military affairs, and in 363 he prepared a great campaign against Persia. While he was outfitting the expedition he attempted to win the inhabitants of Antioch over to his brand of polytheism.

Box 4.2   *Heretics in Early Byzantium*

Heresy became one of the most important issues as Christianity came more and more to dominate life in all its aspects. One crucial feature of Christianity is that, like Judaism and Islam, it is not only monotheist in belief but also exclusivist in orientation. This means that Christianity could not accept the proposition that two differing interpretations of religious truth could both be acceptable: one was (presumably) right and the other wrong. This led to the need to define religious truth and, at the same time, to the concept of heresy – incorrect belief as determined by the contemporary church. With the involvement of the Byzantine state in the enforcement of orthodoxy, heresies and heretics were subject to what we would call official discrimination and severe judicial penalties.

One of the most interesting statements of such penalties can be found in a law issued by Theodosios II in 428, presumably under the influence of the "fire-breathing" Patriarch Nestorios, who was himself to be condemned for heresy a mere three years later:

CTh 16.5.65 (3 May 428). Emperors Theodosius and Valentinian Augustuses to Florentius, Praetorian Prefect.

The madness of the heretics must be so suppressed that they shall know beyond doubt, before all else, that the churches which they have taken from the orthodox, wherever they are held, shall immediately be surrendered to the Catholic Church

. . .

1. Next, if they should join to themselves other clerics or priests . . . a fine of ten pounds of gold for each person shall be paid into Our treasury, both by him who created such cleric and by him who allowed himself to be so created, or if they should pretend poverty, such fine shall be exacted from the common body of clerics of the aforesaid superstition or even from their offertories.

2. Furthermore, since not all should be punished with the same severity, the Arians, indeed, the Macedonians, and the Apollinarians, whose crime it is to be deceived by harmful meditation and to believe lies about the Fountain of Truth, shall not be permitted to have a church within any municipality. Moreover, the Novatians and Sabbatians shall be deprived of the privilege of any innovation [i.e., they cannot build new churches], if perchance they should so attempt. The Eunomians, indeed, the Valentinians, the Montanists or Priscillianists, the Phrygians, the Marcianists, the Borborians, the Messalians, the Euchites or Enthusiasts, the Donatists, the Audians, the Hydroparastatae, the Tascodrogitae, the Photinians, the Paulians, the Marcellians, and those who have arrived at the lowest depth of wickedness, namely, the Manichaeans, shall nowhere on Roman soil have the right to assemble and pray. The Manichaeans, moreover, shall be expelled from the municipalities, since no opportunity must be left to any of them whereby an injury may be wrought upon the elements themselves.

3. No employment at all in the imperial service shall be permitted them except on gubernatorial staffs in the provinces and as soldiers in the camp. They shall be conceded no right at all to make reciprocal gifts, no right to make a testament or last will. All the laws which were formerly issued and promulgated at various times against such persons and against all others who oppose our faith, shall remain in force forever . . .

5. We decree that all the foregoing provisions shall be so enforced that no judge may order a minor punishment or no punishment at all for such a crime when it is reported to him, unless he himself is willing to suffer the same penalty which through connivance he has remitted for others.

The Theodosian Code, trans. Clyde Pharr (Princeton, NJ, 1952), pp. 462–3.

This text makes clear the harshness with which the emperors sought to deal with heresy. Nonetheless, the law shows that heresies were graded in terms of increasing severity and that some of these were essentially tolerated, attempts being made to limit them through the prohibition of the consecration of new clergy and the construction of new churches – apparently the state was willing to allow these believers to conduct their worship in relative peace. The more "serious" heretics – including the Manichaeans who should not be considered Christians at all – were forbidden to assemble anywhere in the empire, and their legal rights (mainly to transmit property) were severely restricted. Nonetheless, there is nothing in the law that curtailed thought or sought to carry out an "inquisition" to ferret out heretics. This is certainly not to deny that there was persecution of heretics – clearly there was – but the state was wary of this and generally sought to encourage orthodoxy through other means.

The Antiochenes, however, refused to listen, and only laughed at the emperor and called him names. Julian's military campaign was at first a brilliant success. The Roman army pushed on to the interior of Persia and even attacked the Persian capital of Ctesiphon. While rallying his troops, however, Julian was mysteriously struck by a spear and soon thereafter died (26 June 363), thus cutting short the military campaign and putting a sudden stop to his broader program. Julian's successor, Jovian, was a Christian, and his religious policy returned to the direction earlier set by Constantine and his sons. We will never know what would have happened had Julian enjoyed a longer reign.

Historians, both ancient and modern, have held widely divergent views of the last polytheistic emperor. Ammianus Marcellinus was a pagan and a contemporary of Julian. Like many of the educated elite, he saw Julian as a heroic figure and the last hope for a return to the policies of the old Roman state. Nevertheless, even Ammianus realized that Julian's character was not free of fault:

He [Julian] was a man truly to be numbered with the heroic spirits, distinguished for his illustrious deeds and his inborn majesty. For since there are, in the opinion of the philosophers, four principal virtues, moderation, wisdom, justice, and courage and corresponding to these also some external characteristics, such as knowledge of the art of war, authority, good fortune, and liberality, these as a whole and separately Julian cultivated with constant zeal.

In the first place, he was so conspicuous for inviolate chastity that after the loss of his wife it is well known that he never gave a thought to love: bearing in mind what we read in Plato, that Sophocles, the tragic poet, when he was asked, at a great age, whether he still had congress with women, said no, adding that he was glad that he had escaped from this passion as from some mad and cruel master . . .

Then there were very many proofs of his wisdom, of which it will suffice to mention a few. He was thoroughly skilled in the arts of war and peace, greatly inclined to courtesy, and claiming for himself only so much deference as he thought preserved him from contempt and insolence. He was older in virtue than in years. He gave great attention to the administration of justice, and was sometimes an unbending judge; also a very strict censor in regulating conduct, with a calm contempt for riches, scorning everything mortal; in short, he often used to declare that it was shameful for a wise man, since he possessed a soul, to seek honors from bodily gifts . . . His authority was so well established that, being feared as well as deeply loved as one who shared in the dangers and hardships of his men, he both in the heat of fierce battles condemned cowards to punishment, and, while he was still only a Caesar, he controlled his men even without pay, when they were fighting with savage tribes, as I have long ago said. And when they were armed and mutinous, he did not fear to address them and threaten to return to private life, if they continued to be insubordinate. Finally, one thing it will be enough to know in token of many, namely, that merely by a speech he induced his Gallic troops, accustomed to snow and to the Rhine, to traverse long stretches of country and follow him through torrid Assyria to the very frontiers of the Medes. His success was so conspicuous that for a long time he seemed to ride on the shoulders of Fortune herself, his faithful guide as he in victorious career surmounted enormous difficulties. And after he left the western region, so long as he was on earth all nations preserved perfect quiet, as if a kind of earthly wand of Mercury were pacifying them.

There are many undoubted tokens of his generosity. Among these are his very light imposition of tribute, his remission of the crown-money, the cancellation of many debts made great by long standing, the impartial treatment of disputes between the privy purse and private persons, the restoration of the revenues from taxes to various states along with their lands . . . furthermore, that he was never eager to increase his wealth, which he thought was better secured in the hands of its possessors; and he often remarked that Alexander the Great, when asked where his treasures were, gave the kindly answer, "in the hands of my friends."

Having set down his good qualities, so many as I could know, let me now come to an account of his faults, although they can be summed up briefly. In disposition he was somewhat inconsistent, but he controlled this by the excellent habit of submitting, when he went wrong, to correction. He was somewhat talkative, and very seldom silent; also too much given to the consideration of omens and portents, so that in this respect he seemed to equal the emperor Hadrian. Superstitious rather than truly religious, he sacrificed innumerable victims without regard to cost, so that one might believe that if he had returned from the Parthians, there would soon have been a scarcity of cattle . . .

He delighted in the applause of the mob, and desired beyond measure praise for the slightest matters, and the desire for popularity often led him to converse with unworthy men . . .

The laws which he enacted were not oppressive, but stated exactly what was to be done or left undone, with a few exceptions. For example, it was a harsh law that forbade Christian rhetoricians and grammarians to teach, unless they consented to worship the pagan deities. And also it was almost unbearable that in the municipal towns he unjustly allowed persons to be made members of the councils, who, either as foreigners, or because of personal privileges or birth, were wholly exempt from such assemblies.

The figure and proportion of his body were as follows. He was of medium stature. His hair lay smooth as if it had been combed, his beard was shaggy and trimmed so as to end in a point, his eyes were fine and full of fire, an indication of the acuteness of his mind. His eyebrows were handsome, his nose very straight, his mouth somewhat large with a pendulous lower lip. His neck was thick and somewhat bent, his shoulders large and broad. Moreover, right from top to toe he was a man of straight well-proportioned bodily frame and as a result was strong and a good runner. (Ammianus Marcellinus 25.4.1–25)

Edward Gibbon, in his *Decline and Fall of the Roman Empire* (chapter 22), has an idealistic view of Julian based on the rational ideas of the Enlightenment:

The reformation of the Imperial court was one of the first and most necessary acts of the government of Julian. Soon after his entrance into the palace of Constantinople he had occasion for the service of a barber. An officer, magnificently dressed, immediately presented himself. "It is a barber," exclaimed the prince, with affected surprise, "that I want, and not a receiver-general of the finances." He questioned the man concerning the profits of his employment, and was informed that, besides a large salary and some valuable perquisites, he enjoyed a daily allowance for twenty servants and as many horses. A thousand barbers, a thousand cupbearers, a thousand cooks, were distributed in the several offices of luxury; and the number of eunuchs could be compared only with the insects of a summer's day. The monarch who resigned to his subjects the superiority of merit and virtue was distinguished by the oppressive magnificence of his dress, his table, his buildings, and his train. The stately palaces erected by Constantine and his sons were decorated with many-coloured marbles and ornaments of massy gold. The most exquisite dainties were procured to gratify their pride rather than their taste; birds of the most distant climates, fish from the most remote seas, fruits out of their natural season, winter roses, and summer snows. The domestic crowd of the palace surpassed the expense of the legions; yet the smallest part of this costly multitude was subservient to the use, or even to the splendour, of the throne. The monarch was disgraced, and the people was injured, by the creation and sale of an infinite number of obscure and even titular employments; and the most worthless of mankind might purchase the privilege of being maintained, without the necessity of labour, from the public revenue. The waste of an enormous household, the increase of fees and perquisites, which were soon claimed as a lawful debt, and the bribes which they extorted from those who feared their enmity or solicited their favour, suddenly enriched these haughty menials. They abused their fortune, without considering their past or their future condition; and their rapine and venality could be equalled only by the extravagance of their dissipations. Their silken robes were embroidered with gold, their tables were served with delicacy and profusion; the houses which they built for their own use would have covered the farm of an ancient consul; and the most honourable citizens were obliged to dismount from their horses and respectfully to salute a eunuch whom they met on the public highway. The luxury of the palace excited the contempt and indignation of Julian, who usually slept on the ground, who yielded with reluctance to the indispensable calls of nature, and who placed his vanity not in emulating, but in despising the pomp of royalty.

Julian was not insensible of the advantages of freedom. From his studies he had imbibed the spirit of ancient sages and heroes; his life and fortunes had depended on the caprice of a tyrant; and, when he ascended the throne, his pride was sometimes mortified by the reflection that the slaves who would not dare to censure his defects were not worthy to applaud his virtues. He sincerely abhorred the system of oriental despotism which Diocletian, Constantine, and the patient habits of four score years, had established in the empire. A motive of superstition prevented the execution of the design which Julian had frequently meditated, of relieving his head from the weight of a costly diadem; but he absolutely refused the title of *Dominus* or *Lord*, a word which was grown so familiar to the ears of the Romans, that they no longer remembered its servile and humiliating origin.

With the death of Julian the House of Constantine came to an end. The rulers who followed were military men: like Diocletian and Constantine, most of them were from the Balkans, and they were not especially sophisticated. The religious controversies (especially Arianism) continued, and pressures grew from the barbarians on the northern frontier. Nonetheless, the late fourth-century emperors determined the way in which the legacy of Constantine would be shaped and passed on to future generations.

Jovian (363–364)

Julian's sudden death left a void of power in the Roman world. Virtually all the members of Constantine's family now were dead, and Julian had stubbornly refused to name a successor. Shortly after his death the senior military commanders met to select the next emperor (remember that the army was on campaign deep in Persian territory at the time). Their first choice was Salutius Secundus, praetorian prefect of the East and a moderate pagan. He was, however, quite old and he refused the position. The commanders' second choice was the Christian Jovian, an officer in the palace guard (*domestici et protectores*); he accepted the position, with some misgiving. Almost immediately after his accession Jovian agreed to a peace with Shapur, the Persian king, allowing him the freedom to return to Constantinople to secure his throne. The treaty was "disgraceful" since it gave up, not only all that Julian had just won, but virtually all Roman conquests since the time of Septimius Severus. This involved the surrender of Nisibis, the most important Roman military stronghold in the East, and all the territory beyond the Tigris. Jovian abandoned the Roman protectorate in Armenia and agreed to pay the Persians a large subsidy in gold.

Jovian rescinded Julian's generally unpopular legislation against the Christians and he openly favored the Christian church once more. He did not, however, persecute the pagans, but allowed all to worship as they pleased. Jovian died suddenly, on 17 February 364, having reigned for only eight months.

Valentinian I (364–375) and Valens (364–378)

The military commanders met again at Nicaea and chose a hardened and successful commander of Pannonian descent, Flavius Valentianus, known in English as Valentinian I. From one point of view, this relatively orderly succession was an indication of the stability of the contemporary political structure. Valentinian, 43 at the time, was crude and poorly educated, but he was an energetic campaigner and as emperor he was nearly constantly on campaign. Within six months of his accession the army besought Valentinian to choose a colleague to help him rule the empire, and he selected his younger brother Valens, who was then 36 years old. Valentinian ruled in the West, from his imperial residence, first in Milan and then in Trier, while Valens ruled the East, from his residence in Antioch.

Valentinian concentrated his attention on the Rhine frontier, where he defeated and pacified the Franks and Alamanni; he also defeated the Picts and Scots in Britain, along with Frankish and Saxon pirates. He also undertook campaigns against the Moors in North Africa. Valens, meanwhile, fought the Goths in Thrace, and in 371 he turned his attention to the Persian frontier, where he was able to re-establish Roman influence in Armenia. In 365 a distant relative of Julian, Prokopios, rose in rebellion and gained the support of a Gothic leader, Athanaric; Valens put the revolt down with special severity.

In 375 Valentinian moved to Illyricum, where he sought to deal with incursions of the Quadi and Sarmatians. Valentinian was undone by his violent temper when, in 375, he met an embassy of Quadi who were seeking terms for a peace treaty. Valentinian found the terms suggested by Quadi to be so infuriating that he lost his temper and apparently suffered a stroke, from which he died (17 November 375). Valentinian had two sons, Gratian (then 16) and Valentinian II (4 years old), and he had already crowned them *Augusti*, so there was no real question that they would succeed their father, but the situation was difficult because of their youth.

Both Valentinian and Valens favored soldiers, especially Pannonians, in their administration, rather than aristocrats and *literati*. They vastly increased the size of the senatorial order, including within this group many individuals of peasant – or even barbarian – origin because of their military ability. During this period the problems of the cities became critical and the role of the *curiales* especially difficult. Julian, it will be remembered, had tried to preserve the *curiae* (city councils) and had restored the property that had been confiscated by Constantine and Constantius II. Valens and Valentinian reconfiscated this property but promised to allow the cities a proportion of the revenue (a kind of revenue-sharing scheme) for the repair of public buildings and other expenses. The state took measures to try to keep the *curiales* in the cities, where they could undertake their civic duties and ensure that the imperial taxes were paid. In the context of the pressures put on them, many *curiales* apparently sought to flee their responsibilities through a variety of means. As a result, the state ruled that *curiales* could not become senators (and thus earn immunity from civic duties) unless they left a son behind who could take over these duties. In addition, *curiales* were forbidden from becoming clerics (Christian priests, etc., who were also exempt from civic duties) unless they surrendered some of their property to the local *curia*. Valentinian and Valens made liberal use of the institution of the *defensor civitatis*. This was an individual, sent out from the central government, who was to supervise civic expenses and act as a kind of public civic patron and protector of the poor – he was to make sure that local needs were being met and that the wealthy were living up to their responsibilities. In some ways this was an intervention of the central government in local affairs, but it is hard to see how the government could have done anything else. Valentinian and Valens were careful administrators, and they seem to have been able to cut state expenditures (and thus taxes), perhaps by as much as one-half.

Valentinian and Valens were convinced Christians. As mentioned, they again confiscated the temple lands that Julian had restored to the pagan cults, but paganism was officially tolerated: only divination and magic were condemned and forbidden (as they always in fact had been, even by most pagan emperors). Public sacrifice was discouraged, but many rites were allowed if their practitioners could show that they were of ancient origin.

Valentinian was apparently not interested in the continuing dispute over Arianism, and he refused to take sides. He was personally a moderate Nicene, and he said that the bishops could meet to discuss religious issues on their own, since this was their business and really did not concern the state. Valens, on the other hand, was a moderate Arian. He viewed Nicene (orthodox) opposition to Arianism as insubordination, and he ultimately resorted to persecution against the orthodox, encouraged in this by the intolerance of the Arian hierarchy and the eagerness for martyrdom on the part of the orthodox.

The Barbarian World

One of the most important phenomena in late antiquity was the relationship between the Roman Empire and the barbarian peoples, especially those who originally lived north of the empire, across the Rhine and the Danube frontiers.

In the simplest terms, these people ultimately conquered the western half of the empire and transformed its culture, language, and institutions. At one time these people – mostly Germanic in language – were thought to be wild, uncivilized, nomadic – true barbarians who descended on the empire and laid it low. Today we know that the situation was much more complex. The barbarians exhibited vast differences from group to group and they were far more affected by Roman culture than we had previously thought. Furthermore, most of the Germanic peoples were settled agriculturalists rather than mobile soldiers.

The Germanic peoples were not the only barbarians known to the Romans. Indeed, to a certain degree, the barbarians par excellence were the Persians, ruled in this period by the dynasty of the Sassanids. The Persians were barbarians in the archetypal sense that they were non-Greeks and non-Romans: the Romans of course always identified their culture with that of Greece, and since for the Greeks the Persians always were the "enemy," the self-defining "other," so too they were for the Romans. Thus, first the Parthians and then the Sassanids were always the powerful enemy on the eastern frontier. But the Sassanids clearly were civilized and highly cultured, a match for the Romans on virtually every level, from culture to military power. They had an organized, monarchic state, a monotheistic state religion (Zoroastrianism), and a ruler who was supported by all the apparatus of religion and state. The Persians were also a serious military threat to the Romans since they had a powerful army, whose primary force was made up of heavy cavalry. Their generals were skilled and they knew all the arts of war, from how to fight pitched battles to how to besiege cities.

The Romans thus had ambivalent feelings toward the Persians. On the one hand they admired and respected them, but on the other they looked down on them as inferior (since they were not Romans) and effete. Certainly the Sassanids posed a threat to the Romans that was unlike that posed by any other enemy.

In the East there were certain other non-Roman people, most of them living outside the empire or engaged in a tenuous relationship with Rome. Thus, some of these people were technically "allies" of the Romans, who were formally connected to the empire by a treaty (*foedus*). Among these were various Arabic principalities and tribes (in Arabia and Syria) and various folk living in the region of the Caucasus, especially between the Black and the Caspian Seas, north of Mesopotamia. Among these were the Lazi and the Iberians. The Armenians had a special place, since their state had been established at an early date, and, indeed, the Armenians claimed that theirs was the first country to accept Christianity. Armenia lay at the northern end of the border between Rome and Persia, and it had long played the role of a buffer state, first dominated by Rome and then by Persia, in succession; whichever of the great powers was stronger tended to dominate Armenia.

In Africa there were many native peoples, who enjoyed a certain degree of autonomy and who could, on occasion, threaten the state. These included the Blemmyes, who lived south of Egypt, in northern Nubia, and apparently maintained their ancient religion against the triumph of Christianity in Egypt.

indigenous

To the west the Moors or Berbers presumably were the autochthonous inhabitants of North Africa, who had been pushed to the mountain fringes by the succession of Punic and Roman domination, but it seems likely that they began to move down into the fertile coastal plain in late antiquity. It is often argued that Donatism was especially welcome among the Berber population of northern Africa.

Christian Culture in the Fourth Century

As the fourth century wore on Christian intellectuals came more and more to dominate the cultural life of the empire. It is remarkable that, prior to the time of Constantine, Christian scholars (such as Origen) had been relegated to the background of intellectual discussion. By the middle of the fourth century, however, less than half a century after the Battle of the Milvian Bridge, Christians were coming increasingly to determine the intellectual currents of the time. It was this, at least as much as anything else, that the emperor Julian had struggled to fight.

The Christians, for their part, had long ago come to accept the premise that Christianity and classical culture were not irreparably opposed, and Christian thinkers (from the Apostle Paul onward) made use of Greek modes of thinking and the principles of Greek logic and philosophy. In the fourth century, however, this tradition broke fully into the open and was represented by thinkers as diverse as Eusebios of Caesarea, St. Athanasios of Alexandria, the Cappadocian Fathers (Sts. Basil, Gregory of Nazianzos, Gregory of Nyssa), St. Jerome, and St. Ambrose of Milan. Eusebios seems to have been the first to connect fully the salvation promised by Christianity and the political tradition of the Roman state, something that was to characterize Byzantine tradition for the next thousand years and beyond. His views of history, the role of the bishop, and the place of the emperor in Byzantine society quickly became the norm. St. Athanasios has already been mentioned as the foremost defender of the orthodox position against the Arians, and his fiery and obstinate opposition to Constantius II and Julian was nearly as important as his carefully argued theological treatises. Likewise, his biography of St. Anthony, the archetypal hermit-monk, set the standard for hagiographical works (lives of the saints).

The Cappadocian Fathers are perhaps most characteristic of these Christian intellectuals. Basil was an important bishop and monastic organizer (see below), his brother Gregory of Nyssa was a subtle philosopher, and Gregory of Nazianzos, who became bishop of Constantinople, was an accomplished orator. Although subtle differences can be discerned among their opinions, on the whole they agreed in their opposition to Arianism and their eagerness to adapt the classical tradition of learning to Christian use. Basil and Gregory of Nazianzos were students together in Athens (along with Julian, the future emperor), while Gregory of Nyssa was a younger brother of Basil. Although they were all strictly orthodox in their theology, they had a profound admiration for Plato and even made considerable use of the heretic Origen. Their theological work had an important influence in the development of ideas that were to be the underpinning of discussion of the Christological debates that took place in the fifth century. At the same time, all three of the Cappadocian Fathers were members of the curial class and they all became bishops who were deeply involved in the social as well as spiritual issues of the time.

The Germanic Peoples

Naturally, we are poorly informed about the prehistory of the Germanic peoples. Literary sources are restricted to views preserved for us by Roman authors, who were obviously biased or who at least had their own point of view. The most famous of these accounts is the *Germania* of Tacitus, written in the early part of the second century AD. This well-known account presents the Germans as ferocious fighters who nonetheless preserved noble traits of honor and fairness and a kind of primitive democracy. Although there may be some reliable information in the *Germania*, it is clear that the work is primarily a moralizing treatise, designed more to shame the Romans into good behavior than to present an accurate view of Germanic society.

The archaeological record for the early Germanic peoples is obviously tantalizing and it is providing us with much valuable information as research continues. One of the problems with the archaeological record is the difficulty in distinguishing one group from another on the basis of archaeological evidence, and we cannot always relate the archaeological evidence to the ethnic groups we know from the written sources. Linguistic evidence, on the other hand, has been a particularly fruitful source of information since we can trace place-names, personal names, and linguistic variants back to a very distant past. Indeed, our understanding of much of the prehistoric period of Germanic society has been based on this linguistic evidence. Unfortunately, some of this material has been used in the twentieth century for political reasons, either to glorify one group vis-à-vis another or to argue that one modern nation has a "right" to live in a certain territory as a result of this historical information.

With a few exceptions, the Germanic peoples who took part in the great *Völkerwanderung* (migrations) were not the same as the German tribes known to Caesar, Tiberius, and the other generals of the early Roman Empire. These latter peoples, living mainly between the Rhine and the Elbe, are known as the West Germans, and during the early imperial period they became increasingly Romanized, so that by the fourth century many of them were scarcely distinguishable from the Romans. Many of them lived inside Roman territory, and the *limes*, the Roman term usually translated as "border," was less a border than it was a broad frontier band, permitting interchange and commerce as much as it prevented invasion. To be sure, some of these West Germanic peoples remained outside the *limes* and they continued to give the Romans trouble. Among these were the Franks, the Alamanni, and the Saxons. The Alamanni, in particular, had invaded the empire in the third century: in the 250s they had crossed the frontier and raided Italy until they were driven out by Gallienus.

The Germanic peoples who caused the most difficulty for the Romans, however, were those we call the East Germans, including people such as the Goths (Visigoths and Ostrogoths) and the Vandals. They had apparently lived in Scandinavia since time immemorial, but perhaps in the second century AD they began to move in a broad arc, swinging across Eastern Europe and coming to rest at the formidable barrier of the Danube. By the 350s, if not earlier, various federations had come to establish themselves in this area just outside the empire. They did not immediately threaten the empire, but instead most of the groups settled down in the relatively open land across the Danube and founded farming villages where they lived fairly peacefully. What set events in motion, however, was the arrival of the Huns on the Danube frontier. The Huns were a Turkic people from Central Asia; they were nomadic mounted hunters and warriors, very different from the settled Germans. The Huns' homeland was far away from the Roman frontier, but there was no effective natural barrier between Central Asia and Roman territory, and, once the Huns set off toward the West (perhaps after having been defeated by the Chinese), there was very little to stop them.

The Battle of Adrianople (8 August 378)

In 375 Valentinian I died, leaving the western part of the empire to his sons Gratian and Valentinian II (who was only a young boy). Valens was occupied on the eastern frontier from about 371 onward. In about 376 the Huns suddenly appeared north of the Danube (in what is now Romania), and the terrified Goths sought safety across the Roman frontier. They offered to settle in Roman territory and serve in the Roman army; Valens thought they would make a good addition to the army and he agreed. Perhaps as many as 200,000 Goths sought to settle within the empire, but the Roman government was not able to meet the vast needs of this immigrant population. Food was promised to them, but it did not arrive or was sold to the Germans by corrupt officials at exorbitant prices. These same officials also seized many Goths and sold them into slavery. Frustrated by this treatment, the Goths rose in revolt in 377 and began to ravage Roman territory in Thrace.

Valens immediately moved his army from the eastern frontier and brought it to deal with the situation in Thrace. Gratian also began to move his forces from the West to meet the threat. Valens, however, was apparently jealous of his young nephew and he received a false report that the Gothic troops were only 10,000 strong. Accordingly, as soon as he arrived in Thrace Valens immediately prepared for battle, hoping to win the victory for himself. Valens' troops, however, were tired from their long march, and they were not able to set themselves up properly for the battle, which took place on a hot plain outside the city of Adrianople (Adrianoupolis) in Thrace.

The Goths drew up the wagons containing their families into a large circle, with cavalry detachments on both sides facing Valens' forces. The Roman skirmishers were driven back in panic by the Gothic soldiers and they ran quickly into the ranks of their own men. Meanwhile, the cavalry on the Roman left wing advanced too far against the enemy, and the Gothic cavalry, which had been held in reserve, was able to strike the left side of the Roman infantry, which had no effective protection. Attacked from the side and the front, the Roman troops were slaughtered at will. Valens and about two-thirds of his army perished at the hands of the victorious Goths.

The situation was catastrophic for the empire: a Roman emperor was killed in battle for the first time in well over a century, there was a power vacuum in the East, the Persian frontier was undefended, and the Goths were at large in Thrace. The Battle of Adrianople also showed that the Germans could defeat a trained Roman army, and it demonstrated the superiority of heavy mounted cavalry. In the crisis the Roman government was temporarily paralyzed, and it was fortunate that the Goths were unable to take advantage of the situation. They had no experience in besieging cities and they had to be content with raiding the Thracian countryside.

Theodosios the Great (379–395) and Gratian (375–383)

After the battle of Adrianople Gratian was left as sole emperor. It was clear that he needed a colleague, since he was young, inexperienced, and completely unable to deal with the military situation. In this context, the state turned to Theodosios, an experienced general. Theodosios' father (also called Theodosios) was from an old Spanish family, and he had been one of Valentinian's primary commanders; he restored order in Britain and put down the rebellion of Firmus in North Africa. The elder Theodosios had, however, fallen from favor under circumstances that are not clear, and he was executed in 375. His son, the younger Theodosios, retired to his Spanish estate, but in the circumstances after Adrianople Gratian had him recalled and proclaimed emperor at Sirmium on 19 January 379. Theodosios was given control of all the East, along with Dacia and Macedonia.

Theodosios had many immediate problems to face, not least of which was the need to recruit new soldiers to fill the ranks depleted by the disaster of Adrianople – he had to replace at least 20,000 troops. Theodosios instituted stringent measures to locate and enroll those who had an obligation to serve in the army. He sought out the sons of veterans (who were supposed also to serve) and enlisted even those who had mutilated themselves in order to escape service.

Meanwhile Theodosios tried to control the Goths who were still ravaging Thrace. He was unable to pin them down to fight a decisive battle, and they continued to raid the farms and villages of the countryside. Theodosios finally signed a treaty with the Goths on 3 October 382. Under the terms of this treaty the Goths were allowed to settle in Roman territory but in return they

Figure 4.1 Missorium of Theodosios I. This large silver disc shows the senior emperor, set in an elaborate architectural frame, with his two sons and heirs to the throne, sitting at a lower level than the senior emperor. Note the soldiers with their shields and the halo of Theodosios. The halo, of course, is not a mark of sanctity, but a symbol of divine support for the rulers. Academia de la Historia, Madrid, Spain. Photo: Scala / Art Resource, NY

were to serve in the Roman army as *foederati* (barbarian allies), apparently contributing about 20,000 men. It had always been Roman policy to ally with foreigners (including barbarians) who might fight for and alongside the Romans. But until this point the foreigners were either treated as allied contingents or they were enrolled one by one in small numbers in Roman units. Now, however, the Goths were enrolled in large numbers and they were allowed to serve under their own tribal leaders. This was an important break with precedent, a policy that was condemned by some contemporaries (see the speeches of Themistios, who was very much opposed to this "barbarization" of the army). Thus, large numbers of Goths were settled along the south bank of the Danube and in northern Thrace.

In the East Theodosios was able to arrange a peace with Persia. Armenia was partitioned between Rome and Persia, the Romans receiving the smaller share. Nonetheless, as a result of this Theodosios was able to control a strategic territory between the upper Tigris and Euphrates, which would be of considerable significance in case of renewed hostilities between the major powers.

In religious policy Theodosios was a rather straightforward Nicene Christian, and his Christianity had a definite western orientation (as one might imagine from his place of origin in Spain). Early in his reign he was frightened by a serious illness, from which he nearly died; as a result he was baptized and was thenceforth enthusiastic in his support of Christianity. In 380 he issued a law saying that all Christians should follow the teachings of the bishops of Rome and Alexandria. This was a simple and clear statement in support of the teachings of Nicaea, and it avoided doctrinal sophistication or doubt: faith was defined by reference to the teaching of individual bishops. Theodosios, however, thought it was wise to call an ecumenical council to put an end to the Arian controversy that had divided the empire for more than half a century and had defied all attempts at compromise. Thus, the first Council of Constantinople was held in May of 381. The council added slightly to the Creed of the Council of Nicaea, but it reaffirmed the teachings of that council and essentially put an end to debate about Arianism in the East. Some individuals, of course, continued to maintain Arian teachings, but the theological controversy finally seemed settled with the resolute decision of both emperor and council. In the meantime, however, the bishop Ulfilas had already been active in converting the Goths to Arian Christianity. Thus, ironically enough, Arianism was to remain a potent force in the West, not among the Roman Christians, but among the barbarians, and it remained a major difference and source of conflict between Romans and barbarians. This was especially important because the bishop of Rome (the Pope) grew in importance and the orthodox bishops in the West came to acquire political as well as religious power. The bishops, of course, regarded the Germans first and foremost as heretics.

Theodosios' policy toward paganism was likewise remarkably straightforward and pragmatic. He seems personally to have accepted Christianity wholeheartedly, and he could not really understand why some would persist in following "false" teachings. As a result, just as he had viewed the Arian controversy in practical terms, he looked at paganism as a "backward" practice, out of keeping with the policies of his times, although he was certainly willing to tolerate the paganism of most of his Germanic allies and he maintained good relations with pagan officials such as Symmachus. Thus, like the Christian emperors prior to him, Theodosios supported Christianity and opposed paganism by preferring Christians for posts in the government and providing financial support to churches, monasteries, and other ecclesiastical establishments, which encouraged the continued growth of Christianity within the empire.

Theodosios did, however, take action against pagan cults and the remaining pagan temples. These official attacks on paganism are chronicled in the laws preserved in the Codex Theodosianus, compiled by the emperor's grandson in

438. These show that there was no such thing as a single "edict of Theodosios" that closed the pagan temples. The situation was far more complicated, and local conditions probably played a greater role than anything else. Laws of 383 and 385 prohibited public sacrifice, but paganism (as a belief system) was not forbidden, and the state had no interest in or ability to intervene in what people did in private. Thus there was no single order to close all the temples, but there is no doubt that when bishops, cities, and individual Christians made requests to close individual places of pagan worship, these were often favorably received by state officials. Many temples undoubtedly were destroyed, with or without official approval. In part because the temples officially belonged to the state, imperial officials were generally supposed to protect them, but temples were frequently attacked by bishops, and even by groups of monks, and administrators commonly looked the other way. Sometimes the local population resisted these actions and tried to prevent the destruction of their temples, and violence often occurred.

One of the most dramatic and most symbolic of these events was the destruction of the Serapeum in Alexandria (see box, pp. 86–7). This temple to the god Serapis was one of the most famous buildings of the ancient world. In 391 Theophilos, the bishop of Alexandria, obtained permission from the emperor to convert the temples of the city into churches. The bishop found an obscene sculpture among the "sacred objects" in the temple of Dionysos and paraded this through the streets in order to make fun of the pagans for their "immorality." The pagans were incensed by this and a riot broke out between the pagans and the Christians. Olympios, a pagan philosopher, gathered together a group of pagans, seized the Serapeum, and turned it into a fortress. The pagans rushed out of the Serapeum and beat up Christians, some of whom they brought back to the temple, where they crucified them. The Augustal Prefect, the chief military official in Egypt, was unable to restore order, and he sought reinforcement from imperial troops. These were dispatched from Constantinople and the revolt collapsed. The Serapeum was then converted into a church. In 391 and 392 Theodosios forbade all pagan cults, in public and private, although again the law certainly could not be strictly enforced.

In the West Gratian at first granted toleration to the pagans, but he changed his mind, probably under the influence of Ambrose, the bishop of Milan. Gratian was the last emperor to hold the title *pontifex maximus* (chief priest of the pagan cult), an honor he resigned in 381 when he removed the Altar of Victory from the Senate in Rome. (Pope Gregory I [r. 590–604] was the first to use this same title as the "chief priest" of Christendom.)

Gratian, however, did not inspire the loyalty of the troops. He was well educated and intelligent, but there was considerable opposition to him. Valentinian had not ruled long enough to establish loyalty to his dynasty, and in 383 a revolt broke out, led by the Spanish officer Magnus Maximus. Gratian was killed on 25 August 383. Valentinian II, then 13 years old, was still emperor, but he was unable to exercise any independent power. Theodosios at first recognized Maximus, but in 387 Maximus invaded Italy, which belonged

Box 4.3   *Destruction of the Serapeum in Alexandria*

The temple of the Egyptian god Serapis in Alexandria was one of the most famous centers of polytheism (paganism) in the ancient world. The Serapeum (or Serapion) remained open for worship well after the time of Constantine, but it finally was turned into a Christian church in 391, during the reign of Theodosios I. This event was regarded by pagans as a particularly serious defeat, an indication that an era had passed. Theophilos (Theophilus), the fiery bishop of Alexandria, set about to silence any opposition to Christianity in the Egyptian capital, but his attack on the pagan shrines quickly turned into a violent clash between Christians and pagans, and imperial officials were unable to control the situation. The destruction of the Serapeum was described by many contemporaries, including the church historian Sozomen, whose account is printed below. From this you should notice how the pagans responded to the insult shown to their religion and the violence of the events that followed. You should also notice how the emperor finally managed to put an end to the uprising.

About this period, the bishop of Alexandria [Theophilos], to whom the temple of Dionysus had, at his own request, been granted by the emperor, converted the edifice into a church. The statues were removed, the *adyta* [the secret places in temples where objects used in worship were kept] were exposed; and, in order to cast disrepute on the pagan mysteries, he made a procession for the display of these objects, the *phalli*, and he made a public exhibition of whatever other objects had been concealed in the *adyta* which really were, or seemed to be, ridiculous. The pagans, amazed at so unexpected an exposure, could not suffer it in silence, but conspired together to attack the Christians.

They killed many of the Christians, wounded others, and seized the Serapion, a temple which was conspicuous for beauty and vastness and which was seated on an eminence. This they converted into a temporary citadel; and hither they conveyed many of the Christians, put them to the torture, and compelled them to offer sacrifice. Those who refused compliance were crucified, had both legs broken, or were put to death in some cruel manner. When the sedition had prevailed for some time, the rulers came and urged the people to remember the laws, to lay down their arms, and to give up the Serapion. There came then Romanus, the general of the military legions in Egypt, and Evagrius, the prefect of Alexandria. As their efforts, however, to reduce the people to submission were utterly in vain, they made known what had transpired to the emperor. Those who had shut themselves up in the Serapion prepared a more spirited resistance, from fear of the punishment that they knew would await their audacious proceedings, and they were further instigated to revolt by the inflammatory discourses of a man named Olympius, attired in the garments of a philosopher, who told them that they ought to die rather than neglect the gods of their fathers. Perceiving that they were greatly dispirited by the destruction of the idolatrous statues, he assured them that such a circumstance did not warrant their renouncing their religion; for that the statues were composed of corruptible materials, and were mere pictures, and therefore would disappear; whereas, the powers which had dwelt within them, had flown to heaven. By such representations as these, he retained the multitude with him in the Serapion.

When the emperor was informed of these occurrences, he declared that the Christians who had been slain were blessed, inasmuch as they had been admitted to the honor of martyrdom, and had suffered in defense of the faith. He offered free pardon to those who had slain them, hoping that by this act of clemency they would be the more readily induced to embrace Christianity; and he commanded the demolition of the temples in Alexandria which had been the cause of the popular sedition. It is said that, when this imperial edict was read in public, the Christians uttered loud shouts of joy, because the emperor laid the odium of what had occurred upon the pagans. The people who were guarding the Serapion were so terrified at hearing these shouts, that they took to flight, and the Christians immediately obtained possession of the spot, which they have retained ever since. I have been informed that, on the night preceding this occurrence, Olympius heard the voice of one singing hallelujah in the Serapion. The doors were shut and everything was still; and as he could see no one, but could only hear the voice of the singer, he at once understood what the sign signified; and unknown to any one he quitted the Serapion and embarked for Italy. It is said that when the temple was being demolished, some stones were found, on which were hieroglyphic characters in the form of a cross, which on being submitted to the inspection of the learned, were interpreted as signifying the life to come. These characters led to the conversion of several of the pagans, as did likewise other inscriptions found in the same place, and which contained predictions of the destruction of the temple. It was thus that the Serapion was taken, and, a little while after, converted into a church; it received the name of the Emperor Arcadius.

Sozomen, *Ecclesiastical History* 7. 17, in *A Select Library of Nicene and Post-Nicene Fathers of the Christian Church* (second series), translated under the editorial supervision of Philip Schaff and Henry Wace, vol. 2 (New York, 1890, reprint Grand Rapids, MI, 1979–86).

to Valentinian II, and Theodosios decided to take action. The senior emperor marched west and in 388 he defeated and killed the usurper. The emperor acted as the protector of Valentinian II and took the young emperor's sister, Galla, as his second wife, but Theodosios was from this time at least the undisputed ruler of the entire Roman world.

Theodosios remained in Italy from 388 to 391, leaving the East in the hands of his son Arkadios, who had been Augustus since 383. In 391 the emperor returned to Constantinople. He left Valentinian II in the care of Arbogast, the Frankish *magister militum*, who had helped Theodosios defeat Maximus. In

392 Valentinian attempted to assert his independence from Arbogast, but he was soon found hanged, and Arbogast quickly proclaimed Eugenius as emperor. On the one hand, Arbogast's action showed how political power in the West had fallen into the hands of Germans. On the other, regardless of how much power a German commander might have, it was unthinkable for a barbarian to claim the imperial title for himself. This is an interesting phenomenon in its own right, and it was one of the clear differences between Romans and barbarians (the other being the difference in religion, with the barbarians being Arians and the Romans orthodox).

Eugenius was a professor of rhetoric and a half-hearted Christian, but he found support among the pagans who were opposed to Theodosios' policy of Christianization; the pagans hoped that Eugenius might be a new Julian, who would favor paganism once again. In 394 Theodosios marched west once more and faced Arbogast and Eugenius at the River Frigidus in northern Italy (6 September 394). Theodosios was victorious and Arbogast and Eugenius were killed. This was the last opportunity for toleration of paganism or a pro-pagan policy in the empire.

In 384 the final chapter was written in the controversy over the Altar of Victory in the Senate in Rome. This altar had come to be a symbol of tradition for the old senatorial aristocracy in Rome, which regarded the altar as a cultural symbol as much as a focus for religious celebration. The altar had been removed, probably by Constantine, and then replaced in the Senate by Julian. Gratian, as we have said, then had it removed once again. Symmachus, the Prefect of the City and one of the leading representatives of old-fashioned aristocratic culture, petitioned the young emperor Valentinian II to have the Altar replaced in the Senate. Symmachus pointed out that the altar was a traditional symbol of Roman culture and he appealed for toleration, since there were "many ways to reach God." This request was countered in an equally famous response by Ambrose, the bishop of Milan, who argued – simply – that the pagans were wrong in their adherence to false gods and that there was only one way to reach God. Despite Symmachus' plea for toleration – which sounds so reasonable to the modern reader – the altar was never returned to the Senate House.

In 390 one of Theodosios' generals, the Goth Butheric, was murdered in Thessaloniki by a crowd who disliked the position that the Germans held in the army. Theodosios responded in typical fashion by feigning mildness and inviting the populace of Thessaloniki to assemble in the hippodrome to celebrate the games. At a given moment Theodosios had his troops set upon the unsuspecting people, and thousands of them were massacred. Ambrose of Milan later intervened and refused to allow Theodosios into the church or to communicate with him. In the end Theodosios was forced to admit his crime and do penance – a notable example of how a stubborn church leader could take the moral high ground and force a powerful emperor to bend to his will. This demonstrated clearly that there were certain things which an emperor – even an orthodox ruler "protected by God" – could not do. It should be noted, however, that this event did not weaken Theodosios' political or military power in any way whatsoever.

Theodosios, like Valentianian I, and – more importantly – Constantine before him, sought consciously to pass power on within his own family, in other words to establish a dynasty. This partly explains the importance of the women in his family, especially his first wife Aelia Flaccilla, although other forces were certainly at play here, including, arguably, a greater role accorded to women generally in the society of the time. Theodosios married Flaccilla, ca. 376, and she bore him three children, including the future emperors Arkadios and Honorius, before her premature death in 385 or 386. She was one of the first Byzantine empresses to be depicted widely on coinage: despite her relatively brief time on the throne, coins were struck in her name at a number of mints and her portrait is clearly meant to provide a recognizable image of the empress. Furthermore, her piety and charity clearly made a mark on the leading Christian spokesmen of the day. The church historian Sozomen credits her with persuading her husband not to meet with the Arian Eunomios in an effort to find some compromise on the Arian question, while Theodoret praises her charity and kindness to the poor and her personal involvement in the care of the crippled. St. Gregory of Nyssa bestowed special praise on her piety and good works, and it is a mark of her standing that the great orator and theologian personally delivered a eulogy at the time of her death. Again, we may suspect some manipulation of Aelia Flaccilla's image by the circle closest to the emperor, but there seems little reason to doubt that the empress impressed contemporaries with the power of her own personality, and she is still revered as a saint by the Orthodox church (her feast day is 14 September).

Theodosios was only 48 years old, but he died early in 395 in Milan. He left the East to his son Arkadios (who was 17 or 18) and the West to his son Honorius (who was only 10); both were the sons of Aelia Flaccilla. As mentioned above, Theodosios had married again, this time to Galla, the sister of Valentinian II (and thus the daughter of Gratian), which connected his family directly with that of his predecessors; with her Theodosios had a daughter, Galla Placidia, who was to have a long and eventful life in the West: wife of Constantius III, mother of Valentinian III, and grandmother of Placidia, who was the wife of Olybrius, emperor in 472.

The Fourth Century as an Age of Change

Although there was little that could be called truly revolutionary in the time from the death of Constantine (337) until the death of Theodosios I (395), the period witnessed significant and long-term change. This change was not sudden but gradual, and to a certain degree it can be seen as the implementation and amplification of the movements and processes that had been set in motion during the reign of Constantine. Thus, in this 60-year period the empire tilted across the religious line, from one dominated by paganism and pagan thought to one where Christianity, Christian institutions, and Christian sentiment had become dominant.

This change was not simply the replacement of one group of gods with another, but a much more radical change in which polytheism – which was by nature generally tolerant of diverse religious traditions and approaches to religious "truth" – was replaced by a monotheist tradition which claimed that it held the only approach to truth and which therefore viewed all divergence as necessarily false and deserving of suppression. One might argue that such a monotheist tradition had always existed, but now it was inseparably bound to the power of the Roman state, which was committed to the maintenance of what was perceived as Christian truth and order. Eusebios of Caesarea may have been the first to understand the full significance of this alliance of the Christian church with the power of the Roman state, but at the time of Constantine this relationship was uncertain and its ramifications anything but clear. During the course of the fourth century, however, as new generations came into power, confident in their own view of the world and certain of the relationship between divine truth and political power, this relationship developed and became normative. The policies of Theodosios the Great were not essentially different from those of Constantine, but they were based on a half-century of imperial certainty in Christian truth and a realization that the agreement made between Constantine and the Christian church had become the basis of Roman power and the Roman way of life: it is significant that, for Romans and barbarians alike, orthodox Christians and *romanitas* ("Romanness") had become identical. The dispute between Symmachus and Ambrose over the Altar of Victory in Rome is often seen as a significant moment in this development, a crisis in which the issue was put into sharp relief.

The fourth century was also one in which the power of the bishops clearly came to dominate the Christian church, and the hierarchy that was normative in later centuries came to the fore. At the time of Constantine, or even Constantius II, this was not a foregone conclusion, but by the middle of the century the bishops had come to represent the church without any opposition from within. This can be seen clearly in the series of councils, culminating in the Councils of Nicaea (325) and Constantinople (381), but also in the many local councils that were held to deal with doctrinal and – even more commonly – administrative issues. The bishops, not surprisingly, came primarily from the curial class, the local aristocracies of the cities of the empire, since the *curiales* were the ones who had the training and the experience that prepared them for the responsibilities of office within the church. Imperial legislation attempted to restrain this "drain" of the *curiales* into the ranks of the clergy, but this was to no effect, both because it was impossible to control the religious sensibilities of the age and also because individuals from this group naturally sought positions of power and influence in society as a whole.

The fourth century also witnessed the development and institutionalization of Christian monasticism. The desire for the ascetic life, of course, is common to most religious traditions, and Christian monasticism had its roots in Jewish asceticism, especially as it was practiced in the period from the Maccabees onward. Thus, there is evidence of Christian ascetics from an early age, individuals who sought to follow the example of John the Baptist – and Christ himself – who had spent time in the solitude and wildness of desert places, seeking direct communion with God as a result of their self-denial. By the third century there were large numbers of ascetics, especially in the deserts of Egypt, devoting their lives to the solitary worship of God and the attempt to reach direct communion with him.

The best-known of the early ascetics is St. Antony (or St. Anthony, ca. 251–356), an Egyptian born to a prosperous family who gave away all his wealth to follow the monastic life. St. Athanasios' biography of St. Antony (written ca. 356–7) provides characteristic details about the ascetic life: Anthony's struggles with demons and miracles became the standard fare of all subsequent ascetic lives. Although Antony attracted a number of followers, all of them lived a strictly eremitic (solitary) life, with each monk living on his own, though they did occasionally come together for worship, group teaching, and admonition.

Pachomios (ca. 290–346, and thus a contemporary of St. Antony) is generally regarded as one of the main influences in the development of cenobitic (communal) monasticism. He was an Egyptian born of pagan parents, who encountered Christians while serving in the Roman army, converted to Christianity, and then entered the ascetic life ca. AD 315. Perhaps because of his experience with the organization of the Roman army, Pachomios sought to provide more structure to the monastic life, and he organized his many followers into various communal monasteries, nine for men and two for women.

Monasticism spread outside of Egypt to Syria and Asia Minor in both its eremitic and cenobitic forms. It reached Constantinople in the mid-fourth century and a number of monasteries with special urban characteristics were established in the city. One of the strongest supporters of cenobitic monasticism was Basil of Caesarea (discussed previously as one of the so-called Cappadocian Fathers). Early in his life Basil traveled to the monastic centers in Egypt and Syria but eventually established himself back in Asia Minor. As a bishop he encouraged monks to devote themselves to an active role in society, and he saw the monastery as a community whose members ought to work together for common goals. He wrote a series of regulations for monasteries that emphasized these concepts, and these had a considerable impact on the development of monasticism, both within Byzantium and beyond its borders.

The role of women in the society of the fourth century has often been discussed, with widely different conclusions. On the one hand, we have already seen that "imperial women," such as Helena, the mother of Constantine I, and Aelia Flaccilla, the first wife of Theodosios I, wielded considerable power and influence and we will see this phenomenon continue, and expand, in the following centuries. What about "ordinary" women? Presumably the greatest change is likely to have come from the growing influence of Christianity, but this influence can be read in two different ways.

On the one hand, Christianity certainly recognized women as human beings in their own right and the spiritual equals of men. It called for the protection of women (and children), especially virgins and widows, and even set up institutions such as orphanages (*orphanotropheia*), monasteries for women (called "nunneries" in the West, but usually referred to simply as "monasteries" or "female monasteries" in Byzantium), and old-age homes (*gerokomeia*). The emergence of the cult of the Virgin Mary probably reflected the piety of women and the acknowledgment of a female element in Christianity. Laws in the fourth century restricted the Roman right of divorce, which has often been seen as a protection of the position of women, since men could not simply divorce their wives without reason.

On the other hand, from the beginning Christianity had an essentially negative attitude toward women, who were (in the person of Eve) regarded as the source of sin in the world and (in the person of every woman) seen as temptation to sin for every man. From the Apostle Paul onward the Church Fathers expressed sentiments that are patently misogynistic, and the monastic movement can be seen as designed in part to "free" men from the temptations of women.

Nonetheless, many modern historians have seen the ascetic traditions of the period as liberating women from the burdens of childbirth and homemaking. In addition, female asceticism did provide some women with an opportunity for administrative experience and not infrequently the exercise of real economic power. Further, by the denial of sexuality and the power of the body, the ascetic movement can be seen as providing women with a new kind of authority over their own bodies that had not generally been granted in previous societies.

We should keep this complex situation in mind as we consider the history of women in the Byzantine centuries. The historical sources were mostly written by men and their subjects normally are men, but there were some distinguished Byzantine women authors, some texts and documents speak of women, and we will do our best in the pages that follow to illuminate the position of women in Byzantine society.

Social and Economic Conditions

Socially and economically the fourth century witnessed considerable recovery from the disturbed conditions of the previous 100 years. The general stability of the political situation was certainly an important factor here, and the advantages of the Constantinian economic reforms had an opportunity to work. It is true that, although the gold coinage remained firm from the time of the introduction of the *solidus*, the copper coinage – which was used normally by most ordinary people – apparently weakened significantly, which probably resulted in considerable increases in prices. Famines and other shortages were certainly known in the major cities, although it is not certain to what degree these were due to economic policies and to what extent these were simply the result of situations – like drought and disease – that were beyond the control of the state.

Certainly the political and economic policies of the time weighed heavily on the *curiales*, the class of local aristocrats in the cities of the empire. As we have seen, Constantine had confiscated the state land on which the finances of local government were based, and cities had to fall back on the generosity of their wealthy citizens. Not surprisingly, after the difficulties of the third century, many of these families had limited resources, and they were not always able to bear the burdens of these expectations. Furthermore, the central government made the *curiales* of each city personally responsible for the payment of the land tax, so these individuals found themselves caught between the financial demands of the central government, on the one side, and the needs of the local city on the other. Spokespersons such as Libanios saw the *curiales* as the heart of ancient Roman civilization, and they decried their demise; the emperor Julian supported this view and sought to restore the vitality of this group. Some *curiales* sought to evade their responsibilities, either by elevation to the level of the imperial aristocracy (the senatorial class), by enrollment in the ranks of the Christian clergy, or even (occasionally) by flight into desert places. Imperial legislation tried to prevent such action, although this can hardly have been an effective check.

Similar legislation was also levied in an attempt to guarantee collection of the tax income owed to the state and to insure that the food supplies delivered to the cities were sufficient to prevent riots that might disturb the stability of the imperial government. Thus, legislation was established that, to a certain degree, "froze" individuals in their place and occupation. This included the semi-free peasants, called *coloni*, who were required to remain on the land they were farming: the idea being that their labor was essential to the ability of the landowner to pay the taxes he owed to the state. In addition, members of some of the most important *collegia* (occupational "guilds") such as bakers, shipowners, pork-producers, and vintners, were supposed to remain in their occupations and their children were to do the same, and many of them were required to provide goods and/or services to the state at a fixed rate, even if that meant the delivery of goods at a loss. The idea behind this was that these individuals provided things that were essential for the peaceful functioning of society, and the state felt it necessary to force their compliance with requests for goods and services. Restrictions on the freedom of the *curiales*, mentioned above, should be seen in the same light. Naturally, these were regulations that could only be enforced with difficulty, and the repetition of rules such as these in the contemporary codes is testimony that they were probably honored more in the breach than in fact. Nonetheless, such regulations must have at least produced an atmosphere of constraint, and they have led many modern scholars to view the age as one of oppression and state control. It is in fact more likely that the regulations are evidence of a society in flux, characterized by rapid and sometimes radical change. The state, especially in the West where it was clearly weaker, sought to constrain these changes, and the result was the legislation under consideration. In the East, however, there is little evidence that such restrictive laws were needed and, even if they were formally "on the books" they can hardly have been enforced. The written sources make it clear that there was considerable movement of people, including traders and government officials (who could make use of the empire's efficient system of communication), but also churchmen and – perhaps most striking of all – wandering teachers and poets and the monks who frequently brought their views from the deserts into the centers of contemporary cities. The fact that the state occasionally sought to limit such movement is merely evidence that it frequently occurred.

FURTHER READING

G. W. Bowersock, *The Emperor Julian*. Cambridge, MA, 1978.

Robert Browning, *The Emperor Julian*. Cambridge, 1975.

Susanna Elm, *Virgins of God: The Making of Asceticism in Late Antiquity*. Oxford, 1994.

Garth Fowden, *Empire to Commonwealth: Consequences of Monotheism in Late Antiquity*. Princeton, NJ, 1993.

B. Guttmann, *Studien zu römischen Aussenpolitik in der Spätantike (364–395 n. Chr.)*. Bonn, 1991.

K. G. Holum, *Theodosian Empresses: Women and Imperial Domination in Late Antiquity*. Berkeley, CA, 1982.

A. H. M. Jones, *The Later Roman Empire 284–602: A Social, Economic, and Administrative Survey*. Oxford, 1964.

N. Q. King, *The Emperor Theodosius and the Establishment of Christianity*. Philadelphia, 1960.

R. Lane Fox, *Pagans and Christians*. London, 1986.

J. H. W. G. Liebescheutz, *Continuity and Change in Roman Religion*. Oxford, 1979.

John Matthews, *The Roman Empire of Ammianus*. London, 1989.

A. Momigliano, ed., *The Conflict between Paganism and Christianity in the Fourth Century*. Oxford, 1963.

N. G. Wilson, ed., *Saint Basil on Greek Literature*. London, 1975.

5
The Fifth Century

| 250 | 500 | 750 | 1000 | 1250 | 1500 |

---

395   Empire divided between East and West
408–450   Theodosios II
431   Council of Ephesos
451   Council of Chalcedon

The House of Theodosios in the East

Theodosios I was the last ruler of an undivided Roman Empire. He held the vast extent of the Roman state tightly in his grasp, largely as a result of the strength of his own character and his experience and determination as a military commander. It is one of the ironies of history, therefore, that the arrangements he left for the administration of the state resulted in what turned out to be its permanent division into two halves, which have (at least to some extent) marked the division of Europe up to the present time. In addition, although Theodosios and his father were military men, raised in the Roman tradition of battle, his successors were all brought up in the palace, and nearly two centuries were to pass before emperors again commonly took the field in person.

As mentioned above, Theodosios had crowned his two sons, Arkadios and Honorius, well before his death and he left no doubt that they were to succeed him on the throne. Arkadios (born 377/8) was, however, only 17 years old when his father died, while Honorius was just 11. Theodosios had already made provision for his sons to be under the tutelage of stronger individuals, the praetorian prefect Rufinos in the case of Arkadios and the patrician Stilicho (whose father was a Vandal) in the case of Honorius. The youth of the two emperors and the intrigues of the individuals behind the throne led to difficulties, especially when coupled with the revolt of Alaric the Visigoth shortly after Theodosios' death.

As will be recalled, Theodosios I had settled the Visigoths in Roman territory just to the north and west of Constantinople, where they lived essentially under the jurisdiction of their own leaders. Partly as a result of continued contact with the Romans, Visigothic society became more complex, and by the 390s the dominant leader was Alaric, who had served as commander of the Visigothic contingent in the struggle against Eugenius. Disappointed that he was not named *magister militum*, Alaric used the opportunity of Theodosios' death to rise in revolt, devastate the areas outside Constantinople, and even threaten the city itself. Rivalry between the eastern and the western courts prevented effective action against Alaric, and he descended into Greece and ravished unprotected cities. On at least two occasions Stilicho's western armies had Alaric at their mercy, but disagreement with the eastern court kept him from acting and he allowed Alaric to escape. Alaric first set himself up as an independent power in the Balkans, and later, in 401, he invaded Italy. These disasters, coupled apparently with the weakness of Arkadios himself, caused changes in the court of Constantinople, with Rufinos being replaced, first by the eunuch Eutropios (396–400), then by Arkadios' wife Eudoxia (400–4), and finally by the praetorian prefect Anthemios (404–8), as the dominant power in Constantinople. Meanwhile, opposition developed against Stilicho in the West, and he was executed in 408. With Rome essentially defenseless, Alaric took the city and sacked it in AD 410.

Stilicho followed the example set by Arbogast, and he was the first of a line of Germanic commanders who dominated the imperial court in the West through the rest of the fifth century. Although they were prevented from becoming emperors by their position as "barbarians," they nonetheless stood as the power behind the throne. It is significant that such a phenomenon did not develop in the East. An important event in this regard was the attempted coup of the general Gainas. Gainas was himself a Goth and he had led a contingent in Theodosios' campaign against Eugenius. Apparently favored by the government over Alaric, he eventually became *magister militum* in 399. His power, however, was feared by many in Constantinople and some of the leading politicians organized opposition to him. As a result of this, in 400 Gainas attempted to seize the city by force: he armed his men secretly and sent them into the city on a supposedly peaceful mission. The attempted coup met with violent resistance from the people of the city, who set upon the Visigoths and eventually massacred a contingent of them. Gainas himself escaped, but he was soon killed by a Hunnic chieftain, and his attempted coup provided a powerful warning that Germanic commanders would have a difficult time seizing ultimate power in the East.

During the reign of Arkadios John Chrysostom served as bishop of Constantinople. John had been raised in Antioch and received an excellent education, but he was attracted by the monasticism of the Syrian desert, and his attitudes were marked by the harshness and asceticism of that environment. He gained a reputation as a powerful public speaker in Antioch and his followers were fanatically devoted to him, frequently breaking into applause at key points in his sermons. John was selected as bishop and brought to Constantinople in 398, where he immediately became involved in the political intrigues of his day, in part because of his uncompromising stand against Arianism and immorality. His open criticisms of the empress Eudoxia led to his condemnation at a church council, but popular outrage resulted in his temporary return, until his enemies forced him into permanent exile in 400.

John was a strong defender of the rights of the see of Constantinople, especially against the claims of the bishop of Alexandria, which had heretofore been the dominant episcopacy in the Roman East. This was an important step in the rise of Constantinople to a position as the first bishopric of the East. John also opposed the tendency of the "Alexandrian School" of Biblical exegesis to favor allegorical or symbolic interpretations of Scripture. John favored, instead, a straightforward, almost literal interpretation of the texts and, always, an uncompromising morality.

Arkadios died suddenly in 408, at the age of only 29 or 30. He left behind his son Theodosios II, who was only 7 years old, although he had been crowned as emperor when less than a year of age. Partly because of his youth at the time of his accession, but also apparently as a result of his own temperament, Theodosios was dominated by stronger personalities, especially by his older sister Pulcheria and his wife Athenais-Eudokia. At the same time, Theodosios' reign was marked by extraordinary peace on the frontiers and the accompanying lack of influence from military men in the eastern capital: the Persians presented no significant threat from the east and the power of Attila and the Huns was bought off by the offering of rich gifts. The main foreign concern of the eastern court was to restore the unity of the empire, largely through diplomatic attempts to win over the western court, in part through dynastic marriages. These attempts eventually all failed, although the East had important allies in the person of Galla Placidia and others. At the same time, this period witnessed what turned out to be significant concessions of territories in the West to the barbarians, and the conquest of North Africa by the Vandals.

As mentioned, the court in Constantinople was marked by a certain internal tension, in large part as a result of the emperor's youth at the time of his accession. The transition from the reign of Arkadios was smoothed by the praetorian prefect Anthemios, who remained in power until 414 or 415. Anthemios was a member of one of the most powerful of contemporary aristocratic families, and the church historian Socrates reports that during the emperor's minority he was the virtual ruler of the East. Anthemios maintained a pro-Persian policy that secured peace in the East; he reformed the food supply

Box 5.1 *Women of the House of Theodosios*

In the early 1980s Kenneth Holum published an important book, examining the apparent paradox that the women of the Theodosian dynasty, in an age apparently dominated by male figures and military events, played a crucial role in politics. He pointed to their importance in the establishment and continuation of the Theodosian dynasty and their individual abilities and accomplishments as important factors in this regard. After Theodosios I the emperors of the dynasty were not apparently strong personalities, so imperial propaganda pointed to the strength and abilities of the empresses as companions in rule and, of course, as those who bore the children who allowed continuation of the dynasty. An examination of the biographies of these women provides some insight into their abilities and accomplishments.

Aelia Flaccila (died 385 or 386): wife of Theodosios I, and mother of Arkadios and Honorius. Like Theodosios himself, Flaccila was a native of Spain and she probably married the future emperor during his temporary retirement there in 376–8, since when she came to Constantinople she had already given birth to two children, Pulcheria (who died as a child) and Arkadios; her second son Honorius was born in 384. Flacilla died about two years later, and her main accomplishment seems to have been that she prevented Theodosios from compromising with the Arian bishop Eunomios of Kyzikos. Nonetheless, she apparently made a great impression on people during the time she was in Constantinople. Gregory of Nyssa, the famous orator and theologian, wrote a funerary speech in her honor, praising her piety but also the role she played in the suppression of Arianism. He compares the death of the empress to the impact caused by great natural disasters such as earthquakes and floods, although her loss was greater because it affected the whole world.

Eudoxia (died 404): Aelia Eudoxia Augusta, daughter of a Roman mother and Bauto, a Frankish general of Valentinian II. She married Arkadios in 396 and bore him five children, including Pulcheria and Theodosios II. She was beautiful and headstrong and she earned the enmity of the fiery archbishop John Chrysostom, who compared her to Jezebel and Salome. Eudoxia succeeded in having Chrysostom exiled twice, but she died of a miscarriage in 404.

Pulcheria (399–453): Aelia Pulcheria Augusta was the daughter of Arkadios and Eudoxia and sister of the emperor Theodosios II. When Arkadios died, in 408, Pulcheria was 9 and Theodosios II 7. At the beginning of the reign the Praetorian Prefect Anthemios was in charge of the regency. In 414 Theodosios crowned the 15-year-old Pulcheria as *Augusta* and she dominated the court from that time on. Pulcheria had taken a vow of celibacy and she persuaded her two sisters to do so as well, so that sources report that the court had all the characteristics of a monastery. She supervised the education of her brother and pursued a policy with interests in the West. Theodosios' wife, Eudokia, challenged her authority, as did the patriarch Nestorios, who refused to allow her to enter the altar area of the Great Church of Constantinople. Pulcheria, however, had her revenge at the Council of Ephesos (431) where Nestorios was condemned and deposed. After the return of Eudokia to Constantinople in 439

Pulcheria's power waned; the "Robber Council" of 449 was a defeat for her and she sought support from Pope Leo I. After Theodosios' unexpected death in 450 Pulcheria held power in her own name, but she agreed to marry the aged senator Marcian on condition he respect her virginity. Pulcheria was influential in the Council of Chalcedon (451) which condemned Monophysitism.

Athenais/Eudokia (ca. 400–460): Aelia Eudokia Augusta, daughter of Leontios a pagan philosopher in Athens, married Theodosios II in 421 and bore him three children, the oldest of whom, Licinia Eudoxia, married Valentinian III. Eudokia was highly educated and a poet of some note; a few of her works survive. She apparently led a faction of religious moderates but these were eclipsed by the power of the empress Pulcheria and Eudokia left Constantinople for the Holy Land in 438. When she returned the next year she regained power but accusations of adultery forced her to return to Jerusalem in 443, where she lived estranged from her husband for the rest of her life. In the aftermath of the Council of Chalcedon in 451 she initially sided with the Monophysites, but was ultimately reconciled with the Chalcedonians.

Galla Placidia (388–450): daughter of Theodosios I, she spent most of her life in the West, where she went with her father in 394. She was captured by the Visigoths at the time of Alaric's sack of Rome in 410 and she married the new king Athaulf in 414. She apparently was able to influence the policy of the Visigoths in favor of Rome. After Athaulf's death the next year she was returned to the Romans, and in 417 she married the *patricius* Flavius Constantius, the primary general of Honorius, who was made *Augustus* in 421 (as Constantius III). The couple had two children, including Valentinian III, who became emperor in the West. Theodosios II refused to acknowledge Constantius III, hoping to unite the whole of the empire under his rule. Constantius, however, died in 421 and Galla Placidia broke with her brother and was accused of treason. She fled to the court of Theodosios II in 423 and, after Honorius' death in the same year, the eastern court sought to use her to gain control over the West. Theodosios' troops, under Aspar the Alan, defeated the western usurper Ioannes and established Valentinian III on the throne in Ravenna, with Galla Placidia as regent. After ca. 425 the Roman general Aetius was the major power behind the throne, as he used alliances, especially with the Huns, to control the various Germanic peoples in the West. Galla Placidia was a significant patron and stimulated church construction, especially in Ravenna.

FURTHER READING

R. W. Burgess, "The Accession of Marcian in the Light of Chalcedonian Apologetic and Monophysite Polemic," *Byzantinische Zeitschrift* 86–7 (1993–4), 47–68.

K. Holum, *Theodosian Empresses*. Berkeley, CA, 1982.

J. M. O'Flynn, *Generalissimos of the Western Roman Empire*. Edmonton, 1983.

S. I. Oost, *Galla Placidia Augusta*. Chicago, 1968.

M. D. Usher, *Homeric Stitchings: The Homeric Centos of the Empress Eudocia*. Lanham, MD, 1998.

Figure 5.1 Coin of Theodosios II. This gold coin was struck in 420–21 to commemorate the victory of the emperor's troops. On the reverse of the coin is a Victory (the old pagan personification of Victory, who iconographically was transformed into the image of an angel) holding a long cross and the words VOTXX MVLTXXX, which represents a prayer of thanksgiving for the twentieth anniversary of the emperor's reign and a prayer for the thirtieth anniversary. Photo: Dumbarton Oaks

of the capital and rebuilt the Land Walls of the city, leaving them in essentially the shape they were to have for the next thousand years. After Anthemios' death power fell to the emperor's sister Pulcheria, who was to play a remarkably dominant role in politics for the next 40 years. By this time (ca. 416) she had already taken a vow of virginity that allowed her a free field of operation, and she devoted herself to her own religious policies and the politics of the imperial court. Along with the bishop of Constantinople, Attikos, she sought to turn the atmosphere of the court into that of a monastery, and she was later credited with requesting that the image of the Virgin supposedly painted by the Evangelist Luke be brought to Constantinople. She personally supervised the education of her brother, the emperor, and she followed a decidedly western policy, ordering the bust of Honorius to be placed in a position of honor in the Senate of Constantinople.

In 421 Theodosios married Athenais, daughter of a pagan philosopher from Athens, who took the name Eudokia after her baptism. She was an attractive and talented woman who wrote poetry of some merit, and she bore the emperor three children. She gathered around herself a circle of educated and powerful people who sought to emphasize traditional culture and Roman secular values. For a time Eudokia dominated life at court, but Pulcheria maintained her own base of power and slowly began to eclipse the influence of her sister-in-law. Eudokia left Constantinople for the Holy Land, first in 438, and then, finally, in 443, after which Pulcheria was once again a major force at court.

Interestingly, the government of Theodosios II seems to have taken a real interest in the fortification of the cities and the countryside of the empire. As mentioned above, the praetorian prefect Anthemios expanded and rebuilt the

Figure 5.2 Northeast gate, Byzantine fortress at Isthmia (reconstruction).
This was a monumental gateway through the Hexamilion, the 8-kilometer wall
across the Isthmos of Korinth designed to prevent barbarians from entering
the Pelopponnesos. This fortification was built in the early years of Theodosios
II's reign and reconstructed on several occasions over the next millennium.
Reconstruction by Charles Pierce. Courtesy of The Ohio State University Excavations
at Isthmia

walls of Constantinople and there is evidence of similar activity elsewhere,
most notably the construction of what was later called the Hexamilion ("six-
mile long" wall), a great barrier across the Isthmos of Korinth in Greece,
designed to block the raids of barbarians such as Alaric at the very end of the
fourth century. The poet Kyros from Egyptian Panopolis, as prefect of the
city, also repaired the walls of Constantinople after a disastrous earthquake
in 437.

The Christological Controversy

During the reign of Theodosios II some of the most important developments
in church politics and doctrine played themselves out. In the fourth century
the major theological issue was the Arian controversy, which essentially involved the relationship among the members of the Christian Trinity: the main
question was whether the Son (Christ) was fully equal to the Father, that is,
whether the Son was "of the same substance (*homoousios*)" with the Father, or
whether he was in some way "less fully God" than the Father. As mentioned
above, the Council of Nicaea decided to accept the teaching that Christ and

the Father were both fully God, and this was confirmed at the Council of Constantinople in 381.

These decisions, however, which were largely concerned with so-called Trinitarian questions (i.e., those concerning relations among the three members of the Trinity), left unanswered equally difficult issues concerning the person of Christ, which are normally called Christological questions. To put the matter very simply, if Christ was fully God (as Nicaea had said) how could he be fully a human being? And if he were not fully a human being, how could his death and sacrifice on the cross be effective in the salvation of mankind? In this regard, the decision of Nicaea seemed to some people to favor a strict kind of monotheism in which the human element was downplayed, and this resurrected older controversies about how God himself should be viewed and how humans were to understand their relationship to him. Naturally, these were difficult questions, and, as in the Arian controversy of the fourth century, they were approached by intellectuals and theologians using the traditions and terminology of Greek philosophy. As we have said before, this philosophical tradition was ideally suited for such a task, although the differing tendencies of the theological schools increased the likelihood of serious disagreement or splits within the church which, given the prevailing view since the time of Constantine and Eusebios, would have serious ramifications for the empire as a whole. The emperor was certain to be involved since he generally believed that the success of his reign depended on the support of God, which (in turn) would largely depend on the emperor's support of correct theological positions and the suppression of heresy.

As one can imagine, the Christological controversy was enormously complex and it involved concepts and distinctions that are not only difficult for us to understand fully but difficult to express accurately without recourse to the technical terminology of Greek philosophy. At the same time, the issues involved touched people directly since they concerned the identity of God and the traditions through which many people in the empire had come to look at the world and their place in it. By the time the controversy broke out many people already had firm ideas about how they envisioned their God, and these ideas were not always easy to change.

As already mentioned, it is common to speak of two different "schools" of theology, that of Alexandria and that of Antioch. Such a distinction is an oversimplification, but it may be helpful to look at the way in which these affected the Christological controversies. The Alexandrian tradition, mentioned above, was based on the ideas of Neoplatonism, as they had been adapted to Christianity in the third century by Origen and Clement of Alexandria. Among the principles of Alexandrian teaching was an allegorical (rather than a literal) interpretation of the Bible (especially the Old Testament) and a strong emphasis on the divinity (as opposed to the humanity) of Christ. The Antiochian School developed in opposition to the ideas of the Alexandrian School, and it emphasized a historical or even literal interpretation of the Bible and the humanity of Christ (while not denying his divinity); the Antiochene tradition therefore stressed the two natures of Christ (human and divine).

Not surprisingly, given the importance of religion in this age, the Christological controversy had significant political ramifications. As would be expected, the emperors understood that they had a responsibility to become involved, since they had been entrusted by God with the protection of the church and its doctrines, and they all seem to have accepted the idea that their own political and military successes were directly related to (indeed largely determined by) their maintenance of correct religious doctrine. In addition, as we have already seen, the important bishops of the period were involved in struggles for power among themselves, something that was of considerable importance, given the increasing political and economic influence that the bishops could wield. The bishop of Rome (the pope) was generally regarded in the fourth and fifth centuries as the most prestigious of the bishops of the empire, in part because Rome was the ancient capital of the empire and in part because of the New Testament story of how Christ had singled out Peter (traditionally the first bishop of Rome) as the "rock" on which the church would be built. In addition, the bishop of Rome had no serious rival in the West (with the possible exception of the bishop of Milan), whereas there were many powerful bishops in the East. There, the bishop of Jerusalem had considerable prestige but little political power, while the chief rivalry was between the large and powerful city of Alexandria and the new (and expanding) imperial capital of Constantinople. The Christological controversy was fought out against the background of the struggle among these ecclesiastical powers.

The Nestorian controversy: the Council of Ephesos (431)

In 428 Theodosios II selected Nestorios as bishop of Constantinople. The new bishop was from the same milieu as John Chrysostom and he was, like his famous predecessor, an ascetic with a reputation as a powerful orator and an outspoken opponent of heresy. From the outset Nestorios earned enemies in Constantinople, in part by his condemnation of games and theaters and his attacks on the Arians; he also earned the enmity of the empress Pulcheria. In 429 Nestorios delivered a famous sermon in which he objected to the use of the term *Theotokos* (literally the "God-bearer," or Mother of God) for the Virgin Mary. Nestorios' own ideas are not very well known, because we hear about them mainly from his enemies, but in general he objected to the idea that God himself could be born as a human being; rather, he preferred to use the term *Christotokos* (the Mother of Christ) for the Virgin. Opposition to Nestorios immediately emerged, led by Cyril, the bishop of Alexandria, and to a certain degree the controversy can be seen as a struggle between the theological schools of Antioch and Alexandria. Nestorios' enemies argued that the bishop taught that there were "two Christs," one who was fully God and one who was also human, and the most serious charge against him was that he separated these two aspects of Christ more than his opponents thought was appropriate. Thus, the two sides were not as far apart as some modern observers might imagine. Both agreed that Christ was both human and divine, but they disagreed about the way in which these two aspects were joined.

The emperor strongly supported his bishop, but he finally agreed to have the issue debated by an ecumenical council at Ephesos (in western Asia Minor) in 431. The council was, from the beginning, essentially under the control of Cyril of Alexandria, and Nestorios was soon condemned and sent into exile. Theodosios II was not at all pleased with this outcome, but in the end he came to accept it. Nestorios had, however, gained many supporters who refused to agree to the condemnation of their leader and who supported his view of the relationship between the divine and the human in Christ. They felt that the decisions of the Council of Chalcedon in 451 (see below) justified their position, and they eventually established their own church organization and their own hierarchy. Most of the adherents of Nestorianism were in Syria, and, since they were persecuted for their belief within the Byzantine Empire, many of them migrated to Persia, Arabia, and even farther east, to Central Asia, India, and even China, where they have maintained churches up to the present.

Monophysitism and the Council of Chalcedon (451)

Thus, the Council of Ephesos was a victory for Alexandrian theology and, just as much, for the bishop of Alexandria. Nonetheless, some theologians in Constantinople feared a revival of Nestorianism in the late 440s, and they pressed their ideas perhaps further than they meant to do. The leader of this movement was the monk, Eutyches, who taught that Christ had only one nature (*physis*) – and this was divine. He was opposed by Flavian, the bishop of Constantinople, but he was supported by Dioskoros, the bishop of Alexandria. This controversy was to be settled at the second Council of Ephesos (449, often called the "Robber Council" because it ended in considerable violence). Dioskoros and his followers did not hesitate to intimidate the delegates to the council, and they therefore exonerated Eutyches and condemned and deposed Flavian, who died soon thereafter as a result of this treatment.

In 450, however, Theodosios II died suddenly in a hunting accident. No preparations had been made for the succession, and power naturally fell to Pulcheria, who had been *Augusta* from 414 and who had many supporters at court, especially those who disagreed with the policies recently advocated by her brother. Pulcheria's supporters, however, felt that she could not rule the empire in her own name, so she was married to Marcian, an aged military officer, who had risen to power as an associate of Aspar the Alan, a powerful barbarian commander who dominated the army in the latter years of Theodosios II. A condition of the marriage was that Marcian respect the empress' virginity. Pulcheria had already been in contact with Pope Leo I about the decisions of the "Robber Council," which she regarded as unacceptable. The Pope and the new emperor Marcian agreed with Pulcheria and a new council was called to investigate the issue again. It was held in October of 451 at Chalcedon, a suburb of Constantinople on the Asiatic shore of the Bosphoros.

From the outset it was clear that the new council would reverse the decisions of the Robber Council, and many of the bishops hastened to claim that they had been coerced by the violence of the Egyptians and their supporters at Ephesos in 449. Pope Leo did not attend the meeting himself, but he sent his legates, who carried with them a statement of faith usually described as the "Tome of Leo," and this was accepted by the council as a proper understanding of orthodox Christianity. The council therefore proclaimed that Christ had two natures (*physeis*), human and divine, and that these were inviolably joined together without division or separation. Its acceptance of the two natures of Christ was thought by some to have gone back to the teachings of Nestorios (and Nestorios himself – who was still alive – claimed that this was the case). At the same time, the council did not really solve the dilemma, since virtually all participants in the debate had agreed that there were two natures in Christ. The disagreement centered rather on the characterization of the way in which the human and the divine natures were joined. In any case, by condemning Eutyches and Dioskoros the council made it certain that large portions of the church of Egypt would refuse to accept its teaching.

From this time we can date a significant split in the Christian church. It is true that schisms had existed before. The Arians had never accepted the Council of Nicaea, but they were marginalized after 381. The Nestorians refused to accept the Council of Ephesos, but they came to live essentially outside the empire. The Monophysites, however – as the opponents of Chalcedon came to be called – lived in some of the most populous and most important parts of the empire, in Egypt and (increasingly) in Syria. Much of the religious history of the next 200 years (and perhaps even beyond) can be seen as a struggle to find a solution, or a compromise, to problems resulting from the decisions made at Chalcedon in 451.

Not incidentally, the Council also elevated the position of the bishop of Constantinople by granting him control over Thrace and much of Asia Minor, while ranking the patriarch of Constantinople second in prestige only to the bishop of Rome: this was certainly a direct affront to the bishop of Alexandria, and it confirmed the position of the bishop of the capital as the most important church dignitary in the East. Additionally, in part as a result of the violent activity of some of the monks, the council declared that all monasteries should be under the supervision of their bishop.

After the council the emperor sought to impose a Chalcedonian (i.e., "dyophysite") bishop in Alexandria, but the Egyptians – including most of the bishops themselves – refused to cooperate, and a new bishop could be imposed only by the force of imperial arms. Opposition was strong in Alexandria, but it was perhaps even greater in the villages and monasteries of the country; despite the dominance of Greek in the cities, country people had continued to speak the Egyptian language, which was written in an alphabet based on Greek and known to us as Coptic. For this reason, historians usually refer to the Monophysite Christians of Egypt as Copts, since their liturgy and theological literature was increasingly written in the Coptic language. Similarly, the Monophysites of Syria are commonly referred to as Jacobites, after their leader Jacob Baradaeus (d. 578), and they increasingly used the local language, Syriac, in their literature and church services. As a result of these divisions, from the time of Chalcedon onward, many of the great cities of the eastern part of the empire had two bishops, one loyal to the emperor and the teachings of the council, and one Monophysite.

At one time historians sought to explain the divisions and strong feelings by reference to "national" sentiments on the part of the "oppressed" subjects of the empire. Such a view is no longer tenable, in part because concepts such as nationalism were unknown to people of the pre-modern age, but there is still reason to see in Monophysitism and similar movements an emphasis on local, as opposed to empire-wide concerns, and to see the revival of local languages and culture as a primary characteristic of the period. Thus, instead of viewing the fifth and sixth centuries as a period of cultural uniformity, we should see it as one of vibrant and quite remarkable diversity: the emperor and many church-men (whose views have come down to us) may have wished to impose unity on the culture of the period, but the reality was quite clearly very different.

Marcian and the Emperors of the Fifth Century

Marcian (450–7), as we have seen, came to power as a result of the sudden death of Theodosios II and the need for Pulcheria to find a male colleague. In addition, Marcian had been associated with Aspar the Alan, a general who operated in both the East and West and who came to play a leading role in Constantinople itself. Nonetheless, Marcian was not just a cipher emperor and his policies went far beyond the issue of religious doctrine. In this regard, he seems to have been in tune with other members of the senatorial class of the East, who did not agree with all the policies of Theodosios II. Marcian was a soldier who had risen from the ranks to attain high office, but he had come to agree with most of the ideas of the senatorial aristocracy. Thus, he abolished the *collatio glebalis*, one of the taxes on land, and reduced some of the pay-ments made by officials at the time of their accession. Theodosios' payment of tribute to Attila and the Huns had galled many senators, and immediately upon his accession Marcian refused to continue the practice. Rather surpris-ingly, Attila hesitated to attack Constantinople, but instead moved westward, where he was to wreak considerable havoc. One might have expected Marcian to have adopted a more pro-western political stance, but he failed to support the western court in its struggle with the Vandals. Nonetheless, Marcian's reign was a success and he left the treasury full at the time of his death. Pulcheria had predeceased her husband, and in 457 the dynasty of Theodosios I came to an end.

By 457 Aspar the Alan was the leading power in Constantinople. Although he was himself not of Germanic origin, he came to represent the interests of the Germanic soldiery and was as close as anything Byzantium was to know to a *generalissimo* of the type that had become common in the fifth-century West. At the time of Marcian's death Aspar was able to secure the choice of Leo I (457–74) as emperor, and he was crowned by the patriarch Anatolios, the first time this practice is recorded. Leo was, like his predecessor, a solider who rose through the ranks and ended up as one of Aspar's personal assistants. Aspar, whose Arianism prevented him from seizing the throne in his own name, sought to use Leo as a compliant tool of his own policy, and there is little doubt that Aspar was the power behind the throne during Leo's early years, leading a successful campaign against the Huns and intervening, with dubious success, in the affairs of the West. Aspar's plan of a naval campaign against the Vandals in 468 failed, due to the incompetence of the commander, Basilikos, who was the brother of Leo's wife Verina. Toward the end of his reign Leo was more successful in the West. In 467 he named Anthemios, son-in-law of Marcian, as *caesar* and sent him to Italy, where he was accepted as emperor and viewed by some as the hope for unity between East and West. After Anthemios was overthrown and killed by the western general Ricimer in 472, Leo seems to have encouraged Julius Nepos to seize the western throne.

Leo was, in the end, a match for Aspar's cunning, and he was able to use the Isaurians as a military balance to Aspar's Germanic troops. The Isaurians were a tribal people who lived in southeastern Asia Minor and who gained a significant reputation as skilled and fearless fighters; by the fifth century they made up a significant part of the eastern army. One of the Isaurian commanders, whose original name was Tarasis but who took the name Zeno, offered his support to Leo. The emperor arranged for Zeno to marry his daughter Ariadne, and he used Zeno to free himself of Aspar's control; in 471 both Aspar and his son Ardobourios were found murdered.

Leo I had no sons, so he looked to his grandson, also named Leo (Leo II, emperor 473–4), to succeed him. Leo II was the son of Ariadne and Zeno; although only 6 years of age, he was crowned as emperor by Leo I just before his death. Then, after Leo I's death in early 474, the young emperor crowned his father Zeno as emperor (474–91) and shortly thereafter died himself. There was some talk that Zeno had killed his son, and the dowager empress Verina formed a plot against Zeno, leading to the acclamation of her brother Basilikos as emperor. The movement against Zeno was directed in part against the role that the Isaurian soldiers had come to play in Constantinople, but Basilikos gave it a religious dimension as he openly promoted Monophysitism. Zeno fled to Isauria in 475 but was able to return to Constantinople, in part with the help of Theodoric the Ostrogoth, who had become the most powerful of the Germanic commanders in the East.

The reign of Zeno witnessed a number of important events in the West, in which the eastern court played little role. Zeno accepted Julius Nepos as western emperor, but was not willing to do anything to help him when he was overthrown, fearing Nepos' connection with the dowager empress Verina. Zeno, however, certainly never recognized the "last" western emperor Romulus Augustulus, and continued to regard Nepos as his colleague until the latter's death in 480. The Ostrogoths continued to cause problems in Thrace, and in 488 Zeno persuaded Theodoric to march on Italy in order to remove Odoacer, who ruled the West in fact, if not in name. The movement of the Ostrogoths to Italy and the establishment of Theodoric in Ravenna were events of considerable importance, in large part because, even though he was a Goth and an Arian, Theodoric had grown up in Constantinople, and he was fully aware of Byzantine ways and the ideals of Byzantine civilization. Although he never had himself proclaimed as emperor, he very much acted the part, arguably the first Germanic ruler to do so. He actively supported the Roman aristocrats Boethius and Cassiodorus, both of whom held official posts in his government and who were influential in the transmission of Roman culture to the Goths. Theodoric acted the part of an imperial patron, and he graced his capital of Ravenna with a number of impressive buildings, including a palace (now destroyed), the church of San Apollinare Nuovo, the Arian baptistery, and his own mausoleum.

Although he was probably himself a moderate Monophysite, Zeno had no real interest in religion. He regarded the split within the church, however, as damaging to the state in many ways, and he worked with the patriarch of Constantinople, Akakios, to end the schism. The *Henotikon* (declaration of unity) was a document, issued in 482, that sought to end the controversy by compromise and by imperial fiat. It ignored the decisions of the Council of Chalcedon and made no mention of the dispute concerning the natures of Christ. It condemned both Nestorios and Eutyches and required that the decisions of the first three ecumenical councils (i.e., before Chalcedon) be regarded as binding. Not surprisingly, the *Henotikon* pleased neither side, since nobody was willing to compromise, and it led only to the creation of yet a third party, the adherents of the patriarch Akakios and those who accepted the imperial edict, who were, in turn, condemned thoroughly by the other two groups. The papacy was of course completely opposed to the *Henotikon* and this led to a formal break between the two churches, usually called the Akakian (or Acacian) Schism, after the name of the patriarch Akakios. The *Henotikon* remained officially in force until 519, but it was not, indeed could not be, enforced. It was, however, a rare example of an attempt by an emperor to impose religious doctrine by imperial decree.

Anastasios I (491–519)

The emperor Zeno died in 491, and power was for the time being in the hands of his widow Ariadne. Going against the wishes of Zeno himself, Ariadne chose

Figure 5.3 Coin of Anastasios I. The emperor issued this large copper coin as part of his policy to improve the Byzantine economy and the condition of merchants and others who relied on small change to make everyday transactions. The emperor is shown on the observe in civilian dress and the large K on the reverse is the Greek number 20, indicating that this was a half-follis. A *follis* was worth 40 of the old, small coins that it replaced. Photo: Dumbarton Oaks

as emperor a relatively undistinguished military officer of dubious ancestry named Anastasios. Anastasios was a dedicated and relatively successful emperor whose long reign brought stability and prosperity to the empire and unquestionably paved the way for the "golden age" of Justinian to follow.

Upon his accession Anastasios immediately set himself the task of placing the Isaurian troops in Constantinople under close imperial control. He was a careful and frugal administrator with a real eye for the details of state finance. He sought to rebuild the cities of the empire in part through the encouragement of trade. He did away with the *chrysargyron*, a tax that fell heavily on commercial interests and – in 494 – he reformed imperial bronze coinage, replacing the nearly worthless small *nummi* with a large coin 40 times their nominal value. This reform was designed, in part at least, to stabilize the bronze coinage on which small-scale commerce depended. Anastasios also removed the burden of collecting taxes from the local *curiales*, placing it instead in the hands of state-appointed *vindices*. Anastasios was an energetic builder and was especially involved in the construction of frontier defenses and churches in various parts of the empire. Despite the expenses associated with these, the emperor's sound financial policies brought their reward, and at his death the treasury is said to have contained 320,000 pounds of gold.

Anastasios seems to have been personally religious and a convinced Monophysite; before his elevation to the throne it was even suggested he might be named Monophysite bishop of Antioch. Throughout his reign he left the *Henotikon* as official state policy, and he made several attempts to nominate Monophysite bishops in important cities. This meant that he had strained relations with the papacy and the West in general; the papacy demanded that all eastern bishops accept the teachings of Chalcedon without reservation, and proposed discussions between the parties were unsuccessful. Anastasios' attempt to impose a Monophysite bishop on Constantinople in 511 led to the revolt of Vitalian in Thrace. Vitalian appears not to have wanted to overthrow Anastasios, but to force him to accept Chalcedon; the rebel, however, was defeated in 515 and the revolt collapsed. Anasatasios was also hostile to Theodoric and the Ostrogoths in Italy; although he recognized Theodoric as king of Italy in 497, disagreements later broke out over Pannonia. The long peace that had characterized the East since the days of Theodosios I was broken in 502 in a war with Persia; although they initially suffered setbacks, the troops of Anastasios ultimately prevailed and peace was signed in 506. Anastasios used the respite to rebuild many of the fortifications in the East, most notably at the frontier city of Dara. The Bulgars, a Turkic people who had moved west from Central Asia in the train of the Huns, overran the Danube frontier, beginning as early as 493, and this led the emperor to construct the Long Walls in Thrace. This was a barrier wall across the whole Thracian peninsula, which placed the first line of defense of Constantinople some distance from the capital. He probably also fortified a number of other cities whose defenses are normally attributed to Justinian.

Religion and Society in the Fifth Century

Byzantine society changed in significant ways during the fifth century. These changes were not so sudden or dramatic as those of the fourth century, which can be seen as real changes in direction. Rather, the phenomena of the fifth century can best be thought of as developments built on the basic system established in the preceding period. They were, nonetheless, important, for they created the forms and systems that were to remain for the rest of the Byzantine Empire and beyond.

The construction of Christian space

By the fifth century, society in the Byzantine Empire had become largely Christian in orientation, although the majority of the population was perhaps still not officially Christian. We can see, in this period, the continued growth of episcopal power, not only from the written sources, but also from the archaeological evidence, characterized by the construction of huge ecclesiastical complexes. These featured not only churches for the worship of the faithful, but also large and lavish living accommodations for the bishop and his staff, and many other rooms and buildings to house the administrative and welfare needs of the church. Since a hallmark of the Christian church in the period was the charity it offered to the poor, the sick, orphans, and widows, storage facilities for grain and other supplies had to be constructed, and these were often built right next to the church itself, as sometimes were orphanages, hospitals, and even monasteries. The churches normally also included plentiful supplies of fresh water and a large enclosed space to the west of the church, called an *atrium*, where crowds could gather for a variety of purposes. The architecture of the churches, as we have seen, was based largely on the traditions of classical architecture, and the new ecclesiastical complexes became centers of everyday activity that rivaled the old *agora* that had been the center of the classical city.

The churches were not simply utilitarian places for worship or for the provision of social assistance. They were also splendid testimony to the triumph of Christianity and the power of the bishops. Members of the aristocracy and the episcopacy (who were often the same people) competed among themselves in the construction of beautiful buildings, replete with lavish decoration inside and out. As we have said, the churches were often the center of large complexes and their height would frequently make them the most conspicuous structures in the city. Entrances to the church complex were often marked with decorated archways opening onto courtyards with fountains, sculpture, and colonnaded porches.

The inside of the churches enclosed enormous open spaces. Building on the techniques developed in Roman basilicas and baths, the architects of these churches clearly meant to dazzle the eyes of the beholder with the height and the width of the enclosed space. Columns were frequently used to support the walls and roof, and these too were arranged in ways that emphasized the majesty of the interior of the building.

Throughout the empire literally thousands of these churches were built in the fourth to the seventh centuries and even the most remote rural building often displayed remarkable richness of decoration. The floors were normally paved with slabs of stone – commonly marble, limestone, or slate – or with mosaic. The latter provided opportunities for a wide variety of decoration, with both abstract and figural decorations used. Interestingly, the mosaic decorations in churches seem to resemble very closely those found in public secular buildings and private villas of the time, and it is clear that scenes from nature, representations of hunting, animal fights, and pagan mythology were considered appropriate for the decoration of the floors of churches. Undoubtedly this is in part because these were the scenes that aristocratic donors liked, but they are also the result of the patterns that the artisans in the mosaic workshops were accustomed to make.

The interior walls of the churches were covered with highly polished multicolored sheets of marble (called revetment) that would have reflected light like a mirror and made the interiors of the buildings look even larger than they were. Alternatively, areas of the walls might be covered with mosaics, usually made with brightly colored stone and even glass and depicting scenes from the Bible, the saints from the early church, or even Christ himself. Large-scale programs were frequently designed in which the mosaics represented theological ideas and/or reflected the liturgical ceremonies that went on in the interior of the building. Thus, for example, it is clear that processions, involving the clergy and sometimes even the ordinary believers, were an especially important part of the services of the church at this time, and processions (often a "heavenly" procession) were frequently depicted on the walls of the buildings.

The interior of churches of the fifth and sixth centuries emphasized both their longitudinal and their vertical elements. Thus, worshipers in many churches (especially those of the basilican plan) would be encouraged to look along the colonnades toward the apse and altar at the eastern end, often far off in the distance. This would indicate to the believer both the distance between God and man, but also, at the same time, the possibility of communication with and ultimately access to the divine. Likewise, most churches of this period emphasized their height, with soaring timber-built roofs and/or masonry vaults and domes. Huge windows with translucent glass let in significant quantities of light that illuminated the otherwise dark interiors of the buildings and reflected, in ever changing patterns, off the variegated surfaces of the floors and walls, many of which would have reflected back and thus magnified the light visible to the worshiper.

In this period churches were not the only public buildings affected by the Christianization of the empire. Christian monuments or monuments with Christian symbols were erected throughout the cities and, of course, churches, monasteries, crosses, and other monuments began to dot the countryside. Wealthy donors in many cities erected columns, fountains, and other monuments that expressed their Christian sentiments. An example of this was the so-called Tetrapylon in Ephesos. This was a group of four columns erected astride one of the main streets of the city, through which all traffic would pass from the city center to the port. On the top of the columns were placed symbols or statues of the four Evangelists, powerfully symbolizing the Christianization of the city and its secular activity. Christian graffiti, including crosses, the Christogram, various letters referring to Christ, etc., are found on the walls, columns, and even streets of all the cities of the age.

The organized church

In this period bishops took the general lead in converting people to Christianity, in part through their charity and through the lavish display of architectural space in the huge urban churches. Virtually all the emperors made donations to the churches and these gifts were commonly transformed immediately into church construction and decoration, into the gold and silver vessels used in the liturgy, and into the elaborate and colorful costumes worn by the numerous clergy. Public processions through the streets of the cities became commonplace, and the music, light, movement, and smells associated with them were certainly attractive to urban dwellers in a way that we – who are bombarded with sights, sounds, and colors – might find difficult to appreciate. The festivals of the church year, which at this time began to emerge in a regular fashion, allowed people to mark time in sequence with the calender of the church, adding to the attractiveness of Christianity and cementing people's attachment to it.

As we have seen, the church hierarchy, which was rudimentary at the time of Constantine, developed and crystallized in the succeeding years. By the end of the fifth century the bishop had come to control all the property and wealth of his see and he was one of the leading citizens of his city, if not the most important. On some occasions bishops were selected from among the monks of the desert, but many such bishops encountered difficulty or even opposition in their cities, undoubtedly in part because of their lack of experience in dealing with imperial and local officials and the responsibilities of power.

Not surprisingly, already in this period the bishops began to play a role beyond their religious charge. The bishops naturally had to organize a kind of ecclesiastical court to decide matters of church practice and belief and, as we have seen, Constantine incorporated the episcopal court into Roman legal practice. In the years after Constantine this practice was restricted to cases where both parties agreed to the arbitration of the bishop. Nonetheless, as time went on it was natural for individuals to bring their disputes to the bishop and by the early sixth century the decision of an episcopal court was again recognized as having the force of law.

On the one hand, given the importance of Christianity, which was generally represented by the organized church in this period, it is easy to understand the influence of the bishop beyond his religious authority. On the other hand, the fact that the bishop was, from an early date, expected to be unmarried or separated from his wife meant that he would commonly not have children and therefore might be expected to avoid temptations to look out for his own welfare or that of his family.

As we have also seen, the growing organization of the church meant that the bishops of the greater cities of the empire (the metropolitans) came to exercise administrative and doctrinal authority over the lesser bishops in their province. This organization provided a certain degree of stability and order within the church, and it set down rules for the selection of new bishops, the investigation of complaints, and the removal of bishops who might have failed in their duties. At the same time, the growth in the power of the metropolitans meant that they frequently came into conflict with each other and, as we have seen, this period is marked by heated struggles among the competing interests of the higher churchmen of the empire.

The holy man and holy woman

A key in this period was the emergence of the ascetic, or the "holy man" and "holy woman," as a central figure in Byzantine society. The phenomenon of the holy person did not simply refer to an individual who lived a holy life:

rather, such a person was thought to have the power to effect a direct contact with God and, by this means, to assist in the salvation of others or, more commonly, to work miracles, especially in healing the sick. This concept had deep roots in the religious tradition of the ancient world; it was present in a non-Christian context during the Roman Empire, especially in the form of the *theurgist*, who claimed to be able to command the divine forces of the universe through his own knowledge and special power. Theurgy frequently verged on what we may call superstition or even "quackery," and many of its practitioners were certainly far from honest.

What marked the holy man (and holy woman) in both a Christian and a non-Christian context was the ability to surpass the "norm" and touch the divine, and the proof of this was the ability to perform "superhuman" acts, which we may for the purpose of simplicity call miracles. Thus, within Christianity the idea of the holy man emerged, in part, from the miracles performed by the Disciples of Christ and described in the New Testament. Thus, it is clear that in Christianity the idea of individual sanctity – the idea of the saint – emerged at a very early time, and this was not normally conceived in terms

Figure 5.4 Funeral stele of an abbot. This stone slab was used to cover a tomb, presumably of an Egyptian abbot. The abbot is shown fully frontal, in a simplified almost two-dimensional manner, with his hands raised in the act of prayer. Limestone, Saqqara, 6th–7th century. Photo: Dumbarton Oaks

of individuals leading a simple "good life," but rather it was expected that the holy person would perform remarkable actions and he or she often become a public person, indeed a kind of celebrity.

In the early years of Christianity it was felt that this special status of sanctity was achieved most commonly through martyrdom, and after the martyr's death the faithful sought to maintain contact with the holy person through the physical possession of the body, parts of the body, or even scraps of cloth or other possessions that had intimate contact with the saint. As time went on and the persecutions came to an end, the phenomenon of martyrdom declined, although some individuals found that the doctrinal controversies provided an opportunity (if not the necessity) for opposition to the state that occasionally resulted in martyrdom.

The man or woman who was regarded as "holy" while still alive thus, in a sense, was a "living martyr," an individual whose role was similar to or the same as that of a saint who had already died. Thus the devotion to the holy man (or holy woman) was parallel to the cult of the saints or that of the martyrs, except that he or she was a living individual who could interact with others in the social and political milieu of his or her day. Much has been made of this phenomenon by Peter Brown and his school, and they have made a significant contribution for this period by taking what was once seen as simply a strange, if not perverse, characteristic of the age and putting it into its broader cultural and social setting. Brown was able to argue, for example, that the rise of the holy man was not simply the bizarre product of a superstitious age. Rather, the phenomenon of the holy man was a response to social and political changes in society. Brown started from the proposition that the fourth to sixth centuries were characterized by the decline of the local urban aristocracy (the *curiales*), who had acted as the primary patrons (protectors) of society. As these secular patrons disappeared, the holy man was seen to fill the void and to provide much the same "services": local leadership, dispute negotiation, and – most important – a means by which ordinary people could approach the representatives of the imperial power, or even God himself. Thus the holy man was not essentially an "odd person who lived in the desert," but rather an individual who, by his ascetic practice, had surpassed the normal limitation of the human condition and who had access to God himself: the miracles and even the extreme asceticism were proof of that. In possession of such power, the holy man could provide help to ordinary individuals, whether this was of a practical or a religious nature.

Monasticism

The figure of the holy man impressed itself on many aspects of contemporary society and – since most holy men could be seen as monks – they naturally had a powerful impact on that institution, in a way that (Brown argued) was to provide an important distinction between society in the East and West. During the fifth century monasticism continued to grow as an institution, and many monks left the solitude of their desert retreats and came into the cities of the empire. Some of these were moved by the need to minister to the poor and homeless, and they provided help in a variety of ways. Monasteries became common in cities, especially as wealthy individuals provided fine accommodations for them in unused mansions. Other monks sought to imitate their ascetic environment in the squalor of the cities, and government authorities developed means to deal with throngs of wandering monks.

Especially interesting was the ability of some bishops to organize groups of fanatically loyal monks in order to intimidate their enemies. Foremost among those who used these tactics were the bishops of Alexandria. The *parabalani*, or "bath attendants," were semi-clerical workers in hospitals and baths, whose dangerous occupation made them careless of their lives and fanatically devoted to their ecclesiastical leaders.

A particular form of asceticism that developed in the fifth century was the *stylite* movement. *Stylites* were ascetics who sought a special form of solitude by ascending to the top of a column, where they spent months or even years, normally standing alone, exposed to all the elements, and connected to the rest of the world only by a ladder. The first and most influential of these was Symeon the Stylite, a shepherd who practiced extreme sorts of asceticism such as living in a dry cistern and chaining his leg to a stone; many of his contemporaries thought he was rather too extreme, and he was expelled from at least one monastery. He then ascended a column at a rural site near Antioch and remained there, and this remarkable feat attracted a considerable following. As people gathered around his column, Symeon sought greater solitude and had the column built higher, until it reached a distance of 16 meters from the ground. His reputation spread, and other monks began to imitate him. After his death in 459 a huge pilgrimage complex was built around the column, at a place called Qal'at Sem'an in the north Syrian desert. The column stood in the center of the complex and four basilicas radiated out from it in the shape of a cross; this complex probably was constructed with imperial funds, and it testifies to how a holy man such as Symeon came to be honored. Symeon had many imitators, perhaps the most interesting of whom was Daniel the Stylite, who decided to mount his own column after visiting Symeon in Syria. Daniel, however, moved to the vicinity of Constantinople and, from his column, took part in many of the pressing issues of the day. Thus, his biographer depicts the *stylite* as an adviser of Leo I and an intermediary between the patriarch Akakios and the usurper Basilikos. He even points out Daniel's superiority to the emperor, for on one occasion, when Leo dared to mount his horse in the saint's presence, the horse threw him to the ground. Other ascetics found ways to match the *stylites* in their religious practices, among them the *dendrites*, who performed their religious observances by living in a tree. The ascetic practices of the monks were in accord with the development of apophatic

Box 5.2 *The Murder of the Philosopher Hypatia*

The life of the philosopher Hypatia is a powerful symbol of strikingly divergent tendencies in the early Byzantine world. She was born, ca. 355/60, in the cosmopolitan center of Alexandria, the daughter of the Neoplatonist Theon, who is the last known member of the famous Mouseion of that city. Like her father, Hypatia was a follower of Ptolemy and was interested especially in mathematics. She was not only an intellectual but also a public figure in Alexandria, mixing her intellect with beauty and political skill that won for her considerable popular fame. Characteristically of the age, even though she was a staunch pagan, she was also known for her virtue, which allowed her to withstand the advance of several would-be seducers. Her popularity earned for her the enmity of Cyril of Alexandria, the fiery and sometimes violent patriarch of the city, and in 415 she was set upon by a band of hospital attendants and stabbed to death with quill pens (or, as below, with tiles). Her violent death has often been seen as an important moment in the end of paganism, and modern commentators have viewed her as something of an unwitting martyr to the cause of classical culture. The fact that a woman was one of the last representatives of pagan learning is also to be noted, although her life of virtue bears many similarities to that of Christian holy women:

> There was a woman at Alexandria named Hypatia, daughter of the philosopher Theon, who made such attainments in literature and science, as to far surpass all the philosophers of her own time. Having succeeded to the school of Plato and Plotinus, she explained the principles of philosophy to her auditors, many of whom came from a distance to receive her instructions.
>
> On account of the self-possession and ease of manner, which she had acquired in consequence of the cultivation of her mind, she not unfrequently appeared in public in presence of the magistrates. Neither did she feel abashed in coming to an assembly of men. For all men on account of her extraordinary dignity and virtue admired her the more. Yet even she fell a victim to the political jealousy which at that time prevailed. For as she had frequent interviews with Orestes, it was calumniously reported among the Christian populace, that it was she who prevented Orestes from being reconciled to the bishop. Some of them therefore, hurried away by a fierce and bigoted zeal, whose ringleader was a reader named Peter, waylaid her returning home, and dragging her from her carriage, they took her to the church called Caesareum, where they completely stripped her, and then murdered her with tiles. After tearing her body in pieces, they took her mangled limbs to a place called Cinaron, and there burnt them. This affair brought not the least opprobrium, not only upon Cyril, but also upon the whole Alexandrian church. And surely nothing can be farther from the spirit of Christianity than the allowance of massacres, fights, and transactions of that sort. This happened in the month of March during Lent, in the fourth year of Cyril's episcopate, under the tenth consulate of Honorius, and the sixth of Theodosius.

Sozomen, *Ecclesiastical History*, 6.15. in *A Select Library of Nicene and Post-Nicene Fathers of the Christian Church* (second series), translated under the editorial supervision of Philip Schaff and Henry Wace, vol. 2 (New York, 1890, reprint Grand Rapids, MI, 1979–86).

Figure 5.5 Qal'at Sem'an. This pilgrimage complex in northern Syria was built around the column of Symeon Stylites the Elder ca. 476–90. Symeon had already died by this time but his fame was such that an unknown donor (possibly the emperor) had a large octagon constructed around the column along with four basilicas radiating out from it. A monastery was constructed in the vicinity and, after the Arab invasions, it was refounded in the tenth century. Photo: Dumbarton Oaks / Richard Anderson

theology, a system of thought that said that God could be known and understood only through personal experience. Toward the end of the fifth century an author identified as Pseudo-Dionysios the Areopagite wrote a series of works that developed the ideas of Neoplatonism into a system of thought that was generally in accord with apophatic ideas and that had a wide influence in both East and West.

FURTHER READING

Peter Brown, "The Rise and Function of the Holy Man in Late Antiquity," *Journal of Roman Studies* 61 (1971), 80–101.

Peter Brown, *The Rise of Western Christendom*. 2nd edn. Oxford, 2003.

Alan Cameron, "The House of Anastasius," *Greek, Roman, and Byzantine Studies* 19 (1978), 259–76.

P. Charanis, *Church and State in the Later Roman Empire*. 2nd edn. Thessaloniki, 1974.

Walter E. Kaegi, Jr., *Byzantium and the Decline of Rome*. Princeton, NJ. 1968.

F. Young, *From Nicaea to Chalcedon: A Guide to the Literature and its Background*. London, 1983.

6
The Age of Justinian

250	500	750	1000	1250	1500

527	Justinian emperor
532	Nika Revolt
533–534	Conquest of North Africa
535–552	Conquest of Italy

The reign of Justinian is commonly regarded as the Golden Age of the early Byzantine period. The emperor and his consort Theodora are two of the best known Byzantine personalities, and during this time the uncertainty of earlier years was replaced by confidence and a new synthesis of ancient and Christian society. Justinian's reign will always be associated with the reconquest of the West that nearly brought about the restoration of the old Roman Empire, and he will always be connected with the construction of the church of Hagia Sophia, one of the pre-eminent symbols of the Byzantine Empire as a whole. Art and literature flourished under his rule, and his officials carried out a remarkably thorough synthesis of Roman law that has served as the basis of the legal systems of much of Europe up to the present day. He was one of the few Byzantine emperors whose ideas about his power were matched by a considerable degree of reality. The personalities of the emperor – and even more, the empress – have been the subject of much discussion, and even the focus of popular novels and films, in large part because of the graphic descriptions provided by the contemporary historian Prokopios. Nevertheless, despite the obvious glories of the age, historians are aware of the crisis that followed almost immediately after the emperor's death, and we may ask to what extent the difficulties of the late sixth and seventh centuries were the result of misgovernment under Justinian. In addition, there can be no doubt that Justinian was an autocrat: he himself would have admitted as much, in large part because he seems to have accepted fully the ideas put forth 200 years earlier by Eusebios of Caesarea: the Byzantine emperor was the representative of God, to whom he alone was answerable, and just as the Kingdom of God was an unquestionable monarchy, so the Byzantine Empire was to be ruled by an emperor with autocratic power. Some contemporaries criticized this aspect of Justinian's character and policy, and many modern historians do the same today.

Background: The Reign of Justin I

The emperor Anastasios had no children, so upon his death in 518 the position was up for the taking. There was turmoil at the court, but power was soon seized by the aged commander of the *exkoubitores* (the palace guard), Justin. Like many of his predecessors, Justin had risen from a humble background in the Latin-speaking areas of the Balkans. He had come to Constantinople in search of his fortune, enrolled in the army, and rose through the ranks, ultimately serving as a commander in the wars of Anastasios I. Justin used his position with the *exkoubitores* and, apparently, his own cleverness and guile, to secure the throne and immediately set out to establish a policy very different from that of his predecessor. For example, he exiled some of Anastasios' supporters and recalled other individuals who had fallen out of favor. Later tradition asserts that Justin's nephew Justinian was the force behind his uncle's throne right from the beginning, and there may be some truth in that, since Justinian was selected to hold the consulship as early as 521.

Overall, Justin's policy was based on a determination to seek peace with the West, meaning the papacy and the remnant of the Roman aristocracy in Italy. The emperors' recent religious policy had rendered these relations difficult and, immediately after Justin's accession, a local church council was held in Constantinople, which asserted a Chalcedonian position and condemned a series of prominent Monophysite bishops; this was followed by a series of similar councils throughout the East. The conndemnation of Monophysite bishops was enforced by the emperor, and many went into exile, especially to Egypt, including Severus of Antioch, who became the leading spokesperson for moderate Monophysitism. By the end of 518 the eastern court sent letters to the pope, seeking an end to the Akakian Schism, which had caused years of disagreement. Difficult negotiations followed, but the schism had effectively been healed and the court of Constantinople was firmly Chalcedonian in sentiment.

Ironically enough, agreement between the emperor and the pope led to worsening relations with the Ostrogothic king Theodoric in Ravenna. As long as the pope and the emperor were opposed to each other Theodoric could feel safe in trusting his orthodox subjects, but now that the two were again on good terms, Theodoric felt threatened. The situation was worsened when Justin decided to push more actively for the elimination of heresy in the East, involving, of course, Monophysitism but also Arianism, the version of Christianity endorsed by Theodoric. Attempts were made to heal relations between Constantinople and Ravenna, and Justin even agreed to share the consulship with Theodoric's son-in-law and presumed heir Eutharic, the first Goth to hold this high office. Meanwhile, Theodoric became more and more distrustful of his Roman subjects, and the result was, among other things, the execution of Boethius in 524. In 526 Theodoric himself died, leaving the boy Athalaric as his heir.

Justin generally maintained a friendly relationship with Persia, although he expanded Byzantine influence by building a series of alliances with Persia's neighbors, including the Lazi and the Iberians, and there was an inconsequential war with Persia right at the end of Justin's reign. According to Prokopios, who hated all things connected with Justinian, Justin was boorish and uneducated, not even able to sign his name, but relying on a stencil held by his officials in order to ratify imperial papers. There can be no doubt, however, that his reign marked an important change of direction in imperial policy, and this was to find full development under his nephew Justinian.

Justinian and Theodora: Early Years to 532

Justinian's real name was Flavius Petrus Sabbatius, but the name on his consular diptych of 521 is Flavius Petrus Sabbatius Justinianus, showing that, before that time, he had been adopted by his uncle Justin, who had brought him to Constantinople some years earlier. Justinian, as he was known to contemporaries, was thus raised in the atmosphere of the capital and, although he held high rank in the army, he obviously received a good education and was equally at home in Greek and in Latin. He was born about 482, and as a young man he already displayed some of the restlessness or even foolhardiness that was to characterize his later life, becoming involved in the violence of the circus factions that was common at the time.

These factions had developed from the associations or companies that supplied horses and trappings for the chariot races in Hellenistic Alexandria and then in imperial Rome. Each of the companies distinguished their entries with individual colors: red, blue, green, white, etc. The circus races (i.e., races in the hippodrome) were enormously popular in Rome, and later in Constantinople and the other cities of the early Byzantine East, and they attracted huge numbers of fans who came to identify themselves with the colors of their favorite charioteers. Thus, by the fifth or sixth centuries the "factions" had come to mean, not so much the companies responsible for providing the horses, but the fans themselves, who were commonly made up

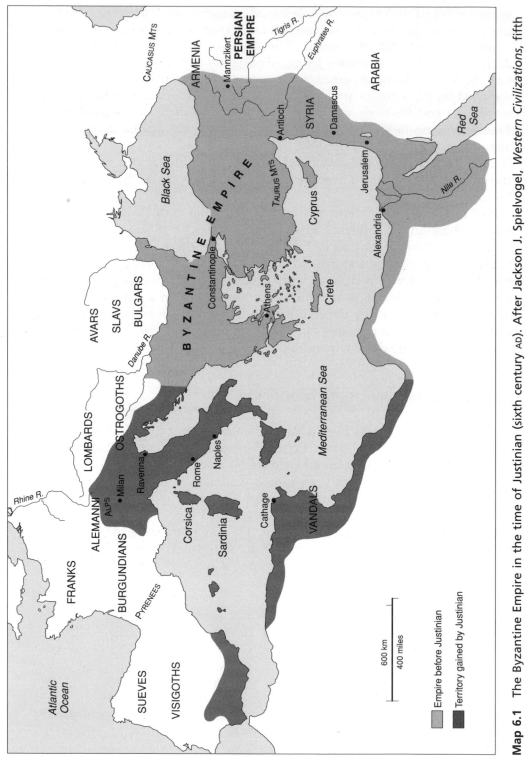

Map 6.1 The Byzantine Empire in the time of Justinian (sixth century AD). After Jackson J. Spielvogel, *Western Civilizations*, fifth edition (Wadsworth, 2003), map 7.4, p. 181

largely of young men who were fanatically loyal to their "color." Just as in modern football games, the fans often engaged in organized chants or shouts, they commonly wore outlandish and immediately identifying clothes and haircuts, and they sometimes engaged in violence, especially against members of opposing factions. This violence not uncommonly spilled outside the hippodrome into the streets, and it had, by the late fifth and early sixth century, become endemic in Constantinople and, to a lesser degree, elsewhere. By this time, the other factions had all but disappeared, leaving only the Greens and the Blues to fight with each other. At one time scholars thought that the factions must have represented ideological or social differences within the early Byzantine cities, since only thus – it was thought – could we explain the violence and the strong attachment people had to the factions. For example, it was once argued either that the Blues represented the interests of the aristocracy while the Greens supported the commercial class, or that the Blues supported a western policy while the Greens had an eastern orientation, and/or that the Blues were Orthodox and the Greens Monophysite. There is, however, little or no evidence for any such identifications, and it seems likely that the factions were simply made up of young men who identified with their own faction for no reason other than group solidarity, and that they engaged in violence in the same way as modern football hooligans. Even the emperors often took sides in factional partisanship and there is reason to believe that Justinian, before he became emperor, was already known as a supporter of the Blues.

Probably early in the 520s Justinian married Theodora, another example of the future emperor's headstrong thinking and willingness to go against tradition. It is true that many of the emperors (and empresses) of the past three centuries had come from humble beginnings, not least the family of Justinian himself, but Theodora would have seemed a most unusual choice for the emperor's nephew, who must already have been seen as a candidate for the imperial throne. Theodora was by all accounts beautiful – and the surviving representations of her (e.g., the San Vitale mosaic in Ravenna) bear this out – and she certainly was intelligent and ingenious, but she was an actress, a profession that in this period was synonymous with prostitution. The *Secret History* of Prokopios tells the story of Theodora's early years in lurid detail. The future empress was the daughter of a "bear-keeper" of the Green faction, a trainer of the wild beasts used in hippodrome performances, and her mother was a dancer and an actress. When her father died and her mother remarried, the family asked the Green faction to appoint the new husband as bear-keeper, but the faction refused; the mother and daughter presented their petition again publicly to the faction in the hippodrome, but the result was the same – until the Blue faction was persuaded to take the stepfather on as their new bear-keeper. Theodora herself became an actress as soon as she was old enough, and, according to Prokopios, she was known for her especially pornographic performances on the stage.

Figure 6.1 The Empress Theodora, San Vitale, Ravenna. This famous mosaic portrait of the empress depicts her with a halo and wearing an elaborate crown and pearl and jewelry-studded garments; she is presenting a richly decorated chalice to Christ. Photo: Scala / Art Resource, NY

Justinian's aunt, the empress Euphemia, objected to the marriage of Justinian and Theodora, even though, ironically enough, she herself had risen from the theater to the imperial palace. In addition, there was a law that forbade a marriage between an actress and a senator (which Justinian was). Nonetheless, after Euphemia's death, Justin promulgated a law that allowed marriage between a "repentant" actress and a senator, and the couple was wed.

Justin crowned Justinian as co-emperor at the beginning of April in 527, and Justinian's succession was smooth after the old emperor's death on 1 August of that year. Justinian took his role as an absolute Christian emperor very seriously, and his early years were marked by the authoritarianism and self-confidence that were to characterize nearly the whole of his reign. He surrounded himself with political newcomers, people like himself, who were strong-willed, ambitious, and willing to break with tradition wherever they thought best. This ruling imperial clique had no patience with the established nobility of Constantinople who, although they too could hardly trace their ancestry back very far, regarded the emperor and his supporters as crude and ambitious upstarts. The imperial clique included the empress Theodora, her friend Antonia, the wife of Belisarios, Justinian's greatest general, Justinian's nephew Germanos, the tax-collector John of Kappadokia, the eunuch general Narses, and the jurist Tribonian. This clique was indeed a formidable group and it was responsible for much of the efflorescence of Justinian's reign.

Some of Justinian's first actions were in the religious sphere, against Manichaeans, Samaritans, and pagans. Renewed laws against pagan sacrifice and prohibition of pagans in the imperial service show that the empire was not entirely Christian by this time, and the conversion of thousands of pagans by John of Ephesos in the 540s testifies to this as well. In 529 Justinian forbade pagans to teach in schools, and this may have led to the closure of the Academy in Athens, one of the foremost intellectual institutions of the period; the professors of the Academy supposedly took flight to the court of the Persian king, who was quite willing to support their activities. The teachers, however, were apparently not happy in Persia, and some of them seem to have returned to Byzantine territory; a clause of the "eternal" peace signed by Justinian and the Persian king Chosroes (Khusro) I in 532 allowed for these teachers to practice their religion in peace within the empire.

Justinian also took action against the Samaritans. They were a strictly monotheistic group who rejected all the books of the Hebrew Bible after the Pentateuch (the first five) and were therefore not accepted by the Jews. Roman tradition, however, viewed them as Jews and left them alone in their settlements in central Israel and elsewhere (including members in Constantinople) even though they had revolted against Byzantine rule at least twice in the fifth century. Justinian attacked them, limiting their right to bequeath property and ordering their synagogues to be destroyed; the result was another revolt in 529. Justinian ruthlessly put down the revolt and destroyed their altar on Mount Gerizim, although the Samaritans were able to revolt again later in the century.

Justinian did not immediately attack heresy, in part because, although he was a Chalcedonian, Theodora strongly supported Monophysitism. The historian Prokopios claimed that the imperial couple feigned this disagreement, in order better to control the religious situation from both sides, but there is no reason to think that this was not based upon sincere belief on the part of both the emperor and the empress. As a result, although Justinian became personally involved in the question of Monophysitism, as we shall see below, he did not persecute the Monophysites and, indeed, he made a deathbed promise to his wife in 548 not to do so – a promise he apparently kept.

Immediately upon his accession Justinian sought to reform the bureaucracy of the state, not so much by reforming its structure (as, for example, Diocletian and Constantine had done), but by making the bureaucracy work more efficiently, especially by rooting out corruption and improving the system of tax collection. Certainly, some of the criticisms of the emperor were the result of his unceasing attempts to close loopholes and eliminate the corruption that had benefited so many individuals, including members of the senatorial order. His greatest accomplice in this task was John the Kappadokian, a ruthless and high-handed official whom Justinian had met well before he became emperor. John was clever and tireless in his rooting out of tax evaders and finding fiscal savings wherever he could, and his critics – not surprisingly – regarded him with hatred and accused him of every possible vice. There can be no doubt that he was rapacious, but it is clear that John met the emperor's needs in an admirable way.

Another aspect of Justinian's attempt to refashion the Byzantine state was in the area of law. As mentioned above, Roman law was "prescriptive" in the sense that it had come to be made up of a series of imperial responses to individual problems and requests for the intervention of the emperor. This naturally led to confusion and serious questions about what the law really meant in certain cases. The Theodosian Code of 438 had gone some distance to solving these problems, but many difficulties remained and – by the time of Justinian – there was considerable legislation that had been issued since the time of Theodosios II. Justinian therefore set out to reform and standardize Roman law, and in 528 he appointed a committee, whose first responsibility was the codification of existing law, along the lines of the Theodosian Code. The head of the committee was the distinguished jurist Tribonian, and in just over a year (529) it published the first volume of the Codex Justinianus. This text, like the Codex Theodosianus, arranged the whole of previous law (back to the time of Hadrian) in categories according to subject, but it was soon itself in need of modification in part because of the considerable legislative activity of the emperor himself.

The Nika Revolt

Before the code could be revised, however, the ambitious reign of Justinian nearly came to an inglorious and sudden end, in the Nika Revolt of January 532. The revolt is named after the Greek word *nika!* ("conquer!"), the cheer of spectators at the races in the hippodrome that became the battle cry of the rioters in 532. The events of the revolt are all but certain, recorded in detail by the historians Prokopios and Malalas. Difficulties began on 10 January 532, when the Prefect of the City arrested some members of the factions for violence and arranged to have them hanged. Fortunately for the condemned, the execution was botched, and two of them survived, one a member of the Blues, one of the Greens, and they were taken off to temporary safety in a nearby monastery. Three days later, when the races were held again, the factions asked the emperor for clemency on behalf of the condemned, and when he failed to respond, the Blues and Greens unexpectedly united and raised the cry of revolt. The rioting spread outside the hippodrome; the *praetorion* (essentially the police headquarters and central jail) was set alight and prisoners released; the authorities lost complete control of the situation and many of the great buildings of the city went up in smoke, among them the churches of Hagia Sophia and Hagia Eirene, the Baths of Zeuxippos, and the Chalke, the great central gate of the palace itself. At this point, if not before, members of the aristocracy joined the side of the rioters and sought to turn the trouble into a revolt against the emperor himself. Justinian realized the gravity of the situation and agreed to the removal of some of the prominent officials who were being blamed for imperial policy: John the Kappadokian, Tribonian, and the Prefect of the City. The riot, however, continued and Justinian ordered his troops, under the command of Belisarios, to attack the rioters, but the soldiers were unsuccessful in their attempt. On 18 January Justinian appeared in the hippodrome and sought to find a compromise, but his offers were rejected, and instead the rioters proposed the nomination of Hypatios as emperor. Hypatios was a nephew of Anastasios, who had a mediocre career as a military officer under Justin and Justinian, but his proposed elevation brought a degree of legitimacy to the movement and clearly transformed the revolt into an attempt to overthrow the emperor. This aspect of the Nika Revolt could hardly have been engineered without the leadership of interested members of the aristocracy. The situation looked desperate, and Justinian was apparently ready to flee, but he was persuaded to hold firm by the encouragement of Theodora; according to a popular account, she told the emperor that he could take flight if he wished, but she would remain since she "found royalty to be an appropriate burial shroud." Cowed by his wife's strength, Justinian again sent Belisarios against the crowd, now assembled in the hippodrome. This time the rioters were no match for imperial troops and a great slaughter ensued: according to our sources, between 30,000 and 35,000 people were massacred and the revolt immediately collapsed. Imperial agents quickly captured Hypatios and some other leaders, and they were immediately executed; arrests continued for some time, incidentally giving the emperor an opportunity to confiscate many estates. The races in the hippodrome, not surprisingly, were suspended and not resumed until about five years later.

On one level the Nika Revolt was typical of the circus riots that had become all too common in the second half of the fifth century. On another level, the riot was a reaction to the authoritarian policies of the emperor, including his attempts to collect taxes and close tax loopholes, as well as his willingness to deal sternly with the violent activities of faction members. In the past half-century it had become common for emperors to favor one of the circus factions over the others, and this produced a kind of stand-off and kept the factions from uniting against the reigning emperor. Justinian and Theodora, however, were willing to oppose the "traditional license" of the people at the hippodrome, and this ran the danger of the factions uniting against the throne. Finally, it is very clear that members of the aristocracy quickly became involved in the Nika Revolt, even if they were not part of it from the outset. The fiscal policies and the ways in which the "peasants and prostitutes" controlled the empire were hardly things that would have affected the ordinary people of Constantinople, but they all served to upset the members of the by now traditional aristocracy, who were jealous of their position and conscious of the superiority they felt to the people who were now in charge of the state.

Over the first five years of their reign Justinian and Theodora had built a government based on an open autocracy run essentially by "outsiders." This had been seriously challenged in the Nika Revolt, but the emperor's victory was ultimately complete and there was no further challenge to his policy, leaving him essentially free to arrange things as he saw fit.

Aftermath: The Building Program

Once securely back in power, Justinian immediately began to implement a long-envisioned plan to fashion the appearance of Constantinople as he wished. The destruction caused by the rioters provided both the necessity and the opportunity to rebuild many of the great structures of the city. We are well informed about the details of this program since the historian Prokopios wrote a work, *On the Buildings,* which praised the emperor effusively for his activity in Constantinople and throughout the empire. Justinian (or perhaps even Theodora herself) had begun the building program before 532, with construction of the important church of Sts. Sergios and Bakchos, either as a palatine chapel or as a refuge for Monophysites in the capital. In the end Justinian built or rebuilt a total of more than 30 churches in the city. The first of the reconstructions was the church of Hagia Sophia, the "Great Church" and cathedral of Constantinople. That Justinian already had this in mind is shown by the fact that construction began only 45 days after the end of the riot. This majestic building, one of the crowning achievements of Byzantine architecture, still survives and has come to symbolize Byzantine civilization for many people.

Justinian's church of Hagia Sophia (Agia Sofia, Aya Sofia, etc.) is the third church of that name constructed on the same spot. It was dedicated, not to a St. Sofia, but rather to the "Wisdom" (Sophia) of Christ. The plan of the building was entrusted to Anthemios of Tralles and Isidore of Miletos, who were not architects but two of the leading scientists of the day, and they came up with a brilliant and daring scheme. The plan of the building combines the longitudinal plan of the basilica with the domed interior space of a centrally planned structure. The floor plan is nearly square, 78 by 72 meters, with huge colonnaded arcades on the north and south sides.

Above the central space is a dome, 100 Byzantine feet (31 meters) in diameter and 62 meters above the floor. On the east and the west are semi-domes and the exterior walls are pierced with windows (now much reduced in size from the originals). The effect on the visitor, even today, when the building has lost much of its interior decoration, is awe-inspiring, and one can only imagine how it would appear, filled with worshipers, thousands of oil lamps, music, the smell of incense, and the color of brightly clad officiants.

Box 6.1 *Anthemios of Tralles and Isidore of Miletos*

It is interesting and characteristic of Justinian that he selected theoretical scientists, rather than architects, to design the church of Hagia Sophia in Constantinople. Later tradition, and even the contemporary historian Prokopios, attribute the building's daring plan and huge domed interior to Justinian and his close connection with God, but it is likely that the design was produced by Anthemios of Tralles and Isidore of Miletos.

Anthemios of Tralles was born into an intellectual family sometime in the late fifth century. He was interested in machines and he wrote books such as *Concerning Remarkable Mechanical Devices* and *On Burning Mirrors*. He was also interested in steam power and actually created artificial earthquakes with this means; he also made artificial thunder and constructed a powerful reflecting mirror. According to Agathias, Anthemios was among the scientists "who apply geometrical speculation to material objects and make models or imitations of the natural world."

Isidore of Miletos worked largely on the books of earlier scientists, issuing a revised edition of the works of Archimedes and writing a commentary on an ancient work on vaulting; he did have some practical interests, however, since he constructed a tool by which he could construct parabolas. Justinian made use of Anthemios and Isidore not only in the construction of Hagia Sophia, but he also consulted them about problems of flooding at the fortified city of Dara, on the upper reaches of the Euphrates.

No buildings other than Hagia Sophia have been certainly attributed to these two scientists. Interestingly enough, the original, relatively flat dome of Hagia Sophia collapsed in 558: its construction apparently surpassed the ability of the materials to support its weight. The dome was repaired and raised some 7 meters and the building was rededicated in 562.

Two comical sculptures in the church of the Panagia (Virgin) Ekatontapyliani on the island of Paros have been connected with the story of Anthemios and Isidore. The sculptures show two overweight individuals supporting the columns of a modern entrance to the church. Two stories are told about these individuals, both connected with the rebuilding of the church on Paros in the sixth century; one says that they are indeed Anthemios and Isidore themselves, one holding his hand over his head to protect himself from the falling dome; the other laughing as the dome collapses. The other legend says that the two figures represent the (unknown) builder of the dome of the church and his (also unknown) teacher; in this story the teacher was jealous of the perfection of the dome and sought to kill his pupil, but the pupil grabbed hold of the master and the two of them fell to their death together. Interestingly, but not necessarily connected with the builders, is another story told about this church in Paros: that it was built with 100 entrances (hence its name Ekatontapyliani, which means the church "with a hundred gates"). But today only 99 are visible; when someone finds the hundredth doorway . . . the world will come to an end!

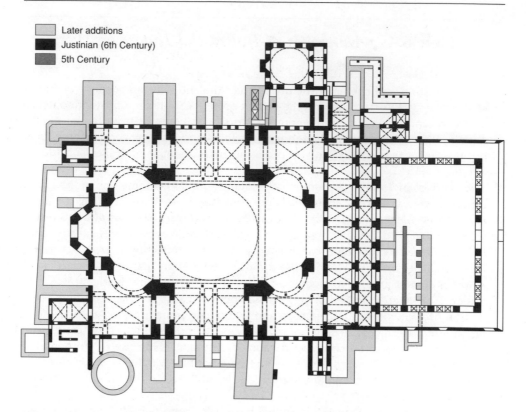

Later additions
Justinian (6th Century)
5th Century

Figure 6.2 Hagia Sophia, plan. The plan of Hagia Sophia tells us a great deal about the building. The core of the building was conceived at floor level as a large rectangle, 78 x 72 meters, with side aisles along the north and south, separated from the central aisle by an enormous colonnade. Thus, in some sense it was a basilica. Four massive piers supported a central dome, 100 Byzantine feet (31 meters) in diameter, and two half-domes on the east and the west

As Prokopios wrote:

> So the church has become a spectacle of marvellous beauty, overwhelming to those who see it, but to those who know it by hearsay altogether incredible. First it soars to a height to match the sky, and as if surging up from amongst the other buildings it stands on high and looks down upon the remainder of the city . . . [The church] is distinguished by indescribable beauty, excelling both in its size, and in the harmony of its measures, having no part excessive and none deficient; being more magnificent than ordinary buildings, and much more elegant than those which are not of so just a proportion. The church is singularly full of light and sunshine; you would declare that the place is not lighted by the sun from without, but that the rays are produced within itself, such an abundance of light is poured into this church.

Justinian rebuilt the church of Hagia Eirene, in a style similar to that of Hagia Sofia, and the church of the Virgin of Pege, just outside the city walls of

Figure 6.3 Hagia Sophia, interior. This view of the interior of Hagia Sophia, looking east toward the apse where the altar was, captures something of the immense inner space of the building. The original dome collapsed in 558 and was rebuilt and dedicated in 562. Earthquakes and the wear of time caused other problems and these were all repaired with the resources available at the time, but the result is that the building today is considerably different from what it was when first built; one aspect of this is that the original windows were much larger, letting in even more light and "opening up" the interior even more than they do now. The Arabic inscriptions and the furniture were added after the building was converted to a mosque in 1453. It is now a museum. Photo: Dumbarton Oaks

Constantinople, at the site of a miraculous spring; this church and the miracles associated with it were the source of the legends of the Virgin as the Zoodochos Pege (Life-giving Spring) and the many ikons depicting her as the "source of life." Justinian also reconstructed parts of the palace and other public buildings damaged in the Nika Revolt, and he placed an equestrian statue of himself in the Augustaion, the notional center of the empire.

Box 6.2 *Anicia Juliana*

When Justinian began his building program in Constantinople he certainly had in mind the activity of Anicia Juliana, and he and all his contemporaries must have judged his work against hers. Juliana was a member of one of the old aristocratic families of Rome. Unlike many of their western colleagues, they had accepted Christianity and they formed close relations with some of the barbarian elites of the period. Juliana's father, Olybrius, married Placidia, the youngest daughter of the western emperor Valentinian III and, in 472, he was chosen as emperor of the West. Olybrius died several months later of natural causes and at an early age Juliana became the heir to a great fortune. She married the Alan Areobindus, who had a distinguished military career under Anastasios I and whom some supporters saw as the leader of a potential revolt against the emperor. When Anastasios I died there was a movement to make Juliana's son Flavius Anicius emperor, but he was passed over in favor of Justin I, the uncle of the future emperor Justinian.

Juliana was pious and dedicated to some of the monastic leaders of her day. She was a determined opponent of the Monophysitism of Anastasios and she corresponded with the pope on this matter. She used her wealth for good works and the construction of many churches in the capital, including that of St. Euphemia and one dedicated to the Virgin. Her greatest achievement was the church of St. Polyeuktos in the capital, built between 524 and 527, a lavish building famed in its day and probably the largest church in Constantinople until Justinian's Hagia Sophia. In later years Anicia Juliana's church was completely destroyed and its exact location unknown until it was excavated in the latter years of the twentieth century. Its remains were identified on the basis of fragments of a poem praising the aristocratic woman for the beauty of the church and comparing her to Solomon:

> She alone has conquered time and surpassed the
> wisdom of renowned Solomon, raising a temple
> to receive God, the richly wrought and graceful
> splendor of which the ages cannot celebrate. How
> it rises from deep-rooted foundation, springing
> up from below and pursuing the stars of heaven,
> and how too it is extended from east to west,
> glittering beyond description with the brightness
> of the sun on both sides! On either side of its aisle
> columns standing on firm columns support the rays of the golden dome,
> while on each side arched recesses scattered on the dome
> reproduce the ever-revolving light of the moon.
> The opposite walls in innumerable paths
> are clothed in marvelous metallic veins of color,
> like flowery meadows which Nature made
> to flower in the depth of the rock, and hid their glory,
> keeping them for the House of God, to be the gift of Juliana,
> so that she might produce a divine work,
> following in her toil the stainless dictates of her heart.

(*Palatine Anthology* 1.10, Loeb edition, vol. 1, pp. 9–11).

Figure 6.4 Bust of an aristocratic woman, probably Anicia Juliana. This woman is depicted as an intellectual, holding a scroll. We cannot be certain if this really is Anicia Juliana, but this is certainly how we would imagine her being portrayed. Photo: Metropolitain Museum, New York

Figure 6.5 Anicia Juliana from the Vienna Dioscorides. This is from a medical manuscript that was made at Juliana's request ca. 512. The hundreds of detailed illustrations of plants in it were copied over and over again during the following centuries. In the image she is pictured between the personifications of Magnanimity (*Megalopsychia*) and Prudence (*Sophrosyne*). Vienna, Nationalbibliothek, Cod. Vind. Med. gr. 1. Photo: Bildarchive d. ÖNB, Wien

According to another story, Justinian asked Juliana to make appropriate dona- tions to his war chests, and she took him to the newly built church, gestured at the gold-plated ceilings, and told him to take what he liked – an indication that she understood that the church was one way for an aristocratic family to protect its wealth from a rapacious ruler.

Anicia Juliana was a member of the wealthy class of the empire who disliked the "upstarts" of Justinian's reign, but it is clear that the emperor and his followers learned well how to imitate the activity and the taste of these wealthy aristocrats.

FURTHER READING

R. M. Harrison, *A Temple for Byzantium*. London and Austin, TX, 1989.

Justinian also carried out a massive building campaign throughout the empire, although it is difficult to know to what extent he was more active than other emperors of this period, and it seems likely that Prokopios, in his wish to praise the emperor, attributed to Justinian the construction of buildings that were the work of his predecessors. Nonetheless, Justinian certainly did build churches and fortifications in many areas. The fortifications were especially important since they were meant to protect areas that were increasingly vulnerable to barbarian attack, and they included not only massive fortifications around urban areas, but also defenses around villages and refuges for people living in sparsely settled parts of the empire. There is reason to believe that the army in this period suffered from a significant diminution in numbers, for one reason or another, and the armies that Justinian dispatched in his various campaigns were much smaller than those available to rulers of the fourth and fifth centuries. For this reason, apparently, Justinian's military engineers constructed powerful fortifications in many places, probably hoping that the defenses would serve to protect people in the absence of large bodies of troops. This defensive policy was, of course, in marked contrast to the emperor's campaigns of reconquest in the West.

The Imperium Restored: Wars of Reconquest in the West

The majority of the West had been lost to barbarian chieftains during the fifth century. This had not happened all at once, and conditions in various parts of the West were very different. In North Africa the Vandals had been in power since 429 and they controlled most of central northern Africa from their capital at Carthage, including most of the islands of the western Mediterranean. The Vandal fleet was able to defeat attempts at reconquest and it threatened the coasts of Italy and even Greece. Despite the foundation of a relatively centralized monarchy under Geiseric and the formation of an elite corps of Germanic warriors, life continued relatively unchanged in Vandal Africa. Relations between the Arian conquerors and the "Roman" population were often strained and there were many confiscations of large properties. Nonetheless, Africa continued to supply grain to Italy, and African manufactured products (such as pottery) found a market throughout the empire. Italy in this period was controlled, theoretically at least, by the Ostrogoths. Theodoric, who died only the year before Justinian's accession, had left his kingdom with a good administration based largely on Roman models, and relationships between the Italian nobility and the Ostrogothic leaders were generally positive. The pope, of course, played a large role in the politics as well as the religion of Italy and (especially after the end of the Akakian Schism in 519) he generally looked to the emperor in Constantinople as an ally against the Arian rulers in Ravenna. The political situation in the rest of the West was far more fluid, although kingdoms had been set up by the Visigoths in the area around Toulouse (and later Spain) and by the Franks in northern Gaul. Indeed, the conversion of Clovis (481/2–511) to orthodox Christianity allowed

Byzantium – as well as the papacy – to regard the Franks as potential allies against the Arian Germanic states to the south.

As a further mark of Justinian's confidence and ability to manage very different affairs at the same time, he opened hostilities against the Vandals in 533, only a year after the Nika Revolt. The pretense for the expedition was a call from the deposed Vandal king Hilderic (reigned 523–30); during his reign Hilderic had promoted good relations with the Orthodox and had recalled many exiled bishops, but he was overthrown by his cousin Gelimer. Using Hilderic's appeal for aid, and remembering the way in which the Vandals had been a problem for his predecessors, Justinian quickly arranged for war. The expedition of about 10,000 men was under the command of Belisarios.

The victory, it turned out, was surprisingly easy for the Byzantines. Gelimer was away from Africa when the fleet arrived and Belisarios was able to make a landing unopposed. Gelimer returned and offered battle near Carthage, but he was decisively defeated and Belasarios was able to enter the city. Another battle was fought in December, but Belisarios was once again victorious. Early in 534 the Vandal king surrendered. Rumors circulated that Belisarios might set himself up in Africa as an independent ruler, but he returned to Constantinople and a great triumphal celebration was held in which both Belisarios and Gelimer prostrated themselves in front of the emperor. Justinian's African war had been a brilliant success, but the situation in North Africa had been destabilized as a result and the native Berber (or Moorish) population, who had already been in revolt against the Vandals, continued to cause severe difficulties. The Byzantine commanders left in Africa built a powerful system of fortifications, many of which still remain, in an attempt to pacify the Berbers, but this goal was never fully achieved and North Africa was not fully reunited into the Byzantine Empire.

Nonetheless, buoyed by his military successes, Justinian immediately laid plans for the reconquest of Italy. The prospects for victory were favorable, since the Ostrogothic monarchy was in turmoil after the death of Theodoric. Theodahad, Theodoric's nephew and king since 534, had an insecure position. Justinian's main force, only half as large as the army that took Africa, landed at Sicily in 535 under the command of Belisarios and quickly took control of the whole island. Early the next year Belisarios marched north and easily took Naples, an event that led to the overthrow of Theodahad and his replacement by Witigis as king. By December of 536 Belisarios had taken Rome, in part with the aid of the pope, but the Gothic counterattack pinned the Byzantines in the city for over a year. As the Byzantines moved closer to a direct attack on Ravenna, the Ostrogoths made contact with the Persian king Chosroes II and offered an alliance. Belisarios was eventually able to take Ravenna in 540, but Justinian had become suspicious at the story that his general might declare himself king of Italy, and he recalled Belisarios to Constantinople. In the meantime, after further internal turmoil, Totila became king of the Ostrogoths in 541 and his military ability caused considerable difficulty for the Byzantines.

In 540 the Persians attacked imperial territory and took Antioch, one of the greatest centers of the empire, a severe blow to Byzantine prestige. In 541 Belisarios was sent to the eastern front, where he was able to halt the Persian advance, but he was again recalled, undoubtedly for political reasons. Meanwhile, in 542 the bubonic plaque ravaged the empire, striking Constantinople and all the great cities and undoubtedly causing psychological as well as demographic damage.

Justinian thus found himself in the difficult situation of having to fight a war on two fronts against increasingly dangerous enemies, and probably with a lower population and tax base. Totila was slowly able to undo most of the conquests of Belisarios, and the Persians were able to defeat the forces sent against them. In the East the war came to focus more on fighting on the periphery (Armenia and Lazika), and in 545 Justinian was able to conclude a five-year peace with Chrosroes, at the cost of paying a relatively minor tribute. In 561 this truce was extended to a period of (supposedly) 50 years and the tribute was reduced. To a certain degree Justinian's policies in the East had been a success.

In the West the war dragged on. Belisarios returned to his command in 544 but at the end of 545 Totila besieged Rome, and at the end of 546 it fell to the Ostrogoths. The city changed hands at least two more times, and the war seemed no closer to a conclusion. Belisarios was again recalled to Constantinople, and, after several plans came and went, Justinian put Narses in command of the imperial forces. Narses was a eunuch of Armenian extraction who had earlier replaced Belisarios in Italy and who had commanded successfully on a number of fronts prior to this time. In 551 Narses set off for Italy with what was then an overwhelming force of 30,000 troops. In the summer of 552 the Ostrogoths were decisively defeated, and Totila died of wounds sustained in the battle. Narses pursued the remnants of the Gothic army south and in October another battle was fought near Naples, which essentially ended all opposition to the Byzantine reconquest. Narses remained in Italy, repulsing a Frankish invasion in 553–4 and securing control of the north. The Byzantines had regained control of Italy, but they accomplished this only after 20 years of war that left the countryside desolate and the Romano-Gothic society of Theodoric in ruins, without replacing it with anything solid. Ravenna remained the capital of Byzantine Italy, and from the end of the sixth century it was governed by an *exarch*, a military commander who held both military and civilian power since the area was constantly subject to barbarian attack.

It is a measure of Justinian's ambition and his confidence in the ultimate success of his endeavors that, just as Narses was completing the war in Italy, the emperor arranged to make the force of Byzantine arms felt in distant Spain. In 551 he responded to the appeal of a Visigothic noble for support in a revolt against the king. Justinian responded with an expeditionary force, and this managed to gain control of a coastal strip of Spain, which the empire was able to hold until the 620s. We now know that this was the "high-water mark" of the Byzantine reconquest, but an observer of Justinian's remarkable military success might well have felt that the restoration of the Roman Empire was indeed at hand.

Theological Controversy

The Monophysite controversy continued to simmer throughout the reign of Justinian. Indeed, as we have seen, long before Justinian's time the battle lines had been drawn and both the Monophysites and the Chalcedonians had developed a theology and – probably more important – a hierarchy, administration, and popular support that made compromise all but impossible. As we have seen, in 519 the Akakian Schism was formally ended, and the pope and the patriarch of Constantinople were formally in communion once again. Nonetheless, in Constantinople a formula was put forward by four Scythian monks in an attempt to find a compromise between the Monophysites (who, it will be remembered, had dominated the court for the previous 37 years) and the Chalcedonians. Their solution was to say that "one of the Holy Trinity suffered in the flesh" – meaning that Christ (a member of the Trinity) had suffered and died; this doctrine is called Theopaschitism (meaning that God "suffered"). This teaching was strongly opposed by one of the dominant monastic communities of Constantinople at the time, the so-called Sleepless Monks (the *akoimetoi*). Theirs was a monastery founded in 405 by a certain Alexander, who encouraged his followers to a literal accomplishment of the New Testament injunction to "pray unceasingly." Despite the opposition of the Sleepless Monks, Justinian seems officially to have supported Theopaschitism and this is clearly stated in a law of 533. The Monophysites, of course, refused to accept the compromise of Theopaschitism, and Justinian for a time used all the resources of the state to persecute them, especially in Syria. The persecution was aimed almost exclusively at the clergy and the monks, many of whom either fled to Egypt, where imperial religious policy simply could not be enforced, or they mingled with the general populace, and the persecution therefore probably had the unintended effect of spreading Monophysite teaching more broadly through all levels of society.

Theodora, it should be remembered, quite openly supported Monophysitism, and from 531 a delegation of Monophysite monks lived under her protection in the Palace of Hosmisdas in the capital. In 532 Justinian organized a conference in Constantinople and invited prominent Chalcedonian and Monophysite leaders, in an attempt to find a solution to the schism. The situation looked promising and in the winter of 534/5 Severus of Antioch came to Constantinople to continue the discussion. The personal intervention of the pope, and Justinian's desire to maintain good relations with the western church on the eve of the war in Italy, spelled the doom of the negotiations, and the emperor returned to force as a means to support the Chalcedonian position.

Frustrated at his failure to achieve unity in the church in the 540s Justinian turned again to persuasion. The issue at this time involved the teachings of three earlier theologians: Theodore of Mopsuestia, Theodoret of Cyrrhus, and Ibas of Edessa. These three, generally speaking, represented the theological school of Antioch, but their teachings were accepted by the Council of Chalcedon. Over time, however, they became a bone of contention for the Monophysites, who felt that they and their works should be condemned, since they felt that they were tainted by Nestorian sentiments. Justinian thus felt that such a condemnation of the "Three Chapters" might be a way to heal the rift with the Monophysites, and he himself wrote a detailed theological treatise to this effect, issuing it as an imperial edict in 543/5. This edict was controversial in the West, and the papacy wavered as to whether to accept it, but the condemnation of the Three Chapters was officially proclaimed at the Second Council of Constantinople in 553. The hopes of the emperor were unfulfilled, since the Monophysites were not impressed and the rift between them and the Chalcedonians remained as wide as ever. Even an emperor as powerful as Justinian could not legislate religious belief to his subjects.

One of the reasons the Monophysites were not moved by these attempts to find a solution is that they were growing in numbers and organization. Much of this was due to a tireless group of Monophysite bishops, foremost among whom was Jacob Bardaeus (whose name means "Jacob in ragged clothes" in Syriac). Jacob was a Syrian monk who went to Constantinople about the time of Justinian's accession, and he apparently found a place in the empress Theodora's circle of Monophysite leaders in the capital. Presumably as a counter to the effectiveness of Justinian's persecution of the Monophysites in Syria, Theodora sought the consecration of Jacob as bishop of Edessa and Theodore in Bostra. Jacob was not able to take up residence in Edessa, but he roamed throughout the East as a missionary for his faith and appointed Monophysite bishops in all the major cities, including many in western Asia Minor. Many of these new bishops were monks from Syria, and from this time onward the Monophysite movement had a definitely Syriac character (except for Egypt, where it was Coptic in nature). Justinian made many attempts to arrest Jacob Bardaeus, but he never succeeded.

Continued Legal Activity

Justinian's activity in the realm of law continued after the brief interruption of the Nika Revolt. The legislative committee, disbanded during the difficulties, was reconstituted and it turned its attention, first, to the *Institutes*, published in November of 533, and then to the *Digest*, published in December. The *Institutes* was designed essentially as a textbook to be used in the teaching of law, especially in the schools of Constantinople and Beirut. The *Digest* represents an even more remarkable achievement, especially given the often contradictory nature of earlier Roman legislation. As a practical handbook, designed to be used by real judges, it quoted and discussed the writings of the classical Roman jurists, cited contemporary legislation, and developed principles on which conflicting legal principles might be reconciled.

The original edition of the *Codex Justinianus* (issued in 529) was made obsolete by these newer works and the continued legislation of the emperor, and it was replaced by an updated version, published on 16 November 534. This detailed legal code, organized in 12 books, formed the basis of law for the rest of the Byzantine era, and it was borrowed and modified in all the areas influenced by Byzantine civilization and even in much of the West. Naturally, Justinian continued to issue laws through the rest of his reign; these were called *Novellae* ("New Laws") and, unlike most of the rest of his legislation, they were issued more commonly in Greek than in Latin. Together, these four summaries of Roman (Byzantine) law, the *Institutes*, the *Digest*, the *Codex Justinianus*, and the *Novellae*, represent one of the high points of worldwide legal activity and they came to be known as the *Corpus Juris Civilis*.

Later Years

Theodora died on 28 June 548. It is impossible to be certain about the impact she had on the age and the reign of Justinian. Certainly, Prokopios depicts her as a remarkably strong personality and even the superior of the emperor in under-handed dealing. She founded many monasteries, churches, and other religious institutions: one of the most famous was the Metanoia (Repentance) monastery, which enrolled reformed prostitutes. Her protection of Monophysite leaders in Constantinople, within the walls of the Palace of Hormisdas, seems beyond doubt, and this certainly indicates a woman of strong character and belief.

After the plague of 542 and Theodora's death a few years later, Justinian's remarkable energy and optimism seem to have waned. This must have been further diluted by the long-drawn-out course of the Italian war, even though that ended, eventually, in a Byzantine victory. Furthermore, as we have seen, the emperor's attempts at religious unity were clearly a failure, and it must have puzzled him to see the Monophysites not only defying imperial orders but also growing in strength as the years passed.

In 558 the dome of Hagia Sophia collapsed, and in 559 the Kutrigur Huns crossed the Danube and pressed as far south as Thermopylae in Greece. When the Huns threatened Constantinople, Justinian again called Belisarios out of retirement and he soundly defeated them. The emperor strengthened the Danube fleet and the Huns withdrew, but this invasion was to be a portent of things to come over the next half-century.

Prokopios, the *Secret History*, and an Evaluation of the Reign of Justinian

As mentioned at the outset, it is difficult to know how to evaluate the reign of Justinian: on the one hand, this period can be seen as the great flowering of the culture and political power of early Byzantine civilization; on the other it can

Box 6.3 *Transvestite Nuns*

The Byzantine tradition was very strong in terms of distinguishing the roles of men and women. Like most pre-modern societies, Byzantium assumed that men would be the "bread-winners," the soldiers, the emperors, while women were thought to have a secondary role in the home. As we have already seen in this book, there were remarkable exceptions of powerful women, but the norm was generally very different and this was especially true in religion, where the church was dominated completely by men. Among ascetics, indeed, spiritual virtue was defined in "manly terms" and it was common to view women as temptresses who would, by their very nature, tend to draw monks away from a life of holiness.

It may be somewhat surprising to note, therefore, that there was a strong tradition in Byzantium to honor a small number of women whom we may call "transvestite nuns." These women were admired because their desire for a holy life was so strong that they overcame the opposition of family members or the general monastic community and, disguising themselves as men, entered monasteries and lived lives of particular sanctity. We obviously have no idea how common such a phenomenon was, but the lives of several of these women are filled with enough particular detail that there is no reason to doubt their general veracity.

One such woman was St. Matrona of Perge (in Asia Minor). She apparently lived in the second half of the fifth and the very early part of the sixth century and she offered notable resistance to the Monophysite policy of the emperor Anastasios I. She grew up in ordinary circumstances, was married, and had a daughter. When she was 25 years old, however, she went to Constantinople and decided to adopt the ascetic life. She put her daughter in the care of a widow and sought to become a nun. She was afraid that her husband would find her in one of the well-known women's monasteries of the city and, while considering this, she had a dream that she was fleeing from her husband and was rescued by some monks. From this she decided that she was destined to enter a male monastery. Thus, she cut off her hair, dressed as a eunuch, and took the male name of Babylas. All that accomplished, she entered the monastery of Bassianos in Constantinople.

According to her biographer, Matrona/Babylas astounded the monks with her feats of asceticism, engaging in strenuous fasts and depriving herself of sleep even more than they did. At one point she was almost discovered when one of the monks (who had recently entered the monastery after a dissolute life as an actor) suspected something and asked why her ears were pierced, something unusual for a man in that age. She came up with a clever answer, saying that she had been a slave and her mistress had dressed her up like a girl and made her wear earrings. The abbot of the monastery, however, learned the truth from a dream; after much consideration he decided that Matrona could not remain in the monastery and he arranged for her to be sent to a female monastery at the city of Emesa in Syria. While she was there she performed the first of her miracles and somehow word got out that she had lived disguised as a man in a monastery, causing people to begin regarding her as a holy person. These events came to the attention of Matrona's husband, who pursued her relentlessly, though the saint was always one step ahead of him, keeping on the move and seeking always to conceal her location. In order to escape detection she spent time in a pagan temple near Beirut, where she was beset by demons and even the Devil himself, who sought to turn the pagans of the city against her. Matrona, however, always prevailed and a number of pagan young women were converted to Christianity and joined her nascent monastery in the pagan temple.

Fear of discovery by her husband and a longing to see the abbot Bassianos led Matrona to return to Constantinople. Bassianos received her and her companions and, inspired by God, he advised them to establish a monastery in Constantinople, apparently for women who would live together in male monastic garb. The monastery founded by Matrona grew and flourished, attracting strong-minded women, some of whom, like the abbess, had to flee from their husbands. At the same time, Matrona attracted the attention of many of the aristocrats of Constantinople, including members of the imperial family, who joined in wondering at her sanctity and the way in which her asceticism was as difficult as that of the monks themselves. One of these nuns was especially wealthy; she enabled the monastery to grow and prosper and for Matrona to provide for the construction of several churches. She lived in her monastery the rest of her life, dying apparently at the age of about 100.

Matrona's desire for a male version of the ascetic life was not unique. There had been others before her and there were others later on. A certain Mary, who apparently lived a century later than Matrona, entered a monastery with her father, who disguised his daughter by cutting off her hair and giving her the name of Marinos. She remained in the monastery, undetected, after her father's death, but the greatest challenge to her position occurred when she was accused of fathering a child. Though she could easily have demonstrated her innocence, she instead chose to maintain her disguise and suffered all the punishments and humiliations this brought along with it. Thus, oddly enough, Mary/Marinos demonstrated her "manly" spirituality by accepting punishment for a crime of a man's sin. Her life was broadly known through the Middle Ages; versions of it were popular in the Latin West, and Arabic, Ethiopian, and Armenian translations were also made.

The phenomenon of the "transvestite" nuns is an interesting one and it can be approached from a psychological or sociological, as well as a religious perspective. It adds a fascinating dimension to our understanding of Byzantine life.

FURTHER READING

Alice Mary Talbot, ed., *Holy Women of Byzantium: Ten Saints' Lives in English Translation*. Washington, DC, 1996.

be viewed as an age of tyranny and fiscal excess that laid the seeds for collapse in the decades to come. Probably these are just two sides of the same issue. The age of Justinian was, in many ways, the fulfillment of the religious, political, and cultural trends that began in the age of Constantine, 200 years earlier. The emperor was supremely confident in his relationship to God and his God-given right to rule the world. Many of his predecessors had felt the same way, but Justinian had the talent and the (hyperactive?) personality to attempt to put the political theories of Byzantium into effect. He was undoubtedly intelligent and single-minded in his desire to defeat his enemies and accomplish his goals. In some of these accomplishments he was brilliantly successful, at least in the short run, and the degree of cultural activity in his time is remarkable by any standard.

The emperor, as we have seen, was the son of a peasant and the nephew of his (possibly illiterate) predecessor. Yet he clearly understood the complex theological and philosophical questions of his day, and he took an active role in them, not only as a law-giver and persecutor, but also as the author of theological treatises. The churches and other buildings constructed under his reign, and to a large degree at his command, are clear testimony of the level of cultural activity. Art in general, poetry, law, and historical studies obviously flourished, and the emperor took a direct interest in such matters. The art of the period is of the highest quality, and it is marked by a conscious blending of the classicizing tradition with the more linear, non-realistic style that had emerged alongside it. In some art forms, such as ivory carving, a realistic, classicizing tradition dominated, but in others, such as painting and sculpture, the figures are less realistic and emphasize more the traditions that had developed in the third and fourth centuries. Overall, however, we can see the art and architecture of the period as a blending of the traditions that had existed, side by side, from the third century onward.

Among the leading poets of the age was Romanos the Melodist (died after 555). He was a Syrian (perhaps of Jewish background) who came to Constantinople in the reign of Anastasios I and wrote ecclesiastical hymns in great numbers – some 1,000 according to Byzantine tradition. He was only the most famous of many poets who wrote hymns as *kontakia*, complex verse sermons in a meter that used stressed rather than ancient accents, normally telling Biblical stories or celebrating individual church feasts. His poetry is dramatic and psychological in manner, involving the worshiper in the emotions that might have been experienced by Biblical figures. Over 80 of Romanos' poems survive, but, unlike some of his less famous colleagues, his works were not incorporated in the liturgy. Only the "Akathistos Hymn," arguably the most famous of all Byzantine hymns, found its way into the Byzantine liturgy – and it is not at all certain that this was a composition by Romanos. The literary evidence, however, suggests that this magnificent poem was written in the sixth century (even though the manuscript tradition assigns it to the seventh or eighth century). This poem, which is still used in the Orthodox liturgy for the

Figure 6.6 Mosaic pavement with a representation of "Apolausis." This pavement from northern Syria came from the formal dining room of a wealthy house of ca. the sixth century. It depicts the personification of "Relaxation and Ease" (*apolausis*), shown in the guise of a woman. The mosaic shows the willingness of the Christian elite of the empire to cling to the trappings and symbols of the classical past, while also showing the characteristic affinity for richly patterned surfaces, reminiscent of oriental carpets. Photo: Dumbarton Oaks

Annunciation (25 March) and throughout Lent, consists of 24 stanzas, each beginning with a successive letter of the Greek alphabet. The first 12 are salutations to the Virgin that retell the Biblical story of the Incarnation; the second 12 are meditations on the mysteries of that event. The whole creates a wonderfully subtle set of interrelated images that conveys much of the spirituality of the Byzantine world.

Aside from Prokopios and Tribonian, both mentioned earlier, many other scholars worked under the reign of Justinian and were influenced by his policies. One of the more important of these was John Lydos (meaning he was from Lydia, in Asia Minor). He was a scholar, well versed in Latin as well as Greek, who came to Constantinople in 511 and secured a post in the civil administration. He was successful in this quest and served for 40 years in the bureaucracy, where he earned the respect of Justinian himself. John wrote a number of important works that indicate his knowledge of the Latin history of the Roman Empire and his belief that the Byzantine Empire of his own day was a continuation of that great tradition. His book *On the Magistracies* is a history of late Roman bureaucracy and it provides many insights on the society and politics of his own day, even suggesting that John may well have had republican (i.e., anti-imperial) sentiments. He also wrote other treatises, one *On the Months*, a study of calendars and time-reckoning, and another *On Omens*, concerning astrology.

Although art and literature undoubtedly thrived in this period and the emperor clearly took a strong interest in these, Justinian's leadership also had more negative aspects. He clearly was stubborn, intolerant, and willing to use force to get his way. The persecution of pagans, Manichaeans, Samaritans, and even Monophysites was especially characteristic of his policy, and the closing of the Academy in Athens (if it indeed took place) is often seen as the most negative aspect of Justinian's intolerance.

Naturally, a crucial aspect of any evaluation of the reign of Justinian is the political and military collapse that took place in the empire almost immediately after his death. We will talk about those events in the pages that follow, but in general terms we have to ask whether we should blame these problems on the expensive, grandiose, and "mistaken" policies of Justinian or whether we should find their causes in the actions of his successors.

Certainly our own ambivalence about the reign of Justinian comes also from the works of Prokopios, our predominant authority for this period, and through whose works we (by necessity) view the emperor. Prokopios of Caesarea was a contemporary of Justinian and, as secretary to Belisarios, he had first-hand information about many of the events (particularly the military campaigns) that he describes. The historian's three main works present three almost completely opposed views of the emperor and his age. The *Wars* is an epic depiction of the wars of the period, written in a highly classicizing style that consciously imitates the ancient historian Thucydides. In this work the emperor does not figure highly, as the main characters are the soldiers and generals engaged in Justinian's attempt at reconquest. The *Buildings* clearly is a work of flattery, written to praise the emperor as a great builder, whose wisdom and close connection to God assure his every success and allow him to surpass all his predecessors. The *Secret History*, on the other hand, is a work of calumny, full of personal attacks on the emperor but even more on Theodora and her friend Antonia, the wife of Belisarios. Much of the book is scandalous and humorous to the modern reader, and the decidedly pornographic depictions of Theodora – notably before she became empress – have won the book both praise and condemnation. Certainly, the *Secret History* is not a balanced account (any more than the *Buildings* is), and many of the details can hardly be accepted as historical truth, interesting as they are. Thus, at one point in the work, Prokopios described the imperial couple in the following words:

Wherefore to me, and many others of us, these two [Justinian and Theodora] seemed not to be human beings, but veritable demons, and what the poets call vampires: who laid their heads together to see how they could most easily and quickly destroy the race and deeds of men; and assuming human bodies, became man-demons, and so convulsed the world. And one could find evidence of this in many things, but especially in the superhuman power with which they worked their will . . . And some of those who have been with Justinian at the palace late at night, men who were pure of spirit, have thought they saw a strange demoniac form taking his place. One man said that the Emperor suddenly rose from his throne and walked about, and indeed he was never wont to remain sitting for long, and immediately Justinian's head vanished, while the rest of his body seemed to ebb and flow; whereat the beholder stood aghast and fearful, wondering if his eyes were deceiving him. But presently he perceived the vanished head filling out and joining the body again as strangely as it had left it.

Neither of Prokopios' depictions of Justinian is fully acceptable, and the author undoubtedly was moved by the necessities of the different genres in which he wrote these books: the *Buildings* is a work of encomium (flattering praise) and the *Secret History* is one of invective (scathing attack). At the same time, there is reason to think that Prokopios had real complaints against Justinian and Theodora, having to do mainly with the way in which these relative "newcomers" ran roughshod over the privileges and sensitivities of the contemporary aristocracy, of which Prokopios apparently felt himself a part. Thus, one can imagine that the undisguised authoritarianism of Justinian's reign upset Prokopios and his social circle, people who still maintained a vestige of republican ideas and who demanded, at very least, to be treated with respect by the emperor and his entourage. Justinian, of course, would have nothing of that. He was a believer in Eusebios of Caesarea's ideal of the God-protected emperor and, just as there was only one God, there could be only one emperor, whose rule was absolute. Justinian obviously controlled the state and imposed his will, but Prokopios was able, to a certain extent, to have the last word, since the *Secret History* presents what is undoubtedly the best-known characterization of the emperor and the empress.

FURTHER READING

Robert Browning, *Justinian and Theodora*. 2nd edn. London, 1987.
Alan Cameron, *Circus Factions. Blues and Greens at Rome and Byzantium*. Oxford, 1976.
Averil Cameron, *Agathias*. Oxford, 1970.
Averil Cameron, *Procopius and the Sixth Century*. Berkeley, CA, 1985.
Glanville Downey, *Constantinople in the Age of Justinian*. Norman, OK, 1960.
J. A. S. Evans, *The Age of Justinian: The Circumstances of Imperial Power*. London and New York, 1996.

W. H. C. Frend, *The Rise of the Monophysite Movement: Chapters on the History of the Church in the Fifth and Sixth Centuries.* Cambridge, 1972.

Geoffrey Greatrex, *Rome and Persia at War, 502–532.* Leeds, 1998.

Susan Ashbrook Harvey, *Asceticism and Society in Crisis: John of Ephesus and "The Lives of the Eastern Saints".* Berkeley, CA, 1990.

Tony Honoré, *Tribonian.* London, 1978.

John Moorhead, *Justinian.* London and New York, 1994.

I. Shahîd, *Byzantium and the Arabs in the Sixth Century.* Washington, DC. 1995.

P. N. Ure, *Justinian and his Reign.* Harmondsworth, 1951.

A. Vasiliev, *Justin the First.* Cambridge, MA, 1950.

7

The Byzantine "Dark Ages": Late Sixth and Seventh Centuries

| 250 | 500 | 750 | 1000 | 1250 | 1500 |

582–602	Maurice
610	Herakleios emperor
628	Victory over Persia
634	Beginning of Arab invasions
636	Battle of Yarmuk

Aftermath of the Age of Justinian

Almost immediately after Justinian's death in 565 (some might say even before), the great edifice the emperor had built up quickly began to crumble. As we have already said, the causes for this are difficult to discern; one has to ask how much of the disaster was caused by the excess of the reign of Justinian and how much was a result of mistakes made by his successors; in addition, we have to be aware that the difficulties that fell upon Byzantium in this period were many and difficult, and one may wonder whether anyone could have done a better job. In the end, the state did survive – and Byzantine civilization with it. And the emperors rebuilt the Byzantine Empire on a new basis, one that was to lead the empire to its greatest days of prosperity and power. But before that recovery the empire was nearly destroyed.

Justin II (565–578)

Justinian and Theodora had no children (although it was alleged that Theodora had children before she met Justinian). Justin II was the son of one of Justinian's sisters, and his wife was a niece of Theodora; Justinian had appointed his nephew to high office in the imperial palace and, when the old emperor died, Justin was easily able to seize the throne.

Throughout his reign Justin relied on the help of his wife Sophia, and she was the first Byzantine empress to appear regularly on coins alongside her husband: the two of them are pictured, seated side by side and dressed in full imperial regalia on the voluminous copper coinage of the reign. Like her aunt, Sophia had a powerful personality and she had a following, in Constantinople and elsewhere, that was especially loyal to her. The emperor and empress appeared as a pair in many sculptures throughout Constantinople and they constructed the *Chrysotriklinos*, which was to become the main throne room in the imperial palace.

In foreign affairs Justin believed that the empire should enforce its policy by the force of arms, so he broke away from the policy of winning the barbarians' support through payment of tribute. Nonetheless, this was a difficult practice to maintain at that particular time. As we have seen, trouble was already brewing on the empire's northern frontier, and the situation first began to unravel in Italy. Only three years after the death of Justinian, in 568, the Lombards, yet another Germanic people, began their conquest of the country. The Byzantines maintained control of Ravenna and the lands immediately around it for some time, and Ravenna remained essentially a Byzantine city; in addition, the Byzantine Empire retained control of most of Calabria and Apulia in the south until the middle of the eleventh century, and Byzantine culture continued to influence the peninsula for centuries to come. Most of the rest of the country, however, was quickly lost to the Lombards. In Rome the popes maintained a precarious independence, relying largely on Byzantine military power to support them against the heretical Germans; the Lombards, it should be remembered, were Arians and there was a long history of antagonism between the heretical Germanic rulers of Italy and their Catholic Roman subjects. This provided the Byzantine emperor with an opportunity to remain involved in the politics of central Italy, although (as we have already seen) this policy had a religious aspect as well, since the popes and the Byzantine emperors did not always agree on matters of faith, and, increasingly, some emperors had to choose carefully between religious policies that might antagonize or please the pope.

During the reign of Justin II military problems were also evident on the Danube frontier, where the Slavs had already begun to settle in Byzantine territory during the reign of Justinian, and in North Africa, where the Berbers remained a thorn in the side of the Byzantine administrators. In the East the situation quickly became critical. As we have seen, Justinian was able to turn his attention to the West largely by arranging a series of treaties with Persia at the cost of very heavy subsidies that contributed to the draining of the state coffers that characterized Justinian's administration. Justin II refused to pay the tributes approved by his uncle, and war broke out, fought at this time largely over Armenia. The results were, for the time, inconsequential, but this was the beginning of a period of some 50 years in which Byzantium and Persia were nearly constantly at war, usually to the disadvantage of the former.

In religious affairs Justin again went against the policies of Justin I and Justinian, seeking once again to find a compromise with the Monophysites. He abandoned the theological ideas of Justinian and advocated a return to the doctrines of the church as they existed before the Council of Chalcedon. He insisted on the recitation of the Creed of the Council of Constantinople in the churches, and he called leading theologians together in an attempt to find a compromise. He even resurrected the idea of the *Henotikon*, forbidding the discussion of issues connected with Chalcedon. All these efforts were for naught, however, and Justin once again turned to force in an attempt to bring the Monophysites back into communion with the official church.

Justin apparently suffered from some kind of mental illness, and his behavior became more and more bizarre: apparently the emperor occasionally bit members of the court, and he would spend hours listening to organ music. Sophia saw the danger posed by this instability, and in 574 she convinced Justin to name the handsome courtier Tiberios as Caesar. From then until Justin's death in 578 Tiberios and Sophia effectively ruled the empire.

Tiberios Constantine (578–582)

During the last four years of Justin II's life Tiberios reversed many of the emperor's policies, purchasing the support of the Avars, for example, with a lavish gift, reducing taxes, and spending money on various construction projects.

After Justin's death, the widowed Sophia sought to maintain her own power, and she apparently demanded that Tiberios (hereafter known as Tiberios Constantine) divorce his wife and marry her. She was, however, outwitted by Tiberios, and her influence began to decline. In foreign affairs Tiberios sought at first to regain Italy through a military campaign against the Lombards. He had to fight wars on three fronts, and he ultimately sought to neutralize the Lombards through political intrigue. Tiberios' most successful general was Maurice, who was able to win significant battles against the Persians. The emperor's focus on the eastern frontier forced him to neglect the Balkans, where the Avars had built up a powerful empire of their own. Among the allies (or subjects) of the Avars were the Slavs, and their first large-scale raids into Byzantine territory seem to have taken place during the reign of Tiberios.

Maurice (582–602)

During his 20-year reign the emperor Maurice seemed as though he might restore some semblance of stability to the Byzantine state. He had already demonstrated his ability as a military commander, and in 582 Tiberios Constantine had made him Caesar; after the older emperor's death, Maurice married Tiberios' daughter. Maurice was a good general in his own right, and the first emperor to take the field himself since Theodosios I. He was careful in his choice of competent generals and administrators to help him, and he was a good and thoughtful ruler, who took steps to reverse the centralization that had characterized state policy since the time of Diocletian, and even more since the time of Justinian. He recognized the reality that the reconquered parts of the West (Italy and North Africa) were under constant military threat and that the governors there needed to have both civil and military power. Thus, he formally created the *Exarchates* of Ravenna and Carthage, ruled by exarchs whose powers combined civil and military authority, which went against the previous tenets of state policy. This arrangement was both logical and necessary, and it probably played a role in the formation of the later *theme* system (a new system of provinces that will be discussed later), but at the same time it did have the effect of making these regions more autonomous than they would otherwise have been, and this created a long-term danger for the stability of the central administration.

Maurice was generally successful in his wars against Persia and in 591 a rare opportunity came his way. There was a dispute for the Persian throne and Chosroes II, the grandson of Chosroes I, sought Maurice's help, fled to Byzantine territory, and may even have married the emperor's daughter. Maurice dispatched several of his best generals to help Chosroes in his ultimately successful attempt to regain the throne. The result was a peace treaty (591), remarkably favorable to Byzantium and actually ceding a large portion of Armenia to the empire. Peace on the Persian frontier allowed Maurice to adopt an aggressive foreign policy elsewhere, and Byzantine influence was at a high point in the disputed area of the Caucusus. Maurice had already, at the beginning of his reign, been able to break up the confederacy of the Ghassanid Arabs, who had been a primary ally of Byzantium along the southeastern frontier against the Persians and the desert Bedouin. As a result of this shift of policy the empire was now able to forge floating alliances with a larger number of Arab groups.

In the West the situation was not nearly so positive. Most of the Byzantine possessions in Spain were lost to the Visigoths by ca. 584, although there still was a presence there until the 620s. North Africa remained officially in Byzantine hands until the Arab conquests of the seventh century, but the area was far from secure, since Berber tribesmen attacked the settled centers and made Byzantine control very difficult. Until this time North Africa apparently maintained the agricultural fertility that had made it the "bread-basket" of the

Box 7.1 *The Marriage of Maurice and Constantina, AD 582*

On his deathbed the emperor Tiberios II Constantine had signified his choice of Maurice as his successor by announcing his engagement to his daughter Constantina. Soon after the elder emperor's death the pair were crowned as emperor and empress, and shortly after that they were married in the imperial palace in a ceremony with special brilliance.

> The royal bridal chamber had been magnificently arrayed within the circuit of the first great precinct of the palace, adorned with gold and princely stones, and furthermore empurpled with crimson hangings of priceless deep-tinged Tyrian dye. The daughter of Tiberius, the virgin bride, preceded the emperor to the bridal throne, as though in hiding, shortly to be seen by the people when the fine curtains were suddenly thrown apart as if at an agreed signal. At once the emperor arrived at the bridal chamber, magnificently escorted by many white-robed men. And so he entered within the lofty curtains to escort the queen to the presence of the onlookers and to embrace her. The emperor's bridal attendant was present; this man was an imperial eunuch, Margarites by name, a distinguished man in the royal household. The queen rose from her throne to honour her bridegroom the emperor, while the factions chanted the bridal hymn. In full view of the people the bride's attendant saluted the bridal pair with a cup, for it was not right to put on crowns, since they were not in fact private individuals who were being married: for this action had already been anticipated by their royal title [in other words, the bride and groom had already been crowned as emperor and empress and they did not, therefore, need the crowns that are a particular part in the wedding ceremony of the eastern church]. (Theophylakt Simokatta 1.10.6–9 [trans. M and M. Whitby, 1986, pp. 33–4])

Maurice had special gold medallions struck to commemorate the marriage and an important group of these has been found. Four of the medallions, along with 12 gold coins, were strung on a belt which might have been worn around the waist or draped from the neck. It is possible, even, that the belt was worn by someone (even the emperor or empress) at the wedding itself. On the obverse of the medallion Maurice is shown holding a scepter and *mappa*, a bag or cloth used in the imperial appearances before the crowd, especially in the hippodrome. On the reverse the emperor is shown in a triumphal four-horse chariot; he holds a globe surmounted by a statue of victory – the symbol of universal dominion – and to his right is the Christogram ("Chi-Rho," the superimposed Greek letters Ch and R, the first two characters in the word Christ).

Less than a year after the wedding Constantina gave birth to the first of the couple's nine children. For a time, she had to share the title of empress with her mother Ino and even Sophia, the widow of the long-dead Justin II. Toward the end of the reign relations between Maurice and Constantina became strained, perhaps as a result of different attachments to the circus factions. Constantina and her three daughters survived for a time after the fall of Maurice, but they were later put to death by Phokas.

western Mediterranean and on which the rich urban life of the region was based. The Berber raids, however, along with general insecurity and possibly climatic change, led to significant desertification, leaving North Africa the poor and nearly resource-less area it has been into modern times.

In Italy the Lombards emerged from a period of internal dissension, first under Autari, who took the title of king in 584, and then Agiluf (590–616), and they were able to stabilize their conquest of much of the country. In 593 Pope Gregory I sought to demonstrate his independence of Byzantine support by signing a peace treaty with the Lombards on his own, but this could ultimately be enforced only in 598 with the aid of the Exarch of Ravenna.

Maurice's concern for the West and his consciousness of the old imperial ideal is evident in arrangements he drew up in 597, when he was seriously ill. He planned to leave his eldest son, Theodosios, to rule the East from Constantinople, while his second son, Tiberios, was to rule the West, not from Ravenna but from Rome. There is even a suggestion in the sources that his two remaining sons were to control other parts of the state, thus reviving, in effect, the idea of the Tetrarchy (although in one family).

Domestically, Maurice experienced considerable difficulty with the circus factions who, under his reign, finally recovered most of the power they had before the Nika Revolt. Indeed, for reasons that are not entirely clear, factional rioting, murder, and destruction of property became endemic at this time, not only in Constantinople but in all the cities of the East. Discontent also spread to the army, giving rise to a dangerous spirit of disobedience and willingness to revolt. Ultimately, this was to spell the end of Maurice.

Maurice was one of the many Byzantine emperors who wrote surviving texts, in this case a military handbook, the *Strategikon*. This was a practical guide for military operations, making use of the emperor's considerable first-hand experience. Interestingly enough, the handbook calls for the replacement of mercenary troops, common in the period, by a peasant militia. The book is also of special importance because of its description of foreign peoples (Franks, Lombards, Avars, Turks, and Slavs).

Since the beginning of his reign the army of Maurice had been on the defensive against the Avars and the Slavs in the Balkans. The Avars were a nomadic, mixed people, perhaps of Turkic origin, from Central Asia and we first hear about them in 558 when Justinian made an alliance with them to help instill order among the barbarians north of the Danube. The Avar confederacy, like that of many other Central Asian conquerors, was militarily powerful but politically unstable and ultimately ephemeral. The Avars were mounted warriors who needed people like the Slavs to fight more conventional infantry battles. The Avar chieftains amassed great wealth, and excavated Avar tombs contain enormous quantities of gold and intricate metalwork, including cavalry accoutrements and ornamental belts; the goods include both local Avar work and items imported from Constantinople.

In 580 the Avars had demanded that Tiberios surrender the important city of Sirmium, which had been for some time the most important city in the

Balkans. The emperor – or in reality Maurice (who, as we have seen, was already in charge of affairs) – refused, but difficulties in the East prevented sending forces sufficient to defend the city, and in 582 the empire agreed to hand it over to the Avars, on condition that the inhabitants be allowed to leave in safety. The fall of Sirmium was a symbol of the military situation: the Danube frontier had essentially collapsed and the Byzantine Empire lost effective control of much of the Balkans.

Maurice, however, did not accept this situation; he devoted significant energy to the area and, year after year, his troops campaigned in the Balkans. The peace with Persia in 591 allowed him to focus even more of his attention there. Imperial troops crossed the Danube, beginning in 593, and the Avar confederation showed signs of dissolution. Nonetheless, the order to the troops to spend the winter of 602 across the Danube led to a military revolt that quickly found support in Constantinople, among both the senators and the circus factions, with the Greens and the Blues uniting against Maurice, whom they regarded as too stern in his control of their activity. Phokas, a low-ranking army officer, led the revolt of the army and marched toward Constantinople, claiming that he was going to put Maurice's son Theodosios (or, alternatively, Maurice's father-in-law) on the throne. In this situation the factions revolted, and this spelled the doom of the emperor. Maurice and his sons were all executed and Phokas was proclaimed emperor with the blessing of the Senate.

Phokas (602–610)

The reign of the emperor Phokas is generally viewed both by contemporaries and by modern historians as one of almost unmitigated disaster. As mentioned above, Maurice, ultimately along with his whole family, was murdered in an especially brutal fashion, and the whole fabric of life in Constantinople seemed to come apart. Although Phokas was initially supported by members of the Senate, his government quickly began a series of what can only be called judicial murders. These naturally gave rise to real conspiracies against the emperor, and these in turn led to a greater persecution of the aristocracy. The Green circus faction, which had initially supported Phokas, turned against him for some reason, while the Blue faction came to support the government. The result was almost continuous violence among faction members, not only in Constantinople but elsewhere as well, and this naturally had a destabilizing effect on society as a whole.

Phokas added to the difficult situation by raising religious issues that inflamed many citizens of the empire. On the one hand, Phokas took a strongly Chalcedonian position, in contrast to the more pragmatic policies of his predecessors, who had not made any prolonged attempt to control the Monophysites. This led to persecution of Monophysites in the East and a natural resistance to imperial policy. In addition, in the late sixth century Pope Gregory the Great

Box 7.2   *Circus Faction Violence under Phokas*

It is difficult to know how to understand or characterize the situation in the Byzantine Empire under the emperor Phokas (602–10). Our sources are almost universally hostile to Phokas and they have nothing but evil things to say about him. It would seem that normal social relations dissolved and there were few institutions that were able to act effectively. Unfortunately, one of those institutions was the circus factions, who had attracted young men and essentially encouraged them to acts of wanton violence for centuries. After the suppression of the factions in the Nika Revolt, they obviously survived, for a time perhaps as "underground" organizations, but in the late sixth century they once again came to the fore, attacking each other and unsuspecting citizens alike.

There has been considerable scholarly interest in the factions, largely in an attempt to understand why they would have attracted adherents and whether they were, in fact, political organizations or simply gangs of hooligans. In the past, many historians saw them as early forms of political organizations, with ideology and a politico-economic agenda. Modern scholarship, however, generally sees them as simple hoodlums. The question is, nevertheless, open to discussion.

The following extract is taken from a sermon given in Thessaloniki in honor of the local St. Demetrios. The speaker sets the scene of the "dark days" in which we live, and uses factional violence as an example of the difficulties of the time. Remember that this is a moralistic sermon that might in fact exaggerate things for effect, but there surely is some truth in the contemporary description:

> You all know only too well what a cloud of dust the devil has stirred up under the successor of Maurice of blessed memory, for he has stifled love and sown mutual hatred throughout the whole east, in Cilicia and Asia and Palestine and all the regions round, even up to the gates of the imperial city itself; the demes [the circus factions], not satisfied with shedding the blood of their fellow demesmen in the streets, have forced their way into others' houses and mercilessly murdered those within, throwing down alive from the upper stories women and children, young and old, who were too weak to save themselves by flight; in barbarian fashion they have plundered their fellow-citizens, their acquaintances and relations, and have set fire to their houses.

Miracula S. Demetrii, translated in G. Ostrogorsky, *History of the Byzantine State*, revised edition (New Brunswick, NJ, 1969), p. 84, n. 4.

had generated a controversy by objecting to the use of the term "Ecumenical Patriarch" (meaning patriarch of the whole empire) by the bishop of Constantinople. Maurice had essentially ignored the controversy, but Phokas supported the papal position and he even addressed an edict to the contemporary pope, Boniface III, expressly recognizing the bishop of Rome as the head of the whole church. Such a position, naturally, did not win any support for Phokas, either from Monophysites or from Chalcedonians, who wished to maintain the prerogatives of the church of Constantinople.

Meanwhile, and perhaps most significantly, the defenses of the empire, built up at such expense by Maurice and his predecessors, essentially collapsed, and the Byzantine state nearly ceased to exist. The first blow fell when Chosroes II used the overthrow of his ally Maurice as an excuse to attack Byzantium, and he bolstered the claim by the assertion that Maurice's son Theodosios (who had, in fact, been killed) was campaigning with him. The great frontier city of Dara was taken and Persian troops marched into the heart of Asia Minor, taking Caesarea and even reaching the shores of the Bosphoros. The Byzantine effort at resistance was hampered by disagreement; at least one Byzantine commander opened the doors of his city to the Persians and assisted at the coronation of "Theodosios" as emperor. Phokas sought to secure peace in the Balkans with a huge payment to the Avar khan, and the result of this was that the Byzantine military presence in the Balkans essentially evaporated and cities were left to their own defenses against plundering groups of Avars and Slavs.

The military debacle, of course, led the emperor to find scapegoats, and his government continued to execute leading commanders and members of the aristocracy. This situation, along with military catastrophe, only encouraged further revolts. One of these was successful in putting an end to the bloody reign of Phokas. In 608 Herakleios, the exarch of Carthage, revolted against Phokas and dispatched a fleet toward the capital. Phokas had no troops to meet the challenge and discontented provincials began to flock to the standard of revolt, which soon was taken over by the exarch's son, also named Herakleios. Egypt joined the revolt and immediately cut the grain supply to Constantinople. Raising supporters as he went, the younger Herakleios arrived outside Constantinople on 3 October 610, and Phokas' government collapsed almost immediately: the emperor was summarily executed and the colors of the Blue faction were burned in an outpouring of popular rage. On 5 October Herakleios entered Constantinople and was crowned emperor by the patriarch Sergios. The empire had a new and vigorous ruler, one of the real heroes of Byzantine history and a fascinating character in his own right, but he immediately had to face a very difficult situation, since nearly all the institutions of state had collapsed and the capital was surrounded by its powerful enemies.

Slavic Invasions and the Causes of the "Dark Ages"

The accession of Herakleios to the throne is a good opportunity to step back and look briefly at some of the major historical issues and problems that affect our understanding of the later sixth and seventh centuries, specifically the question of the Slavic settlement of the Balkans and the issue of the so-called Byzantine Dark Ages.

The problem of the settlement of the Slavs in Byzantine territory is a very difficult one, in part because it has significant political ramifications, not least because the various modern Slavic peoples of southeast Europe generally connect their national origins with this phenomenon.

Until fairly recently, most scholars looked at the Slavic migrations in much the same way as the Germanic invasions were viewed: the various Slavic peoples had some common "homeland" (somewhere northeast of the Byzantine Empire) and, from the second half of the sixth century, they began to conquer parts of former Byzantine territory and establish new homes there. Scholars today know that this phenomenon was much more complex, lasting hundreds of years, and that it is probably incorrect to think of Slavic peoples as clearly defined entities before they came into contact with Byzantium. In addition, it is now generally agreed that the people who lived in the Balkans after the Slavic "invasions" were probably for the most part the same as those who had lived there earlier, although the creation of new political groups and the arrival of small numbers of immigrants caused people to look at themselves as distinct from their neighbors, including the Byzantines.

The sixth-century western historian Jordanes claimed that there were three groups of Slavs: the Venethi, the Antae, and the Sclaveni, each of which, in his time, lived in different areas outside the Byzantine Empire. By the middle of the sixth century Byzantium began to make use of Slavic groups as *foederati*, but many of them simply crossed the Danube and settled on imperial territory on their own. Justinian's considerable effort to fortify this frontier apparently had little effect. The Slavs occasionally joined with the Cotrigurs (or Cotrigur Bulgars) in their attacks on Byzantine territory, and after 576 many of them had become part of the Avar confederation. Although some modern groups would like to trace their descent back to them, the Avars ultimately disappeared as a people. However, the Slavs, in the wake of Avar military action, settled in most parts of the Balkans and they make up the dominant ethnic groups in the region today.

The *Miracles of St. Demetrios* reports that the Slavs attacked Thessaloniki many times, beginning in the late sixth century; although the city was not taken, most of its hinterland was settled by newcomers. Likewise, the *Chronicle of Monemvasia*, an important but controversial history of southern Greece, says that the Slavs occupied most of the Peloponnesos and were independent of Byzantine rule for a period of 218 years, that is, from 587/8 to 804/5. Not surprisingly, the "facts" presented by the *Chronicle of Monemvasia* have been subject to considerable debate, and the text has its defenders and detractors, not least because the issue of the alleged Slavic domination of southern Greece has important ramifications for territorial and self-definitional claims by Greeks and the various Slavic peoples, not to speak of westerners who wish to categorize the peoples of Eastern Europe in one way or another. At least we can say that although this period was clearly one of instability and although new people undoubtedly did move into the area formerly controlled by Byzantium, the idea of the Balkans being "overrun" by Slavs is both simplistic and not

Figure 7.1 Byzantine fortress on the island of Dokos. This now-deserted island off the coast of the Argolid in southern Greece was used as a significant naval way-station and fortress during the seventh century when the Arabs first began to challenge Byzantine power at sea. The island lay astride the commercial and military sea lanes between Constantinople and Italy and it was fortified, at least in part, to help the Byzantines keep this line of communication open despite Arab raids and victories at sea. Photo: Timothy E. Gregory

very helpful for our understanding of the events. Probably more significantly, most of the cities of the Balkan area ceased to exist in the late sixth and/or the seventh century, and social life changed dramatically.

Thus, to return to the broader issue of what happened in the late sixth or the early seventh century, we should try to understand why and how Byzantine political and military control essentially disappeared from most of the Balkans. As an important counterpoint, many cities had previously suffered the fate of Sirmium: we have already seen that Rome was sacked in AD 410 and Antioch was taken by the Persians several times in this period. Nonetheless, in all these cases, the cities were rebuilt, while Sirmium and many other cities sacked in the late sixth and seventh centuries never recovered or did so very slowly over the next four of five centuries. Seen in this way, the invasions of the period were not the "real" cause of the difficulties that followed but one of the results of much deeper problems in the political, economic, and possibly demographic situation of the time. It has, in the past, been easy to put the "blame" for these problems on a variety of culprits. Perhaps most simply, it was easy to blame the "invasions" of the period – first the "Slavs" and then, in the East, the Arabs. Yet, it is easy to see that this explanation cannot be maintained, if only because there had always been "invasions" and military defeats, but the broader polity had survived. Likewise, it is easy to cite phenomena such as plagues and earthquakes – events which surely did happen but whose connection with the apparent abandonment of cities and the precipitous decline in the economy is difficult to determine. Finally, as we have seen, it has become customary to blame Justinian for the events of the last half of the sixth century, citing his alleged fixation on the West (and thus a supposed ignoring of the Balkans and Persia) and his arguably spendthrift policies. But – as we have already said – it is probably unfair to blame an emperor for things that happened well after his death.

In recent years, many historians have come to look at the events of the last half of the sixth century in rather different ways. One approach has sought to view the changes in this period as based on the most fundamental units of society. Thus, scholars such as Alexander Kazhdan have argued that this period witnessed a collapse in the broader city-based or state-based social groupings, which resulted in the identification of individuals with small units such as the family. This change led to the significant weakening of the state. Other scholars have pointed to environmental changes, including the alleged (not fully proven) desertification of much of the southeastern rim of the Byzantine Empire, which had once been a primary producer of grain and other goods and which now became desert. Others look to more practical administrative and military matters, pointing out that the Byzantine state in the late sixth century did not have in place workable institutions for the recruitment and integration of troops, the result being the growing ineffectiveness of the Byzantine army and its inability to defeat the very different enemies who appeared from time to time.

On the one hand, the question of why the Byzantine Empire went, in the span of 50 to 100 years, from the dominant power (economically, culturally, and militarily) in the Mediterranean area to one whose very existence was in question, is simply too difficult for historians to answer in a simplistic manner. Certainly, the combination of civil war, religious dissension, and ineffective leadership had important ramifications. On the other hand, the general condition of the empire and the nature of its enemies (at least until the rise of Islam) had not changed greatly. It is attractive for many to turn to explanations outside the control of human affairs – such as earthquakes, plagues, or even climatic or environmental change. These "explanations" are often favored simply because they are more or less mechanistic and do not necessarily require human intervention (or blame). Nonetheless, attractive as such theories are, the evidence to support them is not, to date at least, very convincing. This is not to say that such disasters did not occur – they certainly did – but just as with the invasions of the period, they had happened before, and the question really concerns whether the empire was able to deal with them.

Furthermore, real questions have arisen about the chronology of the crisis. Traditionally, historians have seen the crux of the problem in the half-century after Justinian. Now, however, many historians have increasingly turned to archaeological evidence and they have come to two very different conclusions. One group sees the onset of decline well before the time of Justinian, in the early sixth century, if not before, and they argue that the decline was not a precipitous collapse after the reign of Justinian, but that it was a much slower phenomenon that developed over many generations. Another, perhaps more vocal, group of historians argues that the difficulties of the late sixth century were not anything insurmountable, but rather problems like those that Byzantium had overcome in many other periods and that, in fact, the Byzantine Empire was in a good condition as it entered the seventh century. In this view, the problems that ultimately developed were the result of the Byzantine inability to deal, initially at least, with the threat posed by the explosive expansion of Islam. Interestingly enough, against the background of these difficulties emerged some of the more creative representations of Byzantine spirituality, such as John Klimakos, who lived on Mount Sinai and developed the apophatic ideas of scholars such as Pseudo-Dionysios into a set of admonitions for daily life and the ascent to God.

Defining something by what it is not?!

Herakleios (610–641)

Herakleios came to the throne in a moment of crisis in 610. The Balkans, as we have seen, were essentially lost to the empire, and the war with Persia was going very badly, since the death of Phokas did not diminish Chosroes' desire for a victory over Byzantium. The army in the East fortunately retained some degree of cohesion and it sought resolutely to deflect the Persian advance. Shortly after Herakleios' accession, however, the Persians defeated the Byzantine army near Antioch, and they moved both into Asia Minor and south, taking Damascus and, in 614, Jerusalem. They sacked the Holy City, destroyed the church of the Holy Sepulcher, built by Constantine, and carried off the Holy Cross (supposedly the actual cross used in the crucifixion) to the Persian capital of Ctesiphon.

Herakleios managed to gain some time through negotiation with his enemies and especially through the payment of an increasingly large subsidy to the Avar khan. In this he was assisted, as in many other ways, by the Patriarch Sergios, who allowed significant quantities of the church treasure to be melted down for the emperor's use. (Some historians believe that at this time Herakleios began a radical reorganization of the state, but most think this took place afterwards, and the so-called *theme* system will be discussed at a later point in this book.)

Herakleios also used this time to train the army in new tactics, especially the use of light-armed mounted archers, and he supervised this personally, against the advice of his ministers, who thought he should avoid taking the field himself. By 622 Herakleios felt he was ready for the counterattack against the Persians. He launched this by striking north into Armenia, forcing the Persians to abandon their fortifications in Asia Minor, and the emperor was victorious in a critical battle on Armenian soil. Over the next few years Herakleios remained on the offensive and he was able to take a number of cities, including the important Persian religious city of Ganzak, where he destroyed the fire-temple of Zoroaster in revenge for the destruction of Jerusalem. The Persians, however, counterattacked, and the most serious threat came in 626, when the

Persians and the Avars combined to attack Constantinople itself. The emperor was on campaign in the Caucusus and the defense of the city was in the hands of the patriarch Sergios. The Persians, under their general Shahrbaraz, encamped at Chalcedon, but they had no ships to transport them across the Bosphoros. These were provided by the Slavs, who knew the technology of basic ship-building, although their vessels – while probably not dugout canoes (as some historians think) – were hardly a match for the ships of the Byzantine navy. The Land Walls of Constantinople were enough to frustrate two Avar direct attacks, and when the Slavs set out to transport the Persians over to the European side, the Byzantine navy sailed out of the Golden Horn and devastated the "armada." Another Avar attack also failed and the siege was called off; Constantinople had been saved, and Herakleios was able to press his advantage into the Persian heartland. He spent most of 627 in a successful attempt to subdue the Caucasus and then surprised the Persians by marching into Mesopotamia in December. A battle near Niniveh was a decisive Byzantine victory and Herakleios pursued Chosroes through northern Iraq. The next year (628) there was a revolt in Persia and Chosroes was overthrown and executed.

Herakleios had won a complete victory. The new ruler, Shahrbaraz, was willing to make remarkable concessions, including acceptance of Christianity and the recognition of Herakleios as his son's protector. Although only a few years earlier it looked as though the Byzantine Empire might disappear, by 628 it had decisively defeated its old rival and was definitely in control of the East. The Holy Cross was restored to Jerusalem and in 630 Herakleios entered the city to celebrate the triumph, one that he had won in large part by his own personal courage, determination, and military skill.

Theological Problems

Like virtually all Byzantine emperors, Herakleios had to deal with religious issues and the way that Christianity seemed to divide his subjects rather than unite them. The issue was particularly acute for him once he had recovered the East, and Monophysitism again became a pressing consideration. The patriarch Sergios took the lead in attempting yet again to find some compromise between the two theological sides. He sought to do this with the doctrine of Monoergism, which taught that although Christ had a human and a divine nature, he had a single "energy." The emperor and the patriarch pushed this compromise and they had some initial success; the pope seemed willing to agree, and several important Monophysite clerics were supportive as well. Sophronios, the powerful patriarch of Jerusalem, resisted and demanded nothing less than the full acceptance of Chalcedon, and soon the position of the Monphysites likewise hardened. Sergios therefore rethought the matter and suggested yet another compromise, proposing the doctrine that Christ had a single "will." Herakleios supported the teaching of Monotheletism (the doctrine of the "single will") and in 638 he officially declared it to be imperial policy in a decree called the *Ekthesis*, which was publicly posted in Hagia

Sophia. This "solution" to the religious problem was no more successful than any of the earlier attempts. Just like the *Henotikon* before it, the *Ekthesis* was rejected by Chalcedonians and Monophysites alike, and it only served to harden the position of the two sides and further undermined the ability of the emperor to determine religious belief by imperial fiat.

Chalcedonian opposition to Monotheletism was led by the remarkable theologian Maximos the Confessor. Maximos was a monk and a follower of Sophronios of Jerusalem, but he accepted appointment as a secretary of the

---

Box 7.3 *The Persistence of Pagan Practice: Canons of the Council in Trullo (691/692)*

It is clear that some practices derived from paganism continued to survive into the Byzantine period. Some of these apparently were connected with ancient festivals of the gods Pan (the so-called Bota) and Dionysos (the Brumalia). These festivals were not any longer closely associated with religion, but rather were opportunities for dancing, drinking, and general carousing – much, perhaps, like the modern Mardi Gras. The bishops assembled for the Council in Trullo were shocked by such behavior and one of the canons (decrees) condemned the festivals, but also provides us with important evidence of the kind of behavior that was apparently still going on, well into the Byzantine Empire:

CANON LXII

The so-called Calends, and what are called Bota and Brumalia, and the full assembly which takes place on the first of March, we wish to be abolished from the life of the faithful. And also the public dances of women, which may do much harm and mischief. Moreover we drive away from the life of Christians the dances given in the names of those falsely called gods by the Greeks whether of men or women, and which are performed after an ancient and un-Christian fashion; decreeing that no man from this time forth shall be dressed as a woman, nor any woman in the garb suitable to men. Nor shall he assume comic, satyric, or tragic masks; nor may men invoke the name of the execrable Bacchus when they squeeze out the wine in the presses; nor when pouring out wine into jars [to cause a laugh], practising in ignorance and vanity the things which proceed from the deceit of insanity. Therefore those who in the future attempt any of these things which are written, having obtained a knowledge of them, if they be clerics we order them to be deposed, and if laymen to be cut off.

A Select Library of Nicene and Post-Nicene Fathers of the Christian Church, second series, ed. Philip Schaff and Henry Wace. Vol. XIV, ed. H. R. Percival (New York, 1890; reprint Grand Rapids, MI, 1955), p. 393.

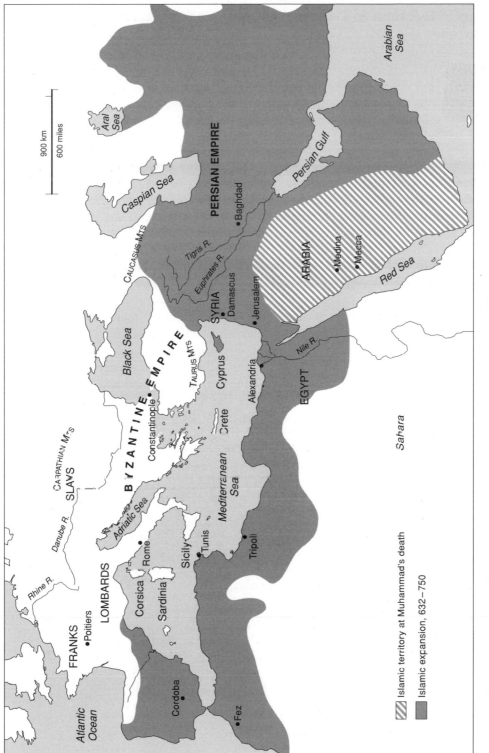

Map 7.1 Islamic conquests. After Jackson J. Spielvogel, *Western Civilizations*, fifth edition (Wadsworth, 2003), map 7.6, p. 187

FRANKS
•Poitiers

LOMBARDS

Rhine R.

Danube R.

CARPATHIAN MTS

SLAVS

Atlantic
Ocean

Corsica

Sardinia

Rome•

Sicily

Tunis•

Fez•

Cordoba•

Tripoli•

Adriatic Sea

Mediterranean
Sea

Crete

BYZANTINE EMPIRE

Constantinople•

Cyprus

Black Sea

TAURUS MTS

CAUCASUS MTS

Aral
Sea

Caspian Sea

Alexandria•

EGYPT

Nile R.

Sahara

SYRIA
•Damascus
•Jerusalem

Euphrates R.

Tigris R.

•Baghdad

PERSIAN EMPIRE

ARABIA

•Medina
•Mecca

Red Sea

Persian Gulf

Arabian
Sea

900 km
600 miles

Islamic territory at Muhammad's death

Islamic expansion, 632–750

court of Herakleios in Constantinople. Speaking out openly against any doctrine other than that of Chalcedon, he publicly denied the emperor's right to be involved in the definition of doctrine. Fearing for his life, Maximos fled to North Africa ca. 630, but from there he kept up a steady stream of invective against Monotheletism and imperial religious policy.

The Arab Invasions

It is a striking irony that Herakleios' total victory over the Persians was followed almost immediately by the permanent loss of virtually the whole of the Byzantine East to the Arabs. As a result of the Persian wars the resources of the Byzantine state were stretched to breaking point, and the emperor must have looked forward to a long period of peace in which prosperity might be restored. On the contrary, in 634 – only six years after Herakleios' victory over the Persians and two years after the death of the Prophet Muhammad – the Arabs broke into Byzantine territory and within two years they had essentially gained control of the Byzantine East, including Syria and Palestine.

This is not the place for a discussion of the origins of Islam and the development of the Arab caliphate; the reader who lacks a basic knowledge of these events would be advised to look at a good summary of early Islamic history. It is clear, however, that the Prophet Muhammad and the early Islamic tradition grew up in a world with strong connections to Byzantium. Muhammad himself was fully aware of both Judaism and Byzantine Christianity, and the Prophet lived on the frontier of the Byzantine Empire, which he almost certainly visited.

Much of the later part of the Prophet's life was devoted to the establishment of a stridently monotheistic new religion among the strongly polytheistic peoples of the Arabian peninsula. This was a difficult task, marked by violence toward the Muslims and many setbacks for Islam. By the time of Muhammad's death in 632, however, most of the peninsula had at least formally accepted Islam, and Abu Bakr, the first caliph ("successor of the Prophet"), could claim at least the formal allegiance of most people living in the peninsula. Abu Bakr's successor was the caliph 'Umar (634–44), who began the military campaigns that led to the rapid spread of Islam and the caliphate.

In 634 'Umar invaded Syria and won a number of victories against Byzantine armies, including the conquest of Damascus. At first the Byzantines had not taken this invasion seriously, since Arab raiders had frequently caused difficulty in that area. By 636, however, Herakleios had become alarmed, and he organized a huge expeditionary force, perhaps as large as 100,000 men, and dispatched it against the Arabs. 'Umar initially pulled back from the north of Syria but offered battle in the Yarmuk Valley (a tributary of the Jordan River in Palestine). Dissension among the Byzantine commanders, the effectiveness of the Arab horsemen, and a sudden duststorm led to the destruction of the whole Byzantine army and left all of Syria and Palestine open to 'Umar's

Box 7.4   *Theophanes on Muhammad and the Origins of Islam* AM *6122* (AD *629/630*)

The growth of Islam was one of the most important historical developments, not only for seventh-century Byzantium, but also for the history of the whole world. The relation between Byzantines and Muslims was always a close one, and the Byzantines naturally regarded the Muslims as the greatest of their rivals. At first, however, the Byzantines were taken by surprise by the sudden rise of Islam, and they generally viewed the new religion as a heretical version of Christianity.

Much of our information on early Byzantine knowledge of and attitudes toward Islam comes from the chronographer Theophanes, a Byzantine monk and a fanatical supporter of image veneration in Byzantium, who wrote shortly after AD 814. His account of the origins of Islam is marked by the acceptance of scurrilous rumor, as well as an acquaintance with a genuine Muslim tradition. Thus, in the passage that follows Theophanes characterizes the revelation of Islam as a calculated ruse on the part of the Prophet, while, at the same time, he clearly follows a Sunni Muslim tradition, since his text makes a point of saying that Muhammad had chosen Abu Bakr as his successor.

Theophanes arranged his material by years, identifying them in a variety of ways, including the regnal years of the most important rulers and bishops, but also the *annus mundi* ("year of the world" or AM), which was calculated in Alexandria on the belief that the world was created in 5492 BC). Nonetheless, in the passage below, Theophanes dates the death of Muhammad to AD 629/30, when, in fact, he died in 632).

In this year died Mouamed [Muhammad], the leader and false prophet of the Saracens, after appointing his kinsman Aboubacharos [Abu Bakr] <to his chieftainship. At the same time his repute spread abroad> and everyone was frightened. At the beginning of his advent the misguided Jews thought he was the Messiah who is awaited by them, so that some of their leaders joined him and accepted his religion while forsaking that of Moses, who saw God. Those who did so were ten in number, and they remained with him until his murder. But when they saw him eating camel meat, they realized that he was not the one they thought him to be, and were at a loss what to do; being afraid to abjure his religion, those wretched men taught him illicit things directed against us, Christians, and remained with him.

I consider it necessary to give an account of this man's origin. He was descended from a very widespread tribe, that of Ishmael, son of Abraham; for Nizaros, descendant of Ishmael, is recognized as the father of them all. He begot two sons, Moudaros and Raias. Moudaros begot Kourasos, Kaisos, Themimes, Asados, and others unknown. All of them dwelt in the Midianite desert and kept cattle, themselves living in tents. There are also those farther away who are not of their tribe, but of that of Iektan, the so-called Amanites, that is Homerites. And some of them traded on their camels. Being destitute and an orphan, the aforesaid Mouamed decided to enter the service of a rich woman who was a relative of his, called Chadiga [Kadîj'a], as a hired worker with a view to trading by camel in Egypt and Palestine. Little by little he became bolder and ingratiated himself with that woman, who was a widow, took her as a wife, and gained possession of her camels and her substance. Whenever he came to Palestine he consorted with Jews and Christians and sought from them certain scriptural matters. He was also afflicted with epilepsy. When his wife became aware of this, she was greatly distressed, inasmuch as she, a noblewoman, had married a man such as he, who was not only poor, but also an epileptic. He tried deceitfully to placate her by saying, "I keep seeing a vision of a certain angel called Gabriel, and being unable to bear his sight, I faint and fall down." Now, she had a certain monk living there, a friend of hers (who had been exiled for his depraved doctrine), and she related everything to him, including the angel's name. Wishing to satisfy her, he said to her, "He has spoken the truth, for this is the angel who is sent to all the prophets." When she had heard the words of the false monk, she was the first to believe in Mouamed and proclaimed to other women of her tribe that he was a prophet. Thus, the report spread from women to men, and first to Aboubacharos [Abu Bakr], whom he left as his successor. This heresy prevailed in the region of Ethribos, in the last resort by war: at first secretly, for ten years, and by war another ten, and openly nine. He taught his subjects that he who kills an enemy or is killed by an enemy goes to Paradise; and he said that this paradise was one of carnal eating and drinking and intercourse with women, and had a river of wine, honey, and milk, and that the women were not like the ones down here, but different ones, and the pleasure continuous; and other things full of profligacy and stupidity; also that men should feel sympathy for one another and help those who are wronged.

Cyril Mango and Roger Scott, *The Chronicle of Theophanes Confessor* (Oxford, 1997), pp. 464–5.

forces. Led by the Patriarch Sophronios, the people of Jerusalem held out against the Arab army, but they too were forced to surrender to 'Umar in 638. The caliph respected the Christian places of worship in Jerusalem and left them in Christian hands, although Muslim shrines were quickly built in the holy city. The Arabs subdued the Persian Empire as quickly as they had taken the Byzantine East, and they moved to conquer Armenia in 640 and Egypt in 641.

The caliph 'Umar began the process of creating a state, which would ultimately have its capital at Damascus, in former Byzantine territory, and in doing so he made use of many Byzantine institutions and, indeed, former Byzantine officials, since the Arabs had no previous tradition of managing a large centralized but diverse empire. In fact, the records of the caliphate were for years

---

Box 7.5 *The Fall of Jerusalem to the Arabs:*
The Nobility of 'Umar and the Patriarch Sophronios

Beginning in 634, the Arabs quickly swept over the whole of the Near East, bringing both the old Persian Empire and all the Byzantine East under their sway. Practically the only place where the Byzantines were able to offer resistance was the holy city of Jerusalem, where the fiery and powerful bishop, Sophronios, was able to hold out against the attack of the caliph 'Umar. Finally, without the likelihood of support from Byzantine troops, Sophronios surrendered the city, taking advantage of the precept of Islam which held that a place which surrendered voluntarily to a Muslim power would be subjected peacefully and not subject to rape and pillage.

The passage that follows, from Theophanes, describes how the transfer of power took place and how caliph and patriarch sought to out-do each other in maintaining their dignity and superiority. Notice also the bias evident in Theophanes and the way in which the patriarch apparently saw the fall of the city in apocalyptic terms: it was a sign that the world was coming to an end:

In this year [634/5] Oumaros ['Umar, the third Muslim caliph] invaded Palestine and, after investing the Holy City for two years, took it by capitulation; for Sophronios, the bishop of Jerusalem, received a promise of immunity of the whole of Palestine. Oumaros entered the Holy City dressed in filthy garments of camel-hair and, showing a devilish pretence, sought the Temple of the Jews – the one built by Solomon – that he might make it a place of worship for his own blasphemous religion. Seeing this, Sophronios said, "Verily, this is the abomination of desolation standing in a holy place, as has been spoken through the prophet Daniel" [Daniel 11:32; cf. Matthew 24:15, Mark 13:14]. And with many tears the defender of piety bewailed the Christian people. While Oumaros was there, the patriarch begged him to receive from him a kerchief and a garment to put on, but he would not suffer to wear them. At length, he persuaded to put them on until his clothes were washed, and then he returned them to Sophronios and put on his own.

Cyril Mango and Roger Scott, *The Chronicle of Theophanes Confessor* (Oxford, 1997), pp. 471–2.

---

kept in Greek, and the earliest Arab coinage imitated Byzantine coins, even so far as depicting a "standing caliph" in imitation of coins showing the emperor in the same pose; only after some time was this human figure removed from the coins, to be replaced by a simple inscription. The same can be said about monumental architecture, since the Arabs had little or no tradition in this regard, and the new rulers naturally employed Byzantine architects and builders in the construction of palaces, mosques, and other public buildings to decorate their cities and places of private retreat. Good examples of the continuity of the Byzantine tradition under the early caliphs are the great mosque in Damascus, the Dome of the Rock in Jerusalem, and the Ummayad palaces in the Jordanian desert.

There is also good evidence of continuity on a more basic level in the archaeological evidence. Close examination of excavations and surveys from both the city and the countryside suggest considerable prosperity in Syria through the fourth to the sixth centuries. This much is in keeping with what we know from throughout the eastern Mediterranean in this period. Excavations at the village of Dehès, however, present a considerable surprise. The apparent prosperity of earlier years allowed the inhabitants, who were apparently farmers, to build quite impressive houses (complete with colonnades along the front) through the sixth century. This construction came to a halt but the Arab conquests left virtually no trace, and life apparently continued without a break at least to the end of the seventh century. There is no evidence of violent destruction at any point, but the settlement seems to have shrunk in size and eventually disappeared, apparently as a result of the rise of the Abassids and the replacement of Damascus by Baghdad as the seat of the caliphate in 750, events that had no direct connection with Byzantium.

The Arabs, thus, did not come as destroyers; in general they respected and admired the culture and the accomplishments of Byzantium (and, equally, of Persia), and they built their own Islamic culture in significant ways on this base. It is often pointed out that the Arabs made use of the writings and ideas of the ancient Greek philosophers, mathematicians, and scientists, and they played a significant role in the transmission of that knowledge to the medieval West (in the twelfth century). What is not always recognized is that to the Arabs these works were "Byzantine," and they borrowed the books from Byzantine libraries, where the manuscripts had been preserved and copied, and translated them into Arabic as an important foundation for their own science and culture.

The reasons for the remarkable expansion of Islam have long been discussed by historians, and many theories have been put forward. The historical discussion is especially difficult because both the Arab and the Byzantine sources are hard to interpret, since they each view the events through the lens of evolving religious traditions. In fact, some recent studies have even argued that Islam emerged only slowly from the Judeo-Christian tradition and that Muhammad's original mission may have been very different from what is pictured in the traditional sources. In general, it is probably useful to distinguish between those factors which weakened the Byzantines (and the Persians) and those which strengthened the Arabs or made them want to leave the Arabian peninsula. In the past, western historians often said that the conquests were caused simply by the religious zeal of the Arabs, who, because they were fanatical Muslims, were all willing to die for the spread of Islam in a holy war (*jihad*). This is highly questionable for a variety of reasons, not least because it is not clearly indicated in the sources.

On the one hand, it is likely that the earliest attacks on Byzantine and Persian territory were simple *razzias*, traditional Arab raids. The *razzia* had for centuries been part of the economic basis of Arabia, and one should remember that large numbers of Arabs had long been settled along the eastern frontier of Byzantium. Many of the Arabs had previously come to abandon their nomadic life in the desert in favor of a sedentary agricultural existence, frequently within the boundaries of the empire. Byzantium had, likewise, long made use of various Arab allies to guard the frontier, and the earliest Islamic attacks presumably fell most heavily on the other Arabs who had made their peace with the Byzantine Empire and who were therefore most seriously disturbed by the sudden attacks.

Futhermore, the new religion of Islam forbade Muslims from making armed attacks on other Muslims, even though there had been a long tradition of such raiding as a "way of life" in the Arabian peninsula. Prevented from carrying out such attacks on fellow Muslims, the newly converted Arabs naturally turned their attention to non-Muslims.

When the new *razzias* fell upon Persian and Byzantine territories, they encountered little opposition. As already mentioned, the long war between Persia and Byzantium (from about 602 to 628) had exhausted both sides and they were ill prepared for a new war from an enemy who came quickly, out of "nowhere." Many of the most productive areas of both states had previously been overrun and burned during the course of the war, and time had not allowed the recovery of their productive capabilities. In this regard the psychological strain of the Arab attacks, so soon after the great war with Persia, must not be discounted.

Historians have often pointed to the weakness caused by the religious split between the Orthodox and the Monophysites, and the dissatisfaction of the latter, as a factor in the Arab success. While this may have been the case, it is difficult at this remove to know how much stock to put in that explanation, especially since there is little evidence that the Monophysites actively assisted the Arabs in any significant way.

Some scholars have argued that the Arabian peninsula was progressively drying up during this period, forcing the Arabs to move into the surrounding territories, driving them, in fact, into territories controlled by Christianized, sedentary Arabs, who in the end came to join the movement into the Byzantine interior. In addition, as we have seen, various scholars now are arguing that the Byzantine world suffered a significant crisis from the middle of the sixth century, as a result of plague and perhaps the overspending of Justinian, and that it was in serious decline already, well before the appearance of the Arabs. Nevertheless, despite the violent shock that the Arab conquests gave to the Byzantine state, there is reason to believe that life in the cities of the East did not actually change much – at least initially – after the conquest. Thus, archaeological evidence now seems to show that many of the great cities continued to thrive after the Arab conquest and that the economy, at least thst of the areas along the coast of the Mediterranean, did not change drastically in the immediate aftermath of the conquest.

The Successors of Herakleios

Herakleios spent his last years sunk in despair, illness, and perhaps even mental disarray. The utter collapse of the East left him unable to act, and the man who had taken the state from defeat to triumph was apparently petrified by indecision and fear. Dissension began to arise in the capital and Herakleios finally died in February of 641.

He left his successors a difficult legacy: the empire was divided internally and had to face a series of challenges from the ascendant Arab caliphate. That the Byzantine state was able to survive this time of troubles is a measure of its deep internal strength and the creation of an institutional structure that would characterize Byzantine society for the next half-millennium. The period is a difficult one to understand, in part because our sources are so poor, but events of crucial importance were taking place. The ultimate failures of the Arabs to take Constantinople or to make permanent inroads in Asia Minor were the beginnings of the long process of Byzantine recovery.

Herakleios had been married twice, first to Favia, who took the name Eudokia, and who bore him the future emperor Herakleios Constantine, also known as Constantine III. After her death Herakleios married his niece Martina (in 613/14), a capable and ambitious woman who earned the enmity of the people and the church, in part because the marriage was generally considered to be incestuous. The patriarch Sergios condemned the union, but Herakleios ignored his opposition and Martina bore the emperor as many as ten children; several of these, however, were mentally incapacitated – a sign to some of God's displeasure.

Herakleios Constantine had been born in 612 and crowned as emperor the next year, so his succession was assured, even though he was in ill health at the time of Herakleios' death. According to the former emperor's will, Herakleios Constantine was to share the throne with his half-brother Heraklonas, the son of Martina, who was only 15 at the time. Herakleios Constantine was popular with the people of Constantinople, but he found the treasury empty (according to one report, he had the tomb of his father opened and his crown removed to be sold!) and he had no military success. Martina clearly found him an impediment to the rule of her own son, and rumors of foul play immediately circulated when Herakleios Constantine died within a few months of his accession.

Martina now felt that she had a clear opportunity to rule in the name of her young son. She supported the teachings of Monotheletism and sought to remove the followers of the recently deceased co-emperor, but opposition arose, both because of her supposedly incestuous marriage and also simply because she was a woman who sought to rule on her own. This opposition was centered especially within the Senate and the army in Asia Minor, and Martina tried to diffuse it by organizing the coronation of Herakleios Constantine's son, Konstans II, who was only 11 years old. This was not enough, however, and a revolt swept her and her son from power. Both were mutilated – the first case of judicial mutilation of an emperor or empress: Heraklonas' nose and Martina's tongue were slit, rendering them incapable of again holding imperial power, and they were exiled to the island of Rhodes (September 641).

The real name of Konstans II (641–68) was Flavios Herakleios, but he was crowned as Constantine and he used that name on his coins. The new emperor, probably because of his youth, was universally known by the nickname of Konstans. During the early part of his reign the Senate exercised unusual power, but by the time he was 18 or so he ruled in his own name and began to take the field himself in command of his troops.

Naturally the first concern of the emperor was the Arab threat, and Konstans devised an aggressive policy, urging his soldiers on with remembrance of the victories of Constantine, the first Christian emperor. Unfortunately for the emperor, the Arabs were increasingly better organized, and in Muawiya, the governor of Syria and then first Umayyad caliph (661–80), they had a leader who devised a carefully thought-out plan to conquer the Byzantine Empire. In 647 he began to make annual raids into Asia Minor. Muawiya was tolerant of Christians and he made use of Byzantine administrators and craftsmen, most notably to help with the construction of a fleet with which he sought to challenge Byzantine naval superiority and strike deep into the heart of the empire. Thus, Muawiya captured Cyprus (649), Rhodes (654), and Kos (654), challenging the Byzantines for control of the southern coast of Asia Minor. Interestingly enough, the Arabs were not able to hold Cyprus, and from this time until the middle of the tenth century Cyprus remained a "condominium" in which both Arabs and the Byzantine officials exercised authority and from which neither power was supposed to launch an attack on the other. This interesting arrangement was probably not unique in this period and indicates the ability of Byzantines and Arabs to interact in a less than hostile way.

Konstans II recognized the danger posed by Muawiya's success at sea, since it meant that the Byzantine heartland of Asia Minor was being caught in the "pincers" of a double threat from the Arabs: attacks by land and a surrounding movement to the south by sea. The emperor organized and personally commanded a fleet that set off to challenge the Arab navy, and the two powers met at the "Battle of the Masts" at Phoenix (modern Finike) in Lycia, off the southern coast of Asia Minor, in 655. The Arabs won a total victory and Konstans barely escaped with his life, disguising himself as an ordinary seaman.

Muawiya, however, was soon preoccupied by internal political events. The latter years of the caliphate of Uthman were marked by civil strife, and the caliph was murdered in 657. Uthman was succeeded by Ali, the nephew of the Prophet and husband of Fatima, Muhammad's daughter. Discontent continued, however, and Muawiya (who had been secretary of the Prophet) was one of Ali's leading opponents. As a result of this struggle Muawiya concluded a peace treaty with Konstans in 659, in which Byzantium was to pay a huge tribute.

Freed temporarily from the Arab threat, Konstans was able to turn his attention to pressing military considerations elsewhere. Indeed, the policy of Konstans II is one of the best indications that the Byzantines had never acknowledged the loss of Italy and the West; the emperor planned to move his residence to Syracuse in Sicily. In addition, taking advantage of the respite in the East (as early as 658), Konstans made a show of strength in "Sklavenia," as the Balkans were then known. This was the first action against the Slavs in 50 years, and shows that Byzantine force of arms, if properly organized and led, was capable of a reconquest of the Balkans. In addition, Konstans began a policy of moving Slavic prisoners to Asia Minor, a practice that was continued by many of his successors in the years to come. Konstans led his army through Greece, spending the winter of 662/3 in Athens. The imperial party moved on to Rome and finally to Syracuse, where the emperor took up residence. Konstans had many enemies, however, and had to face a number of rebellions. His fiscal policies led to considerable opposition in Italy, and his move to the West caused further discontent, especially when Muawiya secured the caliphate in 661 and was able to resume his attacks on Byzantine territory. Konstans was murdered in his bath in 668, the result of a palace coup.

In his religious policy Konstans attempted compromise, but he was unwilling to tolerate any opposition. His desire to strengthen Byzantine power in Italy required the acquiescence of the papacy, and this led to the removal of the *Ekthesis* of Herakleios. His policy was outlined in a statement the emperor signed in 648, called the *Typos*; this did not specifically condemn Monotheletism, but it ordered the removal of the *Ekthesis* from Hagia Sophia and essentially harked back to the *Henotikon* of Zeno, forbidding any discussion of the religious controversy. Of course, this did not solve the problem, and Pope Martin I quickly became involved in the controversy. Before becoming pope, Martin had been a papal emissary in Constantinople, where he supported Maximos the Confessor in his struggle against Monotheletism, and in 649 he called a council in Rome (the Lateran Council) that condemned the *Typos* and excommunicated the patriarch of Constantinople for his support of it. This resistance to imperial policy naturally infuriated Konstans, and the controversy quickly escalated. Konstans took the unusual step of ordering Olympios, the Exarch of Ravenna, to arrest the pope for treason. Olympios, however, came to an understanding with Martin and ultimately proclaimed himself as emperor. Konstans dispatched a new exarch to Rome, and in 653 he had the pope arrested and brought to Constantinople, where he was tried for treason. The pope tried to turn the trial into a forum for discussion of the *Typos*, but this was not allowed and he was condemned to death; the sentence was commuted, however, and Martin was exiled to Cherson, where he died in 655.

Maximos the Confessor supported the pope and condemned the actions of Konstans. As a result, he too was brought to Constantinople, condemned for treason in 655 and exiled, first to Thrace and later to Lazika in the Caucusus, where he died in 662. The opponents of imperial religious policy had been condemned, but they had not been silenced, and Maximos, in particular, continued to write widely in opposition to the intervention of the state in doctrinal matters. In the end, Konstans was able to enforce his will on the church, but Pope Martin and Maximos the Confessor were powerful spokesmen for the independence of the church in the face of what they considered tyrannical imperial behavior. Their example was to play a large role in a controversy that erupted half a century later.

Constantine IV (668–685)

After some initial hesitation Constantine IV, the son of Konstans II, succeeded to the throne. He had been crowned as co-emperor in 654, and he ruled at first with his younger brothers Herakleios and Tiberios. His first act was to go to Sicily to put down the revolt of Mezizios, one of the murderers of his father, but he soon had serious difficulties to deal with on the eastern frontier.

By 668 the dispute within the caliphate had ended, and Muawiya was in firm control. Beginning in 663, the Arabs invaded Asia Minor every year and ravaged it, but each autumn they had to return to their bases in Syria. Muawiya understood that as long as Constantinople remained an impregnable fortress the Arabs would not be able to secure their victories in Asia Minor, and he continued his policy of naval encirclement. In 670 his troops took Kyzikos, on the shores of the Sea of Marmora opposite Constantinople, and in 670 Smyrna. In 674 Muawiya initiated a great siege of Constantinople itself. The siege was based on initial Arab superiority at sea, since the Land Walls of the city were essentially impregnable. The siege dragged on for four years, but the tide finally turned when Byzantine ships sailed out of the Golden Horn and engaged the Arab ships with "Greek Fire" for the first time. This substance, the manufacture of which was a Byzantine state secret not precisely known even today, was shot through a "siphon" and ignited a supposedly unquenchable conflagration. Scholars have proposed various substances as its base, from gunpowder to a petroleum-based mixture; its effect was apparently terrifying and effective for the Byzantine defenders. Although Greek Fire could be used in a variety of circumstances, it was most commonly employed in naval encounters, shot from the decks of Byzantine ships onto the wooden hulls of their opponents.

In the end, the forces of Muawiya had to withdraw (678); although the Arabs were again to threaten Constantinople, this was the high-water mark of Arab power against Byzantium, and from this point on the Byzantines began to recover, certainly in part because of the slow reorganization of the state and the army that was taking place during this period. Muawiya realized that the immediate opportunity had been lost, and he signed a 30-year peace treaty on terms that were far more favorable to Byzantium than those agreed upon earlier in the century. Thus, in broad historical terms, the siege of Constantinople in 674–8 was of considerable importance, and some rank it as more significant than the Battle of Poitiers (or Tours) in 732, when the forces of Charles Martel defeated the Arabs of Spain. The Byzantine victory in 678 was the first significant defeat that the Arabs had experienced since their explosion onto the world scene 40 years earlier, and it has been seen by some as critical in the "defense" of Europe and European civilization. Such a view is largely out of historical fashion, and it is more common for historians to stress the strong interconnections between the Arabs and the Christian powers of early medieval Europe, but there is no question that the Byzantine victory at this point was significant in the survival of the empire itself.

Constantine IV also attempted further to stabilize the situation in the West. He signed a peace treaty with the Lombards, who had made headway in southern Italy, capturing several Byzantine strongholds. He was less successful in the Balkans, and he was forced to recognize the settlement of the Bulgars south of the Danube.

In religious affairs, Constantine followed the lead of his predecessors in attempting to put an end to the religious disputes. He summoned the sixth ecumenical council at Constantinople in 680 to deal with the lingering issue of Monotheletism. By this time, however, most of the Monophysite churches of the East had been lost to the empire, and there was little reason to pursue the seemingly futile quest for compromise. As a result the council decreed that, in keeping with the teachings of Chalcedon, Christ has two "wills" and two "energies" (although these were inseparably united). It condemned Monotheletism and anathematized those who had supported it, including one pope and several bishops of Constantinople; the memories of those who had opposed Monotheletism, including Maximos the Confessor, Sophronios of Jerusalem, and Pope Martin I, were all vindicated.

Box 7.6   *The Miracles of St. Artemios*

According to tradition, Artemios was an Arian imperial official in the fourth century, who persecuted pagans and Orthodox Christians. According to the church historian Philostorgios, he was executed by the emperor Julian the Apostate and his body was brought to Constantinople and deposited in the church of St. John Prodromos (the "Forerunner," usually known as the "Baptist" in the West). There the saint began to perform healing miracles and attracted many people – mostly men who had problems with their reproductive organs.

In the 660s an anonymous author composed a series of apparently eyewitness accounts of these miracles, which were probably read to the afflicted patients as they stayed in the church waiting for the saint to appear and heal them. These stories convey a sense of immediacy and show how the saints were thought to intervene to solve pressing problems of life and death, pain and suffering. They also show that the ancient practice of *incubation* continued in Byzantium. In pagan antiquity the patients slept in a special part of the sanctuary in preparation for the appearance of the god (usually Asklepios), who would heal them. Much the same took place at the church of the Forerunner in Constantinople in the seventh century.

Miracle 1: A certain chief physician, Anthimos by name, had a son about 20 years old whose testicles had become dangerously diseased so that he did not even have the strength to go to the latrines by himself. The father brought him on a litter to the church of the Forerunner where the much-revered relic of the holy and glorious Artemios now lies, and he did whatever all are accustomed to do who are similarly afflicted. Then one night the holy martyr appeared to him in a dream in the semblance of his father Anthimos and said to him: "Let me see what it is that you have." And Anthimos' son, after undressing himself, showed him; once he had done this, Artemios took hold of his testicles and squeezed them forcefully so that he awoke and cried out in pain, still in the grip of the frightening dream. Anxious and worried that the illness was growing worse and after touching the afflicted place, he found himself without pain and his testicles restored to health. (p. 79)

Miracle 7. A certain young man, Plato by name, confident in his youth and, as the young are fond of doing, making a contest over the calibre of his strength, engaged in a wager to lift up the stone of a wooddealer's scales and to set it on his shoulder. After the size of the wager had been set, he picked up the stone and, as he was struggling to set it on his shoulder, all his intestines ruptured in a hernia so that the spectators were astounded by the sight. Now some good men counseled him saying: "Do not entrust yourself to a doctor but go to St. John's in the Oxeia and approach St. Artemios and he himself will cure you. For every day he works miracles in these cases." So after being lifted up by some of them, he was transported by litter, as he was at risk over his life. While waiting a few days and suffering in unbearable pain, he saw St. Artemios in a dream who said to him: "And so, why are you so fond of wagers? See, you have plotted against both your soul and body." And he exhorted him never more to make a wager and, saying these things, he trod on his stomach. The contender awoke from sleep and was relieved of his pain along with his injury. Thanking God and the martyr for this turn of events, he departed for home rejoicing. Whoever had learned of his misfortune, seeing him restored to health, glorified God Who had sped His mercy upon him. (p. 91).

Virgil S. Crisafulli and John W. Nesbitt, *The Miracles of St. Artemios: A Collection of Miracle Stories by an Anonymous Author of Seventh-Century Byzantium* (Leiden, 1997).

Justinian II, First Reign (685–695)

Constantine IV died in 685 and was survived by his wife Anastasia and their two sons, Justinian and Herakleios. Justinian II was only about 16 years of age when his father died, but his elevation was apparently unquestioned. Despite his youth Justinian embarked on a broad and aggressive policy on a number of fronts. Militarily his armies were generally successful against the Arabs early in his reign, although Arab raids deep into Asia Minor forced him to pull back from Armenia and other areas, where he had been able to re-exert Byzantine power. These victories allowed Justinian to campaign with some success in the Balkans, and he continued the policy of population exchange, settling Slavs in Asia Minor and eastern peoples in the Balkans.

Likewise, following the footsteps of his father in religious affairs, he confirmed the condemnation of Monotheletism. In 691–2 he called the Quinisextum Council (Council in Trullo), held in the imperial palace in Constantinople. This council, unlike those that had immediately preceded it, was not primarily concerned with theological controversy, but with the everyday affairs of morality and the governing of the church. The decrees of this council survive and they provide an important window into life in this period, not just for the church and members of the clergy, but also for ordinary laypeople.

Justinian II was extremely pious and he carried out many notable building and iconographic programs, including construction of the Triklinos in the Imperial Palace. Especially significant was Justinian's decision to use a portrait of Christ as the main element on Byzantine gold coins. Previous to this, for one reason or another, the Byzantines had been hesitant to place the figure of Christ directly on the coins, but Justinian reversed this policy and relegated his

Figure 7.2   Gold coin of Justinian II, first reign (692–5). The coin is the first to depict Christ as the main image. The legend on the obverse (front) of the coin reads (in Latin): "Jesus Christ, King of those who rule," while on the reverse "Lord Justinian, the servant of Christ." Christ is depicted with long hair and beard, a representation that became standard in later centuries. Justinian is shown wearing a jeweled garment called a *loros* and he is holding a long cross. Courtesy of the Arthur M. Sackler Museum, Harvard University Art Museums, Bequest of Thomas Whittemore. © President and Fellows of Harvard College

own portrait to the reverse of the coin, a clear indication of the triumph of the Eusebian ideal of the Byzantine monarchy: Christ was the real ruler, while the emperor was his vice-regent and confidant.

Weak Emperors and Near Anarchy (695–717)

Despite Justinian II's success, opposition began to mount, especially to his stringent taxation policies. In 695 a revolt broke out, led by the emperor's most successful general, Leontios, an Isaurian who had fallen out of Justinian's favor. The revolt succeeded and Leontios became emperor. Justinian was mutilated by having his nose cut off; from this time he was known as "Rhinotmetos" ("Slit-nose") and he may have worn a gold "replacement" to hide his disfigurement. The former emperor was exiled to Cherson, on the northern shore of the Black Sea.

Leontios (695–8) ruled only briefly, his reign marked most notably by an outbreak of plague. Leontios dispatched the naval commander Apsimar to North Africa in an attempt to recover that area from the Arabs. The endeavor failed but Apsimar was proclaimed as emperor, and he captured Constantinople with the aid of the Green Faction, and was proclaimed emperor with the name Tiberios II (698–705). Tiberios was active in promoting the defense of the empire, repairing the sea walls of Constantinople, and he intervened militarily in Cyprus and Syria.

Justinian II, however, while exiled in Cherson, had allied himself with the khan of the Khazars, whose sister he married. The Khazars had been established in the Caucasus and north of the Black Sea at least since the time of Herakleios, and they were natural allies of the Byzantines against the Persians and, later, against the Arabs. In addition, they provided the Byzantines with important assistance in controlling the western end of the "steppe corridor," leading from Central Asia to the Danube frontier, always a key area in Byzantine foreign policy.

With the Khazars' help Justinian returned to Constantinople and again seized the throne (705–11). Justinian II was one of only a very few Byzantine rulers to regain the throne, and the only emperor who reigned after having been mutilated. Justinian had his wife Theodora crowned as empress, the first foreign-born woman to hold that honor. During his second reign Justinian II picked up where he had left off, re-establishing a coinage decorated with the bust of Christ and promoting an ambitious foreign policy involving the Lombards, the papacy, and the Bulgars in the West, while the Arabs under Maslama invaded Asia Minor. Justinian dispatched a fleet against Cherson, but the troops revolted and proclaimed their commander Bardanes as emperor with the name Philippikos. Aided by the Khazars, Philippikos captured Constantinople in 711 and Justinian II fled the city.

Surprisingly enough, Philippikos again raised the issue of Monotheletism and called a church council that reversed the decisions recently taken in this regard. Philippikos' reign was militarily unsuccessful and the Arabs had a

Figure 7.3   Gold coin of Justinian II, second reign (705–11). The figure of Christ disappeared from the coinage after Justinian II's overthrow and mutiliatioin in 692. When he recovered the throne in 705, however, the bust of Christ returned to the obverse of the gold coinage. This time Christ was pictured in a very different way: he is young, beardless, and with short curly hair. The reverse shows Justinian along with his young son Tiberios, each of whom is holding onto a long cross. Courtesy of the Arthur M. Sackler Museum, Harvard University Art Museums, Bequest of Thomas Whittemore. © President and Fellows of Harvard College

series of striking victories. Probably for this reason, there was another military revolt and in 713 Philippikos was deposed and blinded.

The court official Artemios was proclaimed emperor as Anastasios II (713–15). He immediately reversed the religious policy of his predecessor, reinstated the councils that Philippikos had condemned, and in 715 made Germanos Patriarch of Constantinople; Germanos, who was an important theologian and author of religious poetry, would play a significant role in the controversies that were soon to break out. Anastasios correctly believed that the Arabs were planning another great attack on Constantinople, and he prepared the city for the siege by strengthening the walls and building up a strong supply of provisions. Nevertheless, yet another military revolt spelled the end of Anastasios II and brought Theodosios III to the throne (715–17). The new emperor may well have been the son of Tiberios II, spared by Justinian II upon his return to power in 705. Theodosios was also aware of the imminent Arab danger, and he signed an alliance with the Bulgar khan Tervel, probably to secure his rear in the event of an Arab siege. Yet another military revolt broke out, however, and with the rise of Leo III, Theodosios abdicated and became a monk.

The Theme System and Administrative Reorganization

During the course of the seventh century important changes took place in the administrative structure of the Byzantine Empire. Essentially these involved the replacement of the system of many small provinces, characteristic of the period since the time of Diocletian, with a number of larger units called *themes*

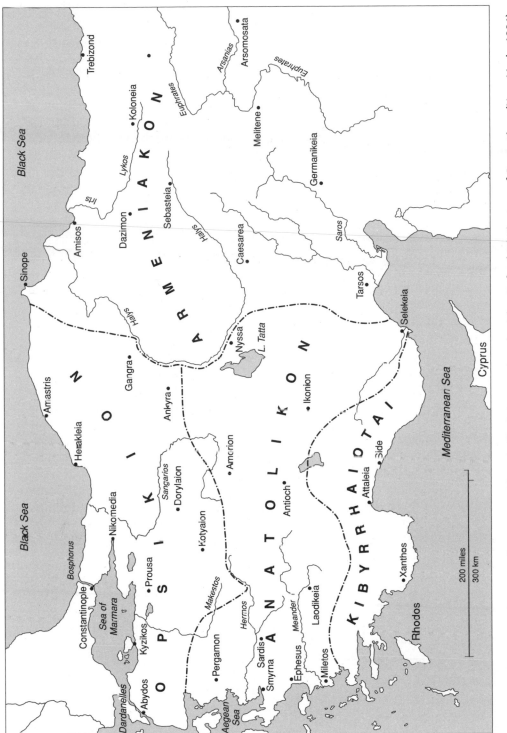

Map 7.2 *Themes in the seventh century. After A. Kazhdan et al., eds.,* The Oxford Dictionary of Byzantium *(New York, 1991), p. 2034*

(themata). By the latter part of the seventh century there were apparently four themes in Asia Minor: the Opsikion, Anatolikon, Armeniakon, and (probably) Thrakesion. It is clear that the themes were essentially military zones, since they were governed by a *strategos*, or general, who had both military and civilian power, and the names of the earliest themes also seem to have been derived from known military units.

There has been considerable disagreement about the date of the creation of the theme system, what it included, and the nature of its implementation. As mentioned above, some scholars, such as George Ostrogorsky, thought that the system had been created as an act of policy by Herakleios, but most think it developed later and more gradually, probably more as a natural response to military collapse in the face of the Arab successes than as a deliberate imperial decision.

The commanders of the themes clearly had considerable power and from the late seventh century onward they frequently rose in revolt against the reigning emperor, so from that perspective the theme system created problems for the empire. On the other hand, the power of the *strategos* and his ability to command his army without waiting for orders from Constantinople were ideal responses to the raids and campaigns of the Arabs in Asia Minor at that time. Over time the larger themes tended to be subdivided into small territories, and themes were organized in newly reconquered territories, first in Greece (the theme of Hellas) and then in more remote areas of the empire.

Ostrogorsky and some others have also connected the rise of the theme system with the institution of the *stratiotika ktemata* (the "soldiers' lands"). In this system the state granted lands that had been abandoned (presumably vacated by their aristocratic owners at the time of the Arab raids in Asia Minor) to soldiers who agreed to arm themselves, provide horses for combat, and appear for military service. Although this system may seem to resemble the western institution of feudalism, it is actually quite different, in part because the state still maintained the right to govern all its territory as a political entity and in part because the farmer/soldiers were not a semi-independent nobility, but simply soldiers who served the empire in return for the use of state-owned land. Ostrogorsky also connected the *stratiotika ktemata* with the villages of independent farmers that he saw as the backbone of Byzantine society and economy from the seventh century onward. Indeed, Ostrogorsky saw the crises of the period, including the Arabic and Slavic "invasions," as an essentially positive force, wiping away virtually all trace of large-scale aristocratic land ownership and paving the way for a direct alliance between the emperors and the peasants. Although many of the details of Ostrogorsky's reconstruction are probably not valid, the basic view of a countryside populated by independent farmers who owned their own land seems correct.

The best evidence for these villages is the so-called *Farmer's Law*, which was probably issued in the later seventh or early eighth century, perhaps even under Justinian II. This law focuses mainly on cattle-raising and the production of various kinds of crops and it makes no mention of large estates, but rather seems to focus on villages of farmers who own their own land and hold a small portion of land in common for the community as a whole.

The emergence of the theme system also meant some changes in the system of administration at the very highest level, in large part because there was no longer any need for the praetorian prefect to coordinate activities among the various provinces; nor was there any longer a place for the *magistri militum* or the other highly placed military commanders of an earlier period. To be sure, from the seventh century onward there often was a commander who, in fact, commanded the main field army when the emperor did not take the field himself, but the *strategoi* of the various *themata* (especially in the early years) commonly served as the main military advisers of the emperor.

Within the central bureaucracy, the major tasks of government fell to the accountants and secretaries who had previously served the praetorian prefects, the so-called *logothetes*. The *logothetes* served at the will of the emperor, but a certain hierarchy and division of authority tended to develop:

> The logothete of military affairs (*logothetes tou stratiotikou*) was in charge of spending for military matters, including armaments and supplies.
> The logothete of the general account (*logothetes tou genikou*) was responsible for most of the taxes of the empire, including the land tax.
> The logothete of the dromos (*logothetes tou dromou*) was originally in charge of the public post, including the dispatch and receipt of imperial orders; in time he took on the task of protection of the emperor, imperial ceremony, and, most importantly, the overall management of diplomatic missions and foreign affairs. By the twelfth century the logothete of the dromos was commonly the most important adviser of the emperor.

Aside from these major *logothetes* there were many other officials in the central bureaucracy, the heads of relatively small departments responsible for the various tasks and accounts required by the state. The changes in the bureaucracy at this time, just like those in the military, resulted in a significant downsizing and decentralization of the administration, although of course the emperor remained at the center of everything that had to do with the state. This did not mean that governmental decision-making was carried out at the provincial level, but rather that the diminished size of the state, and its inability to carry out everything that had been done in an earlier period, meant that the government simply was not as complex as it had been in the fourth to sixth centuries.

FURTHER READING

P. Crone, *Meccan Trade and the Rise of Islam*. Oxford, 1987.
P. Crone and M. Cook, *Hagarism: The Making of the Islamic World*. Cambridge, 1997.
Florin Curta, *The Making of the Slavs: History and Archaeology of the Lower Danube Region, ca. 50–700*. Cambridge, 2001.

W. E. Kaegi, Jr., *Byzantium and the Early Islamic Conquests*. Cambridge, 1992.

W. E. Kaegi, Jr., *Heraclius. Emperor of Byzantium*. Cambridge, 2003.

H. Kennedy, *The Prophet and the Age of the Caliphates: The Islamic Near East from the Sixth to the Eleventh Century*. London, 1986.

P. Pentz, *The Invisible Conquest: The Ontogenesis of Sixth and Seventh Century Syria*. Copenhagen, 1992.

Michael Whitby, *The Emperor Maurice and his Historian*. Oxford, 1988.

Mark Whittow, *The Making of Byzantium, 600–1025*. Berkeley and Los Angeles, 1996.

8

The Isaurian Dynasty and Iconoclasm

250	500	750	1000	1250	1500

717	Leo III emperor
717–718	Arab siege of Constantinople
726	Beginning of Iconoclasm
787	First restoration of ikons
800	Coronation of Charlemagne

Leo III (717–741)

Leo III, like Herakleios, intervened in Byzantine politics at a decisive moment, and he set the state on a sound basis, militarily and politically. His first problem was an Arab siege of Constantinople, which began almost immediately after he seized the throne. After withstanding the siege, Leo began to carry the war to the Arab armies and he succeeded, by the end of his reign, in freeing western Asia Minor from Arab raids. In domestic matters he is best known for his codification of law, the *Ekloga*, and his policy of Iconoclasm. The investigation of the latter is particularly difficult because the Iconophile sources are universal in their condemnation of the emperor, and there are virtually no extant Iconclast sources.

Leo's family had come from Syria and was settled in Thrace as part of Justinian II's policy of population transfers. The appellation "Isaurian" for Leo and his dynasty is thus probably a misnomer. Leo had come to the attention of Justinian II when he helped the emperor regain his throne in 705, and he rose

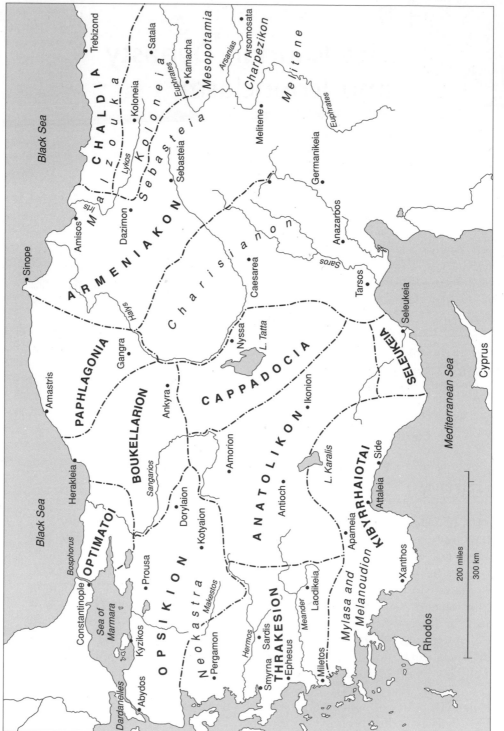

Map 8.1 *Themes in Asia Minor after the seventh century. After A. Kazhdan et al., eds., The Oxford Dictionary of Byzantium* (New York, 1991), p. 2035

to prominence in the army. He became *strategos* of the Anatolikon *theme* under Anastasios II, and during the reign of Theodosios III Leo allied with Ardavasdos, *strategos* of Armeniakon, and seized the throne in 717. He found the capital in a situation of some distress after 30 years of political instability.

Because of the confusion in Constantinople since the death of Constantine IV, the Arabs had made considerable headway in Asia Minor, and the Arab general Maslama (brother of the caliphs Walid, Sulayman, and Yazid [705–24]) planned another direct attack on the capital. The siege of Constantinople began in August of 717, supported by Sulayman's navy. Leo won a victory in Asia Minor and attacked the Arabs from the rear, while the Bulgars (under Tervel) attacked from the west, and Greek Fire again did its work on the Arab fleet. As a result, Maslama withdrew in August of 718 after absorbing heavy losses.

The *theme* system was now fully operational and it provided considerable strength in the face of continued Arab raids. Thus, Leo won signal victories at Nicaea in 726 and Akroinon in 740, so that by the end of his reign western Asia Minor was relatively secure against Arab incursions. In part, Leo's successes against the Arabs were the result of his alliance with the Khazars. The Khazars, who lived north of the Black Sea, could attack the Arabs from the rear, and they had been involved in Byzantine policy at least since the marriage of Justinian II to the khan's daughter. Leo cemented his own alliance with the Khazars by marrying his son Constantine to a Khazar princess.

Just like his predecessors, Leo had to face several revolts, most of them led by *theme* commanders. Leo understood the problems with this system, since he had himself come to power in this way, and he responded by dividing up several of the larger *theme*s into smaller entities, thereby diminishing the power of any individual *theme* commander.

Leo was a careful administrator and an autocrat. Both of these characteristics are shown in the *Ekloga*, a legal codification, issued probably in 726 (or possibly 741). According to the preface of the text, God had entrusted the emperor with the promotion of justice throughout the world, and the new code was part of the emperor's attempt to promote just that. In his view, the current codifications of law were confusing and largely incomprehensible (in part because they were contradictory and still largely in Latin). Judges and lawyers, not only (according to the *Ekloga*) in the provinces, but also in the "God-protected city" (Constantinople) were ignorant of what the law said. The *Ekloga* was a practical handbook designed for everyday use, rather than a treatise that provided a theoretical base for the law. It restricted the right of divorce and provided a long list of sexual crimes. The *Ekloga* also introduced a new system of punishment, including judicial mutilation, but practically did away with capital punishment.

Ikons and the Theory of Ikons

As we have seen, early Christian art had largely avoided the depiction of Christ and the saints, confining itself instead to symbolic representations, probably because of the Mosaic prohibition of worshiping idols. Slowly, however, and especially after the conversion of Constantine, religious pictures began to be employed. Not all Christians accepted these depictions, and, as mentioned earlier, Eusebios of Caesarea was one of those who apparently opposed the new trend.

Box 8.1   *The Theory of Ikons*

John of Damascus (ca. 675–ca. 753) was an Arab Christian, many of whose family worked in the financial administration of the Ummayad caliphate. He was an important Byzantine theologian and wrote a large number of synthetic works in Greek. He was a staunch opponent of Iconoclasm and because he lived outside the Byzantine Empire he was able to express that opposition openly. His works provide the clearest explanation of the Byzantine views on ikons and their place in Christian worship.

In his book, *On Images*, written apparently in 730, right at the beginning of the Iconoclastic controversy, he begins with a consideration of how ikons can be venerated, even though the Second Commandment clearly forbade the worship of "graven images":

> You see that He forbids image-making on account of idolatry, and that it is impossible to make an image of the immeasurable, uncircumscribed, invisible God. You have not seen the likeness of Him, the Scripture says, and this was St Paul's testimony as he stood in the midst of the Areopagus: "Being, therefore, the offspring of God, we must not suppose the divinity to be like unto gold, or silver, or stone, the graving of art, and device of man." (Acts 17.29)
>
> These injunctions were given to the Jews on account of their proneness to idolatry. Now we, on the contrary, are no longer in leading strings. Speaking theologically, it is given to us to avoid superstitious error, to be with God in the knowledge of the truth, to worship God alone, to enjoy the fulness of His knowledge. We have passed the stage of infancy, and reached the perfection of manhood. We receive our habit of mind from God, and know what may be imaged and what may not. The Scripture says, "You have not seen the likeness of Him." (Ex. 33.20) What wisdom in the law-giver. How depict the invisible? How picture the inconceivable? How give expression to the limitless, the immeasurable, the invisible? How give a form to immensity? How paint immortality? How localise mystery? It is clear that when you contemplate God, who is a pure spirit, becoming man for your sake, you will be able to clothe Him with the human form. When the Invisible One becomes visible to flesh, you may then draw a likeness of His form. When He who is a pure spirit, without form or limit, immeasurable in the boundlessness of His own nature, existing as God, takes upon Himself the form of a servant in substance and in stature, and a body of flesh, then you may draw His likeness, and show it to anyone willing to contemplate it. (pp. 7–9)

Later he arrives at the task of discussing the relationship between the image and the original:

> An image is a likeness of the original with a certain difference, for it is not an exact reproduction of the original. Thus, the Son is the living, substantial, unchangeable Image of the invisible God (Col. 1.15), bearing in Himself the whole Father, being in all things equal to Him, differing only in being begotten by the Father, who is the Begetter; the Son is begotten. The Father does not proceed from the Son, but the Son from the Father. It is through the Son, though not after Him, that He is what He is, the Father who generates. In God, too, there are representations and images of His future acts, that is to say, His counsel from all eternity, which is ever unchangeable. That which is divine is immutable; there is no change in Him, nor shadow of change. (James 1.17) (p. 10)

John then went on to say that there are different forms of worship. The highest form, which he describes with the Greek term *latreia*, is reserved for God and only for God. There are, in his view, other, somewhat "lesser" forms of worship, which we might call "veneration" or "religious respect," and these are appropriate for objects such as the Jewish Ark of the Covenant and the Temple in Jerusalem. He goes on, then, to summarize the ways in which he thinks ikons can be used and their appropriateness in Christian worship:

> Of old, God the incorporeal and uncircumscribed was never depicted. Now, however, when God is seen clothed in flesh, and conversing with men, (Bar. 3.38) I make an image of the God whom I see. I do not worship matter, I worship the God of matter, who became matter for my sake, and deigned to inhabit matter, who worked out my salvation through matter. I will not cease from honouring that matter which works my salvation. I venerate it, though not as God. How could God be born out of lifeless things? And if God's body is God by union (*kath' ypostasin*), it is immutable. The nature of God remains the same as before, the flesh created in time is quickened by a logical and reasoning soul. I honour all matter besides, and venerate it. Through it, filled, as it were, with a divine power and grace, my salvation has come to me. Was not the thrice happy and thrice blessed wood of the Cross matter? Was not the sacred and holy mountain of Calvary matter? What of the life-giving rock, the Holy Sepulchre, the source of our resurrection: was it not matter? Is not the most holy book of the Gospels matter? Is not the blessed table matter which gives us the Bread of Life? Are not the gold and silver matter, out of which crosses and altar-plate and chalices are made? And before all these things, is not the body and blood of our Lord matter? Either do away with the veneration and worship due to all these things, or submit to the tradition of the Church in the worship of images, honouring God and His friends, and following in this the grace of the Holy Spirit. Do not despise matter, for it is not despicable. Nothing is that which God has made. This is the Manichean heresy. That alone is despicable

which does not come from God, but is our own invention, the spontaneous choice of will to disregard the natural law, – that is to say, sin. If, therefore, you dishonour and give up images, because they are produced by matter, consider what the Scripture says: And the Lord spoke to Moses, saying, "Behold I have called by name Beseleel, the son of Uri, the son of Hur, of the tribe of Juda. And I have filled him with the spirit of God, with wisdom and understanding, and knowledge in all manner of work. To devise whatsoever may be artificially made of gold, and silver, and brass, of marble and precious stones, and variety of wood. And I have given him for his companion, Ooliab, the son of Achisamech, of the tribe of Dan. And I have put wisdom in the heart of every skilful man, that they may make all things which I have commanded thee." (Ex. 31.1–6) And again: "Moses said to all the assembly of the children of Israel: This is the word the Lord hath commanded, saying: Set aside with you first fruits to the Lord. Let every one that is willing and hath a ready heart, offer them to the Lord, gold, and silver, and brass, violet, and purple, and scarlet twice dyed, and fine linen, goat's hair, and ram's skins died red and violet, coloured skins, selim-wood, and oil to maintain lights and to make ointment, and most sweet incense, onyx stones, and precious stones for the adorning of the ephod and the rational. Whosoever of you is wise, let him come, and make that which the Lord hath commanded." (Ex. 35.4–10) See you here the glorification of matter which you make inglorious. What is more insignificant than goat's hair or colours? Are not scarlet and purple and hyacinth colours? Now, consider the handiwork of man becoming the likeness of the cherubim. How, then, can you make the law a pretence for giving up what it orders? If you invoke it against images, you should keep the Sabbath, and practise circumcision. It is certain that "if you observe the law, Christ will not profit you. You who are justified in the law, you are fallen from grace." (Gal. 5.2–4) Israel of old did not see God, but "we see the Lord's glory face to face." (II Cor. 3.18)

We proclaim Him also by our senses on all sides, and we sanctify the noblest sense, which is that of sight. The image is a memorial, just what words are to a listening ear. What a book is to the literate, that an image is to the illiterate. The image speaks to the sight as words to the ear; it brings us understanding. Hence God ordered the ark to be made of imperishable wood, and to be gilded outside and in, and the tablets to be put in it, and the staff and the golden urn containing the manna, for a remembrance of the past and a type of the future. Who can say these were not images and far-sounding heralds? And they did not hang on the walls of the tabernacle; but in sight of all the people who looked towards them, they were brought forward for the worship and adoration of God, who made use of them. It is evident that they were not worshipped for themselves, but that the people were led through them to remember past signs, and to worship the God of wonders. They were images to serve as recollections, not divine, but leading to divine things by divine power. (pp. 15–19)

From St. John Damascene, *On Holy Images*, trans. Mary H. Allies (London, 1898).

Ikons (*eikones*, "images") were physical depictions of God and the saints, normally two-dimensional pictures, often painted on wood, that were used for devotional purposes. Ikons seem to have originated in the same tradition as that of the cults of the saints and relics; that is, they were not primarily seen as art but as powerful religious "tools" that could help mankind span the enormous gap between the human and the divine.

Despite some misgivings, the use of ikons continued to grow and the decoration of many surviving churches of the fifth and sixth centuries shows that, alongside the continued use of symbols and symbolic representations of Christ (e.g., Christ as a lamb, the use of the Christogram [the Chi-Rho]), churches were commonly decorated with lifelike depictions of Christ, the Virgin Mary, and the saints. There is reason to believe that in the sixth century, especially in the second half, the use of ikons became more widespread, as personal devotion to them increased and as political and religious leaders more and more identified themselves with ikons and used them to help increase their own power. A mark of this was when the Quinisext Council (the Council in Trullo) in 691/2 decreed that Christ should not be depicted as a symbol but rather "in his human form." Also significant was Justinian II's representation of Christ as the main image on Byzantine coins, an indication that the emperor and undoubtedly many of his subjects regarded such images as appropriate and important in maintaining the well-being of the empire.

Ikons were also a personal expression of devotion that was particularly important in the difficult age when many of the institutions of the time were apparently falling apart. Thus, an individual or a family might have an ikon of its own, to which persons might be especially devoted. From an early time ikons were also seen as miraculous and they "localized" the power of God, the Virgin, or an individual saint. Thus, an ikon brought the presence of divine power directly to the individual worshipers, regardless of where they were, and allowed them to "speak" directly to the divine and seek aid for all their needs. Not surprisingly, the ikons, as localized manifestations of the divine, frequently were thought to honor the requests of the faithful, and miracles were often attested and widely praised.

Although the veneration of ikons was probably something that originated in popular devotion and had strong connections with the cult of the saints, it was also supported by significant aspects of the Byzantine intellectual tradition. We have already seen how Neoplatonism was perhaps the dominant philosophical tradition in the early Byzantine period. Neoplatonism, as developed and Christianized, developed a Christian view of images that maintained a close relationship between the prototype (in this case, Christ or the saint depicted) and the image represented in the ikon. This was something very important to the broader Byzantine view of reality, which saw the world "here and now" as an imperfect reflection of the divine perfection of the Kingdom of Heaven, just as the emperor was seen as an imperfect reflection of God, and the empire was a copy of God's everlasting Kingdom. Thus, in terms of the sacred ikon, the prototype and the image were "the same" in significant ways; a prayer or veneration offered to the ikon was, in fact, offered to the original, and the ikon could also "act" on behalf of Christ or the saint, as depicted in the image. These ideas were put forth, refined, and delineated by theologians such as John of Damascus.

In terms of style, the ikons clearly were derived from a variety of traditions. As one might imagine in an image designed for religious use (rather than as a work of art), the figure in an ikon is normally represented frontally, with large, staring eyes that usually look right at the believer. Commonly there was little or no background detail, since the image is designed to facilitate communication between the divine and the worldly spheres, and there was relatively little concern for realism. These artistic conventions most resembled those of Syria and Egypt, especially the so-called Fayum portraits, paintings from Hellenistic and Roman Egypt depicting the dead on their caskets. One may argue that the artistic tradition represented in Byzantine ikons is essentially that of the Hellenistic Near East, but it is clear that the more "realistic" tradition of the Greco-Roman world is also represented, especially in some of the early ikons, probably from Constantinople, now in the Monastery of St. Catherine on Mount Sinai. Ikons might be in any medium, but most were in encaustic technique, painted on wooden panels.

The Outbreak of Iconoclasm

As mentioned above, some people had always been opposed to the production and veneration of ikons, largely because they saw them as a violation of the Mosaic commandment against the making of "graven images." This opposition, however, had never previously formed a movement of any kind, and the emperors had not been involved in the issue in a significant way, except perhaps when Justinian II put the image of Christ on coins and the Quinisext Council forbade the symbolic representation of Christ.

All this changed under Leo III. According to the monk Theophanes, who was very hostile to Iconoclasm (and hence to Leo III and his successors), Leo "began speaking against ikons" in 726 and ultimately ordered that the great ikon of Christ be removed from the Chalke Gate of the palace. This aroused considerable opposition, both in Constantinople and the western provinces. As a result, in 730 Leo summoned a meeting of the imperial council of his advisers (the *silention*) and this declared the veneration of ikons to be illegal and ordered their confiscation. As might be expected, this policy met with considerable opposition. The patriarch Germanos expressed his support of ikons and he was deposed, while the governor of the *theme* of Hellas used the occasion to mount a revolt, which was apparently easily put down. The papacy had always been strongly in favor of the veneration of images, so Leo's policies led to a schism between the two churches. The emperor's officials apparently removed figural decoration from churches and other public places, but there

Figure 8.1 Iconoclasts at work. This miniature from the so-called Khludov Psalter in the State Historical Museum, Moscow, depicts the Iconoclasts removing the sacred images from various places in Constantinople. By permission of the State Historical Museum, Moscow

seems to have been no real persecution of Iconophiles, as those who supported the veneration of ikons may be called.

Modern historians have provided many different explanations for the outbreak of "official" Iconoclasm under Leo III and these have varied significantly. Theophanes (who wrote in the early ninth century) says that Leo's Iconoclastic policy was a result of influence from Jews and Arabs. Even though both Judaism and Islam were both "Iconoclastic" in sentiment, there seems to be no reason to believe that the examples of these religions were the ultimate cause of Byzantine Iconoclasm. Theophanes, to be sure, creates a confusing story, connecting Leo's policy with an Arab vizier and a Jewish wizard, who were supposed to have had an influence on the emperor. Most scholars today doubt any such influence except in the most general sense, even though it seems as though this outbreak of official Iconoclasm followed shortly after the caliph Yazid's attempt to remove ikons in Christian churches under the control of the caliphate.

Some historians have seen the Iconoclastic Controversy as a struggle between the eastern and western parts of the empire, with the East supporting Iconoclasm and the West the veneration of ikons; alternatively, the controversy has been viewed as a struggle between the "oriental" and the "western" (or Greek) elements in Byzantine civilization, with Iconoclasm an expression of the eastern or even "Semitic" tradition and the veneration of ikons an expression of the Greek tradition of representational art. Another explanation provided by modern historians is that Leo used Iconoclasm as an attack on monasteries, since monks were the most ardent supporters of ikons, but this is hardly convincing. Yet another view is that Iconoclasm was simply a result of the emperor's autocratic tendency, since the struggle could be seen as one between the emperor and the ikon, as God's representative on earth. This latter interpretation has perhaps some validity since there is considerable evidence of Leo's strong-minded rule and, like many of the emperors before him, he certainly thought that he could decide matters of belief on his own.

Despite all these theories, the most convincing explanation for Leo's action seems to be his own personal belief. As we have said, many Christians (perhaps primarily in the East) regarded the veneration of ikons as a serious sin, and they presumably felt that God was surely punishing the empire for the growth of this practice over the past few centuries. Thus, in this view, the failure of Byzantium to stem the Arab tide was God's response to the idolatry of Christians who venerated images and placed them in churches and in prominent public places throughout the empire. Leo, it will be remembered, had reigned for nearly ten years before he began to speak openly against the ikons and, when he decided to take action, he apparently did not act directly against the individuals who venerated them, but rather against the public display of ikons – something which might have been taken to displease God more than anything else. Further, Theophanes provides us with information that may help to explain why Leo decided to act precisely when he did. Thus, Theophanes tells us that in the year prior to Leo's first public attack on ikons the empire was struck by the "wrath of God": the island of Thera (in the middle of the Aegean Sea) was wracked by a terrible volcanic eruption that threw out huge flames and floating pumice that was found as far away as Macedonia. We can never be sure, of course, but such an obvious indication of God's anger might easily suggest that something had to be done. If Leo already was an Iconoclast, he may well have been moved to act publicly by this event, and his actions seem well in accord with this interpretation. It is true that some bishops of Asia Minor were already advocating actions to stop the veneration of ikons, and they may well have provided the impetus and the spiritual and theological support for Leo's policies. Nonetheless, the evidence does not suggest that Leo III was motivated by anything other than his own belief that the veneration of ikons was wrong and that, as emperor, he had a responsibility to God and to his subjects to insist on correct religious practice. His own tendency toward autocracy made him act without regard to any opposition and the result was real turmoil within the empire, especially because

Box 8.2 *The* Ekloga *and Byzantine Society of the Eighth Century*

The *Ekloga* of Leo III is a most interesting document because it reveals much of the personality of the emperor and the changes that had been taking place in society since the days of Constantine I. This law code was probably issued in 726 (although possibly in 741), the same year as the beginning of the Iconoclastic Controversy, and it demonstrates the emperor's firm belief that he was responsible, before God, for the good and proper governance of the Roman (Byzantine) Empire.

The provisions of the text are remarkably clear and easy to understand – making it easier for governors in provincial areas to pronounce judgment and assign punishment. The laws deal mainly with day-to-day issues of landowning and personal relations, but large sections reflect the influence that the church and Christian morality had on the society of the time.

One aspect of the code that has attracted considerable attention is the use of mutilation – the cutting off of body parts, including the nose – as a penalty. Some have seen in this the influence of "oriental" (i.e., Near Eastern) practices, and this may be the case, but others have pointed to the preface of the code, which speaks of its "humanization," and point out that the penalty for most of the same crimes in earlier Roman law would have been death. In fact, our understanding of the impact of the *Ekloga* depends to a large degree on our own point of view: on the one hand, the *Ekloga* is harsh and brutal in its punishments, but on the other it allowed people to understand exactly where they stood under the law – arguably for the first time in the history of western civilization (since virtually all earlier systems had been written in ways that would have been essentially unintelligible to most people), and – as mentioned before – it did provide women with protections that they had not enjoyed in previous legislation.

Here are some of the provisions concerning marriage:

> The marriage of Christians, man and woman, who have reached years of discretion, that is for a man at fifteen and for a woman at thirteen years of age, both being desirous and having obtained the consent of their parents, shall be contracted either by deed or by parole [word of honor].
>
> A written marriage contract shall be based upon a written agreement providing the wife's marriage portion; and it shall be made before three credible witnesses according to the new decrees auspiciously prescribed by us. The man on his part agreeing by it continually to protect and preserve undiminished the wife's marriage portion, and also such additions as he may naturally make thereto in augmentation thereof; and it shall be recorded in the agreement made on that in case there are no children, one-fourth part thereof shall be secured in settlement.
>
> If the wife happens to predecease the husband and there are no children of the marriage, the husband shall receive only one-fourth part of the wife's

portion for himself, and the remainder thereof shall be given to the beneficiaries named in the wife's will or, if she be intestate, to the next of kin. If the husband predeceases the wife, and there are no children of the marriage, then all the wife's portion shall revert to her, and so much of her husband's estate as shall be equal to a fourth part of his portion shall also inure to her as her own, and the remainder of his estate shall revert either to his beneficiaries or, if he be intestate, to his next of kin.

As mentioned, the *Ekloga* is probably best known for the severity and brutality of its punishments. Below are some of the regulations for sexual crime. Notice that what is here translated as having one's "nose slit," actually means having the nose cut off – a particularly horrifying and disfiguring punishment.

A married man who commits adultery shall by way of' correction be flogged with twelve lashes; and whether rich or poor he shall pay a fine.

An unmarried man who commits fornication shall be flogged with six lashes.

A person who has carnal knowledge of a nun shall, upon the footing that he is debauching the Church of God, have his nose slit, because he committed wicked adultery with her who belonged to the Church; and she on her side must take heed lest similar punishment be reserved to her.

Anyone who, intending to take in marriage a woman who is his goddaughter in Salvation-bringing baptism, has carnal knowledge of her without marrying her, and being found guilty of the offence shall, after being exiled, be condemned to the same punishment meted out for other adultery, that is to say, both the man and the woman shall have their noses slit.

The husband who is cognizant of, and condones, his wife's adultery shall be flogged and exiled, and the adulterer and the adulteress shall have their noses slit.

From *A Manual of Roman Law: The* Ecloga, trans. E. Freshfield (Cambridge, 1926), pp. 72–4, 108–12. Reprinted in Deno Geanokoplos, *Byzantium* (Chicago, 1984), pp. 266–7, 278.

what he did recalled the worst experience of Christians in which past emperors had tried to impose their own religious views on the empire without consideration of the wishes of the broader public.

Constantine V (741–775)

Under Leo III's son and successor, the Isaurian dynasty reached the height of its power, and Iconoclast policy hardened into outright persecution of the Iconophiles (or Iconodoules, as they are sometimes called).

Constantine V is one of the most interesting of all Byzantine emperors. His rule was generally successful and the emperor was intelligent and determined;

Figure 8.2 Gold coin of Constantine V and Leo IV. The obverse of this coin shows Leo III, the reverse Constantine V with his son Leo IV. The coin was designed to stress the dynastic aspect of political power at this time and to harken back to the founder of the dynasty, Leo III. Thus, the legend of the reverse reads: "Constantine and Leo the Younger," the latter epithet designed to connect the grandson (Leo IV) with his grandfather (Leo III). The appearance of Leo III on the reverse of the coin is a rare instance in which a former emperor appears on Byzantine coinage. Photo: Dumbarton Oaks

yet the Iconophile sources viewed him as their greatest enemy, so his reputation has been blackened beyond that of almost any other emperor. Constantine was born in 718 and the Iconophile sources say that when he was being baptized he defecated in the baptismal font, giving rise to his nickname of Kopronymos ("Dung-name"). He was crowned as co-emperor in 720 and in 732 he was married to Irene, the daughter of the Khazar khan; then, after her death, he married twice again.

Athough Leo III had clearly designated Constantine to succeed him, a revolt broke out immediately in 741, led by his brother-in-law Artabasdos, who apparently opposed Leo's Iconoclasm. Artabasdos initially defeated Constantine, gained control of Constantinople, and sought to establish a dynasty of his own. Constantine, however, defeated him in 743 and regained control of the capital, blinding Artabasdos and his sons.

Once established firmly on the throne, Constantine V continued the successful military policy of his father and he was able to take the offensive in Asia Minor. The Arabs were weakened by their own political problems, which led to the collapse of the Umayyad dynasty and its replacement by the Abbasid dynasty in 750. The Arab capital was moved from Damascus (in Syria) to Baghdad (in Iraq) and the Abbasids were generally less concerned with their western frontier (and warfare with Byzantium) than the Umayyads had been.

Just as the Arab threat began to abate, however, there was a new danger from Bulgaria. Constantine pursued an aggressive policy against the Bulgars and he dealt them a crushing blow at the Battle of Anchialos in 763. At the same time Constantine V almost completely ignored the situation in Italy, in part because he realized that his support for Iconoclasm prevented any rapprochement with the papacy, and this led to a considerable change in the political equilibrium in Italy. Since 726 the papacy had disagreed with Byzantine policy on Iconoclasm and it now saw little difference between the "schismatic" Greeks and the heretical Lombards who had threatened papal possessions over the past two centuries. Previously, the papacy had looked to the Byzantine emperor as a military protector, but Iconoclasm and the lack of interest of the Isaurian emperors led to the collapse of this bond and major changes in relations between Byzantium and the papacy.

In 751 Ravenna fell to the Lombards and the Exarchate of Ravenna ceased to exist. Pope Stephen II was aware of these global changes in policy and military strength; he sought another military protector and found one in the person of the Frankish ruler Pepin, who was a Catholic Christian. This was to have far-reaching ramifications for the West, as papal interests shifted northward to the Frankish Kingdom, and this naturally had a significant impact on Byzantine attempts to maintain their possessions in Italy.

Constantine V was the most ferocious of the Iconoclast emperors. He apparently believed strongly in Iconoclast doctrine and he composed theological tracts himself. While Leo III seems to have supported Iconoclasm as a result of his fairly basic belief in Biblical prohibitions of "graven images," his son was a sophisticated thinker, who had a real grasp of the philosophical and theological issues involved. As a result, an Iconoclast theology was formed, and Christological arguments came to play a dominant role in the controversy. Under Constantine V, Iconoclast theologians began to see connections with the theological disputes of the past 400 years: they argued that images, in fact, raised once again the Christological problems of the fifth century. In their view, if one accepted the veneration of ikons of Christ, one was guilty of either saying that the painting was a representation of God himself (thus merging the human and the divine elements of Christ into one) or, alternatively, maintaining that the ikon depicted Christ's human form alone (thus separating the human and the divine elements of Christ) – neither of which was acceptable. Thus, under Constantine V, the Iconoclastic controversy, which had originally been a debate about church usage and principles of public veneration, suddenly raised again all of the difficult theological issues of the past.

Constantine V summoned a church council, which he naturally packed with supporters of Iconoclasm. This met at the imperial palace of Hiera on the Asiatic shore of the Bosphoros in 754 and proclaimed Iconoclast theology as orthodox, despite the opposition of important theologians such as the former patriarch Germanos, John of Damascus, and Stephen of Mount Auxentios. Although most of the treatises written by the Iconoclasts have not survived, the decisions of the Council of Hiera are preserved, since they were read into and condemned by the later Iconophile Council of Nicaea. Armed with this decision, Constantine instituted a persecution of Iconophiles. He sought to root them out of the bureaucracy and the army, and he struck especially at the monasteries, which were the centers of ikon veneration. In his zeal, Constantine went beyond the teachings of the Council of Hiera and condemned the cult of saints and relics (except, interestingly, those of the True Cross). He is even said to have personally scraped holy pictures from the walls of churches in Constantinople. Although Constantine V was reviled by the Iconophile tradition as the worst of the persecuting Iconoclasts, he was a remarkably successful general and his memory survived among those who continued to respect his military prowess. There is also good reason to believe that Constantine was enormously popular in Constantinople itself, not least because he improved the standard of living within the city and provided its inhabitants with plentiful, inexpensive food.

Leo IV the Khazar (775–780)

Leo IV was the son of Constantine V and his Khazar wife, Irene, so he is often called "the Khazar." He was crowned co-emperor in 751, shortly after his birth, and he survived a conspiracy of his half-brothers, who had hoped to succeed to the throne. Little is known of Leo's reign, but he did campaign against the Arabs in Asia Minor and against the Bulgarians; in fact, he died of a fever in 780 while he was leading the army in person against the Bulgarians. Leo IV was himself an Iconoclast, but he did not continue the violent persecutions of his father, in part as a result of the influence of his wife Irene, who was an Iconophile.

Under the Isaurian dynasty the principle of undivided hereditary rule continued to grow stronger, and, following the precedent of his father and his grandfather, Leo IV crowned his young son Constantine VI as emperor shortly after his own accession, thus assuring the continuity of the dynasty.

The Reign of Irene and the First Restoration of Ikons

Leo IV died suddenly in 780, at the age of only 30. His wife Irene emerged as the regent for her son Constantine VI, who was at the time only 9 years of age. Irene's position was precarious: she was an Iconophile and had already been involved in a movement to bring ikons back into the imperial palace. As a woman, Irene naturally had no military experience, and the army had been the dominant institution of Byzantium for at least the past century. In addition, there were significant rivals for power in the persons of the sons of Constantine V, the younger half-brothers of Leo IV. Irene, nonetheless, emerged as one of the most interesting of the many women rulers of Byzantium, and her character, while perhaps not always admirable by modern standards, was certainly strong and determined. Although her major goal always seemed to be the restoration of ikons, Irene also took a strongly proactive interest in military and political affairs and she was the only Byzantine woman to assume for herself the masculine title of "emperor" (*basileus*). She appointed administrators loyal to herself, starting with the eunuch Stavrakios as *logothete tou dromou*, and appointing as military commanders those who would support her desire to end Iconoclasm. Remarkably enough, her reign began with significant military success against the Slavs and the Arabs, and in 784 she was able to encourage the appointment of her former secretary Tarasios, who was at the time a layman, as patriarch of Constantinople. Tarasios was quickly ordained a priest and almost immediately enthroned as bishop, much to the chagrin of some members of the clergy.

Irene arranged an ecumenical council to carry out the restoration of ikons and the reversal of imperial policy. This council opened in the church of the Holy Apostles in Constantinople in 786. By this time the highest command of the army was loyal to Irene, but members of the *tagmata* (imperial troops stationed in Constantinople) continued to support Iconoclasm and they rioted outside the council, forcing it to disband. Irene realized the importance of these military units and she ordered them transferred to Asia Minor in preparation for a campaign in the East. As soon as they were outside the city, she had them dismissed from the army. Secure in her control of the situation, Irene ordered the council to assemble again in 787, this time in Nicaea, site of the First Ecumenical Council. Under the presidency of Tarasios, the Second Council of Nicaea duly condemned Iconoclasm without any real resistance. Former Iconoclasts were allowed to repent and most were even able to maintain their positions in the church and state; Irene, of course, had a real interest in making sure that her former husband and his family were not severely condemned since her own position depended completely on her relationship with them.

Box 8.3 *The Decree of the Second Council of Nicaea (787)*

The year 787 witnessed the end of the first period of Iconoclasm, as the empress Irene, widow of Leo IV, single-mindedly set about to restore the veneration of ikons. She encountered significant opposition within the army and the organization of the church but dealt with her opponents harshly and ultimately got her way. The following text is part of the final decree of the bishops who met in Nicaea to proclaim the new religious policy. In this proclamation, notice that the bishops refer to the "Catholic Church," meaning the "universal church," which they wish to distinguish from the church of the Iconoclasts. Notice also how much this document reflects the ideas of John of Damascus, for example, in the reference to tradition as passed down through the centuries, and to the distinction between "veneration" (*proskynesis*), which it is appropriate to render to the images, and "worship"(*latreia*), which is due to God alone.

To make our confession short, we keep unchanged all the ecclesiastical traditions handed down to us, whether in writing or verbally, one of which is the making of pictorial representations, agreeable to the history of the preaching of the Gospel, a tradition useful in many respects, but especially in this, that so the incarnation of the Word of God is shown forth as real and not merely fantastic, for these have mutual indications and without doubt have also mutual significations.

We, therefore, following the royal pathway and the divinely inspired authority of our Holy Fathers and the traditions of the Catholic Church (for, as we all know, the Holy Spirit indwells her), define with all certitude and accuracy that just as the figure of the precious and life-giving Cross, so also the venerable and holy images, as well in painting and mosaic as of other fit materials, should be set forth in the holy churches of God, and on the sacred vessels and on the vestments and on hangings and in pictures both in houses and by the wayside, to wit, the figure of our Lord God and Saviour Jesus Christ, of our spotless Lady, the Mother of God, of the honourable Angels, of all Saints and of all pious people. For by so much more frequently as they are seen in artistic representation, by so much more readily are men lifted up to the memory of their prototypes, and to a longing after them; and to these should be given due salutation and honourable reverence (*proskynesis*), not indeed that true worship of faith (*latreia*) which pertains alone to the divine nature; but to these, as to the figure of the precious and life-giving Cross and to the Book of the Gospels and to the other holy objects, incense and lights may be offered according to ancient pious custom. For the honour which is paid to the image passes on to that which the image represents, and he who reveres the image reveres in it the subject represented. For thus the teaching of our holy Fathers, that is the tradition of the Catholic Church, which from one end of the earth to the other hath received the Gospel, is strengthened. Thus we follow Paul, who spake in Christ, and the whole divine Apostolic company and the holy Fathers, holding fast the traditions which we have received. So we sing prophetically the triumphal hymns of the Church, "Rejoice greatly, O daughter of Sion; Shout, O daughter of Jerusalem. Rejoice and be glad with all thy heart. The Lord hath taken away from thee the oppression of thy adversaries; thou art redeemed from the hand of thine enemies. The Lord is a King in the midst of thee; thou shalt not see evil any more, and peace be unto thee forever."

Those, therefore who dare to think or teach otherwise, or as wicked heretics to spurn the traditions of the Church and to invent some novelty, or else to reject some of those things which the Church hath received (e.g., the Book of the Gospels, or the image of the cross, or the pictorial icons, or the holy relics of a martyr), or evilly and sharply to devise anything subversive of the lawful traditions of the Catholic Church or to turn to common uses the sacred vessels or the venerable monasteries, if they be Bishops or Clerics, we command that they be deposed; if religious or lay-persons, that they be cut off from communion.

From *The Seven Ecumenical Councils of the Undivided Church*, trans H. R. Percival, in Nicene and Post-Nicene Fathers of the Christian Church, second series, ed. P. Schaff and H. Wace (New York, 1890; reprint, Grand Rapids, MI, 1955), XIV, p. 550.

In an attempt to mend relations with the West, Constantine VI had been betrothed to Rotrud, the daughter of Charlemagne (Charles the Great), king of the Franks (and later western emperor), and one can only wonder what might have followed had that marriage been carried out. As it happened, Irene broke off the engagement and in 787 arranged a "bride-show" in which she selected a wife, the saintly Maria, for her son. By 790, when he was 19 years old, Constantine sought to rule in his own name and, although a plot against Stavrakios failed, the army eventually came to support him, and Constantine assumed power in his own name. Constantine VI was, however, not a successful ruler, the political situation was divided among various centers of power, and he was eventually forced to recall his mother to the throne. In 795 Constantine divorced his wife and married again, earning the outspoken opposition of the two monks, Plato of Sakkoudion and his nephew Theodore (later known as Theodore of Stoudios). They objected that Constantine's remarriage was illegal under church law and argued that the emperor was therefore guilty of adultery. Theodore's outspoken opposition to the emperor resulted in his exile from Constantinople. This was the beginning of the so-called Moechian (Adultery) Controversy, an issue that was far broader than the mere question of Constantine's marital situation, since it involved an attempt on the part of certain groups within the church to dictate to the emperor what he could and could not do. Not surprisingly, some of the church leaders who wanted to impose stronger penalties on the former Iconoclasts were ranged alongside Plato and Theodore in opposition to Constantine's second marriage.

Meanwhile, the rule of Irene and Constantine faltered in the face of military defeats at the hands of the Arabs and continued friction between mother and son. Finally, in 797 some of Irene's supporters seized the young emperor, blinded him, and Constantine died, probably as a result. In the aftermath Irene was in sole control of the Byzantine state, as we have said, the only empress to use the male form of the imperial title, *basileus*.

Plots continued to haunt Irene, centering on the sons of Constantine V who, although mutilated and exiled, formed a focus for the discontented. The Arabs also had military successes, especially since Irene's policies had weakened the army and drained the treasuries and since the caliph Harun-ar-Raschid (786–809) was one of the strongest and most accomplished rulers the Byzantines were to face. In the West the reign of Irene witnessed an especially important development, when Pope Leo III crowned Charlemagne as emperor at Rome on Christmas Day of 800. This was the culmination of developments that had weakened papal reliance on Byzantium and encouraged the idea that the Franks were the political and military protectors of Italy and the papacy. As we have discussed above, the pope had generally relied on Byzantium as a military power that could neutralize the strength of the Arian Germanic peoples. Over the past 70 years, however, Constantinople had been out of communion with Rome; and what was worse, Leo III and Constantine V had no real interest in the West. At the same time, the Orthodox Franks rose to power, especially under Charles Martel and then Charles the Great.

With the coronation of Charlemagne in AD 800 the "problem" of the two emperors had begun. Up to that point most people believed that there was (or should be) one Christian society ruled by one emperor. Until AD 800 there could be no question that this empire was what we call Byzantium and that it had universal claims that were, to some degree, acknowledged even in the West. Now, with the coronation of Charlemagne the situation was confused. Some westerners claimed that a woman could not be emperor and, thus, the throne in Byzantium was vacant. Both Charlemagne and the papacy realized that the coronation meant a direct challenge to Byzantium in one way or another. The Byzantine Empire saw Charlemagne as a usurper, and Irene's inability to oppose him by force certainly weakened her political position. Charlemagne, meanwhile, realized that his claim to imperial power was meaningless without some acknowledgement from the Byzantines. He therefore sent an embassy to Constantinople offering to marry Irene, and the empress's apparent willingness to consider such a remarkable proposal only caused further distress and opposition in Constantinople.

FURTHER READING

Leslie Brubaker and John Haldon, *Byzantium in the Iconclast Era (ca. 680–850): The Sources. An Annotated Bibliography*. Brookfield, VT, 2000.

Anthony Bryer and Judith Herrin, eds., *Iconoclasm: Papers given at the Ninth Spring Symposium of Byzantine Studies, University of Birmingham, March 1975*. Birmingham, 1977.

R. Cormack, *Writing in Gold: Byzantine Society and its Icons*. Oxford, 1985.

S. Gero, *Byzantine Iconoclasm during the Reign of Leo III*. Louvain, 1973.

S. Gero, *Byzantine Iconoclasm during the Reign of Constantine V*. Louvain, 1977

Glenn Peers, *Subtle Bodies: Representing Angels in Byzantium*. Berkeley, CA, 2001.

J. Pelikan, *Imago Dei: The Byzantine Apologia for Icons*. Berkeley, CA, 1990.

Robert Schick, *The Christian Communities of Palestine from Byzantine to Islamic Rule: A Historical and Archaeological Study*. Princeton, NJ, 1995.

9

Continued Struggle over Ikons

| 250 | 500 | 750 | 1000 | 1250 | 1500 |

815	Restoration of Iconoclasm
843	End of Iconoclasm
860	First Russian attack on Constantinople
863	Mission of Constantine and Methodius to the Slavs

Nikephoros (802–811)

A plot was formed in 802, while ambassadors of Charlemagne were still in Constantinople. Irene was deposed and she withdrew to a monastery she had earlier founded. The conspirators chose as the new emperor Nikephoros (802–11), the *logothete tou genikou* who apparently also had military experience to go along with his administrative skills and who was reputedly descended from the royal house of the Ghassanid Arabs.

Nikephoros was an Iconophile, but he strongly opposed the "monastic party," sometimes called the *Zealots*. One should be very careful not to imagine that there were political parties in the modern sense in Byzantium, but for the purposes of analysis we can group individuals into categories that will help us understand their points of view. Thus, as we have seen, immediately after Irene restored the veneration of ikons, a group of monks demanded severe punishment for Iconoclasts, strict adherence to canon law, and the condemnation of what they considered to be immorality in the imperial palace (the Moechian issue). This monastic or Zealot party was also opposed to the elevation to the episcopacy of those who were laymen at the time, favoring those who had spent long years in the monastic life. Thus, the Zealots were upset when, after the death of the patriarch Tarasios in 806, Nikephoros had him replaced by another layman and former bureaucrat, also named Nikephoros. Theodore of Stoudios, in particular, objected to the ecclesiastical policies of the emperor and he was exiled once again in 809. As a result of his moderate religious policies, the emperor Nikephoros earned the hostility of the monastic writers (mainly Theophanes), who remain our main source of information about the period.

There is no doubt, however, that Nikephoros had considerable experience, and he sought to improve the functioning of the state, both in military and administrative terms, something that was sorely needed after the confusion and occasional laxity under Irene.

Nikephoros wished, in particular, to assure the full and proper collection of taxes, which had frequently been remitted under Irene. In the early ninth century state income was based primarily on the land tax, still calculated on the basis of the quality and the quantity of the agricultural and pastoral land owned by each family. Default in payment was to be covered by the village community as a whole, an institution called *allelengyon*, an important and generally beneficial system, since it was designed to assure the collection of tax by the state while keeping land in the hands of the small farmers. In addition to the land tax, there was a "poll tax," the *kapnikon*, payable by all rural inhabitants of the empire, regardless of whether they owned land or not, and there were also customs duties on goods brought into Byzantium; these latter were very high and reasonably well-regulated, in part because the state was able to force goods to enter the empire through a reasonably small number of border crossings.

Charlemagne tried to force Nikephoros to recognize his claim to the imperial title by exerting military pressure in Dalmatia. Nikephoros, however, worked to re-establish Byzantine power in the Balkans, beginning with the reconquest of the Peloponnesos and the creation of new *themes*: Thrace, Thessaloniki, Macedonia, Kephalonia, Dyrrachium, and the Peloponnesos, all of these in the Balkans. He also made great use of the policy of population transfers, with a focus in the Balkans, settling "loyal" groups and tribes near the western frontiers and removing possibly disloyal elements from areas where they might pose a danger. These settlers in the Balkans seem to have provided the population base for the Byzantine revival in this area in the years to come.

The re-establishment of Byzantine power and the revival of economic prosperity in the Balkans probably went hand-in-hand. Whether these were more the result of imperial policy or developments that had been going on independently at a local level is difficult to say; probably both phenomena were operating together. In any case, we can see some small evidence of the recovery of urban life in the early ninth century in places like Greece. For the first time in two centuries we begin to note the appearance of imported pottery in provincial areas, and there is reason to believe that the urban population began once again to increase. The creation of *themes* in areas of the Balkans and the show of strength made by the emperor may not have had this as their primary goal, but improvement in local conditions certainly must have been affected by these developments.

Nikephoros was forced to negotiate terms in the face of a powerful Arab invasion under Harun-ar-Raschid. He was, however, remarkably successful in the West, re-establishing Byzantine domination of the Dalmatian coast and defeating the Slavs in the Peloponnesos and in the area of Serdica in Bulgaria. The Bulgar Khan Krum became alarmed at these Byzantine successes, but Nikephoros' troops responded by defeating the Bulgars and destroying their capital of Pliska. In 811 Nikephoros led a great campaign against the Bulgars, again taking Pliska and forcing Krum to sue for peace. Nikephoros pressed on with the war, hoping for the complete defeat of Bulgaria. At the moment of his greatest success, Nikephoros and his entire army were caught in an ambush: the emperor was killed, along with many of his generals and a large part of his army. Krum later turned the emperor's skull into a drinking cup with which he had his allies toast his victory. Nikephoros was the first Byzantine emperor to fall in war since the Battle of Adrianople in 378, but his policies and administration strengthened the state in ways that were important for the future.

Michael I Rangabe (811–813)

Nikephoros' successor was his son-in-law, Michael I Rangabe, who held the title of *kouropalates*, giving him a rank just below that of the emperor. Michael I was the first emperor with a proper family name, an indication that aristocratic families were beginning to form as a result of the increased stability of the age. Michael campaigned with his father-in-law but managed to escape the disaster in Bulgaria, and his accession was accepted when he signed a statement, provided by the patriarch Nikephoros, that he would uphold orthodoxy (meaning Iconophile doctrine).

Michael's political policies were in marked contrast to those of Nikephoros I, and he made lavish donations to churches, monasteries, and charitable organizations. He immediately came to terms with the Zealot party, recalled Theodore of Stoudios from exile, and condemned the "adultery" of Constantine VI (which still remained a live issue). Michael's policy was also conciliatory toward the West, allowing direct communication with the papacy, and he planned to marry his son to a Frankish bride. Michael agreed to recognize Charlemagne's claim to the imperial title, and from this time onward the Byzantine emperors regularly took the title *basileus Romaion* (emperor of the Romans) to distinguish themselves from the "lesser" emperors in the West; thus, in the Byzantine view, there still was only one empire, and the western rulers were simply tolerated as a matter of convenience or necessity. Michael was lavish in his grants of money, especially to the clergy, and the state was in a financially difficult situation. In the Balkans Khan Krum was triumphant, and he met with virtually no resistance from any Byzantine army.

Even the monastic chroniclers realized that Michael's position was untenable in the face of obvious weakness, and plots were hatched by those who wished to bring back Iconoclasm, including the unfortunate sons of Constantine V. When Michael tried to take the field against Krum in 813, one of his generals, Leo, *strategos* of Anatolikon, deserted him and seized Constantinople. Michael was deposed and exiled, and Leo V, the Armenian (813–820) was made emperor in his place.

Second Iconoclasm

Leo V clearly felt, along with many in the army, that the military disasters of the past quarter-century were God's punishment of the empire for idolatry after the abandonment of Iconoclasm. The new emperor consciously imitated Leo III in policy and even had his elder son renamed Constantine in order to complete the identification. In the short run Leo's military success was no greater than that of his predecessors, but he met with a stroke of good fortune when Khan Krum suddenly died in April of 814. Leo was able to conclude a peace of 30 years with Krum's son, Omurtag, who was more concerned with his western frontier, where he was threatened by the Franks. The border between Byzantium and the Bulgars was restored to where it had been in 780, and the peace allowed Leo to make some progress in rebuilding the cities of Thrace and Macedonia that had been ravaged in the recent fighting. In addition, there is some evidence that Leo made tentative steps in the direction of introducing the Bulgars to Christianity. This attempt failed completely, but it foreshadowed important developments that were to take place later in the century.

Meanwhile, Leo set about restoring Iconoclasm within the empire. In 814 he established a commission to investigate the issue, under the leadership of John Grammatikos, a young but learned monk who was to be the main intellectual force behind this new Iconoclastic movement. The commission issued an exhaustive argument in favor of Iconoclasm, which the Patriarch Nikephoros refused to sign. The emperor removed the great ikon of Christ that hung over the Bronze Gate of the palace, and in 815 he forced the patriarch Nikephoros to abdicate and go into exile. A council was held in Hagia Sophia that reaffirmed the Iconoclast Council of Hiera (754), and many bishops and monks were exiled, including Theodore of Stoudios. From exile Theodore organized opposition against renewed Iconoclasm and he actively sought the intervention of the papacy, which of course had always remained firmly in favor of the veneration of ikons.

In 820 one of Leo V's old comrades in arms, Michael the Amorian, became involved in a plot against the emperor, apparently largely for personal and family reasons. The plot was detected and Michael was sentenced to death by being tied to an ape and cast into the furnaces that heated the baths of the imperial palace. The sentence was put off until after Christmas, but Michael rallied some of his supporters who, dressed in clerical robes and posing as members of the choir, entered Hagia Sophia during the services for Christmas morning. They stole up to the altar, murdered Leo, and proclaimed Michael as emperor.

The Amorian Dynasty

Michael II the Amorian (820–9) was a soldier and a practical ruler. He was probably himself an Iconoclast, but he wished to discourage dissension over the matter, so he ended the persecution of the Iconophiles, recalled the exiles (including the patriarch Nikephoros and Theodore of Stoudios), and forbade discussion of the issue. Michael II's reign was marked by the revolt of Thomas, probably a Slav settled in Asia Minor. Thomas the Slav had a checkered career and was involved in at least one revolt, but he held high military office in the Anatolikon *theme*. He then revolted a second time and fled to the court of the Caliph Ma'mum (813–33, the son of Harun ar-Rashid), who promised him aid. Thomas put together a heterogeneous force in the eastern frontier districts of the empire. Rather curiously, he claimed that he was Constantine VI, who had been deposed nearly a quarter of a century earlier. He drew to his cause many Iconophiles and all the dispossessed elements in Asia Minor: these included individuals from the Caucasus, Slavs, the poor of the countryside, and the Paulicians. The latter were undoubtedly the most important of the heretical movements of Asia Minor in the Middle Byzantine period; they were dualists, with beliefs that corresponded in many ways to the rigorist movements of earlier times (Montanists, Novatians) and possibly even to the ancient Manichaeans, although there is no reason to think that they represented continuity with any of these. The caliph arranged for the coronation of Thomas by the patriarch of Antioch, and much of the imperial army and navy of Asia Minor went over to his side. Modern historians have been intrigued by this revolt, since it seems to represent one of the few revolutionary movements in the history of Byzantium, but one should probably not overestimate the social aspect of the phenomenon, and it is clear that Thomas' goal was primarily political – the seizure of the imperial throne – and that he had no real program of social change. Thomas controlled most of Asia Minor for two years (821–3) and besieged Constantinople, beginning in December of 821. Like so many before him, however, he was unable to take the city and his forces were scattered by the intervention of the Bulgar Khan Omurtag, who came to the aid of his ally Michael. After this, the revolt quickly collapsed, and Thomas was captured and executed.

The revolt of Thomas the Slav had naturally weakened Byzantium and, although the caliph was not able to take advantage of the situation, Arabs from elsewhere did so. In 826/8 Crete was taken by Arab adventurers from Spain, and in 827/9 Spanish Arabs were able to establish footholds in Sicily. The Arab presence on these two islands was to have serious repercussions for Byzantium. Crete became a base for Arab "pirates" who made the Aegean and its shorelines unsafe for the Byzantines and presumably also disrupted trade in the area. The Arab bases on Sicily were the beginning of a long contest between Byzantines and Arabs for control of southern Italy and Sicily that was also to involve the papacy and, eventually, other powers from Western Europe. The Arabs also used these Sicilian bases to raid Italy and the Balkans.

Michael II maintained his position of religious moderation throughout his reign, but his policies were completely undermined by the Zealot party, under the leadership of Theodore of Stoudios. They would accept nothing short of a full restoration of ikons and condemnation of the Iconoclasts. In this they continued to appeal to the papacy, but when a messenger came to Constantinople with a letter from the pope in support of ikons, the emperor had him mistreated and thrown into prison. Michael also sought to out-do the Zealots by asking for support from the western emperor, Louis the Pious.

Theophilos (829–842)

Michael II was succeeded by his son, Theophilos, who had been crowned as co-emperor in 821. Unlike his father, Theophilos was cultured and learned, since he had been taught by John Grammatikos. In military terms, however, Theophilos' reign was a disaster. He won some victories in the East, but practically everywhere else he was defeated. Palermo fell to the Arabs of Ummayad Spain in 831 and all of western Sicily was in Arab hands by 841. In 839 the Arabs invaded southern Italy, seized Taranto, and thus effectively cut Byzantine Italy in two. Theophilos sought aid against the Spanish Arabs from the German emperor, Louis the Pious, and the caliph Abd ar-Rakhman.

Despite, or because of, these difficulties Theophilos was able to make some administrative changes, generally directed toward the military strengthening of the empire. He repaired the walls of Constantinople, which had deteriorated over time, and he created three new *themes*: Paphlagonia and Chaldia in Asia Minor, and Cherson on the peninsula at the north of the Black Sea. He also formed three defensive districts, called *kleisourai*, along the eastern frontier of the empire.

Under Theophilos Iconoclasm experienced its last real efflorescence. In 837 John Grammatikos became patriarch, and a persecution of the Iconophiles began, directed especially at the monks. Two well-known Palestinian monks, Theodore and Theophanes, were brought to Constantinople, and Iconoclast verses were written on their foreheads with red-hot irons, giving them the name of the *graptoi* ("those who were written on"). It is difficult to know how strong the Iconoclast movement was at this time, whether it was still a vibrant and popular idea or whether its support had diminished. Certainly its strongest argument had been confounded by the military defeats of Michael II and

Box 9.1 *The Poet Kassia (fl. 840)*

Kassia, was, along with Anna Komnena, one of the best-educated of Byzantine women. She was an aristocrat and a nun. Her poetry could be filled with feeling and sensitivity (see the poem on Mary Magdeline below), but it also demonstrated a typical Byzantine disdain for other peoples (see the poem on the Armenians below). According to one tradition, in 830 Kassia took part in a "bride-show" arranged by Euphrosyne, the mother of the emperor Theophilos. Despite Kassia's beauty and accomplishments, Theophilos chose Theodora to be his wife and Kassia entered a monastery. Kassia wrote not only poems, but the religious music to accompany some of them, and several of these survive and are still used in the services of the Orthodox church today:

Prayer of Mary Magdeline

Lord, the woman who fell into many sins
has perceived your divinity
and joins the procession of myrrh-bearing women.
Lamenting, she brings you myrrh, before your burial.
"O!" she cries, "what night falls on me,
what dark and moonless madness of wild-desire,
this thirst for sin.
Take my spring of tears
You who draw water from the clouds,
bend to me, to the sighing of my heart,
You who bend the heavens in your secret incarnation,
I will kiss your immaculate feet
and wipe them dry
with the hair of my head.
When Eve, at twilight in Paradise
heard the sound of your feet, she hid in terror.
Who will trace the abundance of <u>my</u> sins
or your unfathomable judgments, Saviour of my soul?
Do not abandon me, your slave
in your immeasurable mercy."

On the Armenians

The most terrible race of the Armenians
Is deceitful and evil to extremes,
Mad and capricious and slanderous
And full of deceit, being greatly so by nature,
Once a wise man said of them appropriately:
Armenians are evil even when they are obscure.
On being honored they become more evil;
On acquiring wealth they (become) even more evil on the whole;
But when they become extremely wealthy and honored,
They appear to all as evil doubly compounded.

From C. Trypanis, *Medieval and Modern Greek Poetry* (Oxford, 1951), p. 43.

Theophilos, but it would be wrong to think that Iconoclasm's vitality had completely disappeared.

Personally, Theophilos seems to have been something of a romantic, and he had a strong admiration for Arab culture. He even sent emissaries to Baghdad to gain information and architectural ideas from the court there, and there is reason to believe that Byzantine art and architecture in this period were influenced by developments in the caliphate. Theophilos seems to have encouraged learning in Constantinople. When Leo the Mathematician, a polymath with interests in mechanics and communications as well as ancient literature and theology, was invited to the court of the caliph Ma'mun, Theophilos refused to let him go, but set him up as a teacher at public expense in one of the main churches of Constantinople. Theophilos' concern for justice was legendary and there are many stories of him wandering through the streets of the capital, encouraging people to present their problems to him, and then taking action against unjust administrators and judges. The *Timarion*, a satirical work of the twelfth century, undoubtedly reflected this view of the emperor and depicted him as the judge of the dead in Hades. Theophilos probably ordered the opening of provincial mints, for the striking of the bronze coinage that was used in local commerce. This probably had a significant impact on the revival of a monetary economy and the improvement of the overall Byzantine economy at this time.

Theophilos' stepmother Euphrosyne arranged for her son one of the "brideshows" that had been established earlier by her own grandmother, the empress Irene. These rituals, if indeed they are not merely literary inventions, have the character of romance, known in the West in stories like Cinderella. Imperial officials scoured the provinces, looking for girls who met specific qualifications that were written down and captured in a picture. Somehow a small group of finalists was assembled and the emperor made his choice by giving the winner an apple or a ring. In any case, the choice of brides from within the empire was in contrast to the marriage alliances with foreigners that were characteristic of the seventh century, and it reinforced the concept that an empress could come from any social class and from any part of the empire. In the present case Theophilos rejected the beautiful poet Kassia and chose Theodora, the daughter of a provincial military official, apparently not aware that she was, in fact, an Iconophile. The couple had five daughters before the birth of a son, Michael, who ultimately succeeded to the throne.

The Restoration of Ikons

Theophilos died in 842, leaving behind his wife Theodora and his son Michael III (842–67), who was then only 3 years old but who had already been crowned as emperor. Naturally, a regency was established to rule in the name of the young emperor, in this case headed by Theodora, along with the eunuch Theoktistos (*logothete tou dromou*), Theodora's brothers Bardas and Petronas,

Box 9.2   *Digenes Akritas*

Digenes Akritas is often seen as the archetypal Byzantine hero, comparable perhaps to Roland in the medieval West or to Achilles or Aeneas in the ancient world. He is known only from a long poem that is preserved in several different Greek and one Slavic versions. The poem tells the story of Digenes' father, an Arab emir who fell in love with the daughter of a Byzantine general. The emir snatched the girl away from her family, but a reconciliation was made with them and he became a Christian. The poem goes on to talk about the birth and childhood of Digenes (which means "born of two" peoples – the Byzantines and the Arabs; his real name was Basil and the epithet Akritas means "someone who lives on the borders," a "frontiersman"). Digenes has many exploits and daring deeds, fighting brigands, and eventually marrying a beautiful girl and settling down in a lavish house on the Euphrates.

According to the research of Henri Grégoire in the 1930s, the poem reflects conditions and perhaps even specific events on the Byzantine-Arab frontier of the ninth to tenth centuries, and Digenes may have been an actual historical figure. Probably the most striking element is the lack of hostility between the two peoples, who are pictured as more similar to each other than different; they were united in their dislike of the brigands and in their enjoyment of a wealthy aristocratic lifestyle. Although later (probably monastic) editors added pious Christian sentiments to the poem, much of the content shows little concern for religion, and one of the most striking events concerns the hero's adultery and then murder of the woman involved. In addition, the poem provides a certainly exaggerated depiction of an aristocratic house, with its lush garden and ceiling mosaics depicting Old Testament scenes, along with representations from classical mythology and the life of Alexander the Great. The poem also provides information on aristocratic pursuits such as hunting, practicing feats of strength, and of course fighting.

Although *Digenes Akritas* has some of the character of an epic, it more closely resembles the form of romance. As such, in the edited forms in which the poem has come down to us, it is a reflection of the individualism that developed in Byzantium during the eleventh and twelfth centuries.

FURTHER READING

Henri Grégoire, *Autour de l'épopée byzantine*. London, 1975.
Digenes Akritas, trans. John Mavrogordato. Oxford 1956, reprinted 1999.
Digenis Akritis: The Grottaferrata and Escorial Versions, trans. Elizabeth Jefferies. Cambridge, 1998.

and the magister Sergios Nikitiates. Theodora's main goal was the restoration of ikons. Naturally, it was important to preserve, as much as possible, the reputation of Theophilos, since the regency's power depended completely on its relationship to him, and Theodora accordingly circulated the story that on his deathbed Theophilos had repented of Iconoclasm. She felt no need to summon a church council, but in 843 simply assembled a group of officials who accepted the teachings of the Second Council of Nicaea of 787 and deposed the patriarch John Grammatikos. This event is still celebrated by the Orthodox church, on the first Sunday in Lent, as the "Sunday of Orthodoxy."

As time went on, affairs fell more and more under the control of the eunuch Theoktistos, whose career and character have been blackened by later historians. Theoktistos managed the temporary reconquest of Crete, although the island was quickly taken back by the Arabs when quarrels broke out within the regency. Affairs in the church remained somewhat confused, since the regency was concerned to avoid outright condemnation of former Iconoclasts (including members of the ruling dynasty) while the Zealots (including the Stoudites) insisted on nothing less than that. In 847 Theodora chose the monk Ignatios as patriarch of Constantinople; he was a son of Michael I and had been castrated and forced to take monastic vows when his father was deposed in 813. Since Ignatios was a monk, his appointment was welcomed by the Zealot party.

Meanwhile, Michael had been growing up. An appreciation of his character is especially difficult because most of what we know about him comes from later historians who had reason to denigrate the last of the Amorian emperors and who depicted Michael in an unflattering light and gave him the nickname "the Drunkard." It does, however, seem clear that at a young age at least Michael was not especially interested in affairs of state. Michael already had a mistress, Eudokia Ingerina, but Theodora arranged a bride-show where Eudokia Dekapolitissa was chosen as the emperor's wife. Chafing under what he regarded as interference from his mother, the 15-year-old Michael conspired with his uncle, Bardas, who arranged for the assassination of Theoktistos in 855. The next year Michael proclaimed himself sole ruler and exiled Theodora to a monastery.

As mentioned above, the reign of Michael III is difficult to evaluate on the basis of the hostile Byzantine sources, but Arab historians provide a useful counter, since they describe in some detail the military victories under Michael III; and Byzantine popular poetry portrays a ruler, probably Michael himself, who fought heroically and successfully against the Arabs and whose forces pushed well into the interior of Asia Minor.

Ramifications of the End of Iconoclasm

The reign of Michael was marked by important religious and cultural developments that were to have long-term results. Most obviously, the restoration of ikons created a need (and hence a market) for small- and large-scale religious art. Decorative art, of course, had certainly not disappeared during the Iconoclast period, but since representational art had been forbidden this had been restricted in scale and scope. Now, donors vied with each other to find painters and mosaicists who could redecorate churches that had been stripped of figural art and produce ikons that individuals wanted in their homes and in public places. We cannot trace these developments in detail, but one can imagine that artists struggled to recover old techniques and patterns and to form new ones that would meet the needs of society at this time.

In addition, with the Iconoclast Controversy now ended, the Byzantine church was confident and ready to expand its activities and engage in unprecedented missionary activity, especially among the Slavs, some of whom were developing more sophisticated state-based societies and regarded Byzantium as a model for emulation, and who saw organized religion, especially Christianity, as a mark of civilized culture. In addition, and equally important, considerable missionary work needed to be carried out within the empire itself, or perhaps more correctly in the areas that had essentially been lost to the empire in the seventh and eighth centuries.

Further, the end of the Iconoclastic Controversy meant the victory of the monastic movement and the vindication of the hard-line position that many of the monastic leaders had taken. In some ways the situation after 843 was similar to that after the end of the persecutions and the "conversion" of Constantine in the early fourth century: the victorious party could look back to the persecution carried out by their opponents and they could look forward to new ways in which the heroism and determination of the period of struggle could be repeated in new conflicts in the future. This was not only to raise the position of the monks to a new level within society as a whole; it was also to provide for them new roles as "pioneers" and "frontiersmen" and make them heroes and symbols in struggles that were not only spiritual.

On the other hand, even though Iconoclasm was now thoroughly discredited, religious disagreements remained, mainly along lines that had already been drawn at the time ikons were restored over 50 years earlier. In general terms, as discussed above in consideration of events after 787, this disagreement was between the so-called Zealot party, which wanted a strict application of canon law and punishment for all guilty of wrong-doing (including the Iconoclasts), and the so-called Politicians, who were willing to be more lenient, especially in the face of practical realities. As mentioned above, we should be careful not to view these groups as political parties in the modern sense, and individuals were not in any way members of one group or another; rather, this distinction expresses tendencies we can observe that help us understand the religious tensions and difficulties of the period, some of which were ideological, but others were more purely personal. Generally speaking, the Zealots were dominated by monastic leaders, especially associated with the Stoudios monastery, and they developed a tradition of appealing to the pope in cases where they felt the patriarch of Constantinople was in error. The Politicians

too were led by monks – almost by necessity since, after the end of Iconoclasm, virtually all bishops were chosen from the monasteries – but there was
a willingness to allow bishops to be chosen from among (unmarried) laymen
(who were then made monks and consecrated as bishops in a short time) and
they appealed to the theological principle of *oikonomia*, which meant that in
certain cases the strict letter of canon law might not be applied if leniency was
an appropriate response.

As we have seen, the Patriarch Ignatios (although the son of an emperor) could
be regarded as a Zealot and in 858 he was forced to resign when he publicly
condemned what he regarded as immorality among members of Michael's
court. In his place, Michael's uncles chose the learned layman Photios, who
already had built a significant reputation as a scholar. He was reputedly descended from the ancient Greeks and was a nephew of the patriarch Tarasios.
His father had suffered persecution as an Iconophile, but Photios secured a
position at court and took part in an embassy to the Arabs. His appointment
as patriarch naturally angered the Zealots, and Michael's government sought
to avoid political difficulties by seeking the approval of Pope Nicholas I, who
was – as it happened – most interested at this time in expanding the power of
the papacy. The pope dispatched legates to Constantinople and, in 861, they
approved Photios' elevation. Nicholas, however, soon had misgivings about the
situation and in 863 he held a synod in Rome that declared Photios deposed.

The Mission to the Slavs

The so-called Photian Schism was especially serious since it came at a time
when both the papacy and Byzantium were seeking to expand their respective
spheres of interest, especially in the territories settled by the Slavs. In 860
Constantinople had been surprised by an attack from the Rhos; these were a
people, generally recognized as the antecedents of the Russians, who lived
along the river systems that ran north and south, in one direction to the Baltic
Sea and in the other to the Black Sea. The Rhos may originally have been
a Scandinavian military aristocracy – similar to the Vikings – but they had
already gained control over the Slavic peoples who lived in this area, and they
all but certainly represented a mixed population, whose economy was based
partly on trade and raiding along the Russian river system. In 860 the Rhos
descended quickly from the Black Sea and attacked Constantinople. In a
surviving sermon the patriarch Photios describes the alarm felt by the people
of Constantinople and their thankfulness when the enemy fleet was dispersed
by the intervention of the Virgin Mary: in fact, the Byzantine fleet drove them
away. The Rhos were not only a threat to Constantinople, which presumably
could defend itself adequately from such an attack, but, probably more important, their actions north of the Black Sea showed that the Khazars were no
longer able to play the role they had in that region. The Khazars, it should be
remembered, had been the basis of Byzantine military and diplomatic efforts

at the western end of the "steppe corridor" for two centuries, and their decline meant that the Byzantines had to re-evaluate their alliances in this region.

Immediately the court dispatched a missionary embassy to the Khazars, in the hope that by converting them to Christianity, the Byzantines would be able to draw them more closely into the Byzantine fold. This mission was led by Constantine, the later missionary to the Slavs, but he was unable to accomplish his goal, and the Khazars eventually accepted Judaism as their religion. This missionary activity, however, was not totally without result, since it prepared the way for a much greater mission that was soon to come.

In the early ninth century, after the disappearance of the Avar khanate, Great Moravia arose as the first Slavic state in Central Europe. Although the precise location of Great Moravia is uncertain, it was presumably in the area now occupied by the modern Czech Republic and Slovakia. Moravia grew in size and its greatest ruler, Prince Ratislav (846–70), sought to maintain his country's independence from the expansionist tendencies of the Frankish (German) Empire. In 862 Ratislav requested that Constantinople send missionaries to his country to replace the Frankish embassy that was already present and to organize an independent church that would use his subjects' Slavic language, instead of Latin, in the liturgy. This happened, one should remember, at the same time as the dispute between the papacy and Constantinople concerning Photios. Thus, the pope's unilateral declaration that Photios' elevation was invalid (863) certainly encouraged the patriarch to support a Byzantine missionary delegation to Moravia, where the Franks, the papacy, and Byzantium were to be locked in a struggle for pre-eminence.

The mission was led by Constantine the Philosopher (later known as Cyril, or Kyrillos) and Methodios. These two brothers, from the region of Thessaloniki, were already known in Constantinople for their erudition. Constantine had come to Constantinople and attracted the attention of Theoktistos, who helped him attain an excellent education. He became a priest, but was then appointed as teacher of philosophy at the university in the Magnaura (part of the imperial palace). Constantine earned a formidable reputation as a debater and he was able to defeat John Grammatikos in disputation. Later, he presented the cause of Byzantine Christianity at the court of the Khazars and also at the caliph's court at Samarra. Constantine's older brother Methodios held an imperial political position in an apparently Slavic-speaking area of Macedonia, but he eventually became a monk and may have accompanied his brother in the embassy to the Khazars. Both brothers apparently knew the language of the Slavic peoples settled around Thessaloniki (and it is possible that their mother was herself a Slav).

Before leaving for Moravia, Constantine created an alphabet (later called the Glagolitic alphabet), for the Slavonic language that had hitherto been only a spoken tongue. The fact that this alphabet was naturally based on the letters of the Greek alphabet explains the similarity in appearance between Greek and the modern Cyrillic alphabet (named after Constantine/Cyril). While still in Constantinople, Constantine began the translation of the Bible and Byzantine liturgical texts into Slavonic and brought them with him for use in Moravia. The principle of carrying out missionary activity in the language of the local peoples was different from the practice of the Roman church, which insisted on the use of Latin for religious literature and for the liturgy. It naturally gave the Byzantine missionaries a distinct advantage and also set a precedent that was to have important ramifications for the development of culture among the peoples influenced by Byzantium, since the Byzantines did not insist on cultural dominance but instead encouraged the maintenance of local traditions, always, of course, influenced by the culture of the Byzantine capital.

Meanwhile, under the command of his uncle Petronas, Michael III's armies were remarkably successful, especially in the East. Petronas reached the Euphrates in 856, crossed it and attacked Amida some distance beyond. One of the reasons for this was a growing weakness in the caliphate and the emergence of semi-independent emirs along the frontier with Byzantium. In 860 Umar, the emir of Meletine, supported by the Paulicians, attacked deep into Byzantine territory and returned with considerable booty. Three years later, in 863, he attacked again, but was trapped by an army commanded by Petronas (and possibly Michael himself); the emir was killed and his army practically annihilated. In retrospect, this victory was a turning point in the long struggle between Byzantium and the Arabs, and for the next century and a half the Byzantines were to be on the offensive, first arranging for the security of Asia Minor and then gradually attacking Arab positions in the East. The victories of Petronas, of course, also allowed the Byzantines to concentrate their attention in the Balkans and the West.

This was especially fortunate since the disagreement with the papacy (the Photian Schism), the mission to the Slavs, and the need to secure stability in areas north of the Black Sea were to demand all the empire's resources at the time. In the first of these the government of Michael III stood firmly behind the patriarch. The emperor wrote to the pope, asserting the independence of the Byzantine church and demanding that the decision against Photios be rescinded. Photios escalated the conflict beyond the issue of papal supremacy by accusing the western church of errors in practice and in faith. In particular, he pointed to the western insertion of the phrase *filioque* ("and through the Son") into the Nicene Creed's definition of the origin of the Holy Spirit; in the original document, the text had said simply that the Holy Spirit proceeded from the Father, but the addition of the *filioque* meant that the Holy Spirit was understood to proceed from the Father "and the Son." Photios pointed out that this was an innovation in the faith and that it changed the way Christians thought about relationships among the members of the Trinity. The emperor summoned a local council in Constantinople and this condemned the *filioque*, rejected papal interference in the Byzantine church, and excommunicated Pope Nicholas.

Meanwhile, in 863 the Byzantine mission of Constantine and Methodios set off for Moravia, armed with translations in the Slavonic language. The mission was initially successful and, led by Ratislav's encouragement, the country accepted Byzantine Christianity. A local church was organized and the liturgy was celebrated, using the Slavonic language. The Frankish clergy in Moravia, however, hindered the Byzantine missionaries, and Constantine and Methodios sought the assistance of the pope in their endeavor. As a result, in 867 the brothers journeyed to Rome and shortly after their arrival there Constantine died. Methodios returned to Moravia in 870, but he was arrested and imprisoned by the Franks. Ultimately the Byzantine missionaries were expelled from Moravia, since Frankish military power, allied with the papacy, was closer at hand, and the Moravian church ultimately fell under the control of the western church.

The Byzantine missionaries trained in Moravia, however, were able to apply their skills and the translations of holy books in the conversion of Bulgaria. This country, it should be remembered, was ruled by a relatively small Turkic aristocracy, while the vast majority of the population was Slav. In addition, Bulgaria's position was a critical one; the two major military powers in Eastern Europe were the Frankish empire (in the West) and Byzantium (in the East); between them lay Moravia and Bulgaria. Once Moravia accepted Christianity, and at first alliance with Byzantium, the Bulgarians were, in effect, surrounded. In that situation, the Bulgarian prince Boris sent an embassy to the Franks, seeking alliance and missionaries. Michael III, however, dispatched the Byzantine army – fresh from its victory over the Arabs – to the Bulgarian frontier, demonstrating in this period the close relationship between religious and military affairs. As a result, Boris accepted alliance with Byzantium and he was baptized, probably in 864, with Michael standing as his sponsor. The Bulgarian aristocrats rose in opposition to the Christianization of the country and Boris-Michael (as he was henceforth known) put them down savagely, having 52 of them beheaded. The conversion of Bulgaria then proceeded apace, one might say, from the top down, as a result of the baptism of the prince. The church was organized and administered by Byzantine clergy, trained in the Slavonic language, but acting initially on the orders of the patriarch of Constantinople. Although Bulgaria remained politically independent and there would be times in the future when the two states fought especially bitter wars, from 864 onward Bulgaria remained definitively in the Byzantine sphere of influence, and the conversion of the Bulgarians was one of the greatest and most important Byzantine political and cultural achievements.

FURTHER READING

F. Dvornik, *Byzantine Missions among the Slavs*. New Brunswick, NJ, 1970.

F. Dvornik, *The Photian Schism: History and Legend*. Cambridge, 1948.

J. V. A. Fine, *The Early Medieval Balkans: A Critical Survey from the Sixth to the Late Twelfth Century*. Ann Arbor, MI, 1983.

D. Obolensky, *The Byzantine Commonwealth: Eastern Europe, 500–1453*. New York, 1971.

W. Treadgold, *The Byzantine Revival, 780–842*. Stanford, CA, 1988.

A. P. Vlasto, *The Entry of the Slavs into Christendom*. Cambridge, 1970.

10
The Beginnings of the Macedonian Dynasty

250	500	750	1000	1250	1500

867	Basil I founds Macedonian dynasty
893	Symeon tsar of Bulgaria
920	Romanos Lekapenos emperor
922	First efforts to protect peasant landholdings
961	Nikephoros Phokas conquers Crete

The Reign of Basil I (867–886)

In the midst of the missionary activity in the Balkans and the Photian Schism, Michael III fell from power and a new dynasty was established on the Byzantine throne. Basil I the Macedonian was born in Thrace or Macedonia, probably of an Armenian family settled in the area earlier in the century. Basil came to seek his fortune in Constantinople; his physical strength gained him a position at court and his victory over several Bulgarian wrestlers supposedly brought him to the attention of Michael III. He soon married Eudokia Ingerina, the emperor's former mistress, and he was able to supplant the Caesar Bardas, whom he slew with his own hand in 865. Basil became co-emperor with Michael in 866 and the next year he had the emperor murdered in his sleep, emerging in 867 as sole ruler of the Byzantine world and establishing a dynasty that would last for nearly 200 years. The circumstances of Basil's rise were, of course, something of an embarrassment to the later members of the dynasty, and the historians of this period (notable among them Basil's grandson,

Box 10.1 *Byzantine Gold*

The Byzantine gold coin, the *solidus* or *nomisma*, has often been described as the "dollar of the Middle Ages." It kept its value for approximately 700 years and was used as a standard medium of exchange within the Byzantine Empire and far beyond its borders. The Arab caliphate normally did not strike gold coins of its own, instead relying on Byzantine coins, which they called the *bezant*. The *solidus* also circulated widely throughout Europe and was prized by the chiefs and kings of northern Europe as a mark of their wealth and power. Large hoards of Byzantine gold coins have been found widely in Scandinavia.

The *solidus*, of course, was not just a medium of exchange: it was also a primary opportunity for the emperor and his court to communicate with their subjects, and with important figures beyond the frontiers of the empire. From the beginning the Byzantines followed the Roman practice of placing the figure (usually the head) of the emperor (or emperors) on the obverse (the "front") of the coin, occasionally along with symbols or legends that conveyed the ruler's power and achievements. From the middle of the ninth century (after the end of Iconoclasm) the emperor was replaced on the obverse with the figure of Christ, who was thus seen as the "real" ruler of the empire, and he was described in the legend on the coin as "Jesus Christ, King of those who rule." The figure of the emperor, the imperial family, or occasionally a representation of the emperor being crowned by Christ, the Virgin, or a saint, was then placed on the reverse (the "back") of the coin – an indication that the emperor, although less important than God, was still God's representative on earth and unquestioned ruler of the *oikoumene* (the created world).

The most remarkable aspect of the gold coinage was its stability. The *solidus* was originally struck under Constantine I at a weight of 72 coins to a pound of gold (i.e., each coin was 1/72nd of a pound in weight or approximately 4.4 grams), which could also be expressed as a weight of 24 *keratia* or carats.

Through the subsequent 700 years there was no significant variation in the value of the *nomisma* (as it came more commonly to be called). In the sixth and seventh centuries some "light-weight" *solidi* were struck, at a weight of 22 *keratia*, but for the most part the standard 24-carat *nomisma* remained the basic gold coin.

In the middle of the tenth century, however, the emperor Nikephoros Phokas (963–9) struck a new coin that was 1/12 lighter than the standard coin, with a weight of 22 *keratia*. This coin was clearly designed to raise money for the state since it allowed it to make more coins with the same amount of gold and to pay salaries and other state obligations with the new, less valuable coin. This naturally had the effect of devaluing the currency. The lightweight *terarteron*, as the coin was called, apparently circulated alongside the standard full-weight coin (which came to be called the *histamenon*). In the eleventh century, however, a process of systematic devaluation began, which can be documented in the decrease in the fineness of the gold used in the coins. For the most part each ruler allowed the fineness of the gold to fluctuate, perhaps depending on economic and political conditions. Thus, we may note the following values:

Michael IV (1034–41)	24–19.5 *keratia*
Constantine IX Monomachos (1042–55)	24–18 *keratia*
Romanos IV Diogenes (1067–71)	18–16 *keratia*
Michael VII Doukas (1071–8)	16–12 *keratia*
Nikephoros III Votaneiates (1078–81)	ca. 8 *keratia*

From these figures we can see that in a period of less than 50 years the Byzantine gold coins lost roughly two-thirds of their value. There must have been significant effects of this on the economy, and we can be certain that there was considerable inflation, but modern economic developments show that some inflation is not necessarily harmful for the economy and we cannot actually be certain what the long-term effect of this change was on the economy of the Byzantine Empire. Certainly some people, perhaps especially traders, must have been hurt by this, and, certainly, from this time onward the Byzantine *nomisma* lost much of its prestige and universal acceptability. It remained, however, one of the basic currencies of the Mediterranean area and was used by merchants of all ethnicities right to the end of the empire. Probably more seriously, the devaluation of the *nomisma* was a mark that the state itself was experiencing a chronic shortage of income, and this may reasonably be associated with the growth of the power of the large landholders, who were able to escape their duties to pay taxes to the central administration.

For more information on Byzantine coinage and the Byzantine economy, see M. F. Hendy, *Studies in the Byzantine Monetary Economy, c. 300–1450* (Cambridge, 1985), especially pp. 506–10.

Constantine VII) tried to show that Basil was obliged to overthrow the "corrupt" Amorian dynasty, even though this was clearly an illegal act. Constantine VII was, in fact, so concerned to make sure that his grandfather received good "press" that he personally wrote (or had written by a close associate) his biography, the *Vita Vasilii*, which became the standard view of the first emperor of the Macedonian dynasty.

Constantine's biography pictured Basil as a busy administrator and protector of the poor, who was also (despite his rough origins) a significant patron of the arts. Among the emperor's achievements was the construction of the Nea Ekklesia (the "New Church") in the imperial palace in 880. Although this building does not survive, the literary description shows that it was especially sumptuous, with five domes, two exterior fountains, and interior furnishings covered with silver. In the words of his biographer, "This church [was] like a bride adorned with pearls and gold, with gleaming silver, with the variety of many-hued marble" (translated in Cyril Mango, *The Art of the Byzantine Empire*, p. 193).

Basil's first concern was naturally to consolidate his power and secure recognition of his legitimacy. He already had two sons, the elder, Constantine, the

Box 10.2 *Decoration of the Kainourgion Palace*

Among the lavish structures constructed by the emperor Basil I was a residence within the Great Palace called the Kainourgion (the "New Palace"). The emperor's biography, the *Vita Vasilii*, written probably by his grandson Constantine VII, describes the decoration of the residence in some detail, including its elaborate dynastic propaganda. The building was supported by 16 columns, eight of which were of green stone from Thessaly and the others of onychite, whose surfaces were all decorated with relief carving.

What seems to have been a throne-room apparently had a half-dome on the eastern end (just like a church) and the interior of the ceiling was completely covered with glass mosaic tesserae with pure gold filling. Apparently in the half-dome was a representation of Basil himself, seated and accompanied by the figures of his victorious generals, each of which presented to him images of the cities they had captured and brought within the Byzantine Empire. Above the half-dome the emperor's "Herculian labors" were depicted, his deeds in war by which he benefited the citizens of the empire.

Apparently there was a bedchamber attached to the throne-room. The floor of this was paved with stones forming concentric circles, with rivers and eagles in the four corners and the mosaic image of a peacock in the center. The lower courses of the walls were decorated with multicolored stones, while above were bands of flowers made in gold mosaic. In the highest register was a mosaic representation of the emperor, again enthroned, together with his wife Eudokia. "The children they had in common are represented round the building like shining stars, they, too, adorned with imperial vestments and crowns. The male ones among them are shown holding codices that contain the divine commandments (which they were taught to follow), while the female progeniture had been initiated into holy writ and shared in divine wisdom, even if their father had not at first been familiar with letters on account of the circumstances of his life, and yet caused all his children to partake of learning."

On the ceiling of the bedchamber were more mosaics, with a cross at the center. "All round the latter, like stars shining in the sky, you may see the illustrious Emperor himself, his wife and all their children raising their arms to God and the life-giving sign of the Cross and all but crying out that 'on account of this victorious Symbol everything that is good and agreeable to God has been accomplished and achieved in our reign.' There is furthermore an inscription of thanksgiving addressed to God by the parents on behalf of the children, and of the children on behalf of their parents. The one addressed by the parents is conceived in more or less the following words: 'We thank Thee, O God most kind and King of them that reign, that Thou hast surrounded us with children who are grateful for the magnitude of Thy commandments, and so that, in this also, we may give thanks for Thy goodness.' The children's [prayer] is expressed as follows: 'We thank Thee, O Word of God, that Thou hast raised our father from Davidic poverty and has anointed him with the unction of Thy Holy Ghost. Guard him and our mother by Thy hand, while deeming both them and ourselves worthy of Thy heavenly Kingdom.'"

The propaganda here is especially interesting, as is the author's observation that Basil wanted to depict his children's education, even though he had been deprived of such an opportunity, and his notice that care was taken to introduce both the males and the females of the family to "holy wisdom."

Translation from Cyril Mango, *The Art of the Byzantine Empire, 312–1453: Sources and Documents* (Englewood Cliffs, NJ, 1972; reprint Toronto, 1986), pp. 196–8.

Map 10.1 Byzantium in the ninth century. After Jackson J. Spielvogel, *Western Civilizations*, fifth edition (Wadsworth, 2003), p. 183

child of an earlier marriage, and the second, Leo, the son of Eudokia Ingerina; concerning the latter, rumors circulated for years that he was not, in fact, the son of Basil, but rather of Michael III, and this certainly complicated issues later on. Basil moved quickly to secure the legitimacy of his own dynasty, having Constantine crowned as emperor in 869 and Leo in 870. At first there was significant opposition to Basil from the army, which had experienced real success under the old regime. Basil sought supporters wherever he could find them in order to neutralize the opposition, and he found some among the Zealots, who remained opposed to the patriarchate of Photios. As a result, still in 867, Basil had Photios deposed and Ignatios restored as patriarch. This was mainly a political move and Photios was soon employed as tutor to Basil's children. Basil, however, did have interests in the West that were different from those of his predecessors, and for this he needed some accommodation with the papacy. A council was held in Constantinople in 869–70 that included legates from Pope Hadrian II, and Photios was once again excommunicated. The council also met with an embassy from Bulgaria asking for clarification of the status of the Bulgarian church. The issue arose when Boris-Michael found that the Byzantines planned to keep the Bulgarian church closely under the control of the patriarch of Constantinople, and he sought to find a better arrangement through an alliance with Rome. The papacy, however, was no more accommodating than the Byzantines and the Bulgarians sought a solution at the council. In this regard, the patriarchate of Ignatios maintained the policies set by Photios and defended Byzantine interests in the Balkans. Despite the protests of the papal legates, the issue was decided in favor of Byzantium, and the Bulgarian church remained in the sphere of Constantinople. Even though bishops for the new church were still consecrated in Constantinople, Boris-Michael had made a point and used the antagonism between Rome and Byzantium to show that consideration would have to be shown to the interests of the Bulgarian church and to the country as a whole.

In military terms Basil attempted to equal the accomplishments of Michael III, but in this he fell considerably short. He did have some success in Italy, where the Byzantines had made virtually no show of power since the days of Leo III over a century earlier, and where the situation had changed dramatically with the advance of the Arabs and the creation of the Frankish empire in the West. He was able to secure the allegiance of the Lombard Prince of Benevento and the city of Bari, so that a Byzantine foothold in southern Italy was still assured, and late in Basil's reign the able command of Nikephoros Phokas brought considerable success. Unfortunately, however, in Sicily the great city of Syracuse, which had long withstood the Arabs, finally fell to them in 878. Basil's policy of accommodation with the West seems to have been based on the hope of a military alliance with the western emperor Louis II against the Arabs in southern Italy and Sicily, but this eventually came to nothing.

In Asia Minor the Paulicians continued to represent a considerable military threat under their leader Chrysocheir ("Golden Hand"). Basil's brother-in-law Christopher defeated the Paulicians in 872, destroying their capital of Tephrike, and Chrysocheir was murdered by a renegade follower. The movement henceforth ceased to be a military threat. Basil was able to move forward along the Euphrates, consolidating the Byzantine frontier in the East. The continued weakness of the caliphate allowed the development of an independent power in Armenia, which was recognized by both the Byzantines and the Arabs. Basil also was able to occupy Cyprus and to hold it for several years.

In religious policy, Basil realized that the policies of Photios represented the best interests of Byzantium, especially since his attempt at accommodation with the West had largely failed. Thus, when Ignatios died in 877, Photios again became patriarch. The pope agreed to his elevation, and a council in 879 formally settled the dispute and ended the so-called Photian Schism with the total victory of Photios.

Despite his lowly origins and questionable rise to power, Basil was interested in administration, and he was one of the most prolific lawgivers since the time of Justinian. He sought to carry out a complete reorganization of the law, revising the codes of Justinian and supplementing them with more recent laws. This was never fully accomplished, but between 870 and 879 Basil did publish the *Procheiron*, a handbook for the practical use of lawyers and judges. This was followed by the *Epanagoge*, with purpose and content similar to the *Procheiron*, but with much more attention to the political theory behind the legal system. In particular, the *Epanagoge* provided an elegant statement on the relationship between the emperor and patriarch who, together, were responsible for the administration of the world, the one in charge of the administration of secular affairs, the other harmoniously responsible for mankind's spiritual well-being.

The Patriarch Photios

The accomplishments of Photios cannot be compressed into a simple political narrative. He was, of course, deeply involved in the political affairs of his time and his voluminous letters (to foreign rulers as well as religious officials) display his keen knowledge, psychological insight, and determination to support the interests of Byzantium in all areas. We have already discussed his role as patriarch of Constantinople and his support of the emperor and the mission to the Slavs. He was one of the foremost shapers of the expansionist policies that were to characterize the Byzantine state and church over the next two centuries.

Yet Photios was just as important as a scholar. He was influential in the revival of interest in ancient literature in Constantinople and his numerous and varied works provide a valuable insight into the intellectual world of the time. Like most Byzantine intellectuals, he was interested in both secular and religious topics and saw no contradiction between them. His best-known work is the *Bibliotheka* (Library), which contains a description of some 386 books that he and his friends read. Supposedly the book was assembled for his brother Tarasios, who was away from Constantinople, and it therefore represents the tastes and interests of the *literati* at that time. The books described were written by both pagan and Christian authors and they include many works that had survived to Photios' time but are now lost; in this respect the *Bibliotheka* provides invaluable information about ancient literature, as well as providing insight into the intellectual tastes of the ninth century.

Also of considerable importance is his *Lexikon*, a dictionary of words and phrases that he found interesting or problematic. As such, the work provides information about the intellectual climate of the period and the text itself preserves many phrases from lost ancient books, since he commonly quoted whole passages in his discussion. His *Mystagogy of the Holy Spirit* is a detailed discussion of the issue of the *filioque* and argues strongly about the importance of the issue and the fallacies of the western position. He also wrote many

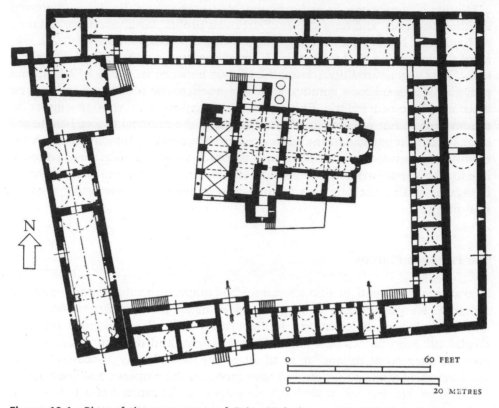

Figure 10.1 Plan of the monastery of Osios Meletios on Mt. Kithairon in central Greece. Byzantine monasteries normally took the shape shown here: a rough rectangle that served as a defensive wall and the location of the rooms that comprised the cells of the monks. A formal reception room and the quarters of the abbot would also normally be located in the exterior circuit. The interior of the enclosure would be dominated by the church, or, often by two churches: one reserved for the monks and the other open to visitors as well. The monastery would also include a kitchen and bakery, along with a dining room (*trapeza*). The latter commonly was a separate building that often was elaborately decorated, although at Osios Meletios these facilities were built into the exterior.

sermons, letters, and other works that provide significant details about life in the period and illuminate aspects of Byzantine foreign policy.

Photios had direct contact with the Arabs, and some scholars think he made use of the libraries in Baghdad during his embassy there. He is an especially good example of the Byzantine scholar-politician who found himself equally at home in the palace and the church. The vicissitudes of his life also provide insight into the complex play of forces at the time, both within and outside of Byzantium. At one time he was condemned by western scholars as the cause of the split between the eastern and the western churches, but this view has now been generally abandoned. Photios is recognized as a saint by the Orthodox church.

The Reign of Leo VI (886–912)

Basil's favorite and first-born son Constantine died in 879, and the emperor was forced, apparently reluctantly, to arrange for the succession of his second son, Leo VI; there were rumors, it should be remembered, that Leo was not the natural son of Basil but of Michael III. Nonetheless, after Basil's death (in a hunting accident) Leo assumed the throne without difficulty, and he began at once to reverse some of his father's acts. Thus, he arranged immediately for the reburial of Michael III with full imperial honors, giving rise to further gossip about Leo's origins. Leo also quickly arranged for the deposition of Photios and his replacement by the emperor's younger brother Stephen, who was only 16 years old. Leo took as his foremost adviser the Armenian Stylianos Zautzes, who was also the father of Leo's mistress (and later wife) Zoe; Zautzes was given the new title *basileopator*.

Despite these reactions against his father, Leo's foreign policy followed the same direction as that of the last Amorians and Basil I. Symeon was now ruler of Bulgaria, and he provided one of the most serious threats that Byzantium was to face. Symeon was a younger son of Boris-Michael, and he had been sent to Constantinople to be trained for a career in the church. He was recalled to Bulgaria in 893 and became *tsar* (from the Roman-Byzantine word *caesar/kaisar*). Symeon was dangerous to Byzantium not only because of his natural ability as ruler and military strategist, but even more because he knew and understood the Byzantines and the power of Byzantine ideology.

War broke out over trade issues. The Byzantines always sought to control points where foreign goods entered Byzantium, and Bulgarian traders had always been allowed to carry out their business in Constantinople. In 893, however, the Byzantines in charge of this trade decided to increase the taxes on Bulgarian goods and to move the market to Thessaloniki; as a result, Symeon decided to force the issue by war and he invaded Byzantine territory in 894. Stylianos Zautzes appears to have suggested that the Byzantines meet this challenge by allying with the Magyars, a Turkic people who were settled to the northeast of Bulgaria, between the Danube and the Dnieper Rivers. As Symeon waged war against the Byzantines in the south the Magyars attacked Bulgaria from the north, forcing Symeon to conclude a truce with Byzantium. Symeon, however, had learned his lessons well in Constantinople and he quickly made a treaty with the Patzinaks (Pechenegs), a people of disputed origins (perhaps Turkic) who settled in the Volga Basin in the late ninth century. The Magyars thus found themselves caught in a vice between the Bulgars and the Patzinaks, and they fled to the west, where they settled in the Danube basin, in the area of modern Hungary, where their descendants have remained until the present day. The settlement of the Magyars, incidentally, had the effect of driving a wedge through the areas inhabited by the Slavic peoples, separating the southern Slavs (Croats, Serbs, etc.) from the Slavs to the north and east. Freed from the pressure of the Magyars, Symeon turned again to

Byzantium, defeating the Byzantine army in 896 before agreeing to a peace treaty in which the Byzantines were obliged to pay substantial tribute to Bulgaria.

Byzantine military activity in the West was naturally weakened as a result of the conflict with Symeon, and in 902 Taormina, the last Byzantine stronghold in Sicily, was lost to the Arabs. Particularly dangerous was the situation in the Aegean, where the Byzantines were not able to provide a vigorous defense against the Arabs. In 904 Leo of Tripoli, a former Christian, led a large fleet from Syria against Constantinople, but he turned and attacked Thessaloniki instead. Thessaloniki, the second most important city of the empire, was not prepared for the onslaught, and it quickly fell. The Arabs slaughtered and imprisoned about half the population and then withdrew. Byzantine military success in Syria produced Arab prisoners who were then exchanged for some of those taken in Thessaloniki. The Byzantine imperial navy sought to reduce the danger of invasion by sea, and attacks were made on Cyprus and Crete, but these were ultimately repulsed, and the Aegean remained subject to Arab incursions.

Meanwhile, the Rhos had come to play a larger role in Byzantine affairs. In 907 the Russian Prince (of Kiev) Oleg brought a large fleet to Constantinople and secured a treaty with the Byzantines that afforded Russian merchants a favorable trading position in Constantinople.

Leo VI is known in Byzantine tradition as Leo the Wise, because of his considerable learning and his works on diverse topics in many styles: political orations, liturgical poems, and theological treatises; he was known frequently to deliver ornate sermons in the churches of Constantinople. He was regarded as "wise" even during his own reign, but his reputation later grew, and he was seen as a prophet and a magician, whose oracles (not really his own, but attributed to him) were thought to foretell the future of the world.

Figure 10.2 Gold coin of Leo VI. The obverse of this coin has a bust of the Virgin praying, with the legend, "Maria" and the abbreviations "MR" and "ThY," which mean "Mother of God." On the reverse is a strikingly realistic image of the emperor with the legend "Leo in Christ Emperor of the Romans." Courtesy of the Arthur M. Sackler Museum, Harvard University Art Museums, Bequest of Thomas Whittemore. © President and Fellows of Harvard College

Leo followed the precedent of Basil I in terms of his legal activity. He set up a legal commission that carried out Basil's intent to codify all of existing Byzantine law. This was accomplished in a work of 60 books that occupied six volumes, variously called the *Exavivlos* or the *Vasilika (Basilika)*. The *Vasilika* was comprehensive, presenting in the Greek language virtually all the laws in the Justinianic Corpus, arranged here (as it had not been before) in a systematic manner. The *Vasilika* thus provided a basis on which all later Byzantine law could be built, and Leo himself began this new tradition with a series of "Novels" (new laws) that dealt with contemporary problems and issues. Both the *Vasilika* and the Novels dealt with ecclesiastical law (canon law) as much as with secular law, and they finally did away with most of the now outdated institutions such as the city councils (*curiae, voulai*) and the Roman Senate. The so-called *Book of the Eparch* and the *Kletorologion of Philotheos* were also issued under Leo's name and testify to his government's interest in organization and the maintenance of public order. The *Book of the Eparch* provided rules and regulations for trade and trade organizations in Constantinople, while the *Kletorologion of Philotheos* was an attempt to regulate officials and ranks at the court in Constantinople.

One of the signal events of Leo's reign was his difficulty in providing an heir to the throne. He had been married early to the pious Theophano (regarded as a saint by the Orthodox church), but she died in 897. Next Leo married his mistress Zoe, the daughter of Stylianos Zautzes, in 898, but she died in 899. The Orthodox church generally allowed remarriage (after death or divorce), but only one time – that is, a person could only be legally married twice. Thus, when Leo was married for a third time, to Eudokia Vaiana (Baiana) in 900, he directly violated the law of both church and state, which he had himself recently reissued in an especially strong format. Leo was, however, in a difficult situation, since the continuation of the dynasty depended on the appearance of a male heir to the throne, and he was willing to accept the disapproval of members of the hierarchy for his action. Unfortunately, however, Eudokia Vaiana also soon died – in 901 – and Leo still did not have an heir. Leo avoided further infuriating the church by yet another marriage, but he took as his mistress Zoe Karvounopsina (Zoe "with coal-black eyes"), who was a member of an important family in Constantinople.

In 905 Zoe gave birth to a son, the future emperor Constantine VII (912–59), and it was crucial for Leo to legitimize the child in order to preserve his claim to the throne. Thus, Leo made an arrangement with the patriarch Nicholas Mystikos that he would separate from Zoe, on condition that the baby be baptized. This was accomplished early in 906, but almost immediately afterwards Leo and Zoe were married and Zoe was proclaimed as Augusta. The patriarch, and much of the church hierarchy with him, were infuriated, and the emperor was forbidden to enter the church. Leo, however, took a page from the book of the Zealots and appealed to the papacy; Pope Sergius III was quite happy to offer a dispensation from canon law, since the emperor's request acknowledged the superiority of the pope to the patriarch of Constantinople.

In the aftermath Nicholas Mystikos was deposed as patriarch, and Constantine VII was crowned as co-emperor in 908. The issue of the Tetragamy ("four marriages") of Leo VI naturally opened all the old controversies between Zealot and Politician "parties," with some interesting new twists. The Zealots were naturally scandalized by the immorality of the emperor, while the Politicians were willing to accept it in light of the need to preserve the dynasty. As long as Leo lived, however, he was able to enforce his will.

The Regency and Romanos Lekapenos

Leo VI died in 912 and, because of Constantine's youth, Leo was succeeded by his brother Alexander (912–13), who had been named as co-emperor some time earlier. Alexander immediately set about reversing his brother's policies, starting with the exile of Zoe from the palace and the recall of Nicholas Mystikos as patriarch. Alexander also refused to pay to Bulgaria the tribute that had been agreed upon by the treaty of 896, and Symeon immediately took the field against Byzantium. In this situation, Alexander promptly died (913).

Constantine VII was the only remaining male member of the Macedonian dynasty and affairs were controlled by a council of regency, initially led by the patriarch Nicholas Mystikos, who of course regarded Constantine as illegitimate. The situation was complex and loyalties were divided, and in the midst of this a revolt broke out, led by Constantine Doukas, commander of the *Scholai* and member of an important military family that had risen to prominence under Leo VI. The revolt nearly succeeded, but Doukas was killed at the moment he was about to seize the palace. Symeon had meanwhile driven through Byzantine territory and stood before the walls of Constantinople (in the summer of 913). Unlike other foreign rulers, who wasted their efforts in futile attacks against the walls of Constantinople, Symeon understood the political situation in the capital and he sought to take advantage of it to control all of Byzantium. The Bulgarian tsar was granted an interview with members of the regency, who agreed to all of Symeon's demands: one of his daughters was to be married to Constantine VII, and the patriarch crowned Symeon as emperor (certainly understood by the Byzantines as emperor of Bulgaria and not of the whole empire).

Shortly after Symeon's departure from Constantinople, however, there was a coup. Zoe returned to the palace as head of the regency, and her government called off the marriage alliance and denied the imperial title to Symeon. Rudely rebuffed, the Bulgarian emperor naturally invaded Byzantine territory, but Zoe refused all concessions. The commanders of the army, however, including Leo and Bardas Phokas, conspired against Zoe, and power was eventually seized by Romanos Lekapenos, son of an Armenian peasant and commander of the Byzantine navy. When the empress' army was unable to accomplish anything against Symeon, Romanos gained control of Constantinople, removed Zoe to a monastery, and in 919 arranged for the marriage of Constantine VII to his daughter Helena. In 920 Romanos was crowned as co-emperor and from this point on he was, in fact, master of the empire.

Symeon's army remained unchecked in the Balkans, and the Bulgarian tsar was furious with the way his plans for control of the empire had been thwarted. Romanos I Lekapenos dealt cleverly with Symeon, refusing to meet him openly in the field, but remaining safe behind the walls of Constantinople and speaking to the Bulgarian as his moral superior, grudgingly granting him the title of emperor of the Bulgarians, but adamantly refusing any consideration of his demands for power within Byzantium. Lekapenos also used diplomacy to distract and defeat his rival. When Symeon sought naval support from the Arabs, the emperor was able to outbid him, and Byzantium and Bulgaria then fought a long struggle for control of Serbia, eventually won by Symeon in 924. His involvement with Croatia, however, under its first king Tomislav, resulted in a disastrous defeat (ca. 926).

After this Symeon appears to have planned further attacks on Byzantium, but he died suddenly in 927, and his son Peter sought accommodation with the empire, at least for the moment. A marriage was arranged between Peter and Maria Lekapena, granddaughter of Romanos Lekapenos, and the empire recognized the legitimacy of the Bulgarian patriarchate that had apparently been recently established. These concessions to Bulgaria were reasonable, and they recognized the considerable military power Bulgaria possessed, but they also led to a prolonged period of peace and Byzantine influence in the whole of the southern Balkans. Serbia, for example, gained independence from Bulgaria, and Prince Časlav allied himself with Byzantium.

During the reign of Peter of Bulgaria a new religious group appeared in the Balkans. These were the Bogomils, who derived their doctrines from a priest called Bogomil who apparently lived in Bulgaria during the first half of the tenth century. They were dualists and believed that the material world, including the Incarnation of Christ, was the work of the Devil; a select group of Bogomil initiates avoided sexual intercourse, meat, and wine. They may have been influenced by Paulicians from Asia Minor who were settled in the Balkans, but this connection is far from clear. Unlike the Paulicians, the Bogomils did not engage in military action against the state, although they resisted all attempts to convert them to orthodox forms of Christianity, and they survived in the Balkans at least until the Ottoman conquest.

Romanos Lekapenos had, meanwhile, solidified his position in Constantinople. He hesitated to remove the legitimate Macedonian emperor Constantine VII, but he had himself proclaimed the senior emperor and his three sons crowned along with him. He appointed John Kourkouas, a talented general, as *domestikos* of the *Scholai* and he married his younger daughters to aristocratic families such as the Argyroi and Musele; the patriarch Nicholas Mystikos, no friend of the Macedonian dynasty, was a natural ally, especially since a church council in 920 had definitively decided in the patriarch's favor in the issue of the Tetragamy. The controversies and struggles that had rocked the Byzantine church for years were at last settled. Ultimately, after the death of Nicholas

Mystikos, Romanos had his 16-year-old son consecrated as patriarch and the emperor was able effectively to control church policy for most of his reign.

Romanos was especially concerned about the growing tendency of the aristocracy (often called simply the *dynatoi* – "the powerful") to gobble up the landholdings of the poor. With the relative stability of the military situation in the empire since the ninth century, the provincial aristocratic families had grown in power and wealth; with their greater opportunity to survive invasions and famines, they frequently found themselves in a position to purchase or to claim by default the land of the poor. The precise course of this development is naturally difficult to trace, and it must have varied from place to place. Furthermore, the exact nature of the relationship between the *dynatoi* and the *ptochoi* (poor) is uncertain, but some of the poor, at least, became *paroikoi*, or dependent tenant farmers. Earlier institutions, such as the *allelengyon*, were designed to protect peasant landholdings, but the situation apparently worsened, and Romanos Lekapenos attempted to reverse the trend toward the sale of such land to the wealthy. His legislation, beginning in 922, targeted the issue of the alienation (by sale or some other means) of peasant land, especially when it had become vacant, and he devised a system of *protimesis* (priority) which laid out clearly the order in which peasant land could be purchased. Thus, relatives, joint-holders, and neighbors were given priority, in carefully designated order; only when no one in these categories was able to purchase the land could it be sold to outsiders. Romanos even realized that there certainly would be violation of these principles and he declared that property illegally acquired would have to be returned, without compensation, subject only to a limitation of ten years (30 in the case of soldiers' land), meaning that land illegally acquired could be demanded back any time before the end of this period. Indeed, it is clear that the legislation was not fully successful, since it had to be reissued, and the underlying problem of poverty and famine, which led to the sale of peasant lands in the first place, was not addressed.

After the amelioration of the Bulgarian threat in 927, Byzantium was able to turn its military attention again to the East, where the Abbasid caliphate continued its decline. Romanos' general John Kourkouas had notable success, leading in 934 to the surrender of Meletine. Kourkouas, however, met a significant adversary in the person of Saif-ad-Daulah, the emir of Aleppo and

Box 10.3 *The Mandylion*

The Mandylion (literally, the "scarf") was one of a class of holy objects called *acheiropoieta* ("not made by hands"). According to a story that is first attested in the sixth century Abgar, the king of Edessa (in Syria), became ill and, learning of the fame of Christ, asked him to come and cure him. Christ, however, pressed his face to

Figure 10.3   The Mandylion. This fresco is from Lagoudera in Cyprus. The inscription reads IC XC, which is the standard abbreviation for "Jesus Christ," and then "The Mandylion." Photo: Dumbarton Oaks

a scarf and his image was miraculously impressed on the cloth. The image was brought to the king, who was immediately cured.

The Mandylion remained in Edessa, even after the Arab conquest. In 944, under Romanos Lekapenos, the Byzantine general John Kourkouas besieged Edessa and he received the holy image as a condition for his lifting of the siege. The Mandylion was transported in triumph through Asia Minor to Constantinople, where it was installed in the palace.

The image was often copied and it was a frequent part of the decoration of a church. Theologically the Mandylion was important because its presence was seen as a proof of the physical reality of Christ's Incarnation (he was a "real" man – fully human – whose features could be directly reproduced through this miraculous means). It was therefore a "proof" used by those who wanted to defend the teachings of the Council of Chalcedon, and its existence was also an argument for the defense of the veneration of ikons.

The depiction of the face of Christ on the Mandylion is certainly that of the Pantokrator (All-ruler) that came to be the standard Byzantine type and had important influence on the medieval West and even into modern times. The Byzantine Mandylion is probably the source of the western tradition of "Veronica's Veil" and perhaps even the "Shroud of Turin." It also may well be associated with what became the standard representation on Byzantine coins in the tenth to eleventh centuries.

Mosul and a member of the Hamdanid family. The empire formed an alliance with the caliphate and the semi-independent dynasty of the Ikhshidids in Egypt against Said-ad-Daulah. The Hamdanid, however, made a successful attack on the empire and invaded Armenia before he turned his attention south to intervene in the affairs of the caliphate.

In 941 the Russians (Rhos) made another surprise attack on Constantinople. Kourkouas returned from the eastern front and defeated the them in a significant land battle, while the Russian fleet was destroyed by Greek Fire. A treaty signed in 944 between Constantinople and the Russians reproduced many of the terms of the treaty of 911, but the balance of power had clearly shifted toward Byzantium.

With the Russian threat temporarily removed, Kourkouas could return to the East, where he won striking victories on the middle Euphrates, taking the towns of Amida, Dara, and Nisibis – places that had last been contested by the Byzantines in the fourth century. Finally, in 944 he besieged Edessa, which resulted in the surrender of the Mandylion, one of the greatest relics in Christianity.

Romanos, however, was unable to enjoy the full results of these triumphs. In 931 the emperor's oldest and most talented son, Christopher, had died. Romanos realized that his younger sons were not really qualified to rule, and he reluctantly seems to have decided that actual power would eventually return to the legitimate emperor, Constantine VII. Determining to pre-empt this, Romanos' younger sons engineered a coup in late 944 in which they deposed their father, exiled him to a monastery, and seized power themselves. In doing do, however, they miscalculated seriously, both on the degree of sentiment in favor of the legitimate dynasty and the cleverness of Constantine himself. A counter-revolt broke out early in 945; the sons of Romanos joined their father in exile, and the legitimate emperor assumed power in his own name.

The Reign of Constantine VII Porphyrogenitos

After 32 years of waiting on the sidelines and at the age of 39 Constantine VII finally assumed power in his own name. Modern scholars often characterize Constantine as bookish and withdrawn, more interested in art and literature than he was in politics. He was clearly interested in culture and he was apparently a painter in his own right. He collected books and official notices, and he was an important figure in the systematization of knowledge that characterized the period. He surrounded himself with a circle of scholars who wrote histories and encyclopedic works on many topics, including even agricultural science. As previously mentioned, he was probably the author of a biography of his grandfather and responsible for significant other historical compilations of the day. Nonetheless, Constantine was also politically aware and he probably was at least partially responsible for the overthrow of the Lekapenoi. He was an

Figure 10.4 Ivory of Constantine VII. Small-size sculpture in ivory was popular from Roman times through the whole of the Byzantine period, especially for images of considerable significance such as those of emperors and religious figures. The emperor shown here in his full ceremonial dress is identified as Constantine VII on the basis of his resemblance to known portraits on items such as coins. He is pictured here, however, as his namesake Constantine I, the first Christian emperor. Photo: Dumbarton Oaks

astute political propagandist, and was determined to use this skill in his own behalf and in the perpetuation of the dynasty.

Almost immediately Constantine had his son Romanos crowned as emperor, thus securing the survival of the dynasty. Romanos, it should be remembered, was the son of Helen Lekapena and thus grandson of Romanos Lekapenos. During the period in which he actually held power Constantine continued to busy himself with scholarship, especially with the compilation of works that would be useful for the administration of the empire and the success of his son as emperor. He apparently compiled the *De administrando imperio*, on foreign policy, the *De thematibus*, on provincial government, and the *De ceremoniis*, on imperial ceremony. He also took an active role in matters of state. He selected as *domestikos* of the *Scholai* Bardas Phokas, brother of the former rival of Romanos Lekapenos, but in general terms Constantine followed the policy that had been set by Lekapenos' government. Thus, Constantine issued further legislation against the alienation of peasant holdings, generally repeating the provision of Lekapenos' laws, although he provided that, in many cases at least, the purchase price had to be returned. Constantine's government also took special steps for the protection of soldiers' lands, laying down principles, for example, that such lands must retain a value of at least a certain amount of gold – obviously there was a tendency to evade the law by selling off all but very small parts of the lands, making it impossible for a soldier or sailor to support himself on the income (which was, after all, the point of the landholdings in the first place).

The Balkans and the West remained untroubled during Constantine's reign, and military action was concentrated in the East, where Bardas Phokas continued the struggle with Said-ad-Daulah. The results were mixed, but the Byzantines met with increasing success after 957 when Nikephoros Phokas replaced his father as *domestikos*. Constantine's diplomatic efforts reached as far afield as the courts of the Ummayyad Caliph Abd-ar-Rahman in Spain and Otto I in Germany. Special importance, however, should be attached to the conversion of the Russian Princess Olga, regent for her young son Svjatoslav, and her visit to Constantinople in 957.

Constantine died in 959, and he was succeeded by his son, Romanos II (959–63). The new emperor, grandson of Romanos Lekapenos, was not especially interested in affairs of state, and he left most decisions to his adviser, the eunuch Joseph Bringas, while the *domestikos* Nikephoros Phokas conducted a series of brilliant campaigns in the East. Both Leo VI and Constantine VII had previously mounted major but unsuccessful attempts to conquer Crete, but in 961 the troops of the *domestikos* finally took the island after a long struggle. After that Nikephoros Phokas returned to the East, where he was remarkably successful, even managing to take Aleppo, Saif-ad-Daulah's capital. Nikephoros, the "Pale Death of the Saracens," as he was known, gained such repute that Arab forces were said to have withdrawn at the mere mention that his armies

Box 10.4 *Liudprand of Cremona in Constantinople*

Liudprand of Cremona (ca. 920–ca. 972) was an Italian diplomat and administrator who served first Berengar II, king of Italy, and then Otto I of Germany (who had annexed Italy to the German Empire). Liudprand was named bishop of Cremona and he played a leading role at the emperor's court. He was familiar with Constantinople because his father and stepfather had undertaken embassies there in the earlier tenth century and he knew the Greek language.

Liudprand made at least two official journeys to Byzantium, one in 949–50 as the representative of Berengar, and the second in 968 as the emissary of Otto I. He wrote reports of each that portray his own lively and sometimes belligerent personality and provide valuable detail about Constantinople and life at the Byzantine court, especially as it was viewed by a foreigner. It is significant that the two journeys turned out very differently, the first a great success and the second a dismal failure, and this certainly is reflected in the tone of the two different works.

Liudprand's *Antapodosis* ("Tit-for-tat") is a general history of Byzantium, Germany, and Italy in his own time and it contains a detailed report of his visit to the court of Constantine VII in 949–50. He was well treated by the scholarly emperor and the two men apparently got on well. He seems to have been genuinely impressed with the splendor of imperial ceremony; this can be seen in his detailed description of how the emperor passed out gifts to his officials and entertained guests (including himself) at a lavish formal dinner. His work also contains information about earlier Byzantine history and relations with Italy and the Rhos, details that may have come directly from the scholarly archives of Constantine VII.

Liudprand's *Narrative of an Embassy to Constantinople* was a report to Otto I about his second embassy to the court of Nikephoros II Phokas in 968. The purpose of this visit was to arrange a marriage between Otto II, the son of Otto I, and a Byzantine princess. At this time, of course, the issue of diplomatic marriages must have been a particularly sensitive one in Constantinople since Nikephoros himself was emperor only because he was married to the widow of Romanos II and guardian of the "legitimate" emperor Basil II. Nikephoros was, in addition, a rough and relatively coarse soldier, confident in his own military strength and his ascetic proclivities. On all these counts, therefore, he was not apt to welcome the invitation from the polite and cultivated Italian bishop. The result is that Liudprand's account of his second visit is as full of detail as that of his first embassy, but the tone is completely different. In the latter case Liudprand describes Constantinople and the imperial court in condescending and hostile terms, commenting on the poverty of the garments and trappings of the court and the mean-spirited way in which he was treated. His description of Nikephoros II is a classic example of propaganda and calumny, so overdone that it becomes humorous. Thus, the report is enormously valuable for the wealth of detail it provides, but its broader purpose, either to cultivate hostility toward Byzantium at the German court or to cover up the failure of the embassy, makes it an important document in the development of hostile attitudes toward Byzantium in the West.

FURTHER READING

The Works of Liudprand of Cremona, trans. F. A. Wright. London, 1930.
J. Koder and T. Weber, *Liudprand von Ceremona in Konstantinopel*. Vienna, 1980.

were on the march. The removal of Said-ad-Daulah's power and the conquest of Crete meant that Byzantine arms were everywhere unchecked in the East and that the Aegean area would be spared the ravages of Arab pirates. This latter was of particular importance in the growth of the Byzantine economy and the ability of Byzantium to "recolonize" many islands and coastal areas that had been either abandoned or very sparsely settled over the past two centuries.

FURTHER READING

L. Brubaker, *Vision and Meaning in Ninth-Century Byzantium: Image as Exegesis in the Homilies of Gregory of Nazianzus*. Cambridge, 1999.

J. F. Haldon, *Warfare, State and Society in the Byzantine World, 565–1204*. London, 1999.

P. Lemerle, *Byzantine Humanism: The First Phase*. Canberra, 1986.

M. McCormick, *Origins of the European Economy: Communications and Commerce, AD 300–900*. Cambridge, 2001.

Steven Runciman, *The Emperor Romanos Lekapenos and his Reign: A Study of 10th-Century Byzantium*. Cambridge, 1929; reprint 1988.

S. Tougher, *The Reign of Leo VI (886–912): Politics and People*. Leiden, 1997.

Arnold Toynbee, *Constantine Porphyrogenitus and his World*. London, 1973.

D. S. White, *Patriarch Photios of Constantinople*. Brookline, MA, 1981.

11

The Apogee of Byzantine Power

250	500	750	1000	1250	1500

963	Foundation of Megiste Lavra, Mount Athos
976	Basil II emperor
989	Conversion of Vladimir of Kiev
1014	Basil II defeats Samuel of Bulgaria
1028	Death of last emperor of the Macedonian dynasty
1054	Split between eastern and western churches
1071	Battle of Mantzikert

Nikephoros II Phokas (963–969) and John I Tzimiskes (969–973)

In 963 Romanos II suddenly died, leaving his young sons, Basil II and Constantine VIII, as nominal rulers: Basil was 5 years old and Constantine 3. Romanos' wife Theophano assumed the regency and she formed an arrangement with Nikephoros Phokas, who had already been saluted by his troops as emperor. Theophano offered Nikephoros her hand in marriage and Nikephoros II Phokas (963–9) became emperor and, at the same time, defender of the rights of the two young emperors "born in the purple." Thus, for the first time in Byzantine history a member of the Anatolian military aristocracy came to the throne.

Nikephoros replaced Joseph Bringas as *parakoimomenos* (chamberlain) with Basil, an illegitimate son of Romanos Lekapenos. The position of *domestikos* in the East was given to John Tzimiskes, who had already won considerable repute as a general, while Byzantine forces in the West were commanded by the emperor's brother, Leo Phokas.

Nikephoros was rugged, physically unattractive, and unusually devoted to monks and asceticism. When not on active military campaign, he lived a life of prayer and self-mortification, and some of his best friends were monks. Among these was St. Athanasios, founder of the monastery of Lavra on Mount Athos, and the emperor was one of the first patrons of that famous center of Byzantine monasticism.

Founding of Mount Athos

From the days of early Christianity it was common for monks to gather in large groups in remote and desert places. These monastic retreats then frequently became holy centers, to which the faithful flocked, either to seek miraculous interventions or simply to share in the sanctity of the holy men and women who lived there. Such mountain retreats in the early Byzantine period were Mount Sinai, Mount Auxentios, and the Wondrous Mountain of St. Symeon the Stylite the Younger. In the eighth century Mount Olympos in Bithynia became the most celebrated mountain center of monasticism. This was a large complex on Ulu Dağ, near modern Brusa, that was founded in the fifth century but it eventually contained some 50 monasteries, all but one of them inhabited by men. The monasteries of Olympos were all independent establishments and they had no common organization, but other similar communities, such as Mount Latros, were monastic confederacies under a single *hegoumenos* (abbot) or *protos* ("first" monk).

Mount Athos, usually called in Greek simply *Agion Oros* (the Holy Mountain) forms the easternmost projection of the Chalkidike peninsula in Macedonia, east of Thessaloniki. It is today a spectacularly beautiful area, in part because it has been spared the traumas of modern development. The mountain itself is near the southern tip of the peninsula, and the rest of the area is rolling woodland mixed with plots of arable land, scored by innumerable streams that rush down from the heights. There are traditions that monks had settled on the peninsula in the early Byzantine period or fled there from the Arab invasions or the Iconoclast persecutions, but these cannot be historically substantiated. The first historical references to monasteries on the peninsula date to the ninth century, and an edict of Basil I in 883 provided imperial protection for the monks from local shepherds.

The crucial event for the development of Mount Athos, however, was Athanasios' foundation of the Great Lavra (Megiste Lavra) in 963 with the support of Nikephoros Phokas. Athanasios was a teacher from Trebizond who settled in Constantinople and formed strong alliances with members of the aristocratic families of the time, including that of Nikephoros Phokas. He

Figure 11.1 Megiste Lavra. This is the *katholikon* (public church) of Megiste Lavra, the oldest monastery in Mount Athos. Photo: Timothy E. Gregory

maintained those connections when he entered the monastic life and ca. 958 he moved to Mount Athos, where he sought to reform monasticism, in part by the foundation of larger monasteries. With the help of Nikephoros II he began a tradition of monasticism on Mount Athos that has lasted to our own time, surviving the fall of the empire by over half a millennium.

The Policies of Nikephoros II and John I Tzimiskes

As a member of the military aristocracy, Nikephoros was opposed to the Macedonian dynasty's policy of restricting the purchase of peasant farms by wealthy landowners. His legislation did not exactly revoke that of his predecessors, but it changed some details that made it clear that the state would no longer pursue a policy of protecting the poor landowners. On the other hand, Nikephoros sought to defend the land of the soldiers and, probably in light of the growing cost of military equipment, he increased the minimum holding of a soldier from four pounds of gold to 12. This probably was a reflection of changes in military technique and the tendency toward heavier (and thus more expensive) armor, and it signaled a significant move away from dependence on a militia of peasants: a farm worth a minimum of 12 pounds of gold was hardly a peasant holding. Further, Nikephoros' religious and ascetic sensibilities were against the growth of ecclesiastical and monastic wealth, and he issued legislation that sought to put a stop to the growth of estates belonging to the church – probably for moral rather than for economic or social reasons.

Even after becoming emperor Nikephoros took the field himself. He fought a long and ultimately successful campaign against the Arabs in Cilicia and then in Syria. His generals took the island of Cyprus in 965 and Antioch and Aleppo in 968. Syria was divided in half; the northern part was annexed by Byzantium, and the south, while independent, was under effective Byzantine control. Thus, Byzantine arms were everywhere triumphant in the East, and areas lost to the Arabs more than three centuries earlier were once more restored to the empire. The situation in the West was more complicated, especially because of the revival of the Western Empire under Otto II, who was crowned emperor in 962 and who involved himself heavily in Italy. Like Charlemagne before him, Otto sought accommodation with Byzantium, and, as we have seen, in 968 he dispatched the bishop Liudprand of Cremona as an emissary to Constantinople, for the purpose of arranging a marriage alliance between his son and one of the sisters of the legitimate Macedonian emperors. Nikephoros treated Liudprand harshly and decisively rejected the offer of alliance.

In the Balkans Nikephoros likewise acted decisively, although in the end not with great success. He rejected Bulgarian demands for the payment of tribute and called for aid from the Russian Prince Svjatoslav (the son of Olga) who had recently destroyed the Khazar state. Svjatoslav easily defeated the Bulgars in 968 and 969, deposed the Bulgarian tsar Boris II, and essentially took the country over. He apparently even considered moving his capital to Little Preslav in Bulgaria. As a result, Byzantium found the Russians on the very border of the empire, a situation that was to vex emperors for some time to come.

Meanwhile, the empress Theophano apparently tired of Nikephoros' physical appearance and his monastic habits, and she formed a plot with the emperor's chief general, John Tzimiskes. The conspirators murdered the emperor in his bedroom in December of 969.

John I Tzimiskes (969–76) was crowned only after he had agreed to the patriarch's demand that he do penance for the murder and separate from Theophano, who was sent away to a monastery. He then married Theodora, the daughter of Constantine VII, and, like his predecessor, he assumed the role of guardian of the young emperors. Civil affairs were left in the hands of Basil the *parakoimomenos*. Tzimiskes had to put down several revolts from aristocratic rivals, and his greatest ally was his brother-in-law, Bardas Skleros. Although Tzimiskes himself was, like his predecessor, a member of the military aristocracy, he sought actively to prevent the alienation of private peasant lands and the transformation of the peasants into *paroikoi*. The legislation to do this was already in place, and Tsimiskes used military power to round up the peasants settled on private estates and force them to return to their villages. In this he can hardly have been fully successful and, in effect, the peasants so treated had become essentially the *paroikoi* of the state.

Box 11.1 *Byzantine Houses*

We actually have very little evidence about what kinds of houses the Byzantines lived in. Naturally these would have varied from time to time, depending on the climate and the economic situation of the owner. In the early Byzantine period ancient Mediterranean house types obviously continued to be built and some of the villas of the wealthy were quite lavish, whether in the city or the country. A number of these villas of the fourth to sixth centuries have been excavated; they were commonly developed versions of Roman houses, with frescoed walls and floors of marble and mosaic. They often had elaborate dining areas and peristyled courtyards. In the sixth to seventh centuries there is evidence that some owners were not able to maintain these lavish buildings, and many of them began to be broken up into smaller units that were presumably rented out to help pay the bills.

In the middle and later Byzantine periods it is clear that some large houses were built, and a few of them have been found in archaeological excavations. Many of these were rectangular, with a courtyard in the center. The ground floor was used for storage, workshops, and stables for animals, while the living accommodations were on the upper floor. The buildings were often of irregular shape and they were crowded along narrow lanes, apparently without any thought for a planned arrangement. The houses were built of poor material and the walls were commonly constructed of two faces of uncut stone filled with a mixture of small stones and dirt; the faces of the walls could be covered with a soil plaster and then whitewashed or even painted. Mud bricks were also frequently used, especially in the upper reaches of a wall. Even the houses of the wealthy might be irregular and the eleventh-century historian Michael Atalliates described his house in Constantinople as a complex of several buildings surrounding a court, with a ground floor and a second story that projected out over the courtyard; it also had a grain mill driven by a donkey and – something that became relatively common in the later Byzantine period – a private chapel.

Although houses would not normally have had running water, arrangements were commonly made for toilets, at least in the city houses of the more well-to-do. The legal documents provide considerable information about these, since sewage and the location of toilets might be a matter of considerable disagreement among neighbors. Toilets that emptied into cesspools often were located in the courtyard of a house. The Byzantines also used chamber pots made of various materials and poorer houses probably had very rudimentary sanitation facilities. Byzantine law forbade throwing human waste out the window, but there are reports that this restriction was not always maintained. The twelfth-century poet John Tzetzes complained that the children and the pigs of the deacon who lived above him in Constantinople "urinated so much that they produced navigable rivers."

In the fourteenth to fifteenth centuries the houses of wealthy Byzantines were influenced by trends from the West, especially Italy, and the houses, for example, at Mystras were characterized by second-story balconies supported by arcades, pointed windows, towers, and large interior halls.

FURTHER READING

Ch. Bouras, "Houses in Byzantium," *Deltion tes Christianikes Archaiologikes Etaireias*, series 4, 11 (1983), pp. 1–26.
Ken Dark, ed., *Secular Buildings and the Archaeology of Everyday Life in the Byzantine Empire*. Oxford, 2004.

Tzimiskes had been left with a difficult situation in the Balkans, where the Russian prince Svjatoslav had secured increasing authority over Bulgaria. In 971 Tzimiskes occupied the Bulgarian capital of Great Preslav and took the tsar Boris captive. He then moved on the city of Silistria, which Svjatoslav had occupied. After a desperate siege and an equally desperate resistance, Tzimiskes prevailed and Svjatoslav was forced to withdraw. He was killed shortly thereafter, and Tzimiskes was in effective control of Bulgaria. Tzimiskes was also able to deal successfully with the western emperor Otto II by agreeing to the marriage alliance his predecessor had rejected but sending, not an imperial princess born in the purple, but his own relative Theophano, who became the wife of Otto II in 972. This marriage was to have a significant effect on East–West relations, especially in the impact of Byzantine ideas on the western court. Theophano had considerable influence on her son, Otto III, who became western emperor in 983, and who copied Byzantine ceremonial and asserted the supremacy of the emperor over the pope.

In the East Tzimiskes sought to consolidate and expand the conquests made by Nikephoros Phokas. In this he was opposed by the Fatimids of Egypt, who had also tried to exploit the power vacuum in Syria. Tzimiskes, however, relieved Fatimid pressure on Antioch and pressed far into Syria and the Holy Land, taking Damascus, Tiberias, Caesarea, and stopping not far from the walls of Jerusalem. He returned victorious to Byzantium, conquering Beirut and Sidon on the way. Unfortunately for the empire, this vigorous and successful emperor suddenly took ill and died, early in 976.

The Reign of Basil II (976–1025)

It was in this context that Basil II, then 18 years of age, at last took power in his own name. It is true that throughout his reign he shared the throne with his younger brother Constantine VIII (two years his junior), but power always was effectively in Basil's hands, and Constantine was content to enjoy palace life and leave the burdens of rule to his brother. For years, at least since the death of Romanos II in 968, members of the military aristocracy, who ruled in the names of the legitimate Macedonian emperors, had controlled the empire. Now, in 976, the *domestikos* Bardos Skleros expected to continue that tradition, and he rose in revolt when Basil II declared himself fit to rule on his own. There followed a monumental clash in which the young emperor displayed his own determination and strength of character, helped as he was by the cleverness of Basil the *parakoimomenos*. Skleros at first defeated all the forces sent against him and by 978 he had all of Asia Minor under his control. The *parakoimomenos*, however, formed an alliance with the head of a rival aristocratic family, Bardas Phokas, nephew of the emperor Nikephoros Phokas, and they were able to defeat Skleros and force him to flee to the caliphate.

During the next few years Basil the *parakoimomenos* was essentially in control, as he had been for years, but Basil II finally sought to establish his independence and, despite a plot by the eunuch for Bardas Phokas to seize power, the emperor triumphed, and the venerable *parakoimomenos* was finally removed from power and exiled in 985.

Meanwhile, taking advantage of the confused situation in Constantinople, a revolt against Byzantine power had broken out in the Balkans, led by the Kometopouloi, the four sons of a provincial governor in Macedonia. This revolt was welcomed by the local people, and leadership was finally assumed by Samuel, the youngest of the Kometopouloi, who was founder of the second period of Bulgarian greatness in the Middle Ages. Even though the focus of power in this state was at Ochrid, in Slavic Macedonia (far from the earlier center at Pliska), both Samuel and the Byzantines regarded it as the direct descendant of the empire of Symeon some 150 years earlier. One of the first things Samuel did was to restore the independent Bulgarian patriarchate that had been abolished by Tzimiskes.

Samuel sought to expand his territory to the south, with attacks on Serres and Thessaloniki, and in 985 or 986 he succeeded in taking Larissa (in Thessaly). Basil II counterattacked in 986, but his forces were defeated. In part as a result of this failure, members of the Byzantine aristocracy revolted. Bardas Skleros returned from exile and again sought the imperial throne and, as before, he was opposed by Bardas Phokas. On this occasion, however, Phokas too revolted and had himself proclaimed emperor (987). Phokas quickly became the main pretender, and by the beginning of 988 he was prepared for an assault on the capital. In this situation Basil II called on the Russian prince Vladimir (the son of Svjatoslav) for assistance. The latter dispatched a force of 6,000 warriors, presumably Vikings from Russia, and, led by the emperor in person, they dealt a decisive defeat to Phokas, who died in battle the next year. Bardas Skleros once again rose in revolt, but this was quickly put down, and Basil II's throne was secured, largely by help from his Russian ally.

As a reward for his assistance, Vladimir was offered Basil's sister Anna as his bride, on condition that the prince and his people accept baptism from Constantinople. This was an enormous compromise by the Byzantines and an indication of how much the emperor valued his alliance with the Russians: no purple-born princess had previously ever been offered to a foreign ruler. Certainly, from the Russian point of view, the alliance was equally positive, and the conversion of Olga (Vladimir's grandmother) some years earlier and the strength of Byzantine arms under Tzimiskes had undoubtedly convinced Vladimir that the future of his state lay in alliance with Byzantium. The Russian Primary Chronicle, of course, explains the conversion in terms of a

Box 11.2   *The Historian Michael Psellos*

Michael Psellos (1018–ca.1081) was one of the greatest of the Byzantine historians, but he was much more than that. He, perhaps more than any other writer, characterizes Byzantine writing and culture. He wrote works concerned with philosophy, theology, rhetoric, law, and medicine, and he published a collection of letters. His broad learning and individualism make him perhaps the best example of the "humanism" of the eleventh and twelfth centuries.

Psellos' original name was Constantine, but he took the name Michael when he entered a monastery. He received an excellent education in Constantinople and held a number of posts in the imperial administration. Psellos was a member of a group of intellectuals who hoped to influence politics under Constantine IX (1042–55) but he fell into disgrace and entered a monastery on Mount Olympos. He soon returned to Constantinople, however, and resumed a place at court, holding the position of *Hypatos ton Philosophon* ("Consul of the Philosophers"), effectively head of the philosophical school of the capital.

Psellos' best-known work is the *Chronographia*, a historical work describing the period 976 to 1078, much of it taken from his own personal observations. The *Chronographia* is arranged as a series of imperial biographies, and the court and the emperors play the central role, with military and foreign affairs generally far from his field of view. Psellos saw the course of history as the result of human character and conflict among individuals rather than as the outcome of divine will. He wrote in the first person and his focus is always from his own point of view. The psychological studies of some of his characters are complex and interesting to modern readers. He apparently sought to understand individuals, including those with whom he did not agree, although on a few occasions his judgment seems somewhat less than fair.

Psellos was a member of what is usually called the civil aristocracy and he understood the politics of the eleventh century from that point of view. His history thus fails to take into serious consideration the military difficulties that developed during that period. With hindsight, therefore, we can criticize his work as a representation of some of the reasons behind the military collapse: a focus on culture, without full realization of the changes in foreign relations, a lack of interest in the so-called military aristocracy and the fate of the peasants who had provided the basis of Byzantine strength for centuries, and a self-centeredness that failed to see the many ways in which traditional Byzantine life was changing or even falling apart.

Even in his historical work Psellos was concerned with philosophical issues. He saw "nature" (*physis*) as the driving force in the universe and some recent research argues that the *Chronographia* was in fact a disguised philosophical work, arguing for the secularization of Byzantine society and the end of the church's role in affairs of state. He wrote a work on the topography of ancient Athens, a paraphrase of the *Iliad*, and a list of illnesses. His multifaceted intellect and his direct involvement in the politics of the day make him one of the most interesting of Byzantine writers.

FURTHER READING

Anthony Kaldellis, *The Argument of Psellos'* Chronographia. Leiden, 1999.

Russian search for a religion best suited to the Russian temperament. This story, which certainly cannot be literally true, says that the prince sent out a body of ten officials to visit the homelands of the great religions of the time: the Volga Bulgars (who were Muslims), the Khazars (who were Jews), the Germans (who were Catholic Christians), and the "Greeks" (who were Ortho-dox Christians). The emissaries found objections in the first two religions, but they reported that in the church of Constantinople, presumably Hagia Sophia, "we knew not whether we were in heaven or on earth. For on earth there is no such splendour or such beauty, and we are at a loss how to describe it. We know only that God dwells there among men." In fact, it is likely that Vladimir realized – as had many of his Slavic predecessors – that alliance with one Christian power or another was all but inevitable and that the Byzantine political tradition provided important benefits for the consolidation of his own domestic power and the cultural advancement of the principality. The Byzantines temporarily rethought the awarding of a purple-born princess to such a ruler, but in 989 Vladimir made a military show of force in Cherson, and the marriage was solemnly celebrated, Vladimir accepted baptism, and the conversion of Russia was begun.

In the view of the historian Psellos, Basil's character had been radically changed as a result of the long struggle with Bardas Phokas, Bardas Skleros, and the landed aristocracy. From a pleasure-loving youth he became a hardened and resolute politician and commander; he was dour and short-tempered and – unlike his forefathers – he had no interest in literature or learning. In keeping with his personality he dedicated himself completely to the task of ruling the empire, and, most important, he never married and had no sons to succeed him as emperor.

In terms of land policy Basil II was, not surprisingly, one of the most outspoken critics of the growth of aristocratic holdings and a defender of peasant rights to keep their farms. In this regard, he restated the policies of his predecessors forbidding the alienation of peasant land, and he even withdrew the provision of a 30-year limit for the return of such purchases. He went even further than his predecessors and took the novel step of making the *dynatoi* (powerful landowners) responsible for payment of the *allelengyon*, the default payment for insolvent peasants that had previously been borne by the community as a whole. He was equally stringent in his attempt to prevent the alienation of peasant land by monasteries and the church. All of these efforts, of course, flew in the face of the dominant economic and social trends of the day, and – despite the emperor's occasionally violent attempts at enforcement – it is questionable whether such a policy could have been successful. Basil's actions, however, were the strongest of the attempts by the Macedonian emperors to defend the peasants against the growing power of the landed magnates.

In foreign affairs, Basil II's greatest challenge was Samuel's revived Bulgarian Empire, and he approached this struggle with the same methodical determination that characterized all other aspects of his reign. In 991 Basil invaded Samuel's territory, but his successful campaign was soon interrupted by trouble in the East, where the Fatimids threatened Byzantine positions in northern Syria. Basil traveled to the East and was able to restore Byzantine supremacy with a significant victory in 995. Samuel, meanwhile, was able to take advantage of Basil's absence and his armies advanced south into Greece, reaching as far as the Peloponnesos. On his return to the Balkans in 1001 Basil embraced the struggle with Samuel. Basil first moved against the old Bulgarian capital of Pliska, and his success there cut Samuel's empire in half. The emperor then turned south into Macedonia, winning victory after victory. After four years of nearly ceaseless warfare the Byzantine Empire was once again supreme in the Balkans, but Samuel still held out and the war continued at a reduced level. Finally, in 1014, a great battle at Kleidion (on the Strymon River north of Serres in Macedonia) resulted in the complete victory of Basil and the capture, allegedly, of 14,000 prisoners. Although Samuel escaped the debacle, he could not survive the aftermath: Basil – afterwards always known as Bulgaroktonos (the "Bulgar-slayer") – blinded the prisoners and sent them off to Samuel in groups of 100 men, each led by a one-eyed guide. When the tsar viewed this sight, he suffered a stroke and died almost immediately afterwards.

There was some further resistance, first from Samuel's son and then from other relatives, but in 1018 Bulgaria surrendered completely and Basil entered Ochrid in triumph. After a struggle of nearly 30 years Basil had accomplished his goal, and the whole of the southern Balkan peninsula was under Byzantine control – for the first time since the seventh century. Contrary to the policies of his predecessors, he did not leave Bulgaria as an allied client state, but rather annexed the center of Samuel's empire, dividing it into *themes*. The outlying areas, such as Croatia and Dioclea (including Rascia and Bosnia), continued to be ruled by native princes, who were seen as Byzantine vassals. Basil sought to respect the special importance of Bulgaria, and, although he suppressed the independent patriarchate of Ochrid, he made the archbishop autocephalous, meaning that he was not subject to the authority of the patriarchate of Constantinople, but, in this case at least, he was directly responsible to the emperor himself.

After his unprecedented victory in the Balkans, and although he was well over 60 years of age, Basil II turned his attention to affairs in Asia, where he successfully intervened in Armenia and established new *themes* and other military districts in a wide arc from north to south, extending well into Mesopotamia. Toward the end of his life Basil turned to the West, where Otto III was well disposed to cooperate with Byzantium. The western emperor had even requested an imperial bride, and an agreement was reached, but Otto died in 1002, putting a halt to this initiative. Basil, meanwhile, reorganized Byzantine territories in Italy, and he was making preparations for a great campaign against the Arabs in the West when he died in December of 1025.

Constantine VIII (1025–1028)

As mentioned, Basil had no heirs, and he was therefore succeeded by his brother Constantine VIII, who had long shared the imperial throne with him, at least in name. Constantine was already old when Basil died, but he resisted pressure from the large landowners and the church to abandon the policies of his brother. In 1028 Constantine fell seriously ill, and only at this point did he take measures for the succession. He also had no sons, but three daughters, the eldest of whom had entered the monastic life. Succession, therefore, was to be passed to his two other daughters, Zoe and Theodora, who themselves, by this time were no longer young. In November of 1028 Constantine arranged for Zoe to marry Romanos Argyros, the Prefect of the City, and in December the last Macedonian emperor died.

Romanos III Argyros (1028–1034)

Romanos Argyros was a member of what we may call the Byzantine civil aristocracy, those families who – although they normally held substantial agricultural properties in the provinces – owed their prominence to their administrative positions at court, meaning that they were, generally speaking, lacking in military experience but were highly educated and fully familiar with classical culture. Despite his administrative experience, Romanos Argyros was hardly successful as an emperor. Apparently filled with delusions of grandeur, he attempted various ambitious schemes, including a military campaign in the East, where the situation was saved only by the intervention of the accomplished general George Maniakis.

Most important, Romanos III completely abandoned the Macedonian emperors' policy concerning landholding. He yielded to the pressure of the *dynatoi*, and the institution of the *allelengyon* was abolished. The old laws against the alienation of peasant holdings remained on the books, but there was no attempt at rigorous enforcement and, as a result, peasant land began to disappear into the increasingly large holdings of the great landowners.

Romanos III made the mistake of ignoring Zoe, the ultimate source of his political authority. As a result she formed a liaison with Michael, a peasant from Paphlagonia, who had been brought to the palace by his brother, the eunuch John the Orphanotrophos, who hoped by this means to gain greater power for himself. In the end Romanos III was murdered in his bath (1034) and Zoe married Michael, who ascended the throne as Michael IV.

Michael IV the Paphlagonian (1034–1041) and Michael V Kalaphates (1041–1042)

John the Orphanotrophos essentially administered the state in the name of his brother. He was a capable ruler, although his ruthless taxation policies earned him a reputation for rapaciousness. John sought to tax the substantial wealth of the *dynatoi*, and for this he earned the support of the civil aristocracy, but his measures naturally were felt more heavily by the poor than by the wealthy, and he did nothing effective to restrict the disappearance of peasant landholding in the provinces.

Partly as a result of John's fiscal policies and partly as a reaction to apparent Byzantine military weakness, revolts broke out in the Balkans. The first of these, under Peter Deljan, sought to restore the empire of Samuel. Although this was suppressed by Michael IV himself in 1041, resentment remained among the empire's Slavic subjects, and the allied principality of Zeta (former Dioclea) was able to establish its independence from Byzantine hegemony.

Meanwhile, Michael IV had fallen ill, and John the Orphanotropos selected a young relative, another Michael, known as Kalaphates. He succeeded Michael IV on the latter's death in 1042. Michael V Kalaphates (1041–2) was headstrong and rash and he destroyed his own base of power, first by exiling the Orphanotrophos and then by sending the empress Zoe to a monastery. The result was a nearly instantaneous rebellion by the people of Constantinople and the church, largely in support of the dynastic principle that accorded priority to the two aged empresses. As a result, Michael V was deposed and blinded and Zoe and Theodora were to rule jointly, an arrangement that fell apart almost immediately.

Constantine IX Monomachos (1042–1055)

After that, Zoe (although then 64 years old) was married for the third time, to Constantine Monomachos, a member of the civil aristocracy and a relative of Romanos III Argyros. Court life at the time was certainly brilliant, and Constantine IX was surrounded by scholars of high caliber, such as Constantine Leichoudes, the poet John Mavropous, the jurist John Xiphilinos, and the philosopher and historian Michael Psellos, whom some have compared with the literati of the later Italian Renaissance. In 1045 the University of Constantinople was refounded with faculties of philosophy and law, and based solidly on the principles of classical education. Psellos was named as head of the university, with the high-sounding title of "Consul of the Philosophers." At court the two empresses ruled jointly with Constantine IX, but they were openly joined in official functions by the emperor's mistress Sklerina (niece of his second wife), who was given the newly created title of *sebaste*.

The dominance of the civil aristocracy under Constantine IX did not mean that measures were taken to limit the power of the military aristocracy in the provinces. Indeed, this period witnessed the continued growth of large landholdings and the tendency for the state to surrender some of its prerogatives to the *dynatoi*. Most notably, the landowners were increasingly given grants of *exkousseia*, which exempted them from the payment of taxes, and many were also granted judicial immunity, so that all legal disputes among individuals living on their land would be settled in their courts. In this respect, the landed aristocracy effectively escaped the control of the state, and this was a significant development in a society that had preserved, from its very beginning, the institution of the sovereign political state. Even where the state maintained control, its functioning was restricted – or we might even say "privatized" – by developments such as the increasing reliance on tax farming, a system in which individuals or corporations formed for this purpose essentially purchased the right to collect taxes in certain areas: they paid a set sum to the state and then attempted to raise more than that amount from the hapless peasants.

An important phenomenon in this regard was the development of the so-called *pronoia* system, which came to dominate landholding over the next several centuries. This was a system that bears some resemblance to the western European feudal system, although there are important differences, which will be discussed below. A grant of *pronoia* (the word means a benefit or a gift) meant that an individual was given a portion of state-owned land in return for some specified service that the landowner rendered to the state. In return, the landowner – the *pronoiar* – was free to administer the territory as he saw fit and to collect all the revenues from the land and any taxes due from it. This system effectively alienated territories from state control, and in that it has certain similarities to western feudalism. The *pronoia* system came into existence by the middle of the eleventh century, but it was not immediately widespread. It was different from western feudalism in several important ways. First of all, despite the effective diminution of state power, the concept of the state never disappeared from Byzantium, and even the *pronoiars* acknowledged the theoretical sovereignty of the emperor. Furthermore, the grant of *pronoia* was supposedly limited to a specific period of time, and it was not supposed to be transferable either by grant or inheritance; it was also not to be divisible, so that land granted in *pronoia* could not be divided up and passed on to the landowners' underlings, as in the medieval West. Nonetheless, the practice of *pronoia*, along with other similar grants, certainly had the effect of limiting the real power of the state, and it presumably placed severe limitations on the income available to the central administration.

The expenses of the state, however, did not diminish significantly, and the emperor finally took the step that previous rulers had avoided for 700 years: they began the devaluation of the Byzantine coinage. Thus, apparently during the reign of Michael IV, base metal was added to the gold used for coins, allowing the state to strike more money with the same amount of precious metal. This provided the state with a temporary windfall in order to meet current expenses, but the long-term results were certainly disastrous. The Byzantine *nomisma* had long been the accepted currency for foreign exchange, and this brought Byzantium a considerable international prestige that could not be maintained with an unstable currency. Furthermore, the economic advantage of debasement to the state could be maintained only through further devaluation of the coinage, and this was a temptation that few future emperors could resist. In modern times we can see the effect of currency deterioration, largely in the form of run-away inflation, something that the Byzantine economy probably experienced. It is, however, difficult to measure the full impact of this phenomenon, in part since the effect of debasement was restricted largely to the gold coinage that was mostly used by the wealthier sections of the population, while the impact on the poor is uncertain. In particular, it is difficult to estimate the effect of debasement on trade, which was not, in any case, the dominant element of the Byzantine economy.

Just as important, the middle of the eleventh century witnessed the decline in the conscript Byzantine army. This was a result of several contemporary phenomena, one of which – the destruction of peasant-soldier holdings – has already been discussed. Further, the government of Constantine IX was decidedly anti-military in its policies, and it failed to provide funds for the army or to reward its commanders for work well done. In its search for ready income the state allowed soldiers to buy off their obligation to serve in the army. The result of this important phenomenon was that the state had to rely more and more on foreign mercenaries, at first Varangians from Russia but increasingly Normans from Italy and France, Anglo-Saxons from England, and others. The most famous of these was the Varangian Dužina, attested from 1034 onward, which enrolled Vikings from Russsia and eventually Anglo-Saxons. This elite guard, whose members had distinctive arms and uniforms, had its quarters in Constantinople but also took part in field campaigns. In addition, Byzantium had to depend more than before on its alliances with foreign peoples who might be used to fight the empire's wars. The decline of the domestic army thus had far-reaching ramifications. There were also administrative repercussions: the *strategos*, commander of the thematic armies, essentially disappeared, replaced by the provincial governor (normally the *kritis*), who had previously been his subordinate.

Several revolts broke out against Constantine IX, led by the successful generals George Maniakis and (later) Leo Tornikis; both of these nearly succeeded in toppling the civil administration, but in both cases fate intervened and the revolts failed. In the meantime, the peace brought by the success of the great military emperors remained generally undisturbed and Byzantine arms – for the moment – remained unchallenged. Nonetheless, the international scene was changing slowly, and new adversaries arrived who would seriously challenge Byzantium in the years to come. By the middle of the eleventh century the Abbasid caliphate had all but disappeared; effective power was now in the hands of various Turkic groups, from the Fatimids in Egypt to the Seljuks on the empire's eastern frontier. In the Balkans, Bulgaria had essentially disappeared, and the Russians turned their attention to the north, leaving the steppe corridor to people such as the Patzinaks, Cumans, and Uzes. Perhaps most menacing of all, the Normans, who had been established in Sicily and southern Italy for some time, began to turn their attention toward Byzantium, and for the first time the empire was to face a direct threat from that direction.

Late in the reign of Constantine IX the definitive split between the eastern and western churches took place, an event that continues to have significance today and that seriously influenced Byzantium's relations with the West from that time onward. It was especially unfortunate for the empire that, just as

Christian Western Europe began to emerge as a real economic, political, and military power, its natural alliance with Byzantium foundered on the rocks of religious disagreement and misunderstanding. The basic cause of the schism was, as previously in the time of Photios, the cultural gulf that had grown over the centuries between eastern and western Christianity: although Byzantines and westerners were all Christians, in basic outlook and in many aspects of their faith they were worlds apart. In addition, the conflict was fanned by historical circumstances and the personalities of the characters involved. The papacy in the mid-eleventh century was in the midst of its greatest period of reform and was locked in the beginning of a struggle with the western emperor for supremacy in Western Europe. Its claims to universality had become an essential part of papal policy in a way that was bound to clash with Byzantine concepts of ecclesiastical independence and imperial universality. The old theological issue of the *filioque* remained unresolved: this was a serious disagreement about the relationship among the three persons of the Trinity; the Latin church argued that the addition of the term "and from the Son" to the Nicene Creed did not change its essence, while the eastern church argued that the difference was fundamental to our understanding of God. There were also liturgical and practical matters such as the issue of a celibate priesthood, fasting on Saturday, and the use of unleavened bread (the so-called *azymes*), all of which were characteristic of the West but not of the East. Over the past several centuries there had been significant disagreements and breaks in communion, most notably the Akakian Schism, Iconoclasm, and the Photian Schism. And overall, the two major halves of Christianity had in large part gone different ways in terms of culture, so that although the two parties believed essentially the same things, they looked at the world very differently and had built up a large reserve of mistrust. Finally, there was the key issue of papal supremacy: the western church increasingly argued that the pope should have administrative control of the whole Christian church, while the easterners denied this and said that the five patriarchs should independently control their respective areas.

Pope Leo IX, the first of the reforming popes of the eleventh century, was strong-willed and proud, outdone in this regard only by his representative in the controversy, Cardinal Humbert. The patriarch, Michael Keroularios, was in all respects a match for his adversaries; early involved in political activity in Constantinople, he had become a monk and, as patriarch since 1043, he brought all his confidence and self-importance to this office. Both sides were uncompromising and ready for conflict, which first broke out over rival claims in south Italy. A papal delegation, led by Cardinal Humbert, arrived in Constantinople in 1054. Encouraged by the emperor's lack of support for Keroularios, the papal party condemned the Byzantines and excommunicated the patriarch and his followers. Keroularios had the full support of his church and the people of Constantinople, and he quickly brought Constantine IX into line, summoning a council that met in the same year, issued a condemnation of all the Roman practices, and excommunicated the papal legates. The break

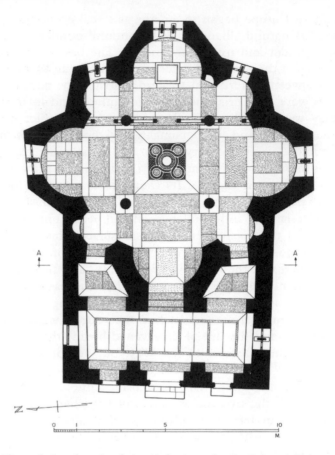

Figure 11.2 Plan of the church of the Holy Apostles in Athens. This small church was built inside the market place of ancient Athens about the year 1000. It was a tetraconch, which means that the four sides of the building ended in an apse; between each of the main apses were smaller subsidiary apses, turning the building into an octagon. The church has a dome supported on four freestanding columns (shown in the plan as four small dark circles surrounding the central square design in the floor). The building was excavated and restored by the American School of Classical Studies at Athens. Plan by W. B. Dinsmoore, Jr., from Alison Frantz, *Agora* 20. *The Church of the Holy Apostles* (Princeton, NJ, 1971), Plate 29. Reproduced with permission from the Trustees of the American School of Classical Studies at Athens

between the eastern and the western churches in 1054 has never been healed. As mentioned above, the two groups believe and practice many of the same things, but the schism has been the cause of much misunderstanding, hostility, and bloodshed ever since, and has remained one of the main points of division between Eastern and Western Europe in recent centuries.

Constantine IX died in January of 1055, and Theodora reigned in her

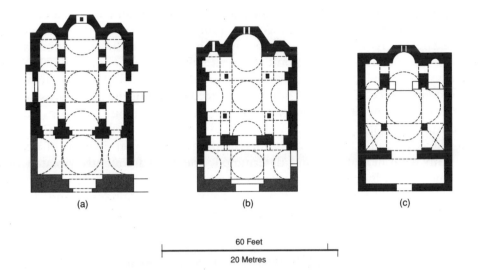

(a)   (b)   (c)

60 Feet

20 Metres

Figure 11.3 Several cross-in-square churches: Kaisariani, St. John the Theologian (both outside Athens), and Ligourio in the Argolid. The "cross-in-square" became the standard church type in the middle Byzantine centuries. This building was elegant, compact, reasonably easy to build, and well suited to the needs of the Byzantine liturgy. The ground plan of the church is essentially a square, but four columns, piers, or a combination of both at the center allow construction of four barrel vaults that run, like the arms of a cross, to the exterior walls. A masonry drum is then built on the central ends of the vaults and this terminates in a dome. Thus, the building is transformed from one that is essentially rectilinear (the square), to one that is curvilinear (the cylinder and half sphere of the dome). This transformation was perceived not only as an architectural phenomenon but also as a spiritual or theological one, as the relatively "weak" form of the lower part of the church is transformed into the "powerful," indeed "perfect" shape of the dome, symbolizing humans' transformation into divine beings

own name until her death the next year. With her passing, the Macedonian dynasty was at last extinct. On her deathbed Theodora nominated Michael VI (1055–7, known as Michael Stratiotikos or Michael the Old), a member of the civil aristocracy who continued the policies of Constantine IX. Not surprisingly, a revolt broke out among the military aristocracy, led by Isaac Komnenos, a member of an important military family from Asia Minor. Disturbances began also in Constantinople, and the patriarch Keroularios joined the insurgents. Michael VI abdicated and Isaac Komnenos (1057–9) was crowned as emperor.

The period since the death of Basil II in 1025 had been marked, as we have seen, by the dominance of the civil aristocracy and a real neglect of the military needs of the state. Isaac Komnenos sought to redress that balance and he made significant moves to strengthen the empire's defenses. A difficult problem, of course, was the lack of funds for the military, and Isaac resorted to extreme measures, including the confiscation of property and the possessions of the church. As we have seen, the patriarch had originally supported Isaac, but the two soon came into conflict, in part over Isaac's confiscation policy, but also over ideological issues, since Keroularios sought nothing less than the full independence of the church, if not the recognition of the superiority of the church to the state; it was even said that the patriarch, on one occasion, put on the purple boots that were one of the main symbols of imperial power. Emperor and patriarch came to a formal understanding of an equal division of power, but both were headstrong and determined, and both frequently violated this agreement. Finally, when Keroularios was out of Constantinople in 1058, he was arrested and a council was quickly summoned to condemn and depose him. Keroularios died shortly thereafter, but Isaac's success was short-lived, since the church and many of the people of Constantinople were offended by his treatment of the patriarch, and the civil aristocracy used this to fuel opposition to the emperor. Ill and disillusioned, Issac Komnenos abdicated in 1059 and retired to the monastery of Stoudios.

The alliance between the leaders of the church and members of the civil aristocracy selected Constantine X Doukas (1059–67) as emperor. Constantine was a member of the distinguished family of Doukas, who at this time represented the civil aristocracy of the capital. He was a devoted follower of Psellos, who became the tutor of his children, and he returned to the fiscal politics of Constantine IX, including the debasement of the coinage and the expenditure of resources in Constantinople rather than on the army. The civil service grew in numbers and expense and the army was completely neglected.

Unfortunately, this neglect of the military came at a time when the enemies of Byzantium were gathering strength on several fronts. The most immediate of these threats was in south Italy, where the Normans under Robert Guiscard were pushing the Byzantines out of their remaining possessions. In the Balkans, Byzantine territory was threatened by attacks from several Turkic groups: the Hungarians from the northwest and the Uzes and the Cumans from the northeast. But ultimately the greatest danger was posed by the Seljuk Turks, who had gained control of Iran and Iraq and virtually the whole of the Near East up to the borders of Byzantium on the west and the Fatimid caliphate of Egypt on the south. Under the leadership of Alp Arslan, the second Seljuk sultan, the Seljuks attacked Armenia and broke into Asia Minor, advancing as far as Caesarea, which they took in 1067.

At this point, Constantine X died, and his wife Eudokia acted as regent for her young sons. Power remained in the hands of the civil administrators but in the end the military situation was so dangerous that even the patriarch, John Xiphilinos, saw the need for accommodation with the military aristocracy, and Eudokia was convinced to marry the general Romanos Diogenes, who ascended the throne as Romanos IV (1068–71).

Romanos IV had to continue to deal with conspirators who wanted to protect the rights of Eudokia's still young sons. His primary concern, however,

Figure 11.4 Coin of Romanos IV (1068–71). This coin shows, among other things, how complicated the dynastic situation had become at this time. Romanos has been forced to accept the three sons of his predecessor Constantine X as his colleagues: Michael VII, Konstantios, and Andronikos. These three are shown on the reverse (the right, in the illustration), with Michael VII in the center. On the obverse Christ is depicted crowning Romanos on the left and his wife Eudoxia on the right. Courtesy of the Arthur M. Sackler Museum, Harvard University Art Museums, Bequest of Thomas Whittemore. © President and Fellows of Harvard College

was to rebuild the army in Asia Minor. As a result of this focus on the East, Byzantine interests in Italy were neglected, and Bari, the last Byzantine stronghold, fell to the Normans in 1071. Romanos made expeditions to eastern Anatolia in 1068–9, but the Seljuks used the opportunity to seize Byzantine cities in the center. In 1071 Romanos led a large army, perhaps as many as 200,000 men, including many foreign contingents, in a monumental effort to drive the Seljuks from Asia Minor; a key element in the army was a group of Norman mercenaries under the adventurer Roussel de Bailleul. In August the forces of Romanos IV met those of the Seljuk Sultan Alp Arslan in a pitched battle near Mantzikert in Armenia. As soon as the fighting began the Norman troops fled the field and the Byzantines were caught in a trap. In a second day of fighting Romanos was moving successfully against the Seljuk center, when his rival Andronikos Doukas promoted a rumor that the emperor had been killed. Panic spread among the troops and many fled. The Seljuks made skillful use of their lightly armed, mounted archers, the Byzantines were thoroughly defeated, and Romanos was taken prisoner.

Modern historians have made much of the Battle of Mantzikert, seeing it as the fatal defeat, from which the empire never recovered. On the contrary, the Byzantine losses were relatively small and Romanos himself was soon released, agreeing only to cede Armenia to the Turks. The real difficulty lay in the aftermath of the battle, in which the army commanders immediately deserted their posts in Asia Minor in a mad scramble for power in Constantinople. As a result the countryside lay open to the Seljuks, who were able to occupy much of Asia Minor and settle in it, virtually without opposition from the Byzantines. Immediately after the battle the Caesar John Doukas proclaimed Michael

Doukas, son of Constantine X, as sole emperor. Romanos IV attempted to reclaim his place, but he lost to the supporters of the Doukas family and was blinded. Michael VII Doukas (1071–8) was generally ineffective, although several important developments took place during his reign. Occupied first with the civil war and inattentive to military considerations, Michael was unable to oppose the Seljuks, who flooded over Asia Minor and established the sultanate of Rum in Ikonion, the first foreign state to occupy part of the Byzantine heartland of Anatolia. About 1074 an alliance was made with the Norman Robert Guiscard, whose daughter was to marry Michael's son Constantine, the presumptive heir to the throne. Throughout the reign of Michael VII the empire remained in dire financial straits. The courtier Nikephoritzes had become the main civil administrator of Michael VII and he used harsh measures in an attempt to restore some form of fiscal stability. These included the regulation of the grain supply of Constantinople, the continued devaluation of the coinage, and a decrease in the size of the *modios*, the main Byzantine measure of grain, by a *pinakion* (about a quarter of a *modios*), a policy that earned for the emperor the nickname "Parapinakis."

Not surprisingly, Michael VII's reign was marked by revolts, the most important of which were by Nikephoros Vryennios in the Balkans and Nikephoros Votaneiates in Asia Minor. The latter secured support from the Seljuks, and entered Constantinople in 1078, shortly after the abdication of Michael VII. Votaneiates had been an effective general, but he was now elderly, and the financial situation forced him to devalue the coinage further in order to make lavish payments to his supporters. In this unstable situation more revolts were inevitable and in 1081 he was overthrown by Alexios Komnenos, who at last managed to provide some continuity and strength on the Byzantine throne.

FURTHER READING

M. Angold, *The Byzantine Empire, 1025–1204. A Political History*, 2nd edn. London, 1997.

S. Franklin and J. Shepard, *The Emergence of Rus, 750–1200*. London, 1996.

P. Stephenson, *Byzantium's Balkan Frontier: A Political Study of the Northern Balkans, 900–1204*. Cambridge, 2000.

12
The Komnenoi

250	500	750	1000	1250	1500

1081	Alexios I Komnenos emperor
1096	First Crusade reaches Constantinople
1143	Manuel I emperor
1185	Death of last emperor of Komnenan dynasty, beginning of collapse of the central state
1204	Fourth Crusade captures and sacks Constantinople

Alexios Komnenos and the First Crusade

Alexios I Komnenos (1081–1118) represents that peculiarly Byzantine phenomenon, the emperor who came along just as the situation was at its darkest, who rescued the empire from military disaster, and set it on a course that it was to follow for the next century. The Komnenoi were a military family from Asia Minor who held prominent commands from the beginning of the eleventh century onward. Alexios was the nephew of the emperor Isaac Komnenos and the son of John Komnenos, who had been *domestikos* of the *Scholai*. Alexios had been a general under Michael IV and Nikephoros III, against whom he revolted and seized the throne. Yet Alexios came to power as a representative of a coalition of aristocratic families: the Komnenoi, the Doukai, the Palaiologoi, and the Melissenoi, and the dynasty of the Komnenoi continued to reflect this aristocratic family alliance in a way that was unprecedented in Byzantine history.

The situation Alexios I found at his accession was certainly not a positive one. Most of Asia Minor had been lost to the Seljuks; the Patzinaks and other local groups were in control of most of the Balkans, and Robert Guiscard and the Normans were preparing to invade Byzantine territories along the Adriatic. Guiscard, it should be remembered, had married his daughter to Michael VII's son, and he used the overthrow of Michael as a pretext to attack Byzantium. Spurious as this claim might be, it could be used by individuals disloyal to the new emperor, and Alexios therefore regarded the Normans as his most serious adversary.

In order to raise a mercenary army Alexios had to pawn the precious vessels of the Byzantine church, and he sought widely for allies against the Normans. The most important of these were the Venetians, the Italian commercial and naval state, which already regarded the Normans as their enemies; this alliance was especially important since the Venetians could supply the naval power that Byzantium now sadly lacked. The Normans attacked Dyrrachium, the main Byzantine city on the Adriatic coast, and they took it in 1081, thus opening Byzantine territory to depredations by the Normans, who reached as far south as Larissa. By a treaty of 1082 the Venetians promised to aid the Byzantines militarily, in return for honors, payments in cash, and most important, the right to trade freely throughout the empire without the imposition of taxes. This important concession was the foundation of Venice's maritime empire. It gave Venetian merchants an advantage over their competitors and seems to have virtually driven Byzantine merchants from the seas. Meanwhile, in 1082 Robert Guiscard was recalled to Italy, and the Byzantines and their Venetian allies were able to regroup. When Guiscard died in 1085 the Norman threat was, for a time, at an end, although Byzantium would yet again meet the Normans in battle, and the price for Byzantine victory, paid to the Venetians, had indeed been great.

No sooner was the Norman threat deflected than Alexios found himself involved in war with the Patzinaks, who moved against Constantinople and stood before the walls of the city in 1090. They formed an alliance with the Seljuk emir of Smyrna, Tzachas, who besieged Constantinople by sea. During the winter of 1090/1 Constantinople endured a dangerous siege, but in early 1091 Alexios allied with the Cumans, who joined with the imperial army in a battle at Mount Levunion on 29 April, when the Patzinaks were nearly completely wiped out.

After this narrow escape Alexios sought to restore Byzantine supremacy in the Balkans. He made a military show in Serbia that resulted in the recognition of Byzantine hegemony, but a revolt of the Cumans prevented the full implementation of the emperor's plans. In Asia Minor, as in Europe, Byzantine power was on the increase, aided largely by the fragmentation of the Seljuk sultanate of Rum into squabbling emirates. A Byzantine reconquest of Asia Minor was not impossible and, along with it, the possibility of a Byzantium restored to the position it had held before Mantzikert.

Nonetheless, at this time a new phenomenon fell upon the Byzantine Empire like a whirlwind. This was the crusading movement, something essentially foreign and strange to the Byzantines, but designed to have a powerful impact

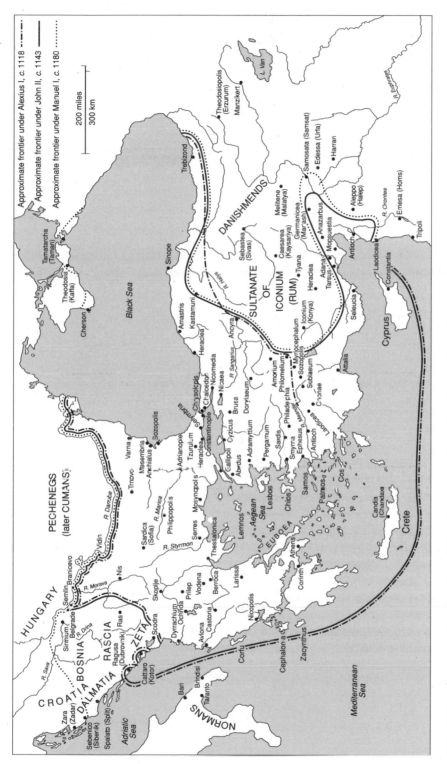

Map 12.1 The Byzantine Empire of the Komnenoi. From *The Cambridge Medieval History*, volume 4, map 5

Approximate frontier under Alexius I, *c.* 1118 — · — · —
Approximate frontier under John II, *c.* 1143 ————
Approximate frontier under Manuel I, *c.* 1180 ·········

200 miles
300 km

on Byzantine history from this time onward. On the one hand, the Byzantines had long been aware of western political and military interests in the East, and, with the arrival of the Venetians and the Normans, they saw the kind of power the westerners could bring. Nonetheless, both the Venetians and the Normans were understandable to the Byzantines – they were foreign powers who recognized Byzantine sovereignty and who generally wished to work within the Byzantine system (perhaps, in the case of the Normans, taking it over as their own). But the Crusades were something totally new for the Byzantines. Not that the Byzantines did not accept a connection between religion and war: they certainly saw their army as the strong arm of the Christian God and they understood that the Muslims waged war in the name of Allah. Indeed, there were phenomena in the Byzantine past where emperors had used religious feeling as a motive for military action. One of these was at the time of Herakleios' wars against the Persians, especially after the latter had carried the Holy Cross off to Ctesiphon, and another was at the time of Nikephoros I Phokas' campaigns in Syria and the Holy Land. But none of these were Crusades in the western sense, primarily seen as religious responsibilities designed to rid the Holy Land of infidel control and to "return" it to the Christians. Rather, the Crusades were a uniquely Western European phenomenon, connected with western concepts of pilgrimage and the universalist claims of the papacy, as well as with the explosive growth of the European economy during the eleventh century and the calls for order and restrictions on war in the West. The fervor that the westerners came to feel for the "recovery" of the Holy Places was something quite foreign to the Byzantines, as were the hordes of peasants, children, and adventurers that descended on the empire as a result of this movement.

Box 12.1   *The Arrival of the First Crusade in the Byzantine Empire: Anna Komnena,* Alexiad

Anna Komnena, daughter of the emperor Alexios Komnenos, describes her impression of the arrival of the Franks (the western Christians) in Byzantine territory in 1096. On the one hand, Anna looked down on the Franks, whom she generally regarded as morally and spiritually inferior, but on the other she was amazed by the huge size of their armies and their great strength and endurance in battle. Especially interesting in this passage is the way the princess compares the Frankish horde to a swarm of locusts and how, she says, the Byzantine soothsayers interpreted this, to the disadvantage of the Muslim Seljuks in possession of most of Asia Minor:

Before he [the emperor Alexios Komnenos] had enjoyed even a short rest, he heard a report of the approach of innumerable Frankish armies. Now he dreaded their arrival for he knew their irresistible manner of attack, their unstable and mobile character and all the peculiar natural and concomitant characteristics which the Frank retains throughout; and he also knew that they were always agape for money, and seemed to disregard their truces readily for any reason that cropped up. For he had always heard this reported of them, and found it very true. However, he did not lose heart, but prepared himself in every way so that, when the occasion called, he would be ready for battle. And indeed the actual facts were far greater and more terrible than rumour made them. For the whole of the West and all the barbarian tribes which dwell between the further side of the Adriatic and the pillars of Heracles, had all migrated in a body and were marching into Asia through the intervening Europe, and were making the journey with all their household. The reason of this upheaval was more or less the following. A certain Frank, Peter by name, nicknamed Cucupeter [Peter of the Cowl], had gone to worship at the Holy Sepulchre and after suffering many things at the hands of the Turks and Saracens who were ravaging Asia, he got back to his own country with difficulty. But he was angry at having failed in his object, and wanted to undertake the same journey again. However, he saw that he ought not to make the journey to the Holy Sepulchre alone again, lest worse things befall him, so he worked out a cunning plan. This was to preach in all the Latin countries that "the voice of God bids me announce to all the Counts in France that they should all leave their homes and set out to worship at the Holy Sepulchre, and to endeavour wholeheartedly with hand and mind to deliver Jerusalem from the hand of the Hagarenes" ["the descendants of Hagar," used by the Byzantines as a synonym for Arabs (or occasionally, any Muslims)]. And he really succeeded. For after inspiring the souls of all with this quasi-divine command he contrived to assemble the Franks from all sides, one after the other, with arms, horses and all the other paraphernalia of war. And they were all so zealous and eager that every highroad was full of them. And those Frankish soldiers were accompanied by an unarmed host more numerous than the sand or the stars, carrying palms and crosses on their shoulders; women and children, too, came away from their countries. And the sight of them was like many rivers streaming from all sides, and they were advancing towards us through Dacia generally with all their hosts. Now the coming of these many peoples was preceded by a locust which did not touch the wheat, but made a terrible attack on the vines. This was really a presage as the diviners of the time interpreted it, and meant that this enormous Frankish army would, when it came, refrain from interference in Christian affairs, but fall very heavily upon the barbarian Ishmaelites who were slaves to drunkenness, wine, and Dionysus. For this race is under the sway of Dionysus and Eros, rushes headlong into all kind of sexual intercourse, and is not circumcised either in the flesh or in their passions. It is nothing but a slave, nay triply enslaved, to the ills wrought by Aphrodite. For this reason they worship and adore Astarte and Ashtaroth too and value above all the image of the moon, and the golden figure of Hobar in their country. Now in these symbols Christianity was taken to be the corn because of its wineless and very nutritive qualities; in this manner the diviners interpreted the vines and the wheat. However let the matter of the prophecy rest.

Alexiad, 10.5, *The Alexiad, of Anna Comnena*, trans. Elizabeth A. Dawes (London, 1928), pp. 248–9.

His own fault?

It is sometimes said that Alexios I brought the Crusades upon himself with letters to Count Robert of Flanders and Pope Urban II, seeking western military aid in his struggle against the Turks. What Alexios had in mind, without doubt, was the dispatch of mercenaries or a military alliance of the kind that Byzantium had long used in its dealings with enemies. Pope Urban, however, at a council in Clermont in 1095, called for a mass movement, under the direction of the papacy, to reconquer Jerusalem, which had fallen to the Seljuks in 1077. Rather surprisingly, the call was enthusiastically received, both by members of the western aristocracy, and by simple lay people, some of whom joined an unscrupulous leader called Peter the Hermit and set off for the Holy Land before the nobles were ready to march. This group, without good leadership and short of supplies, plundered and looted its way through Hungary and the Balkans, arriving in August of 1096 in Constantinople. After attempts to control them failed, the emperor shipped them over to Asia Minor, where most of them were slaughtered by the Turks.

Later in the same year, the noble leaders of the First Crusade began to appear in Constantinople, notable among them Godfrey of Bouillon, Raymond of Toulouse, and Bohemond, the son of the Norman Robert Guiscard. Alexios demanded that the Crusaders pledge their fealty to him in an oath based on western precedent, and most of them did so. Raymond of Toulouse refused, but a compromise was ultimately found in which both Alexios and Raymond promised to respect the life and honor of the other. Alexios, although he certainly had not welcomed the Crusaders, at least sought to control their independence and to guarantee, as best he could, that any territory captured by them would be returned to Byzantine control.

In the spring of 1097 the Crusaders crossed over into Asia Minor, supported by promises of assistance from the emperor, who advised them to seek an alliance with the Armenians. The Crusaders outmaneuvered and defeated a large force the Turks brought out against them and the road across Asia Minor was open to them. The focus of Byzantine expectations was Antioch, since it was the key to the defense of the Euphrates frontier and a city rich with Byzantine associations. The Crusaders ultimately reached Antioch and besieged the city, where they ran into considerable difficulty. Alexios set off himself to relieve the Crusaders, but he ultimately turned back. The Crusaders, however, finally took the city in June of 1098. Rather than surrendering it to the Byzantines, the Crusaders pointed out that Alexios had let them down at a critical moment, and Bohemond seized the city in his own name. Byzantine hopes of a restoration of the empire's fortunes in the East were seen to be false.

Now under the command of Raymond of Toulouse, the Crusaders moved on toward Jerusalem. Raymond, despite his refusal to do obeisance to the emperor, turned over several Syrian ports to Byzantium, while other Crusaders set up principalities of their own in captured territory. Jerusalem fell to the Crusaders on 15 July 1099, but Raymond was disappointed in his hope for reward, as Godfrey of Bouillon was made King of Jersusalem and Defender of the Holy Sepulcher.

Raymond of Toulouse remained on good terms with Alexios, and he helped the emperor deal with a new group of Crusaders who arrived in Constantinople in 1100. Alexios, however, still seethed at Bohemond's seizure of Antioch and – after the Norman rejected Alexios' demand that he surrender the city – the emperor sent an expeditionary force to Syria in hopes of isolating the city and forcing its submission. Bohemond came to see Byzantium as the main threat to his interests in the East, and, leaving his nephew Tancred in charge of Antioch, he went to the West to prepare an invasion of Byzantine Albania, designed to force Alexios to cease his pressure in Syria. In preparation for this Bohemond circulated reports hostile to Alexios and the Byzantines, making use of the stereotypes that the Byzantines were effete and treacherous and claiming that Christians had an obligation to overthrow the schismatic emperor. Bohemond gained the support of Pope Paschal II for his undertaking and the invasion began in 1107. Although at first successful, Bohemond soon found himself hemmed in, for Alexios recalled his best troops from the East to oppose the Norman danger. In the end a treaty was drawn up in 1108 in which Bohemond was left in control of Antioch, but he recognized that he held it as a liegeman of Alexios; and the Normans agreed to recognize the suzerainty of both Alexios and his successor, John Komnenos.

Alexios had managed to deflect the Norman threat and to maintain his claim of suzerainty over most of the Christian East. This claim, however, was without much practical worth and it was bought at the expense of a near-abandonment of Byzantine interests in central Anatolia, where the Seljuks were essentially allowed to maintain and strengthen their holdings. Even in Syria, Tancred was able to take advantage of the disappearance of Byzantine military pressure to secure his control of Antioch, and Alexios was thus moved to seek a military alliance with the Seljuk sultan in Baghdad against the city. This ultimately accomplished nothing but served to confirm Bohemond's propaganda that the Byzantines were willing to conspire with the Turks against Christian interests. Alexios certainly did realize the central importance of Asia Minor, and his generals managed to secure control of much of its western coast. In 1111 the emperor made a serious excursion into central Asia Minor, and he managed to obtain the submission of the Seljuks, although Alexios also agreed to the evacuation of the Greek population from the area, something that was to contribute to the long-term ethnic change in the area.

Alexios Komnenos had a long and militarily successful reign. He rescued the Byzantine state from the threat of imminent dissolution. He faced a series of serious military threats, and, through a combination of diplomacy, personal cunning, and his own military ability, he generally emerged the victor. By the time of his death Byzantium was once again the most powerful state in the eastern Mediterranean. But Alexios had accomplished this by changing some of the basic structures of the Byzantine state, or – perhaps better – he had created new institutions and personal arrangements that replaced the institutions that had characterized Byzantium until that time.

In economic terms, Alexios found himself seriously strapped for cash, especially in the early years of his reign. As mentioned above, he resorted to the expedient of seizing and melting down church vessels, and in the early part of his reign he continued the devaluation of the coins. Around 1092 he was able to restore the value of the coinage and strike a *hyperperon* (as the gold coin was now called) of 21 carats, only somewhat less than the gold before the devaluation of the past century. Hostile critics (such as the historian Zonaras) describe his rapacity and significant increases in taxes, including the introduction of corvée labor. Tax farming had by this time become the norm, and the burden was thus increasingly heavy, but it is difficult to know how to judge Alexios' overall economic policy.

The income realized by these measures was, of course, largely sought for the purchase of mercenaries in order to strengthen the empire's defense. Nonetheless, Alexios tried also to increase the participation of native soldiers in the Byzantine army. The peasant militias were, of course, long a thing of the past, and the military practices of the time demanded the participation of heavily armed, mounted soldiers, who could only come from the ranks of the wealthy. Thus, Alexios tried to tie the system of *pronoia* closely to the responsibility to supply soldiers for the imperial army. What was previously a rather loose and inconsistent system was now connected regularly with the expectation that a *pronoiar* would appear, fully armed, for military service, and, depending on the size of his grant of land, he would be accompanied by a levy of similarly armed troops. As with the beginnings of the *pronoia* system, this modification has frequently been compared or connected to the institution of western feudalism, although, once again, a primary difference is that, under the Komnenoi, the sovereign power of the state was still maintained, at least in theory.

Perhaps the most controversial aspect of Alexios' policy was his treaty with the Venetians (1082), followed by similar concessions to Pisa (1111), and his virtual surrender of trade to the Italian merchants. This has been seen by some historians as a fatal mistake that ultimately ruined the Byzantine economy. Others have pointed out that Italian merchants already had the greatest share of Byzantine trade and that there was little the emperor could have done about it anyway, while still others have pointed to the significant evidence of prosperity in the twelfth-century empire as an indication that the economic strength of Byzantium was hardly destroyed. One theory along these lines is that, while Venetian ships carried the bulk of international transport in the twelfth century, this did not hurt the business of Byzantine traders, who still controlled the bulk of commerce, from port to port, within the empire, and that the increased access to long-distance trade of the Venetians did not harm the Byzantine economy but rather stimulated it to greater production and consumption. The state, however, can hardly have shared in the benefits of any such improvement in the economy as a whole, which must have been split between the foreign merchants and the Byzantine aristocracy.

The reign of Alexios I was also marked by changes within the administrative structure of the state, or at least its system of titles. The old titles had

Figure 12.1 Graffito of a ship from Korinth. Graffiti, both letters and drawings, are often found scratched onto Byzantine buildings. Sometimes these were prayers or curses but ships seem to have been a real favorite and different kinds of ships can often be discerned, suggesting that the person who scratched them on the surface had a particular boat in mind. The ship depicted here is relatively small, with a sail and a round bottom, a well-known Byzantine type. Many of these graffiti of ships may have been votives, silent prayers, perhaps to protect a sailor or a traveler on a sea journey. Robert Scranton, *Corinth 16. Medieval Architecture in the Central Area of Corinth* (Cambridge, MA, 1967), Figure 14 (p. 138), graffito of a round-bottomed boat. Reproduced with permission from the Trustees of the American School of Classical Studies at Athens

essentially lost their meaning in the collapse of the governmental hierarchy, and the nearly wholesale distribution of titles during the course of the second half of the eleventh century. Thus, many of the old imperial titles essentially disappeared, while new and often high-sounding titles were created. For example, the imperial titles of *Caesar, nobilissimus*, and *kouropalates* survived, but were diminished in rank, while the new title of *Sebastokrator*, created by Alexios for his brother Isaac, was superior to all three. Other high-sounding titles were formed by the combination of earlier honors, such as the *protonobilissimos* or *protonobilissimohypertatos*. As the old *theme* army disappeared, the office of *strategos* disappeared as well and the governor of a *theme* was a *dux* and his assistant a *katepan*. The commander of the army was styled the *megas domestikos*, the commander of the fleet the *megas dux*, and the controller of the civil service was the *logothetes ton sekreton*, often known simply as the Grand Logothete.

John II Komnenos (1118–1143)

In his last years Alexios I apparently lost some of his power of command, and his wife, Eirene Doukaina, and his daughter Anna conspired to secure the succession of Anna's husband, the Caesar Nikephoros Vryennios. Alexios' son John Komnenos ultimately prevailed, in part because Vryennios failed to join in the plot and served the new emperor loyally the rest of his life. Nonetheless, the reign of John Komnenos was marked by continued conspiracy, instigated by members of his own family. Conspiracies were not uncommon throughout all of Byzantine history, but to a certain extent John's problems were the result of Alexios I's policy of basing much of his power on the members of his family. While the emperor remained the figurehead and the theoretical center of power, in fact he had become the leader of an alliance of members of the imperial family. John Komnenos sought to end this system and he turned for support to personal servants well outside the circle of the court itself. Most notable of these was John Axoukh, a slave of Turkish origin, the emperor's childhood companion, whom John II named as *megas domestikos*.

Freed, to a certain degree at least, of the interference of his family, John was able to turn his attention to foreign affairs, which were pressing on a variety of fronts. Probably his first priority was to deal with the situation in Asia Minor, and John campaigned there in 1119 and 1120 with some success. His attention, however, was attracted elsewhere when the Patzinaks, who had been quiet for 30 years since their defeat by Alexios, broke into the Balkans in 1122. John responded by offering their leaders gifts, while at the same time attacking their forces that were camped near Veroë (modern Stara Zagora). The battle was closely fought, but the daring of the Varangians won the day and the Byzantines were completely successful. John had become closely involved with Hungary as a result of his marriage to a Hungarian princess, and Byzantine interests on the Danube were dependent on good relations with that country. Nonetheless, beginning in 1128, he had to fight the Hungarians on several occasions in order to maintain the status quo. John's dealings with the Serbs were somewhat more mixed, but Serbia still remained essentially within the Byzantine sphere.

The disappearance of the Norman threat meant that the empire was much less in need of naval help from Venice and John resented the audacity of the Venetians, who often acted against Byzantine interests. John therefore at first refused to ratify the privileged position granted to the Venetians by his father.

Until 1124 the Venetians were occupied elsewhere, but afterwards they turned their attention to Byzantium, attacking the coastline of Asia Minor as well as the island of Kefalonia. In 1126 John decided that he could not fight the Venetians and at the same time carry out his plans to restore Byzantine power in Asia Minor, and he once again ratified Venetian trading privileges.

As a result of the agreement with Venice and victories in the Balkans, John II was finally able to turn his attention to Asia Minor in the period after 1130. Like his father, John's policy had two goals: the recovery of Antioch and the Euphrates frontier, and the restoration of Byzantine control over central Anatolia. Asia Minor at this time was divided between the Seljuk sultanate of Rum, with its center at Ikonion, which controlled the south, and the Danishmends who controlled northern Asia Minor. At this time the Danishmends were very much in the ascendancy, and John waged a series of campaigns against them, unfortunately with little result. He next turned his attention to Cilicia and the territory around Antioch, where the Armenians and the Crusaders had extended their territory at Byzantine expense. Beginning about 1136, John quickly restored Byzantine control of Cilicia and approached Antioch in 1137, where the city was in a difficult situation due to pressure from both the Danishmends and the Muslim forces of Mosul. Raymond of Poitiers, who had just become Prince of Antioch, did homage to John and promised to respect Byzantine territory and cooperate with the emperor in military campaigns. Aided by his Crusader allies, John campaigned in Syria, impressing his opponents with Byzantine power but accomplishing little of a practical nature. His demand that Antioch be turned over to him was frustrated by a popular revolt in the city, and the emperor returned to Constantinople, victorious almost everywhere but with little to show for his effort.

By the 1130s Byzantine foreign policy had to take account of the revival of Norman power in Sicily under Roger II. Aware that the Normans would soon again become interested in Byzantium, John sought an alliance with the German emperors, whose own interests in Italy made them regard the Normans as enemies – and the Byzantines thus as potential allies. Agreement was made, first with the emperor Lothair, and then, after 1138, with Conrad III. This alliance was cemented in 1140 by an agreement for the marriage of Bertha of Sulzbach, sister-in-law of Conrad III, to Manuel Komnenos, the younger son of John II (the marriage did not take place until 1145, after Manuel had become emperor). The emperor felt that Byzantium's future lay in such broad alliances, with the Franks in the West, as well as those in the Levant, and that with this aid he would be able to deal with problems in the Balkans and Asia Minor.

In 1140 John campaigned against the Turks in Asia Minor and prepared yet another offensive against Antioch and the East. Setting off in 1142, John moved speedily through Asia Minor, secured the support of Edessa, and stood before the walls of Antioch. Raymond played for time but ultimately refused to surrender the city. John decided to withdraw to Cilicia for the winter before pressing the siege of the city. In the spring of 1143, however, he was accidentally injured while hunting and died, thus leaving his greatest ambitions and the tasks he had worked at for so long unfulfilled – but presumably well within the grasp of his successor.

Manuel I Komnenos (1143–1180)

John's younger son, Manuel, had already distinguished himself as a competent soldier and a good leader. Probably for this reason, John II ignored normal Byzantine practice and designated Manuel as his heir, passing over his elder son Isaac as he did so. Not surprisingly, there was some doubt about the succession, all the more so since Manuel was proclaimed in Cilicia while his brother was at home in Constantinople. Individuals loyal to Manuel, however, managed to neutralize opposition before it developed and Manuel was welcomed to the city and even reconciled with his brother, who accepted the *fait accompli*.

Once secure on the throne Manuel I attempted to carry out the military plans of his father. In 1144 he sent a joint land and sea expedition against Cilicia and Syria, which met with some success, and in 1146 he attacked Konya (Ikonion), the seat of the Seljuq sultanate of Rum, and again he was reasonably successful, although his siege of Konya was abandoned after a half-hearted attempt.

Meanwhile, a new force gathered on the Byzantine horizon: the Second Crusade. The sentiment of the Byzantines at this moment can easily be gathered from the text of Anna Komnena's *Alexiad*, which was being completed at just this time: in the Byzantine view the goal of the Crusaders, from beginning to end, was not the recovery of the Holy Land, but the conquest of the Byzantine Empire. Manuel learned of plans for a new crusade and he immediately began diplomatic communication designed to safeguard Byzantine interests as best he could. Already in 1146 he wrote to Pope Eugenius III, suggesting that the same arrangements in force for the First Crusade be maintained for the Second – namely that the commanders of the Crusade should swear obedience to the emperor and that they should return former Byzantine possessions to the empire. Manuel also established contacts with the French king, Louis VII, and continued his diplomatic relations with the German emperor, Conrad III. One of Manuel's main goals, of course, was the neutralization of Roger II of Sicily, whom the Byzantines regarded as the most dangerous of the western powers. These negotiations met with considerable success and Roger II was excluded from the Crusade, but, rather surprisingly and in marked contrast to the First Crusade, Conrad III took the cross himself, along with many of his subordinates. This was the first time a major western ruler had taken part in a crusade and it gave the movement a German, rather than a French, flavor, even though Louis VII joined Conrad in the expedition.

The Crusaders arrived quickly, the German contingent reaching Constantinople in 1147. Manuel was very suspicious of Conrad's military intent, even though Conrad was the brother-in-law of the emperor's wife, Bertha of Sulzbach, and he quickly shipped the westerners over to Asia Minor. Although the Crusaders expected opposition only when they reached the Holy Land, they immediately met the armed resistance of the Turks settled in Asia Minor; the Germans were defeated and their army turned back toward Constantinople, where they met up with the French contingent at Nicaea. From this point on the French took the initiative and Manuel arranged to have a fleet carry most of the army to Antioch, thus bypassing all of Asia Minor. Conrad returned to Constantinople, where he was warmly entertained by the emperor. An agreement was made whereby the remainder of the German army, minus the emperor, was sent in Byzantine ships to Acre. Once in the Holy Land, the remnants of the crusading army met with dismal failure and the Second Crusade accomplished nothing.

Manuel I, however, would certainly have been pleased with his success in handling the Crusaders; they had been passed through Byzantine territory with little harm to Byzantium. He exploited the differences between the Germans and the French to his own advantage, and he emerged with Byzantine power unscathed. To the westerners, nonetheless, and even to some Byzantine observers, Manuel had treated the Crusaders shamefully; he had failed to appreciate their "noble goal" but had looked to the narrow interests of the Byzantine state. Thus, in the mind of many westerners Manuel's actions were unconscionable and he was judged largely responsible for the failure of the crusade. To be fair to Manuel, as has already been pointed out, the Byzantines never understood the crusading ideal and they regarded the interests of "Christendom" as identical with the interests of the Byzantine state. These different perceptions were at the heart of differing perceptions of the Crusades and the role of the emperor at the time of the Second Crusade, and they were to have an important influence in growing anti-Byzantine sentiment in the West.

Meanwhile, Roger II chafed at his exclusion from the Crusade, and in 1147 he used the opportunity to attack and plunder the Greek cities of Thebes, Korinth, and Athens, carrying off to Sicily much wealth and the Jewish silk-weavers who had made Greece the center of silk production in the Christian world; he also conquered and held the island of Kerkyra (Corfu) in the Adriatic. In 1148 Conrad and Manuel made an alliance against the Norman kingdom, and Conrad pledged to hand over southern Italy to the Byzantines, as a dowry for Manuel's German wife. Already in 1147 Manuel began preparations for a strike against the Normans, and, realizing the importance of a strong military presence, he renewed Venetian trading privileges within the empire and secured Venetian support for an attack on Kerkyra, which the Venetians naturally regarded as a threat to their own interests. A long and difficult siege followed, during which the Byzantines and the Venetians quarreled, and Roger sought to divert the allies' attention by sending a Norman fleet into the Aegean and by encouraging the Serbs and Hungarians to attack Byzantine territory. In 1149, however, the Normans surrendered Kerkyra to the emperor and Manuel subdued the Serbs and Hungarians, returning to Constantinople in triumph.

Manuel planned to use this victory as a springboard for the recovery of southern Italy and Sicily, and he continued to press Conrad to honor his promise in this regard, but the plans came to nothing in the short run, and Conrad died in 1152. In 1154, however, Roger II died, and the weakness in Sicily and the ambitions of the new German emperor, Frederick Barbarossa, gave the Byzantines an opportunity for action in Italy. Under the command of John Axoukh and with the cooperation of Michael Palaiologos and John Doukas, Byzantine forces secured the surrender of Bari in 1155, along with a number of other coastal towns. An attack on Brindisi failed in 1156, and any immediate attempt at a reconquest of southern Italy came to a halt, but the Byzantines had shown that they could carry the war to Norman territory and that they could still hope to maintain a Byzantine protectorate in Italy. Ultimately, in 1158, Manuel came to terms with William I, the new Norman king of Sicily, probably because by this time Frederick Barbarossa had become alarmed at Byzantine success in the peninsula, and the Byzantine emperor now saw the Norman king as an ally rather than an enemy.

Meantime, virtually all the Crusader states in the East acknowledged at least the theoretical supremacy of Byzantium, and in 1159 Manuel made a ceremonial entrance into Antioch mounted on his horse, while the Latin King of Jerusalem and the Prince of Antioch followed in his train. Manuel had, it seemed, finally solved the problem that the Crusades had caused for Byzantium.

In Hungary Manuel was equally successful, and he intervened in disputes about the succession to the throne, allowing him to consider the possibility of annexing the country once and for all. A treaty of 1164, drawn up with the assistance of the King of Bohemia, gave the emperor considerable influence and eventually led, by 1167, to the subjugation of Croatia, Bosnia, and much of Serbia to the Byzantine Empire. Manuel even considered the possibility of marrying his daughter to the Hungarian prince Bela, to whom he would eventually leave the empire. Dissension, however, broke out in Serbia, about 1166 or 1167, under the leadership of Stefan Nemanja, who rebelled against the empire but was defeated and paraded through the streets of Constantinople in 1172.

Byzantine success in foreign relations ironically had a long-term negative effect, in part because it irritated or neutralized many of Byzantium's allies and raised fears in the West. Especially significant was the fact that there was no real hope of accommodation with the papacy, whose power had grown enormously throughout Europe. Also important was the enmity with Frederick I, who opened negotiations with Kilij Arslan, the Sultan of Rum. Venice, long Byzantium's main ally in the West, had grown fearful as a result of the display of Byzantine power in Italy, along the Dalmatian coast, and in Hungary. Manuel sought to ally Byzantium with Genoa and Pisa, the other Italian naval powers, and in 1171 open conflict broke out with Venice. On 12 March all Venetians within the empire and their ships and goods were seized, resulting in Venetian attacks on Byzantine territory.

In 1176 Manuel moved again against the sultanate of Rum, and the two armies met at Myriokephalon in the mountains of Phrygia on 17 September. The Byzantine forces were surrounded by the Turks and almost completely annihilated. The Battle of Myriokephalon was a disaster on a level with that of Mantzikert a century earlier. Despite his notable successes, Manuel's foreign policy completely disintegrated after 1176, especially in the face of the obvious success of the Turks in Asia Minor.

In economic terms the situation was just as dark, in large part because Manuel's foreign adventures had been expensive and without much in the way of immediate return. Manuel sought to settle foreigners in Byzantine territory, in much the way his father had done, in the hope of making them into soldiers, but the bulk of the army remained mercenary. The state, by this time, had become thoroughly militarized, and military men dominated virtually all aspects of the government, with detrimental effect on society as a whole.

Manuel was himself, however, a great patron of art. He commissioned the paintings in the *trapeza* (refectory) of the monastery of St. Mokios in Constantinople that depicted his ancestors, and similar paintings in the Blachernai and Great Palace also provided excellent examples of an attempt to use art as political and dynastic propaganda. Despite his political and military opposition to the West, Manuel was a great admirer of western culture, and he imitated western court manners, ceremonies, and even feudal jousts and knightly contests.

Andronikos Komnenos (1183–1185)

Manuel I had been married twice, first (as we have seen) to Bertha of Sulzbach and, after her death, to Maria of Antioch, the daughter of Raymond of Poitiers, in 1161. At Manuel's death in 1180 their son, Alexios II, was only 12 years old, and Maria assumed the regency, selecting as her agent Alexios Komnenos, a nephew of Manuel I. Maria remained unpopular in Constantinople, in part because of her western sympathies, and there were several unsuccessful attempts to overthrow the regime, led largely by disgruntled members of the Komnenan family. Ultimately the throne was seized by Andronikos I Komnenos (1183–5), a cousin of Manuel I and his opposite in many ways. While Manuel had supported the military aristocracy and a pro-western policy, Andronikos was an enemy of the aristocracy and he strongly opposed a policy based on good relations with the western powers. His revolt, in 1181, gained strength quickly and, when Andronikos' troops reached Chalcedon, a revolt broke out in Constantinople that resulted in a brutal massacre of the Latins in the city (in May 1182).

Andronikos entered the city in triumph, arranged the imprisonment or execution of his rivals, and was crowned as co-emperor along with young Alexios II in September 1183. The young emperor was eventually murdered, and Andronikos ruled in his own name. The new emperor (he was then 65 years old) made a determined attempt to root out all the evils that beset the state, using whatever means he could to stop corruption and curtail the power of the aristocracy. His methods were often brutal, but generally successful: he is reputed to have said that corrupt officials must "cease either from ill-doing or from living." This application of state power had a generally favorable effect on the Byzantine citizenry, who were released from the worst abuses of the past.

Andronikos had few allies among the aristocracy, especially among the Komnenoi, although some of the Doukai supported him. The landed aristocracy did not generally cooperate with him and he punished corrupt officials with great severity, a policy that only engendered revolts and plots against the emperor; a few nobles even fled to foreign principalities where they stirred up trouble against Byzantium. In addition, it should be remembered, the aristocrats whom the emperor opposed were at the time the very foundation of Byzantine military power.

As a result of these internal difficulties the alliances that Manuel I had built in the Balkans began to come apart. Bela III, the King of Hungary, posed as the avenger of Maria of Antioch, and, allied with the Serbians, attacked Byzantine territory in 1183. The Hungarians withdrew the next year but in the aftermath Stefan Nemanja was able to secure independence for Serbia, and many of the Byzantine cities of the Balkans lay in ruins. The Normans saw this situation as an opportunity to invade once more, and William II, then the Norman king, swept from Dyrrachion eastward, taking Thessaloniki after an especially difficult siege. The population of Constantinople, until then strong supporters of the emperor, abandoned him, and Andronikos was overthrown and torn apart by the mob on 12 September 1185.

With the fall of Andronikos Komnenos the dynasty of the Komnenoi came to an end and with it all attempts to place limits on the independence of the landowning aristocracy. Over the next 20 years the central authority of the state collapsed and local dynasts and petty tyrants became all but independent, dramatically foreshadowing the results of the Fourth Crusade.

The new emperor was Isaac II Angelos (1185–95), a member of an aristocratic family that owed its prominence to the fact that his grandfather had married the youngest daughter of Alexios I. Isaac made little effort to check the power of the provincial aristocracy and he was accused of selling offices and committing other fiscal abuses, raising money, perhaps, for his ambitious building schemes in the capital. He did, however, take the field when necessary, and his general Alexios Vranas was able to halt the expansion of the Normans in the Balkans. Isaac married the daughter of Bela III of Hungary and thus secured some peace from that direction, but a serious revolt broke out in Bulgaria, led by the brothers Peter and Asen, who established themselves in the new capital of Trnovo. The revolt gained support among a population of Bulgarians and Vlachs angered at excessive taxation, and Stefan Nemanja in Serbia used the opportunity to throw off Byzantine rule there.

Although Isaac survived a revolt led by Vranas and he pursued the war against Bulgaria diligently, he could make little headway in the Balkans.

The arrival of Frederick Barbarossa and the German contingent of the Third Crusade in 1189 only worsened the situation, and the rulers of Serbia and Bulgaria were quick to ally themselves with the Westerners against Byzantium. Isaac sought to gain the support of Saladin, who had taken Jerusalem in 1187, and as a result Barbarossa threatened to attack Constantinople itself. In 1190 Isaac was forced to agree to help the Germans on their way to the Holy Land. Barbarossa's death in Asia Minor allowed Isaac to take the initiative in the Balkans, where he met with some success against the Serbs. The treaty that followed (in 1190) acknowledged Serbian independence but sought to keep Serbia in the Byzantine sphere of influence.

In 1191 Richard I Lionheart of England took the island of Cyprus, which had been virtually independent under the adventurer Isaac Komnenos (brother of Manuel I), who had seized the island in 1184; in 1192 Richard sold the island to the Knights Templar and then gave it to Guy de Lusignan, the former King of Jerusalem. From that time onward Cyprus was to be in Latin hands.

Isaac II had difficulties with the Bulgarians and, in 1195, just as he was preparing a new expedition against them, his elder brother Alexios revolted and had Isaac blinded, seizing the throne himself as Alexios III (1195–1203).

Alexios III had none of the dedication to duty that characterized his brother, and the central government was in an advanced state of dissolution. His choice of provincial administrators was questionable at best, and many of them (e.g., Leon Sgouros in Greece) became virtually independent rulers. In the Balkans the situation deteriorated considerably. In 1196 Stefan Nemanja retired, passing the throne to his son, Stefan "the First-crowned" (*zupan* 1195–1217, King of Serbia 1217–27), who was the son-in-law of Alexios III. Byzantium was completely unable to take advantage of this opportunity, and instead the region fell under the influence of Hungary, which encouraged the spread of Catholic power in the Balkans. Bulgaria remained a problem, despite the assassinations of both Asen and Peter, and their youngest brother Kalojan (1197–1207) proved to be one of the most talented rulers of the period. Disturbingly for Byzantium, Kalojan sought to be crowned, not by a representative of the patriarch in Constantinople, but by an emissary of the pope, and the power of western Christianity continued to grow, even in Bulgaria.

Byzantium's most serious challenge, however, came from the German emperor, Henry VI, who had succeeded his father in 1190 and who inherited the (Norman) kingdom of Sicily through his wife. Henry pressed territorial and political claims against Constantinople, demanding the territories the Normans had held in 1185 and using a remote family connection to pose as the avenger of the deposed emperor Isaac II. Alexios III sought accommodation with Henry, and even Pope Innocent III was frightened by the German emperor's claims to world domination. As events turned out, however, Henry died suddenly in 1197 before he could carry out his plans for eastward expansion. After his death the German Empire weakened, and the most powerful political figure in the West was the pope, Innocent III.

Changes in Byzantine Society and Culture

The twelfth century witnessed profound cultural, social, and economic changes that were to have significant effects on the very fabric of Byzantine life for the next 300 years and beyond. All of these, of course, were built on the structures that had existed in the past, and one can certainly see much continuity, as well as change. Perhaps the most important of these has already been briefly discussed in the previous chapter: the growth of the military aristocracy. This should not be seen only in political terms, as it also had many cultural manifestations, not least of which was the militarization of aristocratic ideals, growth in the popularity of military saints, greater significance given to birth and lineage, and even a militarization of the image of the ideal ruler. Indeed, as seen above, there was a strong tendency in the age for the identification of aristocracy with the imperial family and it is not surprising that the ideals of the military aristocracy and those of the emperors were normally one and the same.

Economically, the twelfth century seems to have witnessed a decline in the resources available to the state while, at the same time, the wealth of the empire as a whole seems to have enjoyed a real resurgence. Whether this was due to the impetus given to the economy by the Venetian traders, whether the wealth of the countryside was a direct result of the inability of the central government to collect taxes, and whether these developments were "good" things for Byzantium as a whole are difficult to know at present, although they will certainly repay further consideration.

What seems certain, however, is that in the twelfth century Byzantium enjoyed an economic improvement and what can only be called an urban revival. We have already talked about the importance of cities in understanding the transition from late antiquity to the Middle Ages in Byzantium, and it is clear that there was some degree of urban revival in the ninth and tenth centuries in many parts of the empire. It is also apparent, from both literary and archaeological evidence, that the real urban revival in Byzantium took place in the eleventh through the thirteenth centuries, with significant variations in this phenomenon from region to region of the empire. It is clear that this development was much more widespread in the Balkans, especially in the southern part. Along the Danube, more exposed to barbarian attack, the boom may have been cut short, but in many other areas cities based at least in part on long-distance trade came into being. The anonymous author of the *Timarion* describes in some detail the annual *panigyris* (fair) at Thessaloniki in the middle of the twelfth century, noting that merchants from all round the Mediterranean, from the West as well as Islamic lands, and even from southern Russia, came to the fair to trade and sell goods. The situation among the cities of Asia Minor is more difficult to characterize, in part because so much of the country had fallen into the hands of the Seljuk Turks after Mantzikert. Nonetheless, even there we have evidence of an urban revival in many centers.

> ## Box 12.2 *Western-style Tournaments in Byzantium*
>
> In the twelfth century, after the arrival of the Crusaders in Byzantine territory, western-style tournaments became popular among the Byzantine aristocracy. This corresponded with the growing dominance of military ideals among Byzantine aristocrats at the time. Thus, whereas in earlier centuries the Byzantine aristocracy had been concerned primarily with landowning and/or political matters, by the twelfth century military concerns had become paramount and this included pastimes such as tourneys and "jousts," familiar from the western Middle Ages. The contests, in which the "friendly" combatants dressed sumptuously in ceremonial military gear, were highly formalized but they still often resulted in bloodshed, serious wounds, and not uncommonly deaths.
>
> These military entertainments were particularly popular at the court of the emperor Manuel I (1143–80), who was otherwise significantly influenced by western ideas. The historian Nikitas Choniates described one such tournament arranged for the emperor's arrival in the city of Antioch in 1159. Manuel himself took part in the tournament, dressed in a sumptuous cloak that left his right arm free for action and riding a noble horse that was decorated with golden accoutrements. The emperor was joined by a picked band of Byzantine aristocrats, whom he ordered to dress as beautifully as possible. Opposed to the Byzantines in this ceremonial fight were the knights of the western Prince of Antioch, Reynald of Châtillon. The prince was mounted on a stallion, "whiter than snow," and wearing a long shirt and a golden crown, and he was followed by his best combatants, "all as mighty as Ares and tremendously tall."
>
> Choniates described the tumult of the battle that followed, with knights being unseated, some pale with fear and others rejoicing in their success. He obviously found the spectacle somewhat comic, as the knights fell over each other, and he compared the incongruous sight to how one must imagine the lovemaking of Ares (the fierce god of war) and Aphrodite (the beautiful goddess of love).
>
> ### FURTHER READING
>
> Niketas Choniates, *Historia*, ed. J. L. van Dieten (New York and Berlin, 1975), pp. 108–9.
> A. P. Kazhdan and A. W. Epstein, *Change in Byzantine Culture in the Eleventh and Twelfth Centuries* (Berkeley, CA, 1985), p. 109.

These "new" Byzantine cities were normally built on the sites of the famous cities of antiquity, and they normally continued to be called by the same names: there can be little question that life (whether "urban" or not) had continued in these places since antiquity. But the cities were certainly very

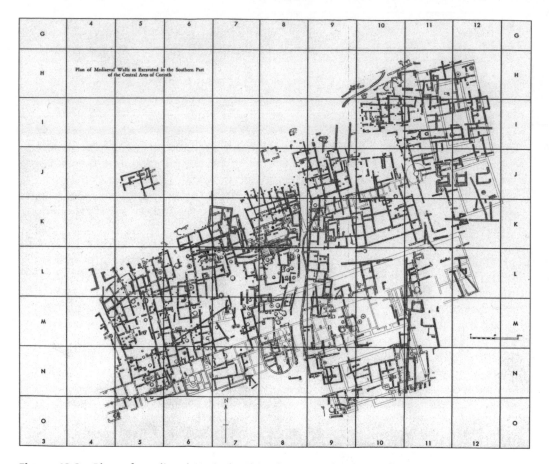

Figure 12.2 Plan of medieval Korinth. This plan provides a good idea of what a Byzantine city would have looked like. Notable is the maze-like arrangement of the streets and the absence of any apparent planning. The houses are small and simple and the only structures that stand out are the churches and monasteries. Robert Scranton, *Corinth* 16. *Medieval Architecture in the Central Area of Corinth* (Cambridge, MA, 1967), Plan VI. Reproduced with permission from the Trustees of the American School of Classical Studies at Athens

different in appearance from their classical predecessors. Commonly the civic center had moved from its original location, and the street-plan had abandoned the gridiron pattern of the Hippodamian plan, replaced instead by what might be described as a warren of winding streets and lanes going off in different directions. New monumental buildings came into existence in the form of churches, sometimes on the foundations of early Christian basilicas, but more often in new places, but these were normally small and would not have stood out strongly against the neighborhoods in which they were set.

It is noteworthy that this Byzantine economic and urban expansion (along, of course, with the question of feudalism) can be paralleled with contemporary

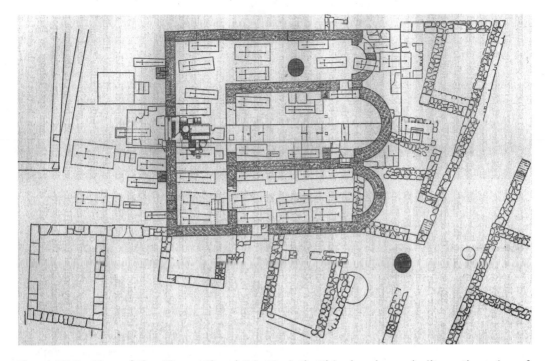

Figure 12.3 Plan of the "Bema Church" in Korinth. This church was built on the ruins of the so-called Bema (speaker's platform) in the forum area of Korinth where, according to tradition, St. Paul was tried by the Roman governor. This elevated space was used as a platform on which the church was built. One can notice the many graves that were set into the floor of the church and its immediate vicinity. Robert Scranton, *Corinth* 16. *Medieval Architecture in the Central Area of Corinth* (Cambridge, MA, 1967), Figure 3, p. 44. Reproduced with permission from the Trustees of the American School of Classical Studies at Athens

developments in the West. Nonetheless, although the similarities are intriguing and greater than have previously been acknowledged, there are important differences. On the one hand, in the West there was an inherent opposition between the feudal aristocracy and the growing power of the emperor and the national monarchs, while in Byzantium no such opposition existed. The Byzantine aristocracy, for all its military inclinations, maintained an identification with and interest in the cities and, while the western national monarchs were able to use the wealth of the cities as a weapon against the aristocracy, no such possibility existed for the emperors of Constantinople.

The wealth of the cities and, even more important, the wealth of the Byzantine aristocracies found expression in works of art and architecture that have left a rich record in the area controlled by the Byzantine state. In part, it can be argued, this was the result of a growing sense of individualism or, perhaps more commonly, "family individualism," that came to characterize the period. This is something we can see in the work of scholars such as

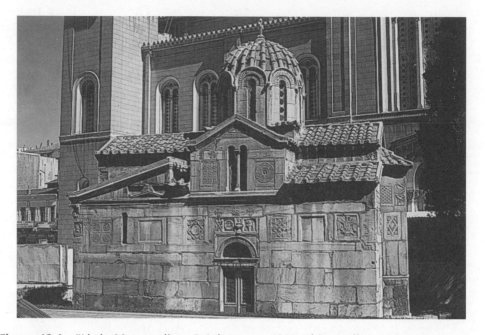

Figure 12.4 "Little Metropolitan," Athens, ca. 1200. This small cross-in-square church in Athens is unusual in that it was built completely of marble blocks, reused from earlier structures. These blocks include a representation of the ancient goddess Athena, allusions to the cult of Eleusis, and the only surviving depiction of the Panathenaic procession. Many ancient funeral reliefs were also employed, frequently modified to include crosses. Photo: Timothy E. Gregory

Psellos in the eleventh century, but it clearly spread outside the capital in the twelfth century and afterwards.

One of the clearest indications of this growth of individuality is in the form of church-building in this period. Indeed, the twelfth century seems to have witnessed an "explosion" in the construction of churches, a phenomenon that confounded earlier historians who were working on the assumption that the period was one of economic collapse. Not only were large numbers of churches constructed in the twelfth century; regional schools of architecture began to develop, some of them in relatively small areas, showing that significant wealth was available in what must previously have been backwaters of the Byzantine Empire. Thus, we can speak of distinct architectural traditions in places such as Macedonia, Cyprus, Central Greece, Attica, and the Argolid. Architectural styles, floor plans, and exterior surface decoration (which came to play a significant role) all varied from place to place and, of course, there was room for significant differences within the individual traditions.

Careful examination also shows significant traces of individualism and individual interpretation of traditional themes in this period in literature and art. Again, this probably was a development from beginnings in the eleventh century, such as the revival of monumental architecture in that century – perhaps connected with the growth of an audience for art. The ideas of the twelfth century, however, showed a new interest not only in ideal forms but also in the natural world. There is evidence, for example, that some were concerned that ikons of saints should actually bear a resemblance to the physical appearance of the original. The same can be seen in literature, which had traditionally been dominated by traditions from antiquity. Influenced in particular by the *Chronographia* of Psellos, historians were interested in the development of personality and the way individuals interacted with the circumstances in which they found themselves. Particularly characteristic in this regard is the *Alexiad* of Anna Komnena, which, though highly classicizing in form, still possesses a keen interest in physical description and detail. Even more, the *Historia* of Niketas Choniates demonstrates the author's self-conscious exploration of the world around him and his interest and curiosity about the human condition.

The same characteristics can be seen in the art of the late eleventh and twelfth centuries. The mosaics and frescoes of the period abandon the abstractness of earlier art and the figures are depicted more in a three-dimensional view and with a real sense of movement. This can clearly be seen in such depictions as the mosaics at Daphni near Athens, Osios Loukas in central Greece, and Agia Moni in Chios, as well as the Communion of the Apostles from the church at Perachorio in Cyprus (third quarter of the twelfth century). Often this change has simply been described as classicism and a return to classical realism, based perhaps on the recovery of Hellenistic period copy-books. Obviously, there is something to such an observation, but the broader question is why patrons and/or artists would prefer such styles, rather than the more traditional two-dimensional depictions of the past. It is characteristic that the great works of art of this period, admired by many who do not like much in the Byzantine tradition, have been ascribed to the genius of the classical tradition rather than to the Byzantines themselves. One may, however, look at the situation the other way round and praise the Byzantines, not only for the maintenance of the Byzantine tradition, but more so for their increasingly individualized use of that tradition and the many others they could claim as their own.

The Fourth Crusade

The question of the causes and the motivation of the Fourth Crusade has long been debated and no real scholarly consensus has emerged as to exactly how the movement designed to conquer the Holy Lands resulted in the capture of the Christian city of Constantinople and the dismemberment of the Byzantine Empire. Nonetheless, the main issues are clear. First, the growing weakness of Byzantium was evident to all, and the events of the past century and a half had created mutual suspicion, if not downright hatred, between westerners and Byzantines. Second, the Byzantines had never understood the crusading ideal and regarded western interests in the East with great suspicion. Third, the Crusaders did not understand the Byzantines' lack of enthusiasm for the

Crusades and their frequent hesitation to provide assistance or, worse yet, Byzantine willingness to work with the Muslims against the Crusaders. Furthermore, there had long been tensions between the papacy and the Byzantine church and state, from at least the mid-ninth century, and the movements for reform that led to the development of the papal monarchy were bound to run foul of, not only the interests of the German emperors, but also the much older institution of the Byzantine Empire. In a simple sense, the papacy and the Byzantine Empire were both based on claims of universal (ecumenical, one might say) sovereignty: each claimed to be God's sole representative on earth. The battleground for missionary activity in the Balkans continued to be real, but popes such as Innocent III looked to secure the acceptance of papal sovereignty from the "schismatic" church of Byzantium. Finally, the Italian merchant republics, most notably the Venetians, had long coveted the wealth of Byzantium. To be sure, since the end of the eleventh century the Venetians had a favored trading position within the Byzantine Empire, but this was something that they had to have reaffirmed at the accession of every new emperor, and some had been reluctant to provide it. Hostility toward the Venetians (indeed to all westerners) was evident in Byzantium, and the riots and massacres of 1171 and 1182 created an atmosphere of increased tension.

In the events that led to the "diversion" of the Fourth Crusade, the personalities of Pope Innocent III and the Venetian Doge, Enrico Dandalo, were paramount, but it is unreasonable to say that the whole thing was a plot, previously thought out. Certainly, all the elements were in place for an attack on Byzantium, and many westerners, especially the Normans and some of the Venetians, had openly talked about the conquest of Constantinople. Mutual hostility, greed, and the weakness of Byzantium were the main factors behind the events, but specific circumstances brought about the actual conquest of Constantinople.

Innocent III proclaimed the Fourth Crusade in 1202, and the Crusaders, under the leadership of Boniface of Montferrat, assembled in Venice, from which they were to sail to Egypt. The Crusaders, however, did not have the funds to pay the Venetians for transport, so an agreement was made, whereby the Crusaders were to stop at Zara, on the Dalmatian coast, which had rebelled from Venice and gone over to the Hungarians; the Crusaders were to assist the Venetians in securing control of the city once again. This was the first diversion of the crusade, and, although the inhabitants of Zara hung crosses on the walls, the city was taken (in 1202). In the meantime, Alexios Angelos, the son of the deposed Isaac II, traveled to the West, seeking aid first from Innocent III and then from Philip of Swabia, the successor of Henry VI of Germany and brother-in-law of the Byzantine prince. Young Alexios made lavish offers to the Crusaders (including a promise to acknowledge the supremacy of the papacy) if they would help him to regain his rightful throne in Constantinople. The Crusaders accepted this proposal, and Alexios joined the Crusade in 1203.

Upon the arrival of the Crusaders outside Constantinople, Alexios III fled the city, and Isaac II and his son Alexios IV were proclaimed as emperors.

Alexios attempted to fulfill the terms of his agreement with the Crusaders, by collecting money and making arrangements to submit to the papacy, but it quickly became clear that neither he nor the weakened empire had the resources to meet these responsibilities. The people of Constantinople became restive, and in January of 1204 a riot broke out in Constantinople, led in part by Alexios Doukas (known as Mourtzouflos), who advocated resistance to the Crusaders. Alexios IV was killed and his father died shortly thereafter in prison. Alexios V Doukas became emperor and began to strengthen the walls and to carry out raids against the Crusaders. Naturally enough this caused the Crusaders to plan an open attack against Constantinople, in this case not to install a pliable puppet emperor, but to take the city for themselves. In March of 1204 they draw up a treaty (the so-called *Partitio Romaniae*) that provided a detailed plan for the division of the empire among the Crusaders and the establishment of a Latin Empire. The forces of Alexios V were able to defeat the first Crusader attack on 9 April 1204, but on 12 April the Crusaders broke into the Golden Horn and attacked the weaker sea walls along the northern side of the city. Despite significant resistance, the Crusaders forced an entry, and Alexios V fled the city. There followed a savage sack of Constantinople, which was still at the time one of the richest cities of the world, and innumerable treasures, books, and works of art were wantonly destroyed. In the carnage many of the manuscripts, Christian relics, and sculptures that had been assembled by the emperors, from the time of Constantine the Great onward, were destroyed, or in some few cases, transported back to the West, primarily to Venice.

FURTHER READING

M. Angold, *The Byzantine Empire, 1025–1204: A Political History*, 2nd edn. London, 1997.

A. Harvey, *Economic Expansion in the Byzantine Empire, 900–1200*. Cambridge, 1989.

A. P. Kazhdan and A. W. Epstein, *Change in Byzantine Culture in the Eleventh and Twelfth Centuries*. Berkeley, CA, 1985.

P. Magdalino, *The Empire of Manuel I Komnenos, 1143–1180*. Cambridge, 1993.

M. Mullett and D. Smythe, eds., *Alexios I Komnenos*. Belfast, 1996.

13

The Aftermath of the Fourth Crusade

250	500	750	1000	1250	1500

1204   Byzantine Empire divided among the Western powers
1259   Beginning of the Palaiologan dynasty
1261   Byzantine recovery of Constantinople

The Latin Empire and the Byzantine Successor States

With the capture of Constantinople and the dismemberment of its territory, the Byzantine Empire had essentially ceased to exist. According to the terms of the treaty between the Crusaders and Venetians, an emperor was chosen for what can now be called the Latin Empire. Although Boniface of Montferrat had been the primary military leader of the Crusade, Baldwin of Flanders was chosen as Latin emperor and he was crowned on 16 May 1204 in Hagia Sophia. The terms of the treaty specified that if a Crusader were elected emperor then the patriarch would be a Venetian, so Thomas Morosini became the first Latin Patriarch of Constantinople.

Thus, the forms of the old Byzantine system remained, but the essence was completely different and it was completely under Crusader control. Furthermore, the old centralized government was replaced by an array of feudal principalities, in theory all of which owed loyalty to the emperor in Constantinople, but which were in fact independent states. According to the *Partitio Romaniae* the emperor was to receive a quarter of the empire, with the remaining three-quarters to be split between the Venetians and the many crusading

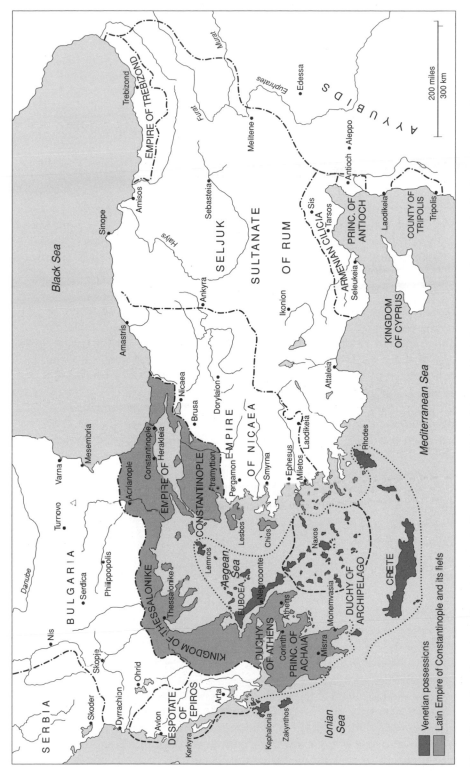

Map 13.1 The situation after the Fourth Crusade, ca. 1214. After A. Kazhdan et al., eds., *The Oxford Dictionary of Byzantium* (New York, 1991), p. 357

Box 13.1 *Destruction of Ancient Art in the Latin Sack of Constantinople*

Despite the poor condition of the empire at the time of the Fourth Crusade, Constantinople was still one of the wealthiest cities of the world. Along with manuscripts and religious relics and monuments, the Byzantine emperors had, over the centuries, decorated Constantinople with many of the great masterpieces of art which had survived from antiquity, although the Christian population of the city naturally had mixed feelings about some of the ancient sculptures that represented pagan gods and goddesses or had mythological themes. Nonetheless it is clear that at least educated Byzantines were aware of the beauty and the historical significance of this rich cultural tradition. Niketas Choniates, perhaps the most important Byzantine historian of his age, describes the lamentable fate of many of these works of classical art and other treasures during the Latin sack of Constantinople in 1204:

> From the very beginning they [the Latins] revealed their race to be lovers of gold; they conceived of a new method of plundering, which had completely escaped the notice of all who had [just] sacked the imperial city. Having opened the graves of those emperors which were in the burial ground situated in the area of the church of Christ's Holy Apostles, they stripped all of them during the night and, if any golden ornament, pearl, or precious stone still lay inviolate in these [tombs], they sacrilegiously seized it. When they found the corpse of the Emperor Justinian, which had remained undisturbed for so many years, they marvelled at it, but they did not refrain from [looting] the funerary adornments. We may say that these Westerners spared neither the living nor the dead. They manifested [toward all], beginning with God and his servants [i.e., the clergy], complete indifference and impiety: quickly enough they tore down the curtain in the Great Church [Hagia Sophia], the value of which was reckoned in millions of purest silver pieces, since it was entirely interwoven with gold.
>
> Even now they were still desirous of money (for nothing can satiate the avarice of the barbarians). They eyed the bronze statues and threw them into the fire. And so the bronze statue of Hera, standing in the agora of Constantine, was broken into pieces and consigned to the flames. The head of this statue, which could hardly be drawn by four oxen yoked together, was brought to the great palace. The [Statue of] Paris [also called] Alexander opposite it, was cast off its base. This statue was connected with that of the goddess Aphrodite to whom the apple of Eris [Discord] was depicted as being awarded by Paris . . . These barbarians – who do not appreciate beauty – did not neglect to overturn the statues standing in the Hippodrome or any other marvellous works. Rather, these too they turned into coinage [nomisma], exchanging great things [i.e., art] for small [i.e., money], thus acquiring petty coins at the expense of those things created at enormous cost. They then threw down the great Hercules

Trihesperus, magnificently constructed on a base and girded with the skin of a lion, a terrifying thing to see even in bronze . . . He was represented as standing, carrying in his hands neither quiver nor arrows nor club, but having his right foot and right hand extended and his left foot bent at the knee with the left hand raised at the elbow . . . He [the statue of Hercules] was very broad in the chest and shoulders and had thick hair, plump buttocks, and strong arms, and was of such huge size, I think, as Lysimachus [Lysippus?] considered the real Hercules to have been – Lysimachus who sculpted from bronze this first and last great masterpiece of his hands. The statue was so large that the rope around his thumb had the size of a man's belt and the lower portion of the leg, the height of a man. But those [i.e., the Latins] who separate manly vigor from other virtues and claim it for themselves (considering it the most important quality) did not leave this Hercules (although it was the epitome of this attribute) untouched.

Niketas Choniates, *Historia*, ed. J. L. van Dieten (New York and Berlin, 1975), pp. 647–51. Translation from D. J. Geanakoplos, *Byzantium: Church, Society, and Civilization seen through Contemporary Eyes* (Chicago, 1984), pp. 371–2.

knights who were to be rewarded for their service in this way. The Latin emperor was given territories in both Asia Minor and Europe, but the greatest power was held by Boniface of Montferrat, who refused to accept the territories assigned to him in Asia Minor but instead seized Macedonia and Thessaly and established himself as king of Thessaloniki. Farther south in Greece, Boniface established himself as lord of Athens, and he put Otto de la Roche in charge of Attica and Boeotia. He also lent his support to William of Champlitte and Geoffrey of Villehardouin, who established the principality of the Morea (the Peloponnesos), which became the most thoroughly westernized of the territories taken by the Crusaders and developed a rich culture of its own, blending western and Byzantine traditions, not much influenced by events elsewhere in the region.

Relations between the Crusaders and the conquered population varied considerably from place to place, but the westerners always were a minority, and the majority of the people retained both the Greek language and Orthodox Christianity. The papacy naturally made strenuous attempts to convert the local population: western monasteries were established in many places, and most churches were theoretically under the control of a Catholic bishop, but in fact these attempts did little other than to strengthen the people in their dedication to age-old tradition. Among the *archontes* (the local Byzantine elite), however, there was a real rapprochement with the Crusader leaders, since many of the *archontes* were incorporated, more or less fully, into the feudal system. Nonetheless, they too, retained the basics of their Byzantine culture and religion, although they accepted many features of western court life.

Figure 13.1 A glazed bowl. Byzantine glazed ceramics developed, beginning in the seventh century, based in large part on models from Persia and even China. A thriving industry in ceramic production developed with many regional centers and different styles. This small bowl, decorated with incising (called *sgraffito*) and colors of green and yellow, dates to the late thirteenth or fourteenth century and comes from the eastern Mediterranean. Photo: Dumbarton Oaks

The Venetians did not want large territories, since their primary interest was trade, and they sought mainly to control the major ports and way-stations along the sea routes between Venice and the East. The Venetians thus took three-eighths of Constantinople itself and many of the islands leading from the Adriatic to Constantinople, including those in the Ionian Sea, many in the Aegean, Crete, and the important ports on the Hellespont.

Beyond the loose control of the Crusader states, what we may call Byzantine successor states began to emerge on the land formerly controlled by the empire. These, to a lesser or greater degree, sought both to replicate the Byzantine administrative machinery and to appeal to Byzantine ideals of political and cultural identity. More specifically, the Byzantine successor states claimed, explicitly or implicitly, that they were the rightful claimants to the Byzantine heritage and that they had the rights to the loyalty and devotion of all who had formerly lived inside its borders. There was, therefore, a natural rivalry not only between Byzantines and Crusaders, but also among those who claimed for themselves the Byzantine heritage.

The oldest of these successor states had actually existed before the fall of Constantinople to the Crusaders in 1204. Owing its independence to the general turmoil within the empire at the beginning of the thirteenth century,

Figure 13.2 Cistercian monastery of Zaraka. In the thirteenth century the Latin Prince of Achaia asked the Cistercian order to establish monasteries in Greece to help in the conversion of the Byzantines to Latin Christianity and to bring the rugged landscape into cultivation. The monastery of Zaraka near the ancient city of Stymphalos was one of those built in this attempt. The substantial remains of a Gothic church, complete with western sculpture, still stand, abandoned when the western mission failed. Photo: Timothy E. Gregory

the so-called Empire of Trebizond (on the southeast shore of the Black Sea), was ruled by the family of the Grand Komnenoi Alexios and David, grandsons of Andronikos I. Locked into the northeastern corner of Asia Minor, the Empire of Trebizond held out for centuries against all enemies, and even outlasted the final collapse of Byzantium in the fifteenth century, but it was destined not to play a larger role on the stage of history.

Ultimately more important than Trebizond was the so-called Empire of Nicaea. This was territory in northwestern Asia Minor occupied by Theodore I Laskaris when Boniface of Montferrat abandoned it to press his claims in Macedonia. Laskaris was the son-in-law of Alexios III and he held the title of

Despot. He sought to organize resistance to Latin rule in Asia Minor, but he was originally pressed with difficulties all around, at first from David Komnenos of Trebizond and then from the supporters of the Latin emperor, who wished to assert his rights in this area. Laskaris was saved, however, when the Crusaders were defeated by the Bulgarian tsar Kalojan in a battle at Adrianople on 14 April 1205. The Latin emperor Baldwin was taken prisoner at the battle, never again to return to Constantinople, and Louis of Blois, Latin claimant to Nicaea, was killed. This left Laskaris free to consolidate his gains and organize a state that laid full claim to the old Byzantine heritage. Abandoning the title of Despot, in 1205 Theodore was acclaimed as emperor; in 1208 he was solemnly crowned by Michael Autoreianos, who had been chosen as patriarch of Constantinople in exile. From this time onward an Orthodox Byzantine emperor and patriarch, resident at Nicaea, opposed their Catholic, western counterparts in Constantinople itself.

Henry, Baldwin's brother and successor as Latin emperor, won some support among the Greeks of Thrace, but his invasion of Asia Minor in 1206 was thwarted by renewed hostility from Kalojan (who, however, died in 1207). At the same time Theodore had to deal with protracted opposition from the Seljuk sultanate of Ikonion (Rum), with whom the deposed emperor Alexios III had sought asylum. The Seljuks concluded a treaty with the Latin Empire against Theodore Laskaris, but the latter ultimately triumphed, and the sultan himself fell in battle with the reviving Byzantine state in 1211. War between the Latin Empire and the Empire of Nicaea continued indecisively until 1214, when a peace treaty was signed, providing for temporarily stable frontiers.

Interestingly enough, although its territories were confined to a small strip of northwest Asia Minor, between those of the Latin Empire and the Seljuk sultanate, the pre-eminence of the Empire of Nicaea was generally recognized among the Balkan Slavs. Thus, in 1219 Sava, the son of Stefan Nemanja, was crowned as the first autocephalous (independent) archbishop of Serbia, and he allied with Nicaea in a struggle to defend an independent Serbia.

The Empire of Trebizond had relied on Latin support in its rivalry with Nicaea, and the peace between Constantinople and Nicaea meant that Trebizond was left without an ally. The result was that in 1214 Theodore Laskaris was able to annex most of Trebizond's western possessions, as far as Sinope, while the Seljuks took Sinope and exercised significant influence in Trebizond itself. The empire of Trebizond was to survive for another quarter-millennium, but it was not again to lay claim to Byzantine universality.

The despotate of Epiros was another Byzantine successor state, and it was to prove a more long-lasting rival to the Empire of Nicaea. Immediately after the fall of Constantinople in 1204 Michael Angelos (cousin of Alexios II and Isaac II) seized control of the northwestern part of the Greek mainland, from Dyrrachium to the Gulf of Korinth. With its capital in Arta, the rulers of Epiros also laid claim to the Byzantine heritage, and they competed equally against the Venetians along the coast, the Frankish kingdom of Thessaloniki in the north, and – ultimately – the Empire of Nicaea, which was its main competitor for the Byzantine tradition. After 1215 the ruler of Epiros was Michael's half-brother Theodore, who proudly took for himself the three imperial names of Angelos, Doukos, Komnenos, and who managed to capture Peter of Courtney, the newly crowned Latin emperor, as he was on his way through the mountains of Albania. Theodore pushed further against the kingdom of Thessaloniki, which had been weak after the death of its founder, Boniface of Montferrat, killed in 1207. By 1224 Theodore was master of Thessaloniki, and one of the Crusader states on Byzantine territory had ceased to exist. After this success, Theodore assumed the imperial purple and styled himself emperor, making him a clear rival to the emperor of Nicaea.

The Empire of Nicaea

In Nicaea Theodore I Laskaris died in 1222, passing the throne to his son-in-law John III Doukos Vatatzes (1222–54). Theodore's brothers sought to claim the throne for themselves, with Latin assistance, but John resolutely put them down. He gained control of most of the islands in the eastern Aegean and responded to an appeal from the people of Adrianople by sending troops to Thrace, establishing his presence in Europe and in effect closing Constantinople in on two sides. At this point, however, Epiros and Bulgaria, which both coveted the same prize, intervened, and Vatatzes was forced to withdraw.

The tsar of Bulgaria, Ivan Asen II, was a formidable power, and he had ambitions similar to those of Symeon of Bulgaria in the tenth century: the conquest of Constantinople and the formation of a Bulgaro-Byzantine state. The Latin ruler, Baldwin II, was a minor, and an alliance was formed whereby Baldwin would marry Asen's daughter. This caused Theodore of Epiros to break his alliance with Bulgaria, but at the battle of Klokotnica in 1230 the Bulgarians prevailed, and Theodore was captured and blinded. He was succeeded by his brother Manuel, who managed to hold on to Thessaloniki, but Asen took over most of Theodore's conquests in Macedonia and Thrace, and he emerged as the most powerful figure in the Balkans. This turn of events caused the Latins to reconsider their alliance with Asen, who therefore allied with Nicaea. Asen and John Vatatzes besieged Constantinople in 1235–6, but Asen soon changed positions once again, and the Bulgaro-Byzantine alliance collapsed. Asen died in 1241 and Bulgarian power declined, in part as a result of the invasion of the Mongols, who ravaged the Balkans and the Near East. Many of Nicaea's enemies, including Bulgaria and the sultanate of Ikonion, were forced to pay tribute to the Mongols, but the Empire of Nicaea emerged unscathed.

John Vatatzes was thus able to consolidate his power in the Balkans, culminating with his seizure of Thessaloniki in 1246 and the capture of most of the territories that Asen II had taken from Epiros. Under the influence of the aged Theodore Angelos, Epiros offered some resistance, but Vatatzes' forces were superior and the rulers of Epiros were forced to recognize him as emperor.

Box 13.2   *Leon Sgouros, Tyrant of Nauplion*

Toward the end of the eleventh century the Argolid, in the northeast Peloponnesos, came under the control of the powerful local family of the Sgouroi. Such phenomena had already become common in Asia Minor. Around 1200 Leon Sgouros succeeded his father as the "tyrant" of Nauplion and began to expand his territory dramatically in the chaos that characterized the Byzantine Empire in the years leading up to the Fourth Crusade. He conquered Argos and Korinth in 1202–3 and defended himself against an expedition sent by the emperor Alexios III. Sgouros then brutally murdered the bishops of Argos and Korinth by having them pushed from the heights of the castle, either at Nauplion or Korinth. His attack on Athens with the aid of pirates from Aigina was unsuccessful: the bishop Michael Choniates managed to hold the acropolis, but the troops of Sgouros burned the lower city. For this and earlier actions Sgouros earned the hatred of Choniates and the reputation of a ruthless and power-hungry ruler. From Athens he moved to the north and in 1204 conquered Euboea and Thebes, crossed through Thermopylae and entered the Thessalian city of Larissa.

In Larissa Sgouros met with the then-deposed emperor Alexios III and his wife Euphrosyne. An alliance was arranged in which Leon married Alexios' daughter, Eudokia Angelina; Alexios hoped that Sgouros would help him regain his throne, while the tyrant sought to consolidate his control over central and southern Greece, essentially independent of the central Byzantine state. The events, however, turned out very differently from what either had expected, since by then the soldiers of the Fourth Crusade had taken Constantinople.

The western army that entered Greece was commanded by Boniface of Montferrat, the King of Thessaloniki, who had not been granted this area in the partition of the empire but who saw a military void and decided to take advantage of it. As Boniface descended into Greece, Sgouros fled to the south, where he tried to make a stand against the Franks at Thermopylae. For the first time after the fall of Constantinople the crusading army met determined resistance. It is impossible to know if Sgouros saw himself as a "new Leonidas," but his violent and reckless temperament does not make this impossible. As it turned out, however, this attempt was unsuccessful because, as the historian Niketas Choniates tells us, the people of that area submitted quickly to Boniface, refusing to resist what they thought was superior force. Sgouros apparently attempted another stand at the Isthmos of Korinth, but this too failed, and he ascended the heights of Akrokorinth, the citadel high above Korinth, to make a last stand. Boniface feared to bypass this famous fortress, so he settled down, from the beginning of 1205, for a long siege.

Faced finally with resistance, at Korinth and Nauplion, Boniface wearied of the campaign, far from his base of power in Thessaloniki. He came to an agreement with the Frankish knights William Champlitte and Geoffrey de Villehardouin, and they were left in charge of the task of subduing the Byzantines in the Peloponnesos. In this they were aided by Michael Angelos Doukas, the ruler of Epiros, who allied with the Franks in their conquest of the region. The siege at Korinth dragged on for years, until Leon Sgouros, apparently despondent and ready for a final act of violent resistance, rode his horse off the side of Akrokorinth and thus died.

Historians have recently spent much energy on the analysis of the frequently contradictory sources on this man and the exact sequence of events, arguing, for example, over whether Sgouros' death took place in 1208 or 1209 and whether it was at Korinth or Nauplion. There are, further, two parallel stories about the cause of his death: the more popular one about his fatal fall from the citadel and another, less romantic one, that he was accidentally killed by a western knight. It is clear that he was a violent, and probably not a very likable, man, but his actions as the only Byzantine to offer armed resistance to the Crusaders have perpetuated his memory. On the one hand he represents a broader phenomenon of the break-up of the Byzantine state well before the arrival of the Fourth Crusade, but on the other he can be seen as the harbinger of the Byzantine resistance that was to develop in the years to come. He was buried in the cathedral church of Nauplion and survived by his widow, the daughter of the equally unfortunate emperor Alexios III. The French version of the Chronicle of the Morea paid Leon Sgouros grudging respect, describing him as a "villainous Greek man," contrasting him to "all the noble Greek men," who surrendered to the Franks without a struggle.

They, in turn, received from him the title of despot, and Epiros continued to exist for some time as a semi-independent Byzantine principality.

Vatatzes cultivated diplomatic relations with the West, in an effort to isolate the Latin Empire politically and militarily. He formed an especially cordial relationship with the German emperor Frederick II and carried out negotiations with the papacy for the union of the churches. Vatatzes was at least originally willing to subjugate the Orthodox Church to the pope in return for alliance against the Latin Empire. In the end, however, these arrangements went nowhere, in part because Vatatzes' military success made western help unnecessary. Vatatzes was especially concerned to restore the system of defensive fortifications in the empire and to strengthen the economy; he tried to restrict imports and dependence on western traders, forbidding his subjects from purchasing luxury imports. John III might well have taken Constantinople himself, but in his later years he suffered from epilepsy and in 1254 he died.

John III was succeeded by his son Theodore II (1254–8), who took the name Laskaris after his mother. Theodore II was an accomplished scholar and author, and he surrounded himself with other men of letters. He was of rather irritable temperament, and he distrusted the leading aristocratic families. As a result there were frequent disagreements between the aristocracy and the emperor, who selected advisers of humble status. Theodore, like his father, suffered from epilepsy and he died in 1258, leaving his 7-year-old son John IV to succeed him. After some maneuvering, the regency was seized by Michael Palaiologos, a member of a great aristocratic family that had risen to prominence under John Vatatzes. Palaiologos assumed the title of despot, but by the

Box 13.3 *William Villehardouin and the*
Parliament of Ladies

Geoffrey de Villehardouin cooperated with several other knights of the Fourth Crusade in the actual occupation of southern Greece. From 1210 onward Geoffrey I was
Prince of Achaia (the Peloponnesos) and he organized the area on a feudal model,
with western knights in control of all the important areas. He was succeeded by his
son Geoffrey II sometime between 1226 and 1231 and then, in turn, in 1246 by his
younger son William (Guillaume) II.

Called "Long-tooth" by some, William II expanded the principality of Achaia to its
greatest extent, capturing Momemvasia and building a castle at Mystras. He was,
however, decisively defeated by the forces of John III Vatatzes, at the Battle of
Pelagonia (Macedonia) in 1259. William escaped from the battle and hid, but he was
captured by the Nicene forces and held prisoner. The new emperor Michael VIII took
Constantinople shortly thereafter and demanded that William cede the whole of the
Peloponnesos to the Byzantines. William refused and he and the other knights also
being held prisoner remained away from their families. Interestingly enough, the
wives and widows of the captive or slain nobles of Achaia met together in what
has come to be called the "Ladies' Parliament." They were tired of the protracted
absence of the men and agreed to some of the Byzantine demands, ceding the major
castles of Monemvasia, Maina, and Mystras. Thus, William gained his freedom but the
events signaled the beginning of a revival of Byzantine power in southern Greece.

beginning of 1259 he was crowned as co-emperor with the young John IV,
whom he essentially ignored for the next two years.

Michael VIII (1259–82) was immediately faced with serious military problems
when Manfred of Sicily, son of Frederick II, allied with Epiros, the principality
of Achaia, and King Uroš of Serbia against Nicaea. Manfred seized Kerkyra
and several of the cities along the Adriatic coast, and the anti-Byzantine alliance
marched into Macedonia. Michael sent his brother, the Sebastokrator John
Palaiologos, to meet the enemy, and in a crucial battle at Pelagonia in 1259 he
decisively defeated them: most of the Latin knights perished on the battlefield,
and the Prince of Achaia, William Villehardouin, was captured.

Michael VIII, now confident of victory, set his sights clearly on Constan-
tinople. Venice was the only power that could hinder his plans, so in 1261
Michael countered this threat by an alliance with Genoa, now Venice's eco-
nomic and naval rival in the eastern Mediterranean; in return for military aid,
Genoa was granted trading privileges and significant tax remissions, similar to
those granted to the Venetians earlier in the treaty of 1082. In July of 1261 the
Byzantine commander Alexios Strategopoulos camped in the neighborhood of
Constantinople and, to his surprise, found the city practically undefended. On

15 July 1261 he took the city and the Latin Empire ceased to exist; a month later Michael VIII made his triumphal entrance into Constantinople and, amid the joyful inhabitants of the city, he made his way along the traditional triumphal route to Hagia Sophia. In September the patriarch performed the second coronation of the emperor, along with his wife Theodora and young son Andronikos, thus assuring the survival of the newly founded dynasty.

Michael had gained control of a city that had suffered considerably from the Latin occupation. Churches had been despoiled and basic services neglected. Michael set about immediately strengthening the defenses of Constantinople, especially the Sea Walls, and rebuilding churches and monasteries. He sought to revive the imperial fleet with the construction of new ships, but his expenses quickly outgrew the resources he had at his disposal, and he was forced to resort to the devaluation of the *hyperperon*, as the Byzantine gold coin continued to be called.

Michael earned the enmity of a group of the clergy when he had his co-emperor John Laskaris blinded at the end of 1261. The Patriarch Arsenios Autoreianos, who had crowned Michael earlier in the year, now excommunicated the emperor, and a group grew up that maintained the legitimacy of the Laskarid, rather than the Palaiologan, line. The patriarch continued his opposition to the emperor over this issue and in 1265 a synod deposed and exiled Arsenios. His followers, the so-called Arsenites, maintained loyalty to the deposed patriarch and their agitation was closely related to the political feeling in support of the Laskarids. Arsenios thus fit the mold of the Byzantine ecclesiastical leader who was mistreated by an emperor for demanding a high standard of moral behavior.

Michael VIII also immediately had to meet strong opposition from the West in the person of Charles of Anjou, brother of King Louis IX of France, who had been selected as King of Sicily and Naples by the papacy. Charles put together a large anti-Byzantine alliance, including the former emperor of the Latin Empire, Prince William Villehardouin of Achaia, the Greek principalities of Epiros and Thessaly, Bulgaria, and Serbia. Fortunately for Byzantium, Michael VIII was a match for Charles of Anjou, and he gained the support of the papacy, first under Clement IV and then Gregory X, both of whom wished to see the reunion of the churches and who thus opposed the plans of Charles for the reconquest of Byzantium. Michael also forged alliances with Hungary, the Tartars of the Golden Horde in Russia, and the Mamlukes in Egypt, thus effectively encircling his enemies with allies who were favorable to the empire. He also managed to play the Venetians and the Genoese off against each other, and finally, he signed independent treaties with the maritime republics for fixed terms, which, although it continued the practice of leaving trade in Italian hands, allowed Byzantium some flexibility and bargaining power in dealing with each of them.

One of Michael's most difficult tasks was the attempt to expand imperial power in Greece. Epiros and Thessaly remained stubbornly independent, and the latter was an especially intransigent enemy of the empire; Michael also devoted considerable resources to his attempt to destroy the principality of Achaia in the Peloponnesos. In all these efforts, however, Michael was hindered by the aid that Charles of Anjou sent to his enemies in the Greek peninsula.

Pope Gregory X, meanwhile, grew tired of the emperor's delaying tactics and insisted that the emperor agree to the union of the churches, and, of course, the recognition of papal supremacy. Michael was compelled to accept, and in 1274 the Council of Lyons formally proclaimed the submission of the Orthodox Church to the papacy. After the imposition of the union opposition grew and reached into every stratum of society. The patriarch of Constantinople refused to accept the supremacy of the pope and he was forcibly removed and replaced with a more pliant bishop, John of Bekkos. The Greek successor states and the Slavic kingdoms all rejected the union and joined in their opposition to Byzantium. In addition, the resistance continued to rally around the blinded John IV as the representative of Laskarid, as opposed to Palaiologan, legitimacy, and the Arsenites kept this issue alive. The emperor's policy of church union, however, did gain time for Michael VIII in his struggle with Charles of Anjou.

In 1281 Martin IV became pope, and he actively supported the ambitions of Charles, going so far as to condemn Michael as a schismatic – although he had of course offered his submission to the papacy and had earned the hatred of many Byzantines for his action. The anti-Byzantine alliance formed once again and King Stefan Uroš II Milutin (1282–1321) of Serbia invaded Macedonia. In this dangerous situation Michael VIII once again relied on his diplomatic abilities. He negotiated an understanding with King Peter III of Aragon, the son-in-law of Manfred of Sicily, who was encouraged to attack Sicily from the rear. Michael also spread Byzantine gold liberally through Sicily, where resentment had developed against Charles of Anjou, especially after he levied special

---

Box 13.4   *St. Sava of Serbia*

St. Sava (1175–1235) was the founder of the Serbian independent church and one of the leading figures of his age. His life was remarkable and full of adventures and achievements of all kinds. It also provides a wonderful view of the relationship between Byzantium and the Christian peoples of the Balkans at the time. He was born the youngest son of Stefan Nemanja (reigned 1165/8–96), Grand Zupan of Serbia, but he abandoned political life, preferring instead to become a monk at Mount Athos, where he lived first at the monastery of Panteleimon and then at Vatopedi. In 1198 his father, who by then had also became a monk at Athos, sent Sava to Constantinople to seek permission to found a Serbian monastery on the Holy Mountain. The emperor Alexios III agreed and Sava became the founder of Hilandar monastery (1208), which still remains today a Serbian monastery at Athos.

In 1207 or 1208 Sava chafed against the Latin takeover of Mount Athos and he fled to the Studenica monastery in Serbia, taking his father's relics with him. Probably while he was there, Sava wrote a *Life* of his father, who was considered a saint immediately after his death. This work was especially important in the early Serbian tradition, not only because it is one of the earliest lives of Serbian saints, but much more because, by glorifying the family of Stefan Nemanja and linking it with the Serbian church and the Byzantine tradition, it provided the Serbian monarchy with an especially strong foundation. In addition, the *Life* of Stefan Nemanja stressed the connection between the kings of Serbia and monasticism, especially as practiced in the monasteries of Mount Athos – since both Stefan and his son Sava became monks.

One of the most interesting aspects of this early part of Sava's career was his relationship with his brother, Stefan the First-crowned (Grand Zupan 1195–1217, king 1217–27). Stefan was first married to Eudokia, niece of the Byzantine emperor Isaac II Angelos and daughter of the future Alexios III. Stefan, however, repudiated Eudokia around 1200 and, about 1207, he married Anna, granddaughter of Enrico Dandalo, the Doge of Venice and one of the leaders of the Fourth Crusade. The reason for these actions undoubtedly was the changing political reality in the Balkans, as Byzantine power weakened and then collapsed in 1204, and Stefan began to lean toward the West for political alliances.

At the same time, Stefan's rule was challenged by his elder brother Vuko, and Sava, in possession of the relics of their father and control of the greatest monastery in Serbia, had leverage in the dispute between his two brothers, which seems to have been settled, temporarily at least, by a kind of division of the kingdom. Meanwhile, Stefan negotiated with the papacy and in 1217 he was crowned king by a representative of the pope. There has been much scholarly controversy about Sava's attitude to this turn toward the West, and it seems impossible now to know how he felt.

What seemed to trouble Sava more was the fact that Serbia lay along the fault line between East and West. In the years after the Fourth Crusade, at a time when conditions were terribly confused. The immediate thought that the westerners would overrun all the East waned, especially with the foundation of the so-called Empire of Nicaea and the despotate of Epiros as successor states, and Serbia – of course – was independent of all the warring states. The church of Serbia, however, was subject to the archbishop of Ochrid, which lay at the time within the despotate of Epiros.

Sava realized that the best hope for the independence of the Serbian church (and perhaps even the Serbian state) lay in alliance with the enemy of Epiros and probably the most serious enemy of the Latins, Theodore I Laskaris, the emperor of Nicaea. As it turned out, Sava and Theodore were distantly related, since the emperor and Sava's father had been married to two sisters. In 1219 Sava journeyed to Nicaea and managed to secure from the emperor exactly what he wanted: he was consecrated the archbishop of the independent (*autocephalous*) Serbian church; henceforth the archbishops of Serbia were to be chosen by the Serbian bishops themselves, without recourse to the patriarch, although they were to honor the patriarch as the first of the bishops of the Orthodox church.

The result of this agreement was of considerable significance: the Serbian church was granted independence. By the same token the independence of the Serbian state was acknowledged and supported, and a strong link was forged between the rising power of Nicaea and that of the Serbian monarchy. At a single stroke the coronation of Stefan was countered by the agreement of 1219.

Sava then set about to strengthen the Serbian character of his church, by replacing Byzantine bishops with local candidates, on the one hand, and, on the other, by providing Slavonic liturgy and literature for the western coastal areas of Serbia, which had been under strong Latin influence. There is no reason to regard Sava as an opponent of Rome, any more than he was an opponent of Byzantium. He was willing to work with both to provide a unified church and culture to his people.

Sava studied Byzantine canon law, which he translated into the Serbian context and which became the basis for Serbian religious and secular law. He also strongly opposed the dualist heresy of the Bogomils, which his father had also fought against. When Stefan the First-crowned died in 1227 and was succeeded by his son Radoslav, there was a danger that the new king might be willing to sacrifice the independence of the Serbian church for political reasons. Perhaps because of this – but also perhaps because Jerusalem had just fallen to the forces of the Third Crusade – Sava set out for Jerusalem in 1229. He visited all the Holy Places and returned home via Mount Athos and Thessaloniki. The early 1230s witnessed turmoil in Serbia, in part because of growing Bulgarian influence, and in 1234 Sava decided to resign, probably for personal reasons. That same year he set sail once again for the Holy Land, narrowly escaping a pirate raid and a fierce storm on his way. He visited Jerusalem, Egypt (then under the control of the Ayyubid dynasty), the monasteries of the Egyptian desert, and Mount Sinai. From there he returned again to Palestine before visiting Constantinople (still then occupied by the Latins). While there he accepted the invitation of Tsar John Asen II of Bulgaria (who was a relative of his) to visit Bulgaria, and during his visit, in January of 1236, he died.

St. Sava's life was a remarkable one and it strongly demonstrates many of the characteristics of the age, the political and religious struggles in the aftermath of the Fourth Crusade, and the rise of the Christian Slavic states of the Balkans. But his importance is the memory he has left to the Serbian people. In the words of Dimitri Obolensky (p. 169), "He remains by far the most popular saint of his people; revered as their ever-present protector, at home and abroad; a familiar figure depicted in icon or fresco in every church of the land, from the grandest of royal *zaduzbine* to the humblest wayside chapel; and, far transcending the bounds of religion, he is a national hero, endlessly celebrated in legend, poetry, and song." There is a fresco of him at Mileseva monastery in southwestern Serbia, where the saint's body was brought for burial.

FURTHER READING

Dimitri Obolensky, *Six Byzantine Portraits*. Oxford, 1988, pp. 115–72.
Graham Speake, *Mount Athos: Renewal in Paradise*. New Haven and London, 2003.

taxes to help pay for the expedition against Constantinople. At the end of March 1282 a rebellion broke out in Sicily against Angevin rule, the notorious Sicilian Vespers. Charles, who was ready to attack Constantinople, was forced to divert his expedition to Sicily in a vain attempt to put down the revolt. When the Aragonese fleet arrived in August of the same year they drove the Angevins from the island and Charles was unable again to threaten Constantinople.

FURTHER READING

A. Angold, *A Byzantine Government in Exile: Government and Society under the Laskarids of Nicaea (1204–1261)*. Oxford, 1975.
D. Geanakoplos, *Emperor Michaeol Palaeologus and the West, 1258–1281: A Study in Byzantine–Latin Relations*. Cambridge, MA, 1959.
D. Gill, *Byzantium and the Papacy, 1198–1400*. New Brunswick, NJ, 1979.
Steven Runciman, *The Sicilian Vespers*. Cambridge, 1958.

14

The Beginnings of Decline

250	500	750	1000	1250	1500

1321	Beginning of civil war
1331	Stefan Dušan king of Serbia
1389	Battle of Kossovo
1391	Manuel II emperor

Andronikos II (1282–1328)

Michael VIII died in 1282, leaving the empire in what appeared to be very good condition. To be sure, Byzantium had re-emerged onto the stage as a major player in international affairs. Nonetheless, his successors were completely unable to maintain the political and military power of Michael's empire, and it is an open question to what degree his policies were responsible for this decline. On the one hand, Michael had expended enormous energy to restore Byzantium to a position of power, and this had possibly weakened the broader fabric of the Byzantine economy and state. On the other hand, we must be careful when we blame the successful Michael VIII for the failures that took place under the rule of his successors. Ostrogorsky is clear in his assessment of the situation: "In reality there were more deep-seated reasons to account for the rapid decline of Byzantine power . . . The internal weaknesses of the state were incurable and increasing external pressure drove Byzantium irretrievably toward catastrophe" (p. 479). In Ostrogorsky's view, the rise of the Ottomans and Serbia took place at a time when the state had been weakened by the expenditure of Michael VIII, and he notes that "these momentous factors in foreign and domestic politics, and not the personal qualities of its rulers, which really account for the decline of Byzantium" (ibid.).

Upon the death of Michael VIII, the throne passed without incident to his son Andronikos II (1282–1328), whose long reign was marked by significant difficulties and defeats for Byzantium. At this time the practice of using members of the imperial family of the Palaiologoi as provincial governors became widespread, so that they were effectively semi-independent rulers of parts of the empire. In this one may note the ultimate victory of the Byzantine nobility, which had long sought power that was essentially personal and independent of the central state. This phenomenon was associated with western concepts of political power, and the desire of the emperor's second wife Irene (Yolanda) of Montferrat to divide imperial territory among her sons was regarded as a sign of western influence, according to the contemporary historian Gregoras. Irene was ultimately unsuccessful in this, although she was able to marry her daughter Simonis to the Serbian king Milutin, and she continued to negotiate with him after her estrangement from her husband. Andronikos was clear in his rejection of Irene's demands for what amounted to the abandonment of the Byzantine idea of the state, but he allowed the growth of the de facto independence of the great landowners which, in turn, weakened the state economically, since they were normally able to avoid payment of taxes to the central government. The old system of *pronoia* had survived and had been used by the emperors of Nicaea, and Michael VIII made the grant hereditary. The practice became more widespread under his successors, and the obligation of the *pronoiar* to perform a service for the state weakened notably.

More than most emperors, Andronikos II depended on his eldest son, Michael IX, who had been named co-emperor in 1281 and crowned in 1294 or 1295. Michael was an energetic and generally competent commander, and Andronikos shared power with him willingly, leaving most military matters in his hands.

Upon his accession, Andronikos II was forced to cut costs, and he did so first in the military, reducing significantly the size of the army and essentially eliminating the Byzantine navy, placing his hopes at sea entirely in his alliance with the Genoese. He later was able to restore the military, to a certain degree, as a result of increasing state revenues. He was able to do this by the introduction (apparently in 1304) of the *sitokrithon*, a supplementary tax on land, to be paid in kind, and the elimination of some tax exemptions. These measures were not altogether successful, but they did allow the emperor to purchase mercenaries, pay off especially dangerous enemies, and maintain a surprisingly small military force, including a total of only 3,000 cavalry.

Andronikos was especially interested in religious affairs. He was opposed to the failed policy of union with Rome, and he abandoned the policy of his father, who had seen the papacy as a basis for securing western support. The Sicilian Vespers had put an end to the workability of this policy, and immediately on his accession Andronikos repudiated the union and restored the traditional position of the Orthodox church. Unfortunately for Byzantium, however, as soon as this obstacle between the emperor and the church was removed, dispute broke out yet again between the Arsenites, who continued to revere the memory of the deposed patriarch, and those who supported the more moderate policies of the emperor. Andronikos made a gesture to the Arsenites in 1284 and allowed the body of Arsenios to be brought back to Constantinople, where it was regarded with honor by his followers. The dispute dragged on, however, until the patriarch Niphon was finally able to negotiate a compromise and the schism came to an end in 1310.

Andronikos took considerable interest in the administration of the church, reorganizing dioceses and regulating monasteries. One of the more important of these actions was his decision of 1311 by which the *protos* of Mount Athos, who presided over all the monasteries on the Holy Mountain, was no longer to be appointed by the emperor but by the patriarch of Constantinople. In this and in many other ways the Byzantine church maintained or even expanded its authority, far outside the increasingly narrow territory controlled by the Byzantine state.

In fact, after suffering from the raids of the Catalan Grand Company early in the fourteenth century, the monasteries of Mount Athos enjoyed a new era of prosperity and importance. During this period the monasteries received many large grants of land, some from private individuals, but even more from the emperors, and these were far-flung, including properties in Serbia, Wallachia, and the islands of the northern Aegean, and not only fields but also some urban properties. The records from the administration, rental, and sale of these holdings, many of which survive, provide especially important information about society in this period (not just the monasteries, but agricultural and commercial life, along with the daily existence of the peasants). Several new monasteries were founded, including those of Gregoriou, Dionysiou, Pantokrator, and Simonopetra. This period also witnessed the development of "idiorrhythmic monasticism," in which the monks lived more or less according to their own rules, frequently worshiping together in the church of the monastery but taking their meals separately and not uncommonly owning private property.

Not surprisingly, Andronikos' foreign policy focused largely on the few Latin claimants to power in the Byzantine sphere. For example, as already mentioned, he took as his second wife Yalonda of Montferrat, the daughter of the last titular Latin ruler of Thessaloniki, who gladly surrendered his claim to his daughter and her children. After the Sicilian Vespers most of the significant western powers had lost interest in the East; those who maintained some hope of intervention were players of the second rank: Philip of Tarentum (son of Charles II, King of Naples) and Charles of Valois, brother of Philip IV (the Fair) of France and titular Latin emperor of Constantinople. Although each of these sought to intervene in Byzantine affairs, none was successful; their alliances with Epiros and Thessaly only prompted Andronikos to respond, relatively successfully, with military force.

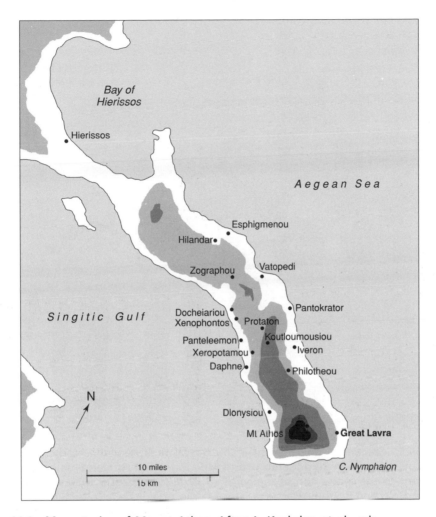

Bay of
Hierissos

Hierissos

Aegean Sea

Esphigmenou

Hilandar

Zographou

Vatopedi

Singitic Gulf

Docheiariou
Xenophontos   Protaton

Pantokrator

Panteleemon
Xeropotamou
Daphne

Koutloumousiou
Iveron

Philotheou

N

Dlonysiou

Mt Athos   Great Lavra

C. Nymphaion

10 miles

15 km

Map 14.1 Monasteries of Mount Athos. After A. Kazhdan et al., eds.,
The Oxford Dictionary of Byzantium (New York, 1991), p. 224

Under Milutin (1282–1321) Serbia provided challenges as well as opportunities for Byzantium at this time. Attacks on Macedonia caused Andronikos to
seek a marriage alliance with Milutin: a proposed marriage with the emperor's
sister Eudokia failed, when the latter refused to cooperate. Both Andronikos
and Milutin sought the alliance, however, and both finally overcame local
opposition, and in 1299 the Serbian king was married to Andronikos' daughter
Simonis (who was only 5 years old at the time). This marriage, although it
failed to produce an heir, was the beginning of an intense period of interaction
in which Byzantine influence in Serbia reached a high point. Byzantine architects, painters, scholars, and missionaries found their way to Serbia, and the
Serbian court became a significant factor in the spread of Byzantine culture

Figure 14.1 Gracanica. This impressive church was built near the modern town of Pristina by the Serbian king Stefan Uroš II Milutin in 1311. It stands as an important monument to the conversion of the Serbs to Byzantine Christianity and to relations between Slavs and Byzantines in the later Middle Ages. The architecture is sophisticated and complex and the fourteenth-century frescoes on the interior are well-preserved, including portraits of members of the Serbian royal family. This church, like many other religious buildings in the Balkans, has been damaged and is still threatened by sectarian violence designed, in part, to remove the historical traces of one group or another from a contested landscape. Photo: Dumbarton Oaks / Slobodan Curcic

into the northern Balkans. As had often happened in the past, the Serbian rulers saw the connection with Byzantium as a means to help solidify their control over the local aristocracy and to provide important symbols of their power and control of their own territory.

As mentioned above, Andronikos had committed himself to alliance with Genoa. In 1294 war broke out between Venice and Genoa, as they struggled for dominance in the East. This devolved into a war between Venice and Byzantium, as the Genoese withdrew from the conflict and even signed a peace treaty with Venice in 1299. Without a fleet of its own, Byzantium could not effectively resist the Venetians, and in a peace treaty signed in 1302 the Venetians retained all their old trading privileges. The Genoese, meanwhile, did not lose their position, but they fortified their settlement in Galata, across the Golden Horn from Constantinople, and in 1304 the Genoese general Benedetto Zaccaria seized the island of Chios, which they were to hold for years.

The Byzantines experienced the greatest difficulty in Asia Minor. The Mongol invasions, which had brought some relief to Byzantium in previous reigns, caused many refugees to pour into Asia Minor from the East. Perhaps because of the recapture of Constantinople and the shift of attention to the West, the empire had paid less attention to Asia Minor in the years since 1261. As a result, Byzantium was able to offer little resistance to the Turkic people who spread across the countryside, and by the beginning of the fourteenth century virtually all of Asia Minor, with the exception of the great cities, had been lost to Byzantine control. Instead, Asia Minor was divided into a great many independent Turkic principalities, not least of which was that of Osman (1288–1326), founder of the Ottoman dynasty, in Bithynia.

Box 14.1   *The Condition of Asia Minor at the End of the Fourteenth Century*

Manuel II Palaiologos (1391–1425) was a clever and hard-working emperor, but he also found himself compelled to go to war as the vassal of the Ottoman Sultan Beyezid I. While on campaign with the sultan, Manuel kept in touch with his friends in Constantinople by writing and receiving letters. These letters were read aloud, within a narrow circle of highly educated men who appreciated the compositions, not so much for the information they conveyed as for their careful rhetorical composition. In several of these letters, written during a difficult campaign in Asia Minor, the emperor vividly described conditions in the former Byzantine heartland. The following passages provide elegant testimony of how Asia Minor, the former core of the Byzantine Empire, had changed completely, especially as a result of the Turkish occupation:

Letter 16, to Cydones
Asia Minor, winter 1391

A great expanse of land has your letter traversed; after passing over mountains and fording rivers, it has finally found us here in a tiny, little plain, encircled by a chain of precipitous mountains, as a poet would say, so that it barely suffices as an encampment for the army. In appearance and in reality it is an extremely savage place. Apart from a little wood and some murky water, it cannot provide us with anything. It has been deserted by the inhabitants, who have fled to the clefts in the rocks, to the forests, and to the mountain heights in an effort to escape a death from which there is no escape, a very cruel and inhuman death without any semblance of justice. For every mouth which is opened in answer is immediately closed by the sword. Nobody is spared, neither very young children nor defenseless women . . .

The small plain in which we are now staying certainly had some name when it was fortunate enough to be inhabited and ruled by the Romans [Byzantines]. But now when I ask what it was, I might as well ask about the proverbial winds of a wolf, since there is absolutely nobody to inform me. To be sure, you can see many cities here, but they lack what constitutes the true splendor of a city and without which they could not really be termed cities, that is, human beings. Most of these cities now lie in ruins, a pitiable spectacle for the people whose ancestors once possessed them. But not even the names have survived, since they were destroyed so long ago . . .

You have heard of the city of Pompey [Pompeiopolis], beautiful, marvelous, extensive; rather, that is how it once was, for now you can barely make out its ruins. It is situated on the banks of a river which is crossed by a stone bridge, adorned with colonnades, marvelous for their size, their beauty and their skillful construction. Indeed, this city and these magnificent remains offer no less evidence why the Romans bestowed on its founder the surname of "the Great" [that is, Pompey, the Great, as he was called] than the many victories which amply justified this title. Now, after leaving this city and then the city of Zeno behind us, with Sinope off to the left and the Halys on the other side, we have already been marching for many days, using the sun for our guide. For we must head directly toward the rising sun if we are not to lose our way.

George T. Dennis, *The Letters of Manuel II Palaeologus.* Corpus Fontium Historiae Byzantinae 8 (Washington, DC, 1977), pp. 42–3.

Andronikos did not have the military resources to counter the Turkic threat, so he sought aid from allies. He first joined forces with the Alans, whose foray into Asia Minor was a complete failure. In 1303 he then allied himself with Roger de Flor, the commander of the Catalan Grand Company, a band of mercenaries from Spain who had previously fought for various western leaders. Andronikos made Roger Caesar and married him to his niece Maria Asen. In 1304 the Catalans had some notable success in northwestern Asia Minor, but they also attacked the Byzantine population, especially when the emperor was not always able to supply their agreed-upon payments. They crossed over to Europe and continued their ravages, which were only amplified after the assassination of Roger de Flor in 1305, perhaps on the orders of Michael IX. The co-emperor took the field against the Catalans but was decisively defeated, and for two years the Catalans ravaged Thrace before they descended into Macedonia.

These difficulties gave the Bulgarian tsar Theodore Svetoslav (1300–22) the opportunity to seize Byzantine strongholds on the Black Sea, and Charles of

Valois renewed his efforts in the East, coming to terms with Venice, Serbia, and even the Catalan Company. The Catalans, however, had their own interests at heart; they conquered Thessaly, and at the Battle of the Kiphissos in Boeotia (1311) they defeated Walter of Brienne and killed the majority of the knights of Frankish Greece. The Catalans set themselves up as the rulers of Athens, which they held for the next 70 years. As a result of this, western plans against Byzantium collapsed, and, oddly enough, the success of the Catalans gave Byzantium the opportunity to strengthen its position in the Morea (Peloponnesos), which was henceforth to be an important outpost of Byzantine culture and power.

Civil War

Andronikos' son Michael IX died in 1320 at the age of 43. Previous to this a serious break had occurred between the old emperor Andronikos II and his grandson and namesake, Andronikos III. The younger Andronikos, son of Michael IX, had already been crowned co-emperor, but his frivolous lifestyle and violent behavior caused the elder emperor to exclude him from the succession. Members of the aristocracy, such as John Kantakouzenos, who held offices in the provinces, used the crisis as an opportunity to revolt against the rule of Constantinople, and in 1321 Andronikos III assumed leadership of this movement. Unencumbered by fiscal responsibilities, he offered lavish gifts and exemptions to his supporters, and the old emperor was forced to come to terms with his grandson, whom he accepted as his co-ruler in 1325. Civil war broke out again in 1327 and came to involve the Slavic kingdoms, as Serbia supported the elder and Bulgaria the younger Andronikos; in addition, the civil war allowed large numbers of Albanians to flood into imperial territory, where they remained essentially independent for a time. In large part because of opposition to Andronikos II's austere financial policies, Andronikos III's popularity grew; in 1328 he was able to enter Constantinople unopposed, and he forced his grandfather to abdicate.

Andronikos III (1328–1341)

John Kantakouzenos, who had been one of Andronikos III's greatest supporters, essentially held the reins of state under the new emperor, while Andronikos devoted himself primarily to military affairs. Kantekouzenos sought to craft a workable foreign policy based upon the reality that Serbia and the Ottoman state had become the most powerful of Byzantium's rivals, while the threat from the West had seriously weakened. Kantakouzenos also sought to eliminate Byzantium's dependence on Genoa by construction of a fleet, which was paid for in large part by contributions from the nobility. In Asia Minor the

Ottomans had continued their advance, taking Bursa (Prousa), which henceforth became their capital. Kantakouzenos allied the empire with the remaining Seljuk emirs, whose existence was likewise threatened by the Ottomans.

In the Balkans Byzantium allied with Bulgaria against Serbia, and this led to a trial of strength between the two Slavic kingdoms at Velbuzd in 1330. The battle was a complete victory for the Serbs, who now came to dominate the whole of the southern Balkans. Soon thereafter the new Serbian king, Stefan Uroš IV Dušan (1331–55) made peace with the new Bulgarian tsar Ivan Alexander (1331–71), and he was able to move victoriously into Byzantine Macedonia. One by one the cities of Macedonia fell to Dušan: Ochrid, Prilep, Strumica, Kastoria, and Vodena (Edessa). In 1334 a peace treaty was signed, according to which the Serbs were left in control of most of their conquests.

The situation was, if anything, worse in Asia Minor, where Nicaea and Nikomedia fell to the Ottomans, leaving only a few outposts still in Byzantine hands. Just as seriously for the future, after their conquest of Bithynia, the Ottomans constructed a fleet and began to threaten Byzantine possessions from the sea. For the time being, however, the renewed Byzantine navy was equal to the task of defending the capital and even made headway in the Aegean, as Chios and Phocaea were taken from the Genoese, and a western fleet intent on the capture of Lesbos was driven off. Byzantium was meanwhile able to extend its authority in Thessaly and Epiros, where the last survivors of the independent Byzantine successor states recognized the authority of Andronikos III.

Renewed Civil War

When Andronikos III died in 1341, his son and heir John V was only 9 years old. Almost immediately civil war broke out once again. On one side was the party of the patriarch John Kalekas and Alexios Apokavkos, who were in control of the regency in Constantinople; on the other was the party of the Grand Domestikos Kantakouzenos, the friend and ally of Andronikos III, whose greatest support was among the provincial aristocracy. Kantakouzenos had himself crowned emperor, as John VI, although he always maintained that he was supporting the legitimate emperor John V. In this context of political confusion a new and highly divisive controversy broke out, which had religious, social, and political consequences.

Hesychasm and Social Unrest

The controversy had deep roots in monastic practice and theory. Byzantine monks had always sought *hesychia* (tranquility) as a means to communion and union with God. Hescychasm as a specific ascetic practice was promoted particularly by Gregory of Sinai in the early fourteenth century in Thrace and especially in the monasteries of Mount Athos, where he introduced the so-called Jesus Prayer (the words: "Lord Jesus Christ, Son of God, have mercy on me"). Hesychast monks lived a strict ascetic life, including special exercises, breathing, and recital of the Jesus prayer, that supposedly led to ecstasy and a vision of Divine Light, which was identified with the Light that was visible on Mount Tabor at the time of the Transfiguration of Christ. In other words, the hesychasts claimed that they could actually see God himself.

The practices of the hesychasts and their claim to see God earned the enmity and ridicule of many theologians, led by the monk Varlaam of Calabria. Varlaam was a thinker of considerable ability who, although born of an Orthodox family in southern Italy, was influenced by the western logical systems of Scholasticism. He became abbot of the Akataleptos Monastery in Constantinople and was an adviser of Andronikos II on religious matters. Around 1335 he began to attack the hesychasts, arguing that the Light on Mount Tabor was created (and thus not eternal) and making fun of his opponents for their practice of looking at their navels, calling them *omphalopsychoi* ("people with their souls in their navels").

The main defender of hesychasm was Gregory Palamas, who answered Varlaam's criticisms by making a distinction between the essence of God, which is unknowable and inaccessible to humans, and the uncreated "energies" of God – which are God just the same. The latter are comprehensible by humans and they include the Light of Tabor. Thus, in Palamas' view, mankind, although a creature, can comprehend and "participate" in God himself. Palamas' thought was firmly based in the *apophatic* tradition of Byzantine theology, which said that no logical system was satisfactory to understand God, but that God might be perceived through direct experience. In this respect he was not so much opposed to Scholasticism as he was to the idea that logical systems could actually define God.

The controversy continued for several years. In 1341 Andronikos III called a council that provided Palamas with a clear victory. The death of the emperor a few days later, however, threw the question into doubt again. Varlaam renewed his attacks, and the religious dispute began to take on a political aspect, with Kantakouzenos and his party generally supporting Palamas and the hesychasts, with the patriarch Kalekas and Apokavkos in opposition. As the latter gained the upper hand, hesychasm was condemned, and Gregory Palamas was imprisoned and excommunicated.

The controversy, however, soon had social as well as political ramifications connected with the struggle for the throne. Kantakouzenos was supported by the aristocracy, and the regency of Apokavkos relied on the support of the urban poor, first in Constantinople and later in the cities of Thrace and Macedonia, where real hatred for the aristocracy had developed. In Thessaloniki the poor and the sailors were organized as a party called the Zealots (not to be confused with the Zealots of the tenth century) which, in 1342, drove out all members of the aristocracy and the governor appointed by Kantakouzenos, establishing a government that was essentially independent. The Zealot party naturally supported the regency in Constantinople against Kantakouzenos in the struggle for supremacy. Although the historian Gregoras characterized the Zealot regime as "mob rule," it would be a mistake to see this primarily as a class war, and it is equally misleading to see hard and fast connections between this conflict and the dispute over hesychasm. Thus, although there is some evidence that the Zealots in Thessaloniki ridiculed the Christian liturgy, they certainly had no interest in the suppression of hesychasm.

Kantakouzenos, meanwhile, was deprived of most of his support and he turned to Serbia for assistance. Stefan Dušan was willing to help, and, beginning in 1342, he aided Kantakouzenos in a series of unsuccessful attacks on several Macedonian towns. Kantakouzenos, however, was recognized in Thessaly and Epiros, which led to a split with Dušan, who then switched sides and allied with the regency in Constantinople, arranging the marriage of his son Uroš to the sister of John Palaiologos. Kantakouzenos then found support from the Seljuk emir Omur, and, with the aid of the Turks, he was able to make notable progress in Thrace, although an attack on Thessaloniki failed. In Constantinople Apokavkos was killed in a prison revolt in 1345, and Kantakouzenos was assured of victory. He was crowned as John VI in 1346 and assumed the regency for the legitimate emperor John V, who had to remain in the background for a further ten years.

The Zealot government in Thessaloniki survived for a time but descended into greater violence against the aristocracy, many of whom were thrown from the walls of the city and massacred by the mob. In 1349 the Zealots sought to surrender the city to Stefan Dušan, but this failed and Kantakouzenos entered the city in 1350 along with Gregory Palamas, who had been elected bishop of the city.

The victory of Kantakouzenos also meant the triumph of hesychasm. In 1351 a council met in the Blachernae palace of Constantinople and proclaimed the orthodoxy of Palamas' theology and condemned Varlaam. Controversy continued on the issue, but hesychast teaching was from then on officially recognized and it was the basis of the thinking of the most influential theologians of the Byzantine church until the end of the empire and beyond.

Stephan Dušan and the Ascendancy of Serbia

The Serbian king Stefan Dušan gained the greatest advantage from this period of civil war in Byzantium. He controlled all of Macedonia except for Thessaloniki, and he declared himself emperor of the Serbs and the Greeks, crowned with this title by the independent patriarch of Serbia in 1346. Dušan therefore shared the same goals as Symeon of Bulgaria in the tenth century: he wanted to establish a joint Slavo-Byzantine empire. Dušan was especially favorable to the monasteries of Mount Athos, which lay inside his territory; he visited Athos himself, and he imitated the Byzantine emperors in his gifts to

Figure 14.2 St. Merkourios. This dramatic depiction of the military saint Merkourios is from the Protaton church in Karyies, Mt. Athos. It dates to the early part of the fourteenth century. According to tradition, Merkourios was a Christian military officer who was executed by the emperor Decius; interestingly, another tradition developed that – returning from the dead – he killed the apostate emperor Julian. Photo: Dumbarton Oaks / I. Djordjevic, with thanks to Miodrag Markovic

the monasteries. His reign witnessed the strongest wave of Byzantine influence in Serbia itself as Byzantine officials were integrated into the Serbian administration and Greek was used as the language of the chancellery.

After Kantakouzenos' victory in the civil wars, Dušan continued his advance in Greece, completing his conquest of Epiros and Thessaly. With very little effort he had doubled his territory, controlling an empire that stretched from the Danube in the north to the Gulf of Korinth in the south. Approximately half of this empire was Greek-speaking, and Dušan himself took special interest in the Greek part of his realm, leaving the administration of the northern territories to his son Uroš. Dušan was also especially interested in the infrastructure of his empire and its legal system. He promulgated a legal code in

Figure 14.3 Presentation of the Virgin. The cycle of the life of the Virgin was a favorite topic in Byzantine art. It represents an event, not mentioned in the canonical New Testament, in which the parents of the Virgin bring her to the Temple in Jerusalem, where she was welcomed by the priest Zacharias. In this scene the Virgin can be seen being presented by her mother, while in the upper right she appears again, inside the temple, being given bread by an angel. Particularly lifelike are the paintings of the women who stand behind the scene and who look piercingly in all different directions. From the Protaton church in Karyies, Mount Athos, early fourteenth century. Photo: Dumbarton Oaks / I. Djordjevic, with thanks to Miodrag Markovic

1349 and again in 1354 that was built essentially on Byzantine models, serving to place his rule on a sound footing and creating a base for the development of the Serbian state in the future.

As emperor, John VI Kantakouzenos maintained the same policies he had promoted while adviser and claimant to the throne. Members of the imperial family were appointed to positions in the provinces as the best way to prevent governors from declaring independence. Thus, Kantakouzenos appointed his eldest son Matthew as the ruler of Thrace and his second son Manuel as the

Despot of the Morea. In this way he also sought to create a dynasty of his own, parallel and in rivalry to that of the Palaiologoi.

Kantakouzenos continued to seek independence from the Genoese, and to that end, he again raised what private funds he could for another reconstruction of the Byzantine fleet. He also sought to undermine the Genoese trade monopoly in Constantinople by lowering tariffs for Byzantine merchants, but the Genoese reacted militarily and destroyed the Byzantine navy in 1349.

Byzantium's enemies realized that Kantakouzenos was not the legitimate emperor, and they therefore sought to undermine his power through support of John V Palaiologos. The legitimate emperor himself began to grow restive with the tutelage of Kantekouzenos and he sought power in his own name. In order to placate the young emperor Kantekouzenos granted John V the territories formerly given to his son Matthew, while transferring to Matthew the areas around Adrianople. Not surprisingly, however, civil war broke out again in 1352 between these two semi-independent principalities. With the support of

---

Box 14.2   *The Monasteries of Meteora*

The visitor driving west from the Thessalian metropolis of Larissa in Central Greece crosses through an enormous plain, unusual in Greece. In the early summer the fields are covered with wheat and in the fall with cotton. Extremes of temperature and weather are common, with searing heat in summer and bitter cold in winter, accompanied by driving rain and – not uncommonly – snow. This is an area that seems far from the coasts of the Aegean Sea and very much a part of the Balkan world. Storks can be seen perched on chimneys, and in the town of Trikkala there is an impressive Byzantine fortification and one of the largest surviving Ottoman mosques in Greece.

Beyond Trikkala a series of strange rock formations slowly begin to rise sharply out of the flatness of the plain, many well over 200 meters high. As one approaches, the rocks divide into pinnacles and towers that seem tortured and almost alive, dark grey in color and filled with caves. In this remarkable setting are the monasteries of Meteora, once large in number, although today fewer than ten still cling to a precarious existence on the tops of precipitous crags. Meteora, located above the Byzantine town of Stagoi, thus became one of the last Byzantine monastic centers. Like Mount Athos, Meteora survived the fall of Constantinople and remains the most visited Byzantine monastic complex and one of the few places where the traditions of Byzantium come face to face with the modern world.

Thessaly was a major center of wealth during the whole of the Byzantine period, in large part because of its agricultural productivity. Slavs and Vlachs settled in the mountainous area and the Latins gained control of the east after 1204. The western part of the plain, however, remained in Byzantine hands, ultimately under the control of John I Doukas, who established an independent principality in Thessaly, which survived until it was brought again under the control of Constantinople in 1335.

Figure 14.4   Meteora, the skete of Doupiani. These caves in the northwest corner of the plain of Thessaly apparently housed the first hermits in the area. Photo: Timothy E. Gregory

It was in this period that monasticism really developed at Meteora. According to local tradition monks had inhabited the caves in the vicinity since early Byzantine times, but there is no solid evidence of this. The first historical indication of monasticism refers to a loose grouping of monks living in the *skete* (*asketerion*, "hermitage") of Doupiani, presumably in the caves around one of the central rock outcrops, probably in the early fourteenth century. Difficulties at Mount Athos, including the dangers posed by Turkish pirate raids, provided the special impetus for the development of Meteora, as monks fled to the relative security of northwestern Thessaly. The earliest surviving church is in the rock-cut monastery of the Hypante, founded in 1366/7.

The most important monastery at Meteora was the Great Meteoron, founded in the late fourteenth century by Athanasios of Meteora. Athanasios was from Neopatras, the most important city of Thessaly at the time, but he studied in Thessaloniki and Constantinople and made contact with some of the leading monastic figures of the

Figure 14.5 Meteora, church of the Metamorphosis (Transfiguration) in the Great Meteoron. This is the east end of the church, part of the original *katholikon*, built by John Uroš Paliologos, son of the Serbian tsar, who took the monastic name Ioasaph. Photo: Timothy E. Gregory

day. After a time in Crete, he moved to Mount Athos and then, ca. 1340, to Meteora, where he established a monastery at a place called Platylithos (the "broad rock") at the center of the Meteora "forest of stone." In the 1380s, when Serbia dominated Thessaly, John-Ioasaph Uroš, son of Symeon Uroš, became the abbot of the Megalo Meteoron and founded a church dedicated to the Transfiguration, whose eastern end survives in the rebuilt *katholikon* (the public church) of the monastery.

In the course of the fourteenth century other monasteries were built at the Meteora: Agios Stephanos and Agios Nikolaos Anapavsas, and new foundations were made through the sixteenth and seventeenth centuries, under Ottoman control, when the monasteries reached a number of some 23 or so, and several of the churches were painted by important artists including Theophanes of Crete.

Fifty years ago the monasteries of Meteora were in a state of decay, with only a few monks in each of the six or so that were still inhabited. The intervention of the Greek state from the 1960s onward saved the physical structures, and the revitalization of the monastic tradition in more recent years has assured a continuity of function. The Meteora, however, have become a major tourist attraction and hotels, camping sites, and expensive restaurants cover the hills in the surrounding countryside. The monks make an attempt to preserve their way of life, but the Meteora, which was once far removed from the currents of major world events, are now on

Figure 14.6 Meteora, the monastery of Rousanou. One of the more dramatic of the Meteora monasteries, which fits snugly onto the top of its pillar of stone. This monastery was founded in the sixteenth century and has well-preserved frescoes of that century. Photo: Timothy E. Gregory

the major tourist road from Europe into Greece, and it is difficult to know exactly what the future will bring.

FURTHER READING

D. M. Nicol, *Meteora: The Rock Monasteries of Thessaly*. London, 1975.

Turkic mercenaries Kantakouzenos was initially successful, but John V appealed to Serbia and Bulgaria for assistance and Dušan sent a contingent of cavalry, while the Kantakouzenoi were aided by the Ottoman sultan Orchan (1326–62) the successor of Osman. The Turks ultimately defeated the Serbs, and in 1353 Kantakouzenos abandoned the fiction of support of the legitimate dynasty and had his son Matthew proclaimed as co-emperor while John V was deposed.

Meanwhile, Orchan abandoned Kantakouzeonos, seized the city of Kallipolis on the Hellespont, and prepared to invade Thrace. Partly as a result of the panic that ensued in Constantinople, John V took heart once more, allied with the Genoese corsair Francesco Gattilusio, and in 1354 seized Constantinople. The conspirators forced John Kantakouzenos to abdicate and enter a monastery. Thus, at the age of 25 John V Palaiologos was sole ruler in Constantinople.

As the monk Joasaph, John Kantakouzenos wrote a number of important works and continued to involve himself in the political disputes of the day until his death in 1383. Members of the Kantakouzenos family were able to hold out in the provinces, and Manuel Kantakouzenos at first sought to organize an alliance to overthrow John V and, after renouncing the throne in 1357, he devoted himself to the reorganization and strengthening of the Despotate of the Morea.

Cultural Developments of the Fourteenth Century

Despite the political and military difficulties, the fourteenth century witnessed many cultural developments that were built especially on the phenomena of the twelfth century and the experience of the Crusader dominance of most of the empire. These were based partly on the individualism and secularism of the twelfth century, including the development of a distinct Byzantine aristocratic culture, but this was then enriched (if that is the right word) by contact with the similar but very different world of the Latin West. In the end, the Latin conquerors who came to the central lands of the Byzantine Empire were absorbed into a truly multicultural environment. That was evident in the thirteenth century, but the results in the fourteenth century were much richer still. Obviously this differed from region to region, and we must always remember that the cultural achievements of this period were built largely on the labor of the farmers and tradespeople, whether they were Byzantine or Latin.

One can see the results of these developments in a variety of ways, from the growing sophistication of Byzantine philosophy and theology as a result of contact with western ideas (as discussed above) to trends and changes in architecture and art.

Byzantium as an Ottoman Vassal: the Reign of John V

Perhaps fortunately for John V, Stefan Dušan, one of Byzantium's most serious enemies, died suddenly in 1355 and his successor Stefan Uroš (1355–71) was not able to hold together the empire his father had built. As a result, a number of weak Greco-Serbian principalities sprang up in the Balkans, but Byzantium was not able to take advantage of the vacuum in the region, and it was increasingly clear that the real power was the Ottoman Turks, who first set foot in Thrace in 1354.

It is questionable how much Ottoman policy in Europe was actually directed by the sultan and how much was the work of independent Turkish warlords, but in 1361 Turkish forces took Dydimoteichon and by the end of the decade the important city of Adrianople. Significant numbers of Ottoman settlers moved into Thrace, seeking land in the newly conquered territories. Murad (1362–89), the son of Orchan, had grand ambitions for the Ottoman state and he slowly brought most of the rulers of the Balkans under his sway.

In this situation John V sought western aid through the old expedient of holding out the prospect of a union of the churches. In 1355 he sent a letter to Pope Innocent VI at Avignon, making all kinds of extravagant promises on

Box 14.3 *St. Anastasia the Poison-curer*

This fresco is from the narthex of the church of the Panagia (Virgin Mary) Phorbiotissa of Asinou in Cyprus. This important building was constructed in the early twelfth century by a certain Nikephoros, who held the high rank of *magistros* at the imperial court during the reign of Alexios Komnenos; the title does not allow us to tell precisely what duties Nikephoros had, but it attests his importance in Constantinople. Other inscriptions in the church show that this same Nikephoros retired to Asinou, where he founded a monastery and became its first abbot. The main dedicatory inscription reveals the donor's motive: "I, Nikephoros *magistros*, a poor suppliant, erected this church with longing, in return for which, I pray that you will be my patron in the terrible day of Judgment."

The fresco of St. Anastasia is in the narthex of the church and it was painted in the fourteenth century. The saint is depicted holding a cross in her right hand and a white bottle of medicine in her left. The donor of the fresco was a certain Anastasia Saramalina, who is shown on a lower level than the saint and of a smaller size. She is praying to the saint, with her hands extended in the usual gesture that indicates supplication. The donor is dressed in rich white clothes under a cloak that is fastened at the neck. Her head-covering is of the same material as her clothes (presumably silk) and is derived from western fashion. The artist was concerned to depict Saramalina in a realistic fashion, showing her face wrinkled by old age. Both figures have their faces fully frontal (i.e., looking at the worshipers in the church), although the donor is obviously meant to be facing the saint.

St. Anastasia is depicted as calm and self-confident, obviously ready to help those who call upon her. Little is known about this saint; she may be remotely connected with a Roman saint who was martyred in the Diocletianic persecution, but there is

Figure 14.7 St. Anastasia the Medicine-healer (Pharmakolytria). From the church of the Panagia (Virgin Mary) Phorbiotissa of Asinou in Cyprus. St. Anastasia is shown with her bottle of medicine, ready to offer aid to sufferers. Below her and shown much smaller is the donor, Anastasia Saramalina, who is dressed in clothing that show the western European influence on Cyprus in the 13th and 14th centuries. Photo: Dumbarton Oaks

another tradition assigning her to Thessaloniki. Her powers included not only release from physical poisoning but also (and probably more commonly) from the ill-effects of magic spells.

FURTHER READING

D. Winfield and E. J. W. Hawkins, "The Church of Our Lady at Asinou, Cyprus," *Dumbarton Oaks Papers* 21 (1967), pp. 261–6.

condition that the pope send military help to the beleaguered empire. The pope did nothing and John formed an alliance with his cousin, Amadeo VI of Savoy, who planned a crusade to conquer the Holy Lands and assist Byzantium into the bargain. The crusade actually did set off in 1366 and managed to take Kallipolis from the Ottomans. John sought a church council to discuss union, but Pope Urban V dismissed this idea, suggesting instead that the Byzantine emperor come to Rome. Perhaps moved by the loss of Adrianople, John V did make a journey to Italy, and in October of 1369 he made a personal profession of the Catholic faith and submitted himself publicly to the authority of the pope. John remained for some time in Rome and then in Venice, not returning to Constantinople until the autumn of 1371. Unfortunately, the abasement of the emperor did not result in any aid from the West.

In the absence of the emperor, the situation in the Balkans deteriorated further. The successors of Stefan Uroš, Vukasin and his brother Jovan Uglesa, attempted to organize opposition to Ottoman expansion, and on 26 September 1371 (about a month before John V's return) the Serbs confronted the Ottoman army at the Maritsa River near Cernomen. The Serbian forces were annihilated and the whole of the southern Balkans lay open to the Ottomans. John V saw the lesson from this battle, and shortly after his arrival in Constantinople he sought a treaty with the Sultan Murad, hoping that in this manner the Ottomans could be persuaded to leave Byzantium in possession of its few holdings in Thrace. As a condition of this treaty, however, John had to recognize the sultan as his superior and to pay regular tribute and contribute troops to the Ottoman army when asked to do so. Thus, in a short period John had submitted himself to two of Byzantium's enemies, first the pope and then the Ottoman sultan.

In this era of Byzantine dependency upon the Ottomans, relations between the Byzantine and the Ottoman aristocracies were close; this was made clear in the unfortunate events that marked the rest of John V's reign. A vicious disagreement broke out between John V and his son, who had already been crowned as the co-emperor Andronikos IV. In 1373 Andronikos joined with Sultan Murad's son Savci Çelebi in a joint revolt designed to overthrown both their fathers. The revolt was savagely put down, Savci Çelebi was probably killed, and Andronikos and his young son John (later VII) were imprisoned and partially blinded. John V elevated his second son Manuel as co-emperor, but in 1376 Andronikos escaped from prison and, with help from the Genoese and the Ottomans, seized the throne, in turn imprisoning John V and Manuel. The same scenario was reenacted after another three years and the elder emperor was again in power, while Andronikos established himself in Galata. This standoff was presumably ended in 1381, when an agreement was made in which Andronikos was reconciled to his father, accepted as heir, and the succession of his son, John VII, was assured. John V's son Manuel, now left outside the succession, fled to Thessaloniki, from which he gained control over much of Thessaly and Epiros. The sultan regarded Manuel as a serious enemy, since he had broken his oath of vassalage to the Ottomans, and he sent one of his most trusted generals to take Thessaloniki. Manuel sought to make a resolute stand, but he received no outside assistance, and the inhabitants of the city seemed willing to surrender it, so in 1387 the emperor left the city to its own resources, and Ottoman troops entered the gates without opposition. Manuel later appeared in the sultan's court (in Bursa) as a suppliant and was restored to his father in Constantinople.

This whole series of events highlights the continued infighting within the Palaiologan family and their apparent inability to cooperate in a manner to make the most of the resources the Byzantines had. It also shows the way in which the Ottoman sultan controlled internal Byzantine politics, since in each case – although the Byzantine claimant sought the support of the Genoese or the Venetians – the sultan made the final determination, selecting, normally, the side that offered him the greatest monetary payment.

Murad meanwhile continued his expansion northward in the Balkans. He took Sofia in 1385 and Nis in 1386. In that same year the sultan was forced to return to Asia Minor to deal with an invasion from the east. Byzantium might have used the occasion to reassert its independence, but John V was aged, and the events of the past 15 years had rendered him essentially impotent. The opportunity, however, was seized by the Serbian nobility, led by the prince Lazar, the most powerful figure from 1371 onward, and Vuk Branković, ruler of the area of Kossovo, along with the prince of Bosnia Tvrtko I. In the absence of the sultan, their forces had some success, inspiring Bulgaria to proclaim its independence of the Ottomans. Murad returned to the Balkans and dealt with the situation in a characteristically methodical fashion. He gathered a large army, in part made up of levies from the Christian peoples of the region, and forced the Bulgarians to submit. The Serbs and their allies sought to make a desperate stand on the plain of Kosovo (Kosovo Polje), on 15 June 1389. This battle, which sealed the fate of the Balkans for centuries to come, has come to play a critical role in legend and heroic tales, especially for the Serbs, and it is difficult to separate fact from romantic fantasy. The Ottomans were commanded by Murad himself, while the leader of the Serbs was the prince Lazar. It seems that the Serbs were seriously outnumbered and they suffered from internal dissension and a lack of confidence. Lazar was at first successful, but at a critical moment – according to the legend at least – Vuk Branković deserted his companions, and the Serbs were stopped by Beyezid, the sultan's son and heir. Murad was killed in the battle, but Beyezid led the Ottomans to a complete victory and slaughtered many of the vanquished, including Lazar himself.

As sultan (1389–1402), Beyezid carefully organized the new territory, imposing a head tax, or *haradj*, on all non-Muslim inhabitants and forcing the Christian princes to swear personal fealty to himself. Lazar's son Stephen Lazarević was regarded as the leader of the Serbs, and he faithfully maintained his loyalty to the sultan to the end of his days.

After the Battle of Kossovo Constantinople was completely isolated and surrounded by Ottoman territory, in both Europe and Asia; the only significant territory remaining in loose Byzantine control was the Morea (Peloponnesos), controlled by Byzantium from 1262 and organized as a despotate after 1349.

Beyezid was a ruler of immense ability and ambition, and, even more than his father, he was able to exploit disagreements in the Byzantine ruling family for his own ends. Byzantium experienced some relief, as Beyezid occupied himself with a show of military force in Asia Minor, but he soon conspired with Andronikos' son John VII, who was able to seize Constantinople with Ottoman help. The aged John V, however, refused to give up, and he retook the throne with the help of his son Manuel. Beyezid peremptorily summoned both younger emperors, Manuel and John VII, to assist him in his campaigns in Asia Minor, and the two Byzantine princes were forced to take part in the subjection of Philadelphia, the last Christian city to defy the sultan in western Asia. John V, meanwhile, barely survived these events and he died in 1391 a broken and weak man.

Manuel II Palaiologos (1391–1425)

Hearing of his father's death, Manuel escaped the watchful eye of the Turks and returned to Constantinople, where he was immediately hailed as emperor. Beyezid, sultan from 1389, accepted the *fait accompli*, but he imposed new restrictions on Constantinople and forced the new emperor to join his nephew John VII and the Ottoman army in a long and arduous military campaign in Asia Minor. Toward the beginning of 1392 Manuel returned to Constantinople and soon thereafter married Helena, daughter of the Serbian prince of Serres, Constantine Dragas. Manuel himself was a talented and intelligent ruler who might have flourished in different circumstances. He had the literary and theological tendencies of his grandfather, John Kantakouzenos, and he attempted to make the most of what was a very difficult political and military situation, maintaining the dignity and the traditions of the Byzantine Empire as much as possible. The successive patriarchs of Constantinople strongly supported the emperor and the central place of Byzantium in the overall world order. Thus, when Basil, the Prince of Moscow, forbade the commemoration of the emperor in the Russian liturgy, saying "We have a church; an emperor we do not have," the patriarch reacted strongly and answered Basil with a letter setting out the traditional doctrine of the position of the emperor as the ruler of the *oikoumene*.

Hungary remained the only other Christian power in southeast Europe that so far had escaped the Ottoman yoke, and in 1393 the Hungarians encouraged the Bulgarian king, John Sisman to revolt against the Ottomans. Beyezid reacted immediately and re-established his control over Bulgaria, ending its vassal status and ruling it thenceforth as a province (*pashalik*) of his empire – a fate that many of the Balkan vassals imagined would soon be their own. In 1394 Beyezid began a blockade of Constantinople, and the population was reduced to starvation, relieved only by a shipment of grain brought by the Venetians. The Christian powers still controlled the sea, and Constantinople once again sought its salvation from the West, but the situation was serious for the city.

In 1392/3 the Turks conquered Thessaly and by 1395 Wallachia had become tributary to the Ottomans. The invasion of Thessaly showed both the Greeks and the Latins of central Greece and the Peloponnesos that they too were threatened by Ottoman expansion. These events finally encouraged the West to lend some aid, and a new crusading spirit swept through Europe. Led by Sigismund of Hungary, an army of some 100,000 soldiers (much larger than those of the earlier crusades), made up the so-called Crusade of Nikopolis that gathered in Hungary in 1396. The approach of the crusading army caused Beyezid to lift the blockade of Constantinople, and he rushed away to the Danube. The crusaders – as in the past – disagreed about the conduct of the war, with the Hungarians advocating caution but the French calling for a direct attack on the Turks. Initially the crusaders met with some success, but on 15 September 1396 disaster struck as the French cavalry was led into a trap and massacred, and the whole of the crusading army dissolved in flight.

With the end of this threat, Beyezid resumed the siege of Constantinople and in 1397 an Ottoman army marched from Thessaly into central Greece and the Peloponnesos, meeting with virtually no opposition and taking Athens and Argos before returning to Thessaly. At least some of the Venetians, meanwhile, seem to have come to understand the seriousness of the threat, and they promised military and financial support to the Byzantines. Manuel sent delegations to all the rulers of the West, seeking aid and receiving vague promises of money and armies. Charles VI, King of France, was especially interested, since he had recently become overlord of Genoa (and hence he controlled Genoa's trading interests and colonies in the East). Marshal Charles Boucicaut, a veteran of the Crusade of Nikopolis who had been captured and ransomed, was sent with a small force of 1,200 soldiers that forced its way through the Ottoman blockade and landed at Constantinople in 1399.

Boucicaut was immediately aware that a much larger force was necessary to defend the city, and he persuaded Manuel to return with him to Europe to seek such support. The marshal was also able to convince John VII to become reconciled with his uncle and rule the city in his absence. As a result, Manuel II took his family and set off for the West. This strange embassy, lasting more than three years, is one of the more ironic events in the long history of the empire. Manuel's visit was in stark contrast to that of his father some years earlier, not only because the Ottoman threat was much more real, but also because western scholars had now become infatuated with Greek learning and they looked upon the Byzantines as the purveyors of that culture. In addition, Manuel was an attractive and proud ruler and, although he came seeking western help, he did so with pride and he did not raise the issue of church union nor offer once again to subject the Byzantine church to the rule of the pope. Manuel traveled through Italy; in 1400 he reached Paris and, toward the end of the year, London. There he was warmly received by King Henry IV, who made grandiose promises and actually gave the emperor a small sum (which had probably been collected by his predecessor). Optimistic that he would receive military support from the English, Manuel returned to Paris early in 1401. There he continued to carry out negotiations for military aid, but after a year of frustration he finally began to realize that nothing would be forthcoming and that he would have to return to Constantinople empty-handed. Meanwhile, the emperor passed his time writing treatises of a literary and theological nature – testifying to both his erudition and to his continued allegiance to the Orthodox church.

Meanwhile, in Constantinople the French troops of Boucicaut continued to hold out against the Ottomans, but the population was driven to despair from hunger. Some – even the regent John VII, the Genoese, and the patriarch himself – were accused of collusion with the Turks, although there is no clear evidence of this. Beyezid, meanwhile, was confident he would take the city, and he is reported to have sat at a distance, marking out the various parts of Constantinople he would give to his lieutenants. Finally, as the situation became even more desperate, the miracle the Christians had been waiting for took place. Rumors began to reach Constantinople and the West that a great leader of the East (perhaps a Christian) had arisen and was defeating the Turks. This was Timur-lenk, known in English as Tamerlane, the Mongol chieftain whose armies swept from Samarkand into Afghanistan and India, north into Russia, and west into Georgia, Armenia, and Asia Minor. There they encountered the independent Turcoman emirates that had not yet been incorporated into Bayezid's empire, and then, in 1400, they entered Ottoman territory, taking the city of Sivas (Byzantine Sebaste) and massacring its inhabitants. Interestingly, there is evidence that the Christian powers, perhaps even Manuel himself, had long been aware of Timur's power, and they had hoped that he might become their ally against the Ottomans (and, indeed, that he might become a Christian himself).

Timur decided on a massive invasion of Anatolia, and in 1402 Bayezid brought a great army to meet him, abandoning the siege of Constantinople as a result. The Battle of Ankara on 28 July 1402 was a complete victory for the Mongols: some 15,000 Turks and their Christian allies are said to have been killed and Bayezid himself was captured. He died the next year in captivity, and his empire lay in shambles. Timur ravaged all of Asia Minor, taking Smyrna and massacring its inhabitants. Diplomatically he sought the support of the emirs, who had remained at least partly independent of the Ottomans, and he encouraged the sons of Bayezid to fight each other over the succession. The most successful of these was Suleiman, who managed to find his way to Europe, which remained untouched by the Mongols, and he established himself at Adrianople.

Timur, however, was not ultimately interested in the administration of his conquests and in 1403 he left Asia Minor. He returned to Samarkand and then set off to conquer China, where he died in 1405. Tamerlane was gone, but the empire of Bayezid was shattered and divided, and, of course, the siege of Constantinople was now forgotten. The Byzantine Empire had been given another lease on life, and only the future could tell whether it would be able to take advantage of the respite to build its strength again.

Manuel II was naturally encouraged by the news of Tamerlane's victories, but he was still slow to return to Constantinople, and he made a great procession from Paris to Venice, and then on to the Morea, where his family had been staying. He finally arrived in the capital toward the middle of 1403. Meanwhile, Bayezid's son Suleiman came to an understanding with the regency of John VII in Constantinople. The situation of the Ottomans was reflected in the terms of the treaty, in which Byzantium was no longer required to pay tribute, Mount Athos and Thessaloniki were restored to the empire, and Suleiman even declared himself the vassal of the emperor, seeking only to be left alone in his possession of Thrace. Upon his return Manuel confirmed the treaty and sealed it by marrying his illegitimate niece (the daughter of Theodore I, Despot of the Morea) to Suleiman. Rivalry broke out again between John VII and his uncle, but an accommodation was made and John became the governor of Thessaloniki and Thrace.

The weakness of the Ottomans and the warfare that soon broke out among the sons of Bayezid further aided the Byzantine recovery, and Manuel sought to establish unified control by the establishment of his young sons as Despot of the Morea (after the death of his brother Theodore in 1407) and of Thessaloniki (after the death of John VII the next year). The civil war lasted for ten years, and Manuel made the best he could of the situation. In the end he sided with Bayezid's son Mehmed in his struggle with his brothers for control of Thrace, and the Serbs and some other Christian groups joined him in this. Mehmed I (1402–21) ultimately prevailed, Manuel was rewarded by the renewal of all the provisions of the earlier treaty, and Mehmed was beholden to him and well disposed to the Christian princes of the Balkans.

Manuel, however, was already in his sixties and it was clear that the Turks were still the greatest power in the region. The emperor sought, however, to solidify his control, especially in the areas he had assigned to his sons, and in 1414 he undertook an extended tour of his domains. He traveled to Thessaloniki and then sailed to the Morea, pausing at the Isthmus of Korinth to rebuild the Hexamilion, the wall nearly six miles long that he hoped would help keep the Turks out of the Peloponnesos. This was a remarkable achievement, and the Venetians congratulated him on his success. Manuel journeyed on to Mistras and finally returned to Constantinople in 1416.

Manuel meanwhile maintained a formally friendly relationship with the Sultan Mehmed (sometimes called a "gentlemen's agreement"), and Mehmed was in fact busy with the task of restoring Ottoman control in Asia Minor and putting down minor revolts (some of which were, in fact, aided by Manuel). Manuel renewed his negotiations with the western powers, but the rivalry between Venice and Hungary and the weakness of the papacy doomed these attempts to failure.

The year 1421 was eventful for Byzantium. Manuel was by now old and he crowned his son John VIII as co-emperor and heir. Soon thereafter the Sultan Mehmed died suddenly in uncertain circumstances and was succeeded by his son, Murad II (1421–51). Manuel and his son disagreed as to how to react to the change of regime: the old emperor was in favor of an alliance with Murad, but John VIII sought to exploit the situation by supporting a rival. Murad quickly prevailed and he furiously attacked Constantinople, determined to take the city and punish the Byzantines for their perfidy. This siege was serious, but the old emperor played his last hand by once again stirring up rivals to the sultan, forcing Murad to lift the siege, and finally, in 1424, to sign a peace treaty that provided a temporary respite but placed Constantinople again in the inferior position as a tribute-paying vassal of the sultan. The situation had returned, more or less, to what it had been 22 years earlier. The opportunity for a Byzantine recovery had passed.

FURTHER READING

M. Angold, *A Byzantine Government in Exile: Government and Society under the Laskarids of Nicaea (1204–1261)* (Oxford, 1975).

J. Barker, *Manuel II Palaeologus (1391–1425): A Study in Late Byzantine Statesmanship* (New Brunswick, NJ, 1969).

E. Freyde, *The Early Palaeologan Renaissance. 1261–c.1360* (Leiden, 2000).

D. Geanakoplos, *Emperor Michael Palaeologus and the West, 1258–1281: A Study in Byzantine–Latin Relations* (Cambridge, MA, 1959).

A. Laiou, *Constantinople and the Latins: The Foreign Policy of Andronikos II, 1282–1328* (Cambridge, MA, 1972).

A. Laiou-Thomadakis. *Peasant Society in the Late Byzantine Empire: A Social and Demographic Study* (Princeton, NJ, 1977).

D. Nicol, *Byzantium and Venice: A Study in Diplomatic and Cultural Relations* (Cambridge, 1988).

D. Nicol, *The Despotate of Epiros, 1267–1479* (Cambridge, 1984).

D. Nicol, *The Last Centuries of Byzantium, 1261–1453*, 2nd edn. (Cambridge, 1993).

G. Soulis, *The Serbs and Byzantium during the Reigns of Tsar Stephen Dusan (1331–1355) and his Successors* (Washington, DC, 1984).

S. Vryonis, *The Decline of Hellenism in Asia Minor and the Process of Islamization from the Eleventh through the Fifteenth Century* (Berkeley and Los Angeles, 1971).

15

The End of the Empire

250	500	750	1000	1250	1500

1438–1439	Council of Florence and union of churches
1449	Constantine XI emperor
1453	Fall of Constantinople

The Reign of John VIII Palaiologos

On 21 July 1425 the emperor Manuel II Palaiologus died at the age of 75. His passing was deeply mourned by his subjects, for he had preserved them, more or less without harm, but also without bowing to the demands of the West or raising again the specter of submission of the Byzantine church to the papacy.

Manuel was succeeded by his son John VIII Palaiologos (1425–48), who inherited a multitude of problems. Perhaps the most stable portion of the empire was the Morea, where, indeed, three of his brothers then resided. But the situation in Thrace had recently become much more serious. Thessaloniki had been in Venetian hands since 1423, and there was some hope that, under their control, it would again become a wealthy center of trade and culture. But there was dissension within the city, and the Venetians despaired of maintaining its defenses, so the situation was bleak when Murad brought his forces before the walls in March of 1430. Many citizens wished to surrender immediately, but the Venetians demanded that the city be defended – before sailing off to safety with their ships. After a short siege, the city fell and was subject to a terrible sack; the early Christian church of the Acheiropoietos was turned into a mosque. The second city of the Byzantine Empire had fallen to the Turks.

Sinan Pasha, the Ottoman governor-general in Europe, moved against Ioannina in the West. Unlike the population of Thessaloniki, the people of Ioannina accepted Sinan Pasha's offer of surrender, and as a result they exchanged their freedom for the protection of their property, churches, and lives.

The twin Ottoman successes of 1430 seriously frightened the western powers, especially Venice and Hungary. The ruler of what was left of Serbia was now George Branković, and he now swore loyalty to King Sigismund of Hungary and made preparations to withstand the Ottoman onslaught from a new fortified capital at Smederevo on the Danube near Belgrade.

The Despotate of the Morea in the Fifteenth Century

The Despotate of the Morea, with its capital at Mystras (close to ancient Sparta) flourished politically and culturally in the fifteenth century and provided one ray of optimism in the military difficulties of the age. Born of a fusion of Crusader and Byzantine culture in the years after the Fourth Crusade, the Despotate of the Morea came to be ruled as an *appanage* (essentially an independent territory linked by family ties to Constantinople) by junior members of the imperial family. The castle of Mystras, just a short distance west of ancient Sparta, was built in 1248 by William II Villehardouin, the Frankish Prince of Achaia, to guard the plain of Lakonia from the wild tribes that dwelled on Mount Taÿgetos. The castle was surrendered to the Byzantines in 1262 (after the Battle of Pelagonia), and a city soon grew up below it, as the inhabitants of Sparta fled there to enjoy the greater protection of the fortifications. Ruled at first by governors who were changed every year, from 1308 onward they held office for longer periods. These governors were important individuals, first the father of the future emperor John Kantakouzenos, and then Andronikos Asen, son of the former tsar of Bulgaria and great-nephew of Andronikos II. John VI created the Despotate of the Morea in 1349 and appointed his son Manuel Kantakouzenos to a long rule there. John V then appointed Theodore I Palaiologos, who ruled from 1381 to 1407, and from then on the Despotate was an appanage of the Palaiologan family. From 1407 until its capture by the Turks, the Despotate was ruled by the sons of the emperor Manuel II, first Theodore II (1407–43), then the future emperor Constantine XI (1443–9), and finally Thomas and Demetrios Palaiologos (1449–60). By 1429 the Despotate had gained control of the whole of the Peloponnesos, but the Ottomans took advantage of competition among the sons of Manuel II to raid the Morea, despite continued efforts to fortify and defend the Isthmus of Korinth.

In the early fifteenth century Byzantine culture experienced a significant revival at Mystras, sparked in part by the cultural mixtures that had characterized the area and also, perhaps, the freedom the city enjoyed from the intellectual domination of the capital. Writers, philosophers, architects, and painters gathered in Mystras to enjoy the patronage of the despot and the wealthy families and monasteries of the city. Many churches were constructed, representing a blend of traditions and, perhaps, even consciously pointing back to the tradition of the early Christian basilica. The churches were painted in a style that was possibly the most lively and realistic of the Byzantine period. The artists, whose names are unknown, used colors that were lighter and more varied than those normally seen in Byzantine art, and many of the compositions sought to convey emotion and psychological subtlety.

The emperor Manuel II and his son Theodore, who was despot after 1408, were strong supporters of intellectual life at Mystras, where there was a blend of classical and traditional religious, and even monastic, culture. Among the intellectuals who lived and worked at the court in Mystras were Isidore, later bishop of Kiev, Bessarion, later bishop of Nicaea (both of whom became cardinals in the Roman church), and Georgios Scholarios, who, as Gennadeios II, became the first patriarch of Constantinople under Ottoman rule. The greatest of these intellectuals, however, was the philosopher Georgios Gemistos, who took the surname Plethon in imitation of Plato (Platon in Greek), whom he admired and sought to follow. Plethon already had a distinguished career behind him, as intellectual and adviser to the emperor, when he arrived in Mystras by 1409. He wrote voluminously, and most of his works are on strictly philosophical topics, but, like Plato before him, he felt he had a real political duty to promote his ideas for the well-being (or even the salvation) of society.

Plethon was not the first of the Byzantines to point out the connection between Byzantine and ancient Greek culture, but he put that point eloquently and clearly. "We are," he wrote, "Greeks [Hellenes], as our language and ancestral culture show." Thus, to Plethon, as to many Byzantines, "Greekness" was not a matter of blood or descent, but rather determined by language and culture. Plethon was also willing to call himself a Hellene, the term that had long been used by the Byzantines to refer to the pagans. This did not trouble him and, unlike most of his contemporaries, he was unabashedly in favor of the (certainly impossible) task of restoring classical paganism as the religion of the empire!

Plethon was apparently moved by what he saw at Mystras, and he regarded the Morea (Peloponnesos) as a possible center for a revived Hellenism that would, in turn, help revive the whole of the Byzantine Empire. He wrote:

No country can be found which is more intimately and closely connected with the Greeks than is the Peloponnesos . . . It is a country which the same Greek stock has always inhabited, as far back as human memory goes; no other people had settled there before them, nor have immigrants occupied it subsequently . . . On the contrary, Greeks have always occupied this country as their own, and while they have emigrated from it, owing to the pressure of population, and have occupied other and not inconsiderable territories, they have never abandoned it. (Nicol, *Last Centuries*, p. 343)

Plethon also proposed real policies for the defense of the Peloponnesos and the revival of the empire. Some of these were eminently practical, such as repairing the defense of the Isthmus of Korinth and creating a standing army of native soldiers, but others were impossible to realize, such as the prohibition of private property and the creation of an authoritarian monarchy. He recommended that one-third of all produce be given to the state and drew up proposals for the encouragement of trade and domestic industry, an indication that he realized that the domination of Byzantium by foreign economic interests and those of the Byzantine wealthy few were at the heart of the weakness of the Byzantine state. Needless to say, there never was a chance that these latter reforms would ever be implemented.

The Council of Florence and the Crusade of Varna

John VIII was now emboldened to hope that aid from the West might really be forthcoming, and he entered into negotiations with the papacy. This was, of course, a period of considerable disagreement in the Western church, when the so-called Conciliarists sought to take power away from the pope and put it in the hands of church councils. This was a point of view similar to that of the Byzantines, and John was able to hope that they might be more understanding in dealing with the Eastern church. Pope Eugenius IV was successful in getting the Byzantine emissaries to set off, late in November 1437, for a council that was to meet at Ferrara in Italy.

The Byzantine delegation was distinguished indeed: it included the patriarch, Joseph II (the first patriarch of Constantinople to attend such a meeting in the West). Among the supporters of a union were Bessarion, a distinguished theologian recently made bishop of Nicaea, and Isidore, who had just been named bishop of Kiev and All Russia; those opposed to union included Markos Eugenikos, then the bishop of Ephesos. The dispute was, of course, fundamentally theological and – as always – cultural, but in the 1430s a new element had emerged, the intellectual power of the Italian Renaissance and its fascination with all things Greek. This intellectual excitement was appealing to some Byzantine theologians, while to others it was yet another sign that the westerners were willing to take things from the Greeks but were unwilling to understand the needs of the empire or the importance of the Byzantine theological tradition. The lay leaders of the Byzantine delegation were at least as distinguished as the clerics, including the emperor John himself, his brother Demetrios – and, most notably, Plethon; they were accompanied by Plethon's friend, the theologian and lawyer, Georgios Scholarios, the Platonist Amiroutzes, and the Aristotelian Georgios of Trebizond.

The Byzantine party arrived in Venice, to a great welcome, early in 1438, and made its way to Ferrara, and the council began its deliberations in early April of that year. The discussion was generally on a high level, but difficult for both sides; debate dragged on and the cost to the papacy mounted, so that at the end of 1438 the council was transferred to Florence, where the wealthy Medici family was willing to help underwrite the cost. The major differences between the two sides were essentially the same as before: the procession of the Holy Spirit and the supremacy of the pope. Some of the Byzantine prelates objected that it was unfair that they be expected to give in on all points, and some sources suggest that they were essentially starved into submission. In the end, the patriarch and all the Byzantine prelates – except for Markos Evgenikos – signed a statement of union on 5 July 1439; of the secular representatives, only the emperor had to agree.

The schism had formally been healed, but most of the bishops and the laity in the East were steadfastly opposed, and Markos Evgenikos became a popular hero for his resistance. In return for agreement to what came to be called the Union of Florence, the pope agreed to send an army to defend Constantinople from the Turks. Almost immediately, however, difficulties emerged in the East as many bishops opposed the union, and some who signed began to change their mind. As mentioned above, the leader of the resistance was Evgenikos, but when he died Georgios Scholarios took his place.

Meanwhile, Murad II continued his conquests in the northern Balkans. Smederevo fell in 1439, Belgrade in 1440, and in 1441 the Ottomans invaded Transylvania. The promised crusade was hastened by these events, and the forces of the papacy, Venice, and the Duke of Burgundy promised to set sail in 1444. Leaders of the Christian resistance in eastern Europe were the Polish King Ladislas III, who had become ruler of Hungary, and the Hungarian general John Hunyadi. In addition, a local leader had emerged in Albania, raised as a Muslim and given the name "Iskender beg" (Alexander) by the sultan for his prowess. Skanderbeg, as he was known by the Albanians, escaped from Ottoman control and organized resistance from the mountain fastness of his homeland. At the same time, Constantine, Despot of the Morea and brother of John VIII, organized the defenses of the Peloponnesos and seized Athens from the weak Florentine family of the Acciajuoli.

In July of 1443 the long-awaited crusade finally set off from Hungary, while the fleet sailed up the Danube from the Black Sea. Murad II was busy with a revolt in Anatolia, and the Crusaders were able to march quickly south and take Nis and Sofia. In 1444 the leaders of the crusade sent ambassadors to the sultan and a truce was arranged for ten years. George Branković, the leader of Serbia, kept his part of the bargain, but the emissaries of the pope, along with King Ladislav, broke the treaty and marched further into Ottoman territory, reaching the Black Sea near Varna. Murad returned quickly from Anatolia, outwitted the crusader fleet, and arrived at Varna with a huge army that annihilated the outnumbered Christian force. Thus ended the Crusade of Varna and any real hope that Byzantium would receive help from the West. At the same time, many Byzantines realized that the goal of the crusade was Constantinople and they felt a real sense of relief when it came to a bad end. John VIII could do nothing more than congratulate the sultan on his victory. John Hunyadi remained at large, with a fairly large army, but he was decisively

defeated at a second battle at Kossovo in 1448. George Branković survived these
difficulties with much of his power intact, but Byzantium had fallen to a level
of virtual insignificance in world politics. The efforts of John VIII to secure
support from the West had failed completely, and on 31 October 1448 he died.

The Fall of the City

John VIII had no children, and he apparently thought long and hard about his
successor. In the end he chose his brother Constantine, who was then 44 years
old and Despot of the Morea. He was clearly the most talented and ambitious
of his brothers and had demonstrated ability in his energetic actions to defend
and develop the Morea. Frequently known by his mother's surname Dragas or
Dragatzes, Constantine XI was destined to be the last emperor of Byzantium.
In January of 1449 he was proclaimed emperor at Mystras and was never
formally crowned by the patriarch, even after his arrival in Constantinople, in
part because the patriarch was still loyal to the Union with Rome, and the new
emperor did not wish to encourage further dissent on this issue.

Constantine entered Constantinople in March of 1449 and immediately
sought the approval of his elevation from the Sultan Murad. The emperor confirmed his brothers Thomas and Demetrios as co-rulers of the despotate of the
Morea, but they almost immediately began to feud over control of the region.

Constantinople itself was divided over the issue of Union with Rome. The
emperor formally approved the Union, since he continued to hope that it
might somehow lead to military assistance from the West. Some of the members of the court energetically supported the emperor in this matter, while
others were opposed but were willing to keep silent for the well-being of the
state. The great majority of the clergy and the laity, however, were steadfast in
their opposition. Leaders such as Georgios Scholarios, who had become a
monk with the name Gennadeios, and John Evgenikos, the brother of Markos,
continued to maintain a position hostile to Rome. In 1451 the patriarch of
Constantinople, Gregory III, grew tired of the controversy and he withdrew
from the city and took refuge in Rome; the city was without a patriarch.

In this situation Byzantine diplomacy focused itself on the need to find a
suitable wife for the emperor (his previous two wives had died), who might bring
the empire a sizable dowry and an heir to the throne. Nothing ultimately came
of this, but in February of 1451 the situation of the empire changed dramatically
when Sultan Murad II died. He was succeeded by his son Mehmed II, who
was then only 19 years of age. He already had considerable experience, since
his father had no other surviving son and had early left many affairs of state to
Mehmed. These, however, had not all gone well, and many Christian rulers
hoped that his youth and lack of earlier success would alleviate the threat all
felt from the power of the Ottomans. They were seriously mistaken.

The Byzantine government shared in this misconception, and, when Mehmed
was occupied with a revolt in Anatolia, it sought to defend the claims of a

Figure 15.1 Sultan Mehmed II. The personality and policies of Mehmed II have been broadly discussed, and it is clear that his actions had far-reaching consequences, not only in terms of the conquest of Constantinople, but also in the arrangements that were to govern the Balkans for the succeeding four hundred years. This portrait by the Italian artist Gentile Bellini (1429–1507) depicts him very much as a Renaissance prince. National Gallery, London. Photo: Erich Lessing / Art Resource, NY

weak pretender to the Ottoman throne. Mehmed reacted swiftly, told the Byzantines that they had broken the recent treaty they had signed, and, in the spring of 1452, began the construction of a great fortress on the European side of the Bosphoros: Rumeli Hisar ("Roman Fortress") was to match Anadolou Hisar ("Anatolian Fortress"), built by Mehmed's grandfather Beyezid on the Asiatic shore, to complete the encirclement of Constantinople by the Turks.

It was clear that the sultan was preparing for a final assault on the city. In this situation Constantine could do little other than seek to store up provisions and make whatever appeals he could to the West. He made promises to Hungary and Aragon and attempted to elicit the assistance of the merchants of

Ragusa. The great Italian maritime republics had essentially lost interest in the fate of Constantinople, in part because they had already made their own arrangements for the promotion of their trade with the Turks.

In October of 1452 Cardinal Isidore arrived in Constantinople as papal legate. He brought along with him 200 archers from Naples to aid in the defense of the city, but his real goal was to have the Union of Florence formally proclaimed there. The anti-Unionists, led by Gennadeios, resisted steadfastly, and at a meeting in the imperial palace in November they were allowed to sign a formal statement of protest. But the emperor and the papal party persevered and, on 12 December 1452, a formal ceremony was held in Hagia Sophia in which Orthodox and Catholic clergy both participated, and the decrees of the Council of Florence were read out. The bulk of the people continued to worship in the churches whose priests were opposed to the Union. In the words of Steven Runciman, "Had the union been followed quickly by the appearance of ships and soldiers from the West its practical advantages might have won it general support . . . But, as it was, they had paid the price demanded for Western aid, and they were cheated" (p. 72; cf. Nicol, p. 377: "It seemed that, in the end, when their backs were to the wall, they had allowed the Latins to win the last round of the battle of wits that had begun with the Fourth Crusade").

Within the city people were well aware of the coming siege. The great cannons of Rumeli Hisar could be heard up the Bosphoros, and in November of 1452, when a Venetian ship failed to heed the order not to pass through the straits, it was sunk. The ship's crew was brought before the sultan, who ordered them decapitated; he had the captain impaled and displayed his body along the roadside. Spirits in Constantinople must have been low, and the historian Doukas quotes the official Loukas Notaras as saying "Better the Sultan's turban than the Pope's cap," meaning that it would be better to surrender to the Turks rather than agree to the Union. Nonetheless, Constantine urged his citizens on, and he worked with them through the winter as they sought to patch up the walls of the city. The biggest danger, as he well knew, was the Turkish cannon. Gunpowder had been used in Europe for the past hundred years, but it had not been very effective in turning the tide of war. Both Constantine and Mehmed, however, were interested in the use of cannon. In 1452 a Hungarian engineer named Urban came to Constantinople and offered the emperor his services; Constantine, however, had neither the funds to pay him his salary nor the resources to allow him to build the weapon. Urban, therefore, offered his services to the sultan; when he told Mehmed that he could build a cannon that would break the gates of Babylon itself, the sultan offered him a salary four times what he was asking and put at his disposal all the resources he would need. Urban then constructed the massive cannon that sank the Venetian ship in the Bosphoros and then set about to construct one twice its size for the attack on Constantinople. The weapon was constructed at Adrianople, and, according to one source, when finished, it had a length of over 26 feet and a diameter over 8 feet at the front; the cannonballs weighed

1,200 pounds each! After successful test-firing at Adrianople, in which the first shot traveled over a mile, the cannon began its journey to Constantinople, drawn by 60 oxen with a team of 2,000 men required to keep the great weapon steady. Other cannons were built and sent to the siege, although none of them was as large as the first.

Meanwhile, the Sultan's troops began to assemble around the city, marching overland, and eliminating every remnant of Byzantine resistance. The Greek historian George Sphrantzes claimed that the Turkish army numbered

---

Box 15.1   *The Fearful Cannon*

Probably the greatest factor in the Siege of Constantinople in 1543 was the battery of huge cannons that Mehmed II brought up against the aged city walls. The Greek historian Laonikos Chalkokondyles tells us that the cannons were made by a Hungarian founder named Urban who had previously worked for the Byzantines, but when they could no longer pay his salary he offered his services to the sultan, who promptly put him to work on the artillery he hoped would take Constantinople.

The cannons were made in Adrianople and the whole of the sultan's European army had to go to that city to bring them to the vicinity of Constantinople. It took a force of 60 oxen and 2,000 men to pull the largest of these. Mehmed stationed his two largest cannons at key points, one opposite the emperor's palace, the other at the Gate of Romanos.

The Ottomans, however, had a tactic designed to instill fear in the hearts of the defenders. They placed two small cannons beside the huge cannons mentioned above. The smaller cannons were fired first and did what damage they could with their relatively small projectiles, weighing "only" half a talent each. Then the huge cannon was fired, using a ball that weighted 3 talents (over 160 pounds; interestingly, one western account says that the cannonball of the large cannon weighed 1,900 pounds and was over 16 feet in circumference). Chalkokondyles reports that the sound of the large cannon was so loud that it could be heard about five miles away. This cannon could naturally not be loaded very quickly, so it was fired only seven times a day, with the first shot each day just before dawn. The smaller cannons were, apparently, fired between 100 and 120 times a day.

Not surprisingly, this bombardment had an effect and Chalkokondyles says that much of the outer wall was brought down, along with four of the towers. The Byzantines, for their part, had some cannon of their own, but the largest of these burst when it was first fired. The others were not small, apparently able to fire projectiles weighing one and a half talents, but the historian tells us that the vibrations from the firing did more damage to the walls than they did harm to the Turks.

Ultimately, much of the wall was battered down, but the defenders bravely raced out each evening to fill the breaches. Finally, when the Turks made a last attack, at a critical moment in the fighting, the Genoese leader of the defenders, Giovanni Giustiniani, left his post when he was hit by cannon fire and the city fell.

200,000, while a more reasonable estimate is 80,000 men. Within the city there was a serious shortage of defenders: Sphrantzes put the number at 4,773. The Land Walls of the city, long the empire's best defense, were in reasonably good condition, but they had two serious weaknesses: their very length (approximately four miles) made them difficult to defend by a small force, and their size and construction, although still formidable, had not been designed to withstand a gunpowder assault that had the power to break them down through unprecedented force.

The other hope of the city was the arrival of help from the outside. All too little was forthcoming. Mehmed ordered his general Turahan to cross into the Morea and ravage the countryside, preventing the despots from aiding their brother. The relatively weak Christian powers of the Balkans (Alphonso of Aragon, John Hunyadi of Hungary, and George Brancović of Serbia) provided no assistance, and the European powers were either unable to provide aid or they had lost interest. Aware of the lessons of history, Mehmed understood that Constantinople could only be taken by a power that controlled the sea, so he constructed a navy of considerable size to counter any attack from western maritime powers. Finally, in February of 1453, Venice decided to send two ships to Constantinople, with 800 soldiers, and these set sail at last in April. The pope followed suit and said he would send five ships, and the Genoese one; assuming that these ships had been able to escape the Ottoman blockade, they were already too late, and their force was also too small to do anything to help the situation.

The defense of the city was entrusted to the Grand Duke (Megas Doux) Loukas Notaras, Demetrios and John Kantakouzenos, and Nikephoros Palaiologos, all of course under the overall command of the emperor. The Venetians of the city provided their full support, and many members of the Genoese and Catalan communities threw in their lot with the Byzantines. A number of adventurers appeared as well, most notable among whom was the Genoese Giovanni Giustiniani Longo, who was given general supervision of the defense along the Land Walls.

The Byzantines celebrated Easter of 1453 in relative peace, but on Easter Monday, 2 April, the first elements of the sultan's army arrived before the Land Walls; the emperor at once ordered the great boom across the mouth of the Golden Horn to be put in place to seal the harbor from attack. On 6 April the artillery barrage began on the Land Walls; the Turks fired on the walls during the day and the defenders rushed out at night to repair the damage. The defenders had some successes: an attempt to force the boom at the Golden Horn was beaten off and likewise an attack on the Land Walls; on 20 April three Genoese ships commissioned by the pope, along with a freighter with a load of wheat from Alphonso of Aragon, were able to break through the Ottoman blockade and enter the Golden Horn.

Given this state of affairs, Mehmed determined to take extraordinary action. He constructed a road behind Galata, from the Bosphoros to the Golden Horn; carts were placed on rails along the road, drawn by oxen, and the ships

Figure 15.2 Siege of Constantinople. This depiction of the siege of Constantinople, from the Romanian church of Moldovita, is actually meant to show the seventh-century siege by the Avars and Slavs. But it is clear that the artist had the fifteenth-century siege more directly in mind, as shown by the prominent appearance of cannon. Especially interesting is the appearance of bishops on the walls of the city, along with the Mandylion, prominently displayed in the back of the scene. Photo: Dumbarton Oaks / Ihor Sevćenko

were loaded on the carts and transported into the Horn. The efforts of the defenders to set the ships afire came to naught, and on 22 April the Ottoman fleet appeared in the Horn; a huge pontoon was constructed and artillery set up on it. The defenders now had to consider the possibility of an attack at any point along the whole of the circuit of the city instead of being able to concentrate their attention on the Land Walls, and difficulties of communication naturally ensued. The Otttomans, by contrast, were able to bring to bear their overwhelming numerical superiority and to bombard the walls in the Horn, where they were structurally inferior.

The defenders held out resolutely, and the emperor was able to confiscate church and private wealth in order to buy food. In the meantime, the help the Byzantines sought from abroad almost arrived, not from the West but from the East, in the form of revolts from the sultan's subjects in Asia Minor. It became clear that the siege could not be prolonged indefinitely and that Mehmed would have to take the city or face a difficult situation in his own realms. He offered the emperor terms: the Byzantines should peacefully surrender the city and either remain in Constantinople with the payment of tribute or leave and settle somewhere else. Despite the advice of some of his counselors, Constantine was determined to stay and fight with his people. The sultan was also now able under Muslim law to promise his soldiers the traditional right to plunder the city after its collapse.

On Monday, 28 May, Mehmed gave his soldiers a day of rest, in preparation for a massive attack. In the city, the omens of doom were everywhere, but the people assembled in the evening at Hagia Sophia and all, including both supporters and opponents of the Union, the emperor and Cardinal Isidore, took part in the last Christian liturgy in the Byzantine capital.

The Ottoman attack began in the early hours of Tuesday, 29 May. The poorly equipped irregular troops attacked first in large numbers; wave after wave they struck the weakest sections of the Land Walls, but Giustiniani and his men held firm. As the better-armed regular troops took their place, the Turks attacked also the walls on the Golden Horn, but the defense held firm. The sultan then ordered the Janissaries to attack; these picked troops were well-equipped and fresh and the fighting was thick and furious. Just before dawn Giustiniani was wounded and he was carried from the front line. Although his injuries were not fatal, the Genoese troops thought he was dying or that he was giving up the fight, and they pulled back. The Janissaries seized the moment and one of them reached the top of the wall. He was immediately struck down but others quickly followed. Even this attack, however, might have been thrust back, but at the same time a small body of Janissaries discovered that the small Kerkoporta Gate had mistakenly been left open. They rushed through, climbed up to the top of the wall and raised the Ottoman standard. The Turks pressed forward through the two breaches; they quickly opened other gates and their comrades swarmed in.

The emperor Constantine did what he could to rally his troops. Some left the field to try to defend their families. Others, like the emperor, rushed forward to meet the foe. Constantine removed his imperial regalia and met the Turks near the Gate of St. Romanos. He was never seen again.

Many of the Italians fled to their ships, and a few got away, but the majority of the inhabitants were left to their fate. The rape and pillage began immediately, as the soldiers of the sultan claimed their reward. Churches were despoiled, houses were ransacked, and the treasures that had escaped the plundering of the Crusaders now fell to the hands of the Turks: the ikon of the Virgin Odegetria, supposedly the work of St. Luke, was destroyed, jeweled covers were removed from books before they were burned, and mosaics and frescoes were gouged and hacked. The survivors were rounded up and carried off as slaves, although many killed themselves rather than fall into the hands of the conquerors. There is no reliable account, but contemporary estimates held that 4,000 people were killed and 50,000 led into slavery. Christian legend maintained that Hagia Sophia, the Great Church of God, would not fall to the invaders, but that as they approached its doors the Angel of God would appear and strike them down. Thus, some of the survivors rushed to the church and barred the doors. When the Turks arrived, they burst into the building, killing the old and infirm and taking the others prisoner. The priests of the church had, meanwhile, continued their celebration of the Christian liturgy uninterrupted by the fall of the city. According to tradition, as the Turks gained control of the church, the priests picked up the sacred vessels, the walls of the sanctuary opened, and the priests moved into the interior of the building, from which they will emerge once more to resume the liturgy when the building once again becomes a Christian church.

In the late afternoon, the sultan entered the city and ordered an end to the plunder, which had essentially been accomplished already. He rode to Hagia Sophia and offered mercy to those he found still huddling in the building, which he ordered immediately transformed into a mosque. Mehmed had a Muslim cleric ascend the pulpit and proclaim a Muslim prayer, and he himself ascended the altar of the former cathedral and worshiped Allah.

In the aftermath Mehmed demanded for himself the choicest of the plundered treasures and the most noble of the captives. Some of the latter he kept in his palace or gave to Muslim allies. He discovered a number of Byzantine aristocrats and administrators, including the Grand Duke Loukas Notaras and his family. At first the sultan treated all the prisoners with generosity, but he soon changed his mind and had all the males executed. Mehmed was especially concerned to discover the body of the emperor Constantine, in part because he wanted to make sure that he had not escaped to lead an uprising at a later time. Although a thorough search was made and severed heads and bodies were washed and examined, and although a corpse wearing stockings with an embroidered eagle was at first said to be that of the emperor, Constantine's body was never discovered. The fact of his apparently complete disappearance has allowed later tradition to view him as the "Marble Emperor," who is not dead but waiting, somewhere out of time, to return and restore the Byzantine Empire.

Box 15.2 *Byzantium and the Italian Renaissance*

Close connections had always existed between Byzantium and Italy, and indeed much of southern Italy had been a Byzantine possession until the eleventh century. As a result, many important buildings and works of art in Italy and Sicily were strongly influenced by the Byzantine tradition. In the last century of the Byzantine Empire, however, and in the years following the fall of Constantinople, these connections increased and, perhaps ironically, as Byzantium weakened and finally collapsed, Byzantine culture had a powerful impact on developments in Italy. This was, in part, the result of the strong economic relations between Byzantium and the Italian maritime republics.

The Byzantine impact on the Italian Renaissance was enormous and it is impossible to imagine the Renaissance without the participation of Byzantine scholars. The Greek language, of course, was essentially unknown in the medieval West, and as a result most of the works of Greek antiquity were unknown or known only through Latin (or Arabic) translations. The "rediscovery" of the Greek language effectively began in the fourteenth century, spurred on by the poet Petrarch (1304–74) and his disciple Boccaccio (1313–75), who translated the *Iliad* into Latin. In 1360 the first professor of Greek was appointed at the University of Florence, and in 1397 Manuel Chrysoloras attained that chair. Chrysoloras (ca. 1350–1415) was a remarkably talented individual, a true "Renaissance man." He was a friend of the emperor Manuel II and undertook many diplomatic missions to the West, primarily to seek military aid. He was also a scholar of considerable ability and insight. He wrote a textbook on Greek grammar and an interesting *Comparison of Old and New Rome*, in which he demonstrated an interest in and sensitivity to the works of art in Rome (although he ultimately concluded that the "New Rome" – i.e., Constantinople – was more beautiful). He was an accomplished teacher and in Italy he came into contact with scholars and students interested in learning Greek. Leonardo Bruni's statement that Chrysoloras restored Greek literature to Italy is certainly an exaggeration, but he was important nonetheless.

· Other Greek teachers followed Chrysoloras to Italy, frequently for diplomatic or commercial purposes. Perhaps the most influential of the early visitors was Plethon (ca. 1360–1452), who was a member of the Byzantine delegation to the Council of Ferrara-Florence in 1438–9. In Florence he had contact with Italian scholars and he discussed the ideas of Plato with them. This was a fundamental event for the development of the Renaissance, which from this point on saw Platonism as the basis of philosophy. Among those who attended these discussions was the Florentine politician Cosimo de' Medici who in 1441 founded the Platonic Academy in Florence, the institution that is often seen as the most important in the development of Renaissance thought. The relationship between Byzantium and Italy was not one-sided, however, with Greek scholars only going to Italy. The Italians themselves began to come to Byzantium, in search of knowledge of the language but even more in order to bring back Greek books. In 1418, for example, the Sicilian Giovanni Aurispa went to Constantinople in order to study Greek and collect manuscripts. In 1423 Aurispa returned to Venice with 248 books by classical Greek authors, most of which were unknown to the West. Among these were the *Iliad*, the works of Demosthenes, Plato, and Xenophon, along with a tenth-century codex that includes seven plays of Sophocles, six of Æschylus, and the *Argonautica*.

After the fall of Constantinople many well-to-do Byzantines fled Constantinople and established themselves in Italy, especially in Venice, which in the 1470s had a population of some 4,000 Greeks. Among these immigrants were some scholars. John Argyropoulos went to Italy in 1456 on a diplomatic mission but he was offered the opportunity to teach Greek in Florence and he immediately accepted. Theodore Gaza of Thessaloniki taught at Ferrara, Naples, and Rome, Demetrius Chalkondyles of Athens at Padua, Florence, and Milan, and George of Trebizond in Rome. These scholars not only encouraged the study of ancient Greek authors among Italians (and westerners generally); they also carried out important research and publication themselves, including the translation of Greek works into Latin.

In some ways the most important of the Byzantine scholarly émigrés was Bessarion, who came from Trebizond and became a monk in Constantinople. He headed the

Byzantine delegation at the Council of Ferrara-Florence and eventually became a Catholic. He was named a cardinal, settled in Italy, held many important ecclesiastical positions, and was even a serious candidate to become pope on two occasions. He was a prolific scholar in his own right, writing in both Greek and Latin, and he founded an academy in Rome that produced translations of ancient Greek authors. He was an avid collector of Greek manuscripts and eventually willed his vast collection to Venice, where they became the core of the Marciana Library there. Venice was the location of the press established in the 1490s by Aldus Manutius. This publishing company issued most of the early printed editions of Greek and Latin classical works, dictionaries, and texts of Byzantine authors. Many of these were written, translated, or edited by Byzantine émigré scholars and they had a powerful effect on the spread of knowledge about both the Byzantine and the ancient worlds.

FURTHER READING

D. A. Geanakoplos, *Greek Scholars in Venice*. Cambridge, MA, 1962.
Jonathan Harris, *Greek Emigrés in the West, 1400–1520*. Camberley, 1995.

FURTHER READING

Morea

A. Bon, *La Morée franque. Recherches historiques, topographiques et archéologiques sur la principauté d'Achaie (1205–1430)*, 2 vols. Paris, 1969.
Steven Runciman, *The Last Byzantine Renaissance*. Cambridge, 1970.
Steven Runciman, *Mistra: Byzantine Capital of the Peloponnese*. London, 1980.
C. M. Woodhouse, *Gemistos Plethon: The Last of the Hellenes*. Oxford, 1986.
D. A. Zakythinos, *Le Despotat grec de Morée, I: Histoire politique, II: Vie et institutions*, 2nd edn. by Chryssa Maltezou, 2 vols. London, 1975.

Fall of Constantinople

Frantz Babinger, *Mehmed the Conqueror and his Time*, trans. Ralph Manheim. Princeton, NJ, 1978.
D. M. Nicol, *The Immortal Emperor: The Life and Legend of Constantine Palaiologos, Last Emperor of the Romans*. Cambridge, 1992.
E. Pears, *The Destruction of the Greek Empire and the Story of the Capture of Constantinople by the Turks*. London, 1903.
Steven Runciman, *The Fall of Constantinople 1453*. Cambridge, 1965.

16

Byzantium after the Fall of the City

250	500	750	1000	1250	1500

1461	End of the Empire of Trebizond
1553–1617	Vincenzos Kornaros, author of *Erotokritos*
Nineteenth century	Revolutions against Ottoman Empire, establishment of Byzantine "successor states" in the Balkans

One may say that the Byzantine Empire ended on 29 May 1453 when Constantinople fell to the Ottoman Turks. On the other hand, several Byzantine political entities survived the catastrophe and, certainly more important, the Byzantine ideal and Byzantine cultural traditions lived on and are still with us today.

The Byzantine Survivor States

The despotate of the Morea survived the fall of Constantinople only because it was distant, and the sultan did not immediately turn his attention there. The brothers Thomas and Demetrios Palaiologos, who ruled in different parts of the Peloponnesos, fell once again to quarreling, with Thomas still hoping for aid from the West and Demetrios willing to call in the Turks against his brother. Mehmed finally decided to take action himself and in 1460 he set out for the Morea. Demetrios surrendered at once, exactly seven years after the capture of Constantinople; Thomas held out a little longer, but he fled to Italy before the end of the year, and the despotate of the Morea ceased to exist. Thomas was the only member of his family to have heirs, and Palaiologoi

Box 16.1 *The Emperor Turned to Marble*

Many "signs and prodigies" preceded the Fall of Constantinople in 1453, including most spectacularly a lunar eclipse that took place only a few days before that event. In addition, there were many predictions that, despite the desperate situation of the empire after the appearance of the Ottomans in Europe in 1354, the city would be saved by divine intervention. According to one of these predictions, the Turks would enter the city, slaying the "Romans" as they advanced. They would reach the Column of Constantine in the center of the city, but at that moment an angel would descend and give a sword to a mysterious unknown individual, saying "Take this sword and avenge the people of the Lord!" The course of the battle would then change and the Byzantines would drive the Turks from the city, pursuing them as far as a place called the "Red Apple Tree" on the borders of Persia. Of course, the situation turned out rather different from the prophecy.

Many of the Orthodox people of the Balkans and Asia Minor, however, continued to believe that the Byzantine Empire would be resurrected. Based on popular traditions and passages from the Old Testament (such as the prophecies of Daniel), stories began to circulate about this awaited event. According to one:

> And again, Five-hilled City [Constantinople] you will rule.
> Many indeed look at the dead and completely plundered [city],
> But no one actually sees
> That you will appear as if [awakening] from sleep
> And you will hold the scepter of this empire.

One of the most popular of these stories had to do with Constantine IX Palaiologos as the "Emperor turned to Stone." According to this tradition, the body of the last emperor was never found after the end of the siege in 1453. This was explained by the theory that he was not in fact killed in the battle but that an angel turned him to marble and hid him in a cave close to the Golden Gate of Constantinople. And there he would remain until that time when the angel would return and restore his body to human form. Constantine would then enter the City through the Golden Gate, the entrance that previous emperors had always used when they returned to celebrate a victory in war, and he would drive the Turks as far as the Red Apple Tree. In one account:

> O emperor Constantine, what happened to you?
> Some say that you died with your sword in your hand.
> I heard others say that you were drawn out
> By the all-holy right hand of God.
> May you be alive and unburied.

The fall of Constantinople made an enormous impression on all the people of the "East" and similar prophecies circulated, interestingly enough, among the Arabs and the Turks, not to speak of the Slavic Orthodox Christians. According to a Russian version of the story, a "blond people" would join with the survivors of the Byzantines to defeat the Turks. These "blond people" were originally probably thought to be the western Europeans, but from at least the beginning of the sixteenth century, they were normally identified with the Russians. Other details were commonly provided that focused on a kind of "stoppage of time" when the city fell, but a restoration of the rightful state eventuates at the proper moment. Thus, one very well-known story told about the priests of Hagia Sophia, who melted into the core of the building when the Turks broke into the sanctuary, from which they will emerge once more, still singing the words of the interrupted liturgy. Similarly, another story told of a monk who was frying a fish when the city fell and that the cooking of the fish will be completed only at the moment that the Christians again take control of Constantinople.

Such stories, of course, provided hope to the defeated people of Byzantium and their descendants, but they also may have engendered false hopes and dangerous military adventures over the centuries. In any case, it is clear that not everyone believed in these prophecies. Thus, in 1618 Matthew Myreon could write, sarcastically:

> We hope in the "blond people" to save us,
> To come from Moscow to free us.
> We put our hope in the oracles, in the false prophecies,
> And we waste our time in worthless words.

FURTHER READING

Michael Herzfeld, *Ours Once More : Folklore, Ideology, and the Making of Modern Greece*. Austin, TX, 1982.

descended from him continued to live on in the West, occasionally surfacing to raise their claim to the throne of Byzantium.

Meanwhile, as we have already mentioned, the so-called Empire of Trebizond continued to exist on the southern shores of the Black Sea in eastern Asia Minor. This tiny state, it will be remembered, had come into existence just before the Fourth Crusade and it had maintained its independence from the Latins, the Turks, and the resurgent power of the Empire of Nicaea in the thirteenth century. The territory of this state was a small coastal strip, protected from the great powers of Asia Minor by the defenses of the city of Trebizond and the great wall of the Pontic Mountains. Thus, up until the middle of the fifteenth century Trebizond maintained its independence against the Otttomans. Murad II had ambitions to capture it, but these were foiled by the diplomatic maneuvers of the emperor John IV Komnenos (1429–59/60?). After the fall of Constantinople, John IV made alliances with his neighbors, especially the White Sheep Turkomans, but he died before the attack finally came and was succeeded by his brother David Komnenos. David's diplomatic ambitions were even wider than those of his brother, and he made contacts with the Duke of Burgundy and the pope, discussing even the possibility of a new Crusade to liberate Jerusalem. David approached Mehmed II with a request for the remission of tribute paid by his brother, and this and the web of alliances that the Empire of Trebizond had built up caused the sultan to move. In the winter of 1460 he put together an enormous expeditionary force, numbering 60,000 cavalry and 80,000 infantry. Supported by the Ottoman fleet in the Black Sea, this force marched to eastern Asia Minor, took Sinope, and made a demonstration of force in Armenia before descending into the territory of Trebizond. There was no alternative to surrender, and on 15 August 1461 the last Byzantine state ceased to exist. The emperor David and his family were taken to Adrianople and initially treated well, but the sultan could not allow the line of the Grand Komnenoi to exist, and in 1463 he ordered them all to be executed.

The Italian maritime republics, as usual, made the best of the situation after the fall of Constantinople. As we have seen, they had already made trading agreements with the Ottomans and they sought primarily to maintain their economic presence in the East. Venice, which had invested most in its territories in the East, preserved them the longest. The Venetians' foremost concern, of course, was to preserve the naval way-stations from Venice to Constantinople and the Levant, but they also had many land-based territories in Greece. Indeed, Venice remained the primary rival of the Ottoman Empire in the Mediterranean until the dissolution of the republic in 1797. Many of the Venetian territories were not originally held directly but were given to Venetian adventurers under the loose authority of the state, but the tendency as time went by was for Venice to assert direct sovereignty. In central Greece Negroponte (Euboia) fell to the Turks in 1470 and Nafpaktos (Lepanto) in 1499, while in the Peloponnesos Korone and Methone (Coron and Modon) were held by the Venetians until 1500 and Monemvasia until 1540. Of the great islands Cyprus remained a Venetian possession until 1571 and Crete until 1669; the Ionian islands had an ever-changing fate, but overall they remained in Venetian control until the end of the republic.

Genoa, Venice's main rival in the commercial setting of the later Byzantine Empire, lost its holdings somewhat earlier. The Genoese kept Lesvos until 1462 and Chios until 1566, although as Turkish vassals, and the duchy of Naxos in the Cyclades (then in the hands of a Veronese family) was extinguished in the same year.

Byzantine Christians under Ottoman Rule

Needless to say, the Christian communities of the former empire continued to exist, both in Asia Minor and the Balkans, in part because the Muslim Ottomans were bound to recognize the Christians as a legitimate entity, following a "religion of the book." For them, the most important event was Mehmed's decision to restore the patriarch of Constantinople as the head of the *rum milet*, as the community of Greek-speaking Orthodox was known. The former patriarch, Gregory III, had long been in exile, and, in any case, the sultan was wary of a unionist bishop since he continued to fear that the Greek Christians might collaborate with the West against the Ottoman state. For this reason he sought out Georgios Scholarios, now the monk Gennadeios, who had become a slave. Mehmed offered him the patriarchal throne; after some consideration, Scholarios accepted, and he was enthroned as Gennadeios II in January 1454, not in Hagia Sophia (which was now a mosque), but in the church of the Holy Apostles. The sultan, just like the emperor before him, took part in the ceremony and handed the patriarch his staff of office. Significantly for the future, the Orthodox Christians of the former emperor had found a rallying point in the person of the patriarch and the Orthodox church.

This situation was, of course, a result of the overall Islamic view of the world and the Ottoman system of administration. Theoretically at least, the Ottoman Empire was based on Islamic sha'ria (law) which viewed only Muslims as full members of the community. On the other hand, Muslim tradition clearly recognized the rights of the various peoples of the Book, including all Christian groups, and held that they were to be governed essentially by their own religious leaders, in this case the bishops. The *milet* system therefore encouraged the maintenance of the ethnic Christian groups that had already developed in the Byzantine period, for example, the *rum milet* (Orthodox Greek-speaking peoples), Serbian, Bulgarian, Romanian Orthodox *milets*, independent *milets* for the Armenians, and the non-Orthodox Jacobites and Copts.

Thus, within the Ottoman Empire the role and the power of the Orthodox church were, if anything, increased as a result of the conquest. The clergy were not subject to taxation, the organization of the church was unchanged, and the hierarchy enjoyed considerable prestige. Indeed, the bishops and the patriarch now had additional responsibilities, since they were political, as well as religious, leaders and they had an interest in ensuring the stability and success of the Ottoman regime. This encouraged the church to be politically conservative and to support the status quo. In addition, the church had come to symbolize for the Orthodox people of the Balkans the glory and the tradition of the Byzantine Empire. The empire had obviously disappeared, but the church retained not only the culture of Byzantium but also – and probably more importantly – a political structure that assured its own preservation and the maintenance of an institution closely associated with Byzantium. This had important repercussions as far as the heritage of Byzantine culture was concerned. That culture had always been infused with Christian meanings and interpretation, but there also was a strong practical and secular tradition in Byzantium and even – one might argue – a tradition that could be called anti-clerical. This secular tradition in Byzantine culture was less than useful to the educated clergy that dominated the higher offices of the church, and it was therefore not stressed and perhaps even suppressed, and the perception of Byzantine culture that emerged into modern times was one that was dominated almost exclusively by religious considerations, so Byzantium has consistently been seen – even today – as a society that was thoroughly and fundamentally religious.

The Ottomans wished to place the Slavic churches within the Ottoman Empire under the authority of the patriarch in Constantinople, as the mirror of the control the sultan had over the whole of the empire. In reality, however, a tradition of ecclesiastical independence had already grown up among the Slavs of the Balkans, and they were unwilling to give that up. They naturally retained their own languages, liturgy, and literature, and they were, practically speaking, independent of the patriarch. In any case, from the eighteenth century onward, national sentiment made such control impossible.

Russia

In Russia, of course, the situation was different, because the new political center of Moscow lay far beyond the control of the Ottoman state, and there were important points of friction between the two powers, first in the Black Sea, and ultimately at the point of contact at the northeastern extremity of Ottoman power in Europe, in Romania, Reuthenia, and Byelorussia. As we have seen, the conversion of Russia to Christianity came from Byzantium, and until the very end of the empire, most of the Metropolitans of Kiev and All Russia were Greeks. In the fifteenth century the Russians exhibited some independence when the Grand Prince of Moscow rejected Isidore of Kiev because he accepted the Union of Florence, and they eventually elected a metropolitan on their own, loyal to the Orthodox tradition.

After the fall of Constantinople, the Grand Prince Ivan III married Zoe Palaiologina, the younger daughter of Thomas Palaiologos, in 1472. Zoe, known to the Russians as Sofia, thus brought a close connection between the last imperial family of Byzantium and the ruling family of Russia, and indeed some Russians had been speaking for a time about the "mantle" of Constantinople passing to Moscow. In the early sixteenth century the monk Filofei of Pskov wrote that the "two Romes" (Rome and Constantinople) had fallen, and Moscow had become the "Third Rome." This was clearly seen in an apocalyptic sense, prefiguring the end of the world, and the Russian aristocracy never adopted the idea that Moscow had taken on all the ideology of Byzantium. Nonetheless, there were many ways in which Russia could see itself as the inheritor of the Byzantine imperial tradition and the protector of the Orthodox people who lived under Ottoman control.

In 1547 Ivan IV, grandson of Ivan III and Zoe Palaiologina, was crowned as tsar in a ceremony modeled on that of Constantinople, but it is significant that, unlike Slavic rulers such as Symeon of Bulgaria, he made no move to call himself emperor of the Romans, but rather styled himself "tsar of all the Rus," and he sought formal recognition of his coronation from the Patriarch of

Constantinople. The patriarch in this case, Joasaph, sanctioned the elevation, but only on condition that the actual coronation be performed by a representative of the patriarchate (something that was never done). In 1558, in fact, the patriarch Jeremiah II traveled to Moscow, and the tsar suggested that he abandon Constantinople and take up permanent residence in the nearby city of Vladimir. Jeremiah declined this offer, but the result was the creation of the patriarchate of Moscow, which was clearly seen as the restoration of the Pentarchy (the system of five patriarchs), Moscow replacing Rome, which had strayed from communion with the other Orthodox churches.

Thus, in many significant ways the two major poles of the Byzantine heritage were the Patriarch of Constantinople (and to a lesser degree the bishops and other patriarchs who were nominally under his control) and the Grand Prince, and later Tsar, of Russia. Each of them had powers of their own and both derived strength and inspiration from the Byzantine tradition; neither was, however, devoted to the restoration of the Byzantine state, for practical and ideological reasons. A major difference between the tsar and the patriarch, of course, was that the Patriarch of Constantinople was a subject of the sultan, while the Tsar of Russia was independent. This, in fact, had far larger ramifications, because in the Balkans, the Ottoman conquest had resulted in the elimination, not only of the Orthodox Christian states, but also in the essential disappearance of the former aristocracy, who had served as the major patrons of Byzantine culture. They were replaced, of course, by an Ottoman aristocracy that was almost completely Muslim (see the exceptions below) and that supported institutions and projects that were connected with Islam.

The Continuation and Development of Byzantine Culture

That is not to say that many elements of the Byzantine tradition did not survive during the Ottoman period: architecture is perhaps the best example here, and the marvelous mosques of Sinan and the other master architects of the sixteenth century can certainly be described as continuing the Byzantine tradition of monumental construction in the service of God. Likewise, post-Byzantine painting also continued, without a break, the trends begun in the Byzantine period.

Art historians have singled out two major traditions existing well before the fall of Constantinople that one may call the Cretan and the revived Macedonian schools of painting. Both of these continued after 1453, the latter already divided into sub-groups, roughly along regional – or one might argue – national lines, and the former a more unified tradition that was increasingly influenced by Italian art, in part because Crete was controlled by Venice and because a prosperous Venetian aristocracy there supported painters. Theophanes the Cretan (d. 1559) was the greatest member of this school, and his student Domenikos Theotokopoulos gained fame and attention in the West as El Greco (ca. 1541–1614). Theophanes worked primarily on Mount Athos and his paintings are characterized by tall, lean, austere figures.

Figure 16.1 Panagia Lactans. A fine example of a post-Byzantine ikon that exhibits strong influence from the West, particularly from Italy. Especially in places such as Cyprus, Crete, and the Ionian Islands, Venetian cultural influence was strong and painting was influenced by both the Byzantine and the western tradition. Photo: Dumbarton Oaks

After the fall of Crete to the Ottomans in 1669 many painters fled to the Ionian Islands, where the tradition survived but slowly declined. Thus, while one approach to Christian art after the fall of Constantinople was to combine the traditions of Byzantium with the new techniques and interests of the West, another was to stress, perhaps rigidly, the maintenance of Byzantine subject matter, style, and methods of painting, especially as it had been carried out by the so-called Macedonian school in the thirteenth and fourteenth centuries. This revision to a more naturalistic depiction came to dominate post-Byzantine Orthodox painting in Russia as well as throughout the Balkans in the late seventeenth and eighteenth centuries. One of the most influential of these painters was Dionysios of Fourna (in Thessaly), who worked in the middle of the eighteenth century.

Figure 16.2 Last Judgment from Vatopedi Monastery, Mt. Athos. Scenes of martyrdom and the Last Judgment, depicting the punishment of the damned and the rewards of the saved, were very popular in the post-Byzantine period, especially in monasteries. This representation is from the exonarthex (the outer entranceway) of the main church of the monastery of Vatopedi on Mt. Athos. Photo: Dumbarton Oaks / Ploutarchos Theocharidis

Among the most important institutions that assured the survival of the Byzantine tradition were the monasteries. To be sure, monasteries had existed throughout the Byzantine period, and they always played an important role in economic as well as religious and intellectual life. That importance was redoubled after the fall of Constantinople, in part because the monasteries were among the very few Byzantine institutions that survived intact, and as *waqfs* (religious foundations) they were generally given the full protection of Ottoman law. Many also received special privileges – normally remission of taxation or confirmation of landholding – from individual sultans. Thus, monasteries maintained, and often increased, the substantial landholdings they possessed, and they frequently engaged in trade and other economic activities. They also served, to a certain degree, as intellectual centers, given the reality that there were no non-Muslim institutions of higher learning in former Byzantine territory and that learning generally fell to a low level.

The monastic life did provide individuals – men and women alike – with an opportunity for administrative responsibility and activity that was difficult to find in the secular world, and some of the more talented individuals naturally

Figure 16.3 Detail from the Last Judgment. This is a detail from another scene of the Last Judgment, from the church of Voronet in Romania in the sixteenth century. This section of the painting depicts the fate of the saved, characterized by King David in the center of the composition, playing a lyre, while an angel pulls the soul of an individual in the form of a child from a dead man's mouth. In the bottom right one gets just a hint of the torments in store for the damned. The artistic tradition of this fresco is derived from the Macedonian school, with its faithfulness to the Byzantine tradition. Photo: Erich Lessing / Art Resource, NY

gravitated there. Likewise, since they were often wealthy, the monasteries were often able to serve as patrons, especially for architects and painters and thus, to a certain extent, they made up for the disappearance of the Christian aristocracy in the Balkans.

Certainly the most important of the monastic establishments of the post-Byzantine world were those on Mount Athos. These flourished and grew, and the Ottoman era represents their efflorescence. The same could be said of the monasteries of Meteora in Thessaly. Both Athos and Meteora were made up of a number of essentially independent monasteries that could occasionally work together on common causes, and they preserved the unique characteristic of Byzantine monasticism, which stressed the physical proximity of several monastic communities and independent anchorites who lived side by side in essentially the same "wilderness." Other monasteries throughout the Balkans also prospered under the Ottoman Empire, and their importance was increased by the fact that, as under Byzantine rule, all bishops were chosen from among the ranks of the monks, who not surprisingly often maintained close ties with their former monasteries.

The Decline of the Ottoman Empire

Among the reasons for the survival of the Byzantine tradition are the social and economic changes that accompanied the decline of the Ottoman state from the late seventeenth century onward and the creation of local aristocracies in the Balkans, some of whom were Christian and who looked to Byzantium as the origin of their culture. In the countryside, this was based on large-scale landowning and/or warfare, in the islands it was the result of commerce and shipping, while in the capital there developed a small, Greek-speaking aristocracy. These individuals often had humble origins, and they frequently imitated western and Ottoman culture, but at the same time they provided important economic support for elements of the Byzantine tradition such as church building and decoration. The Phanariotes, as the elite in Constantinople were called (from their homes near the patriarchate in the Phanar [lighthouse] quarter of Constantinople), came partly from the city itself, but also from among the Hellenized peoples of Romania and Albania. They served as diplomats and interpreters, and in this capacity they often exercised considerable influence and power. Ultimately the Phanariotes gained control of the Danubian principalities of Wallachia and Moldavia, which they ruled essentially as viceroys of the sultan.

As has often been pointed out, the elements of post-Byzantine culture may be separated into two "layers," that of formal (higher) culture and that of popular (or folk) culture. The line between these is frequently blurred, but the distinction may be a useful one, and it is possible, once again, to see a significant difference between Russia and the Balkans in this regard. On the one hand, the Russian acceptance of Byzantine culture, which was mostly characterized by religion, has often been seen as a singularly unfortunate event for the Russians, largely because – so it is argued – they came to accept the elements of Byzantine religion ready-made (as it were) and already characterized by a rigidity that was enforced both by the power of the Russian state and by an unbending and "unthinking" acceptance of the Orthodox tradition. Such a characterization is certainly wrong and blatantly unfair, in part because it fails to take into account the many ways in which the Russians modified the Byzantine tradition to suit their own needs. Nonetheless, some aspects of Russian culture were certainly dominated by Byzantine elements. As already mentioned, there is little reason to imagine that Russia accepted a role as the "Third Rome," but its culture was profoundly affected by the liturgy, which permeated every aspect of life and which brought Byzantine literature and spirituality to people at all levels of society. This did lead to Russians looking at many things in an eschatological view that was only part of the way the Byzantines saw the world.

In the Balkans, in part because the institutions that supported higher culture had largely collapsed, the Byzantine tradition was continued by the church (and the monasteries) and as a result much of Byzantine culture was either "ecclesiasticized" or it fell into what we would probably call "folk culture." Thus, the languages spoken in the Balkans continued to develop, just as they had under Byzantium, and phenomena such as festivals or fairs, attitudes toward the supernatural, and music and poetry continued to be essentially Byzantine in character. Only in Venetian-dominated Crete, with its own tradition of aristocracy until 1669, did self-consciously literary developments take place, with poetry such as the *Erotokritos* of Vinsentos Kornaros.

In the late eighteenth century, partly as a result of the Enlightenment, a political face was put on the Byzantine heritage, both in Russia and in the Balkans. The Byzantine heritage and especially the political ideology of the Byzantine Empire were seen by some as a call to war with and/or independence from the Ottoman Turks. Naturally this same heritage could be used by others, especially in the church, to recommend obedience to the Ottoman state. Perhaps ironically, among those who sought the overthrow of the "Turkish yoke," the Byzantine tradition was used to create two very different visions of the future: the first and most common was to see the replacement of the Ottoman Empire by what was essentially a revival of the Byzantine Empire, dominated perhaps by the Phanariotes, but multi-ethnic and multi-religious, with Constantinople as its center. This was, for example, the view of Regas Feraios and some of the Phanariotes themselves. By the early part of the nineteenth century this view had been largely replaced by an idea that stressed the connection between Byzantium, the individual Orthodox churches, and the concept of nationhood that had developed almost entirely in Western Europe. In this view, the Byzantine tradition could be used to help define various national groups, in part by fixing the circumstances of their conversion to Orthodox Christianity, and these groups, as nations, could be seen as having a natural right to an independent existence. Naturally, the creation of what were essentially "national" churches aided the acceptance of this idea. Thus, perhaps ironically, the Byzantine tradition could be used to support both the idea of a multi-ethnic state and that of national self-determination, although the latter view certainly won out and has been the background of the political history of the Balkans and Eastern Europe for the past two centuries. It should be pointed out, however, that this idea has very little direct connection with Byzantium itself, which certainly did not view itself as a "nation" in the modern sense and was – as we have seen – fully multi-ethnic and, in many ways, tolerant of different cultures.

The "Heirs" of Byzantium

The Greeks, Russians, Armenians, Ukrainians, Romanians, Bulgarians, Serbs, and other Slavic peoples, both in their own countries and in the international diaspora which they have experienced, are the direct cultural heirs of Byzantium. They have all been, in one way or another, intensely aware of that heritage and

Box 16.2 *Kornaros and* Erotokritos

Vinsentos Kornaros (1553–ca. 1617) was born near Sita in western Crete, the son of a Venetian-Cretan aristocrat. He moved to Candia (now Heraklion) and held various government positions, including inspector of health during the plague of 1591–3. He became a member of the "Academy of the Peculiar," a literary society founded by his brother.

Kornaros was probably the author of the long verse novel, the *Erotokritos*. This product of the so-called Cretan Renaissance is an important work in its own right, but also provides an important bridge between the literature of the Middle Ages and that of modern times. The *Erotokritos* draws inspiration from the popular chronicles and romances of Byzantine literature, but is also strongly influenced by western literature, such as the French novel, *Paris et Vienne,* and Ariosto's *Orlando Furioso.* The poem has over 10,000 lines, but the story (derived largely from the French work mentioned above) is simple. Erotokritos, the adopted son of a king, fell in love with the princess Aretoussa, but their relationship was forbidden by the social conventions of the day. When the king learned about the situation, he exiled Erotokritos. The young man, however, aided by magic intervention, was able to aid the king in an especially difficult battle, thereby gaining possession of his love. Kornaros, however, is able to bring this banal story to life through his use of vivid language, lively dialogue, and rich references to folk traditions. The following is a brief selection depicting the moment at which the two lovers were parted:

> She was speaking on one side [of the window], he on the other; the same suffering gripped them both, one pain, one storm. No longer had they time to speak of their misfortune; the dark moment came when they had to part. Lightning flashed and thunder rolled in the west when he opened his lips to say good-bye, and the place shook from the pain it felt when they held hands and said good-bye. Who can describe how the young girl stood there dazed at that moment and how the young man looked? They had no mouth, no lips to say good-bye, no eyes to see nor ears to hear. But time was pressing; the day had come, and full of passion they pressed each other's hand. And a great marvel happened to that window; the stones and the iron bars wept at that moment, tear-drops rolled down from the stone and the iron; Aretousa found them there and they were warmer than blood. But time was pressing; Erotocritos left with a bitter sigh that shook the land. Arete was left alone with Phrosyne and then a dreadful thing happened: she fell and swooned on the lap of her nurse, not knowing if she were dead or living.

From Constantine A. Trypanis, *The Penguin Book of Greek Verse* (Harmondsworth, 1971), pp. 492–3.

its role in making them who they are. Modern commentators, both within and outside the Orthodox church, have seen the Byzantine historical tradition as separating Orthodox Christian peoples from their powerful neighbors in Catholic or Protestant Western Europe, on the one hand, and the Muslim Turks and Arabs, on the other. The attitude of the "heirs" to the Byzantine tradition has often been ambivalent, since Byzantium is sometimes seen as something "medieval" (which of course it chronologically was) and "backward" (which it was not); modernizers have often argued that the Byzantine concern for religion has prevented the Orthodox people from taking advantage of technological and other developments of the contemporary world and that this holds them up to ridicule from more "advanced" cultures. One sees this tendency clearly in Greece along the fault lines between *Hellenismos* (based on the classical tradition) and *Romiosyne* (based on the Byzantine tradition).

Indeed, in the Orthodox areas there is not surprisingly an acute awareness of the "superiority" of the modern West – in technology, wealth, and military power – and a rarely spoken fear that the reason that Orthodox countries have not "developed" in the same way is because of the Byzantine tradition. Westerners, of course, have often been happy to encourage this kind of thinking, in

Box 16.3   *Byzantium and* The Brothers Karamazov

One of the first places where the ordinary modern person is apt to encounter Byzantine civilization is in the works of nineteenth- and twentieth-century Russian literature. The novels, plays, and poems of Tolstoy, Dostoyevsky, Chekhov, Pasternak, and Solzhenitsyn have countless references to Russian religion and its close connections with the religion of the Byzantine Empire. The omnipresence of the village priest and his frequent failure to meet the expectations of a fully Christian life is a commonplace in Russian literature, and the monastery features frequently in important passages. This was true not only of the authors well known in the West, but also in the so-called folk novelists of the nineteenth century who have gained greater interest in recent decades.

Perhaps most interesting in this regard is Alyosha, the idealistic "hero" of Dostoyevsky's *The Brothers Karamazov*, and his relationship with the abbot Zossima. Alyosha was the youngest of the three brothers and the most sensitive. His mother died when he was only 4 and he grew up in a foster-family, far from the crazed world of his licentious, alcoholic father. The first event that Dostoyevsky describes concerning Alyosha was that he had a vivid memory of a single moment with his mother: a summer evening with the rays of the setting sun slanting across a room, and the ikon of the Virgin with a lamp before it in a corner, and his mother crying and suddenly embracing the young boy. Later, when he was 19, Alyosha decided to enter a monastery, attracted so the author tells us by the personality of the "elder" Father Zossima. Dostoyevsky then describes in some detail the origin of the position of the elder within Byzantine Christianity and its development from the days of early asceticism to the great monasteries of Mount Athos. Father Zossima had been a military officer but had later joined a monastery. Now he served as a spiritual adviser and healer whose spiritual power made him known far and wide. He was personable and affable and those who consulted him always came away with happy faces. Alyosha wondered at the faith people had that Father Zossima would be able to heal them, but he reasoned that the elder was the very manifestation of love and that his example was precisely what was needed to transform the world into one of justice and love among all mankind.

The details Dostoyevsky provides of the role of the elder and his standing in society reflect very much what we know about the role of holy men and women in Byzantium. Likewise, the author does not discuss the daily round of prayer and fasting in the monastery, but instead focuses on the character of Zossima and, even more, the attitude of the young Alyosha toward him. Zossima is pictured in his role as would-be arbiter in the disputes among members of the Karamazov family and as dispensing good advice to the throngs of pilgrims who came to visit him. Small details, such as Zossima's gift of a small ikon to a woman, the arrangements for Father Zossima's burial, and the debate over whether the bodies of saints remain uncorrupted reinforce the book's connection with Byzantium.

The Brothers Karamazov, of course, focuses on the murder of Alyosha's father and the relations among the three brothers, and its concerns were with the political, social, and intellectual issues of the latter part of the nineteenth century, but Father Zossima stands behind – or perhaps above – the whole scene. An important section of the book is a digression on the elder's earlier life and the personal realizations, set off by a duel with another officer, that led him to become a monk. Zossima is shown not only as a healer but as a prophet who could foresee the terrible things that were going to befall the Karamazov family but he reacted to everything with wisdom and love, in ways that very much resemble the actions recorded in the biographies of Byzantine saints.

After Zossima's death the novel follows on to deal with the central issues of the book: moral responsibility and the struggle between faith and reason. But, even though Dostoyevsky's feelings on these issues are quite clear, his use of symbols (such as the repeated image of individuals bowing down and almost "embracing" the earth) and the way in which many of the religious authorities are pictured in a negative light, show that the author leaves many of the answers ambiguous, in a way that would have been attractive to Byzantine thinkers. This is not to say that the main focus of *The Brothers Karamazov* is Byzantium: it certainly is not. Yet a careful reading of the book (and many others) can provide a useful insight into the nature of the Byzantine tradition.

FURTHER READING

Simon Franklin, *Byzantium, Rus, Russia*. Studies in the Transmission of Christian Culture. Aldershot, 2002.

part as a result of the anti-Byzantine attitudes that have been characteristic of the West for the past thousand years. Indeed, one does not have to look far in contemporary politics and journalism to find the term "Byzantine" associated characteristically with all that is "wrong" about the Balkans and Russia.

The direct heirs of Byzantium are torn in this conflict of ideas, for they often are ready to admit with the critics that their Byzantine heritage (often associated with stale religious traditions and "backwardness") has "held them back." On the other hand, Byzantine culture clearly survives in the cities and villages that were once part of the Byzantine Empire (and increasingly in the diaspora), and ordinary people often feel closely and personally attached to it. Further, the eastern Christians can often detect in the strident words of westerners the image of the Crusades, especially the sack of Constantinople in 1204 at the hands of their Christian "brethren." In a way that most westerners would not imagine, the "memories" of the Crusades and the attendant "colonization" of most of the Byzantine Empire are still very much alive.

This is not to say that more recent events have not played a role here as well, since eastern European Communism was remarkably able to dismiss religion while embracing the concept of the Byzantine Empire as part of its tradition. In addition, the experiences of the Balkan wars at the beginning of the twentieth century, the terrible inter-communal clashes during and after the Second World War, and the events associated with the break-up of Yugoslavia in the 1990s have all influenced the ways in which Byzantium and the West are viewed. Some western commentators have argued, for example, that the Balkans are "inherently" unstable and ethnic violence so great as a result of the religious divisions that go back to the Middle Ages and the period of the Ottoman Empire. As the events described in this book have shown, however, nothing could be further from the truth. The Byzantine reality (as opposed to the western perception of it) was not one of instability or exclusivity, but rather one of stability and inclusiveness, inclusiveness of a kind that would not, for example, understand either wars of a crusading nature or efforts at "ethnic cleansing," both of which are very far from the Byzantine tradition.

The peoples of Russia and the Balkans are not, of course, the only heirs of Byzantium. In significant ways all of modern western culture has been strongly influenced by Byzantium, both in the historical contributions that it made to the development of the West (phenomena such as the blending of Christian and classical culture, the preservation of classical Greek literature and learning) and the creation of significant cultural achievements in its own right. In addition, the peoples with "proximity" to Byzantium might also be considered rightful heirs: the Turks, the Albanians, the Arabs, and, to a significant degree, even the Italians. The Arabs and the Turks are special cases in point since the culture of the former developed alongside and in concert with Byzantine culture, while that of the latter has been influenced in many ways by the culture of Byzantium in its last centuries and the years of afterglow. It should not come as a great surprise to realize that Byzantium shares many elements of its culture with its two great adversaries.

Figure 16.4 Modern "Byzantine" fresco. In the nineteenth and the first half of
the twentieth century, church art in former Byzantine areas was dominated by
imitations of western art: rather weak attempts to produce "fashionable" realistic
depictions of Christ and the saints, with colors and style drawn mainly from Italy.
From the 1970s onward there was a notable and conscious revival of the
Byzantine tradition by artists who sought to reproduce the style and the technique
of the Byzantine tradition. At its best, this revival produces some impressive
pieces of art, although there naturally is a tendency to careless repetition and a
"mass-produced" feel to the work. Photo: Timothy E. Gregory

   Beyond this, the history of the Byzantine Empire can (and I think should)
provide a valuable mirror for the West: Byzantium is the "other" Europe, the
other face, if you will, of western civilization, helping the West to see better
what it is and what it is not. Byzantium is the "alternative" West, showing how
things "might" have turned out differently for Western Europe in different
circumstances, and providing valuable lessons of ways the European tradition itself can be seen and "turned" in different directions. The study of the
Byzantine Empire thus can provide someone who is not a direct cultural
"heir" of the empire with a different way of understanding the West (meaning,

here, the western tradition, of which Byzantium is unquestionably a part), a way that requires, if nothing else, enlarged definitions of what the West actually is. This is something extremely important as people ask themselves about the role of technology in our culture, the dehumanization that seems so universally part of a globalized world, and the direction and fate of such institutions as the European Union. In general, those who weigh these issues tend to see things in bipolar terms: that the future should be "one way or another," and one is either "for us or against us," which in a fundamental way is simply another way to say that "East is East and West is West . . ." Yet, the history of Byzantium shows that this is not the case: there are (at least) third ways, middle ways, indeed a whole world of ways, and alternate ways of thinking and acting are very much a part of our common human heritage that we should both treasure and use as examples for emulation.

George Ostrogorsky did not end his still standard *History of the Byzantine State* by exulting with Leakey that Byzantium fell to the Turks, its inhabitants "wrangling about theology until the end." Instead, he took a very positive tone, arguing that Byzantium had performed a crucial historical service, preserving the culture of classical antiquity until the West was "ready to receive it." Although I agree with Ostrogorsky about the importance of this phenomenon in general terms, I think that the significance of Byzantium is not in what it preserved but in what it created, and most importantly in the rich set of (often quite contradictory) ideas and principles it espoused: a society that was remarkably religious and yet surprisingly secular, almost always at war but with a clear preference for negotiation and diplomacy, a world that respected learning but where most people were illiterate, eschatological but at the same time remarkably practical. And the list can go on. The creation of *apophatic* (or "negative") theology and the concept of *oikonomia* go against the standard view of Byzantium as a culture dominated by narrow-minded monks and petty court officials. Rather, phenomena such as "playfulness" in painting and architectural design, sophistication in philosophy and science, and a varied tradition of saints (and saints' lives), from the women who dressed in monks' clothes to Symeon Stylites, demonstrate the breadth, depth, and richness of Byzantine culture and society.

FURTHER READING

M. Aymard, "To Vyzantio meta to Vyzantio – To Vyzantio pera apo to Vyzantio," in E. Bibikou-Antontiadi, Z. Bompair, A. Guillou, D. Simon, J. Howard-Johnston, F. Bourgarella, J. Le Goff, M. Aymard, eds., *Vyzantio kai Evrope*. Athens, 1996, pp. 107–14.

Lowell Clucas, ed., *The Byzantine Legacy in Eastern Europe*. East European Monographs. Boulder, CO, 1988.

John Meyendorff, *Rome, Constantinople, Moscow: Historical and Theological Studies*. Crestwood, NY, 1996.

D. M. Nicol, *Meteora: The Rock Monasteries of Thessaly*, 2nd edn. London, 1975.

Steven Runciman, *The Great Church in Captivity: A Study of the Patriarchate of Constantinople from the Eve of the Turkish Conquest to the Greek War of Independence*. Cambridge, 1968.

Maria Todorova, *Imagining the Balkans*. New York and Oxford, 1997.

S. Vryonis, "The Byzantine Legacy and Ottoman Forms," *Dumbarton Oaks Papers* 23–24 (1969–70), pp. 251–308.

John J. Yiannias, ed., *The Byzantine Tradition after the Fall of Constantinople*. Charlottesville and London, 1991.

Glossary

Acheiropoieta: literally, "things not made by hand," that is, miraculous objects that were thought to have appeared on earth through divine inspiration; examples were the Mandylion and various ikons, normally of Christ or the Virgin.

Akoimetoi: see "Sleepless Monks."

Alexandria, theological school of: theological tradition that preferred the allegorical or spiritual interpretation of Scripture and an emphasis on the divinity of Christ; heavily influenced by *Neoplatonism* and the teachings of Origen; important followers of this tradition were Clement of Alexandria, Hierokles, Hypatia, and John Philoponos.

Allelengyon: literally "mutual security," the system in Byzantium whereby communities of small farmers were jointly responsible for payment of taxes to the government; in the early eleventh century Basil II made wealthy landowners liable for the tax debts of the poor, a system that was abolished by Romanos III.

Antioch, theological school of: theological tradition that preferred the literal interpretation of Scripture and an emphasis on the human aspect of the person of Christ: important "members" of this tradition were Theodore of Mopsuestia, Theodoret of Cyrrhus, Ibas of Edessa, and Nestorios; opposed to the theological school of Alexandria.

Appanage: a term taken from western feudalism to describe a territory given to a junior member of the ruling family as a nearly independent grant, with the local ruler maintaining his own court, administration, and fiscal system; the system was common in Byzantium from the thirteenth century onward and characterized the breakdown of the central state.

Apophatic theology: sometimes called "negative theology," as opposed to "cataphatic theology," the tradition that the human mind can say nothing positive about God; this tradition, derived largely from Neoplatonism and developed through the Cappadocian Fathers and Pseudo-Dionysios the Areopagite, believed that knowledge of God was derived from experience; it is essentially therefore mystical theology.

Ascetic: an individual who seeks to reach God through physical, mental, and spiritual training, commonly involving extreme deprivation of the body.

Atrium: in the context of church architecture, the large, enclosed, frequently colonnaded space at the west of a church that allowed large numbers of people to congregate in the area of the ecclesiastical complex.

Autocephalous: referring to bishops who were independent of higher episcopal authority, especially the five traditional patriarchs, and others such as the bishops of Cyprus and Bulgaria.

Basileopator: literally, "the emperor's father," a title created by Leo VI for his father-in-law Stylianos Zautzes, implying the tutelage of an older man for an under-age emperor.

Basileus: Greek term meaning "emperor"; from the time of Herakleios onward, this was the normal title of the Byzantine emperor. From the early ninth century onward the emperor was regularly styled "Basileus Romaion" (emperor of the Romans), to distinguish him from emperors in Western Europe.

Bulgars: Turkic-speaking peoples, originally from Central Asia, who first appeared on the Danube frontier in the late fifth century, and who settled within Byzantine territory in the seventh century. As they mixed with local people and adopted a Slavic-based language, they developed a civilization of their own, significantly influenced by that of Byzantium. The so-called First and Second Bulgarian Empires, of the tenth and eleventh century respectively, both threatened the Byzantine Empire and participated in the spread of Byzantine culture in the Balkans and Russia.

Caliph: Arabic *khalifa*, meaning "successor" of the Prophet Muhammad; from the time of Abu Bakr the caliphs held both political and religious authority, theoretically over the whole of the Muslim world.

Caesar: originally the family name of Julius Caesar, the term was applied from the time of the Tetrarchy onward to junior co-emperors, often (but not always) with the expectation that they would succeed to the throne.

Cenobitic: the form of monasticism in which the monks live and pray together, normally in a monastery.

Chalcedonian/Chalcedonianism: from the Council of Chalcedon (451), otherwise called, *dyophysitism*, the belief that there are two natures (*physeis*) in the person of Christ, the human and the divine, and that these are inseparably joined. This doctrine came to be the official teaching of the Orthodox church, in opposition to *Monophysitism*, despite many attempts to heal the split.

Coptic: the language of ancient Egypt as it was spoken in Roman and Byzantine times and written in an alphabet based on Greek; the term is also used to refer to the Monophysite Christians of Egypt.

Diptych: pairs of panels of wood, ivory, or other materials joined together so that they could be opened to view some content within; the most famous were those used to announce appointment to high office, such as the consulship; emperors also issued diptychs, apparently with five leaves, to announce their accession.

Domestikos: the head of a department or division in the church, the civil administration, or the army. Probably the most important was the *Domestikos* of the *Scholai*, who in the Middle Byzantine period was essentially the commander of the imperial army.

Dynatoi: literally "the powerful," usually applied to the landowning aristocracy, especially in the context of the struggle over the alienation of peasant land in the tenth and eleventh centuries, but also later.

Equites: in the Roman and very early Byzantine period, members of a wealthy class who controlled many of the offices of the state, considerably lower in prestige than the *senators*, but far above the station of ordinary citizens.

Eremitic: the form of monasticism in which the monk lives a solitary life by himself or herself, normally in a remote place such as a desert or a mountain.

Eunuchs: castrated males; Byzantine law forbade the practice, and some eunuchs were imported from abroad, but it is clear that it was not altogether uncommon in Byzantium; eunuchs held important positions in the church and all branches of the government, including the army, especially in the palace; the use of eunuchs declined from the period of the Komnenoi onward.

Exarch: name given to governors in Ravenna and in Carthage, from the end of the sixth to the middle of the seventh century; in distinction to the powers of governors in the system of Diocletian and Constantine, the exarchs had both civil and military power.

Exkoubitores/Exkoubitoi: the imperial guard, the bodyguard of the emperor, created by Leo I and extant through at least the eleventh century.

Exkoussia: the practice of freeing landowners from certain obligations to the state, most commonly the payment of taxes.

Filioque: the term meaning "and from the Son," concerning the procession of the Holy Spirit, added by the western church to the text of the Nicene Creed; this was one of the most important theological points of dispute between the papacy and the Byzantine church.

Foederati: originally (fourth–fifth centuries), barbarian tribes settled on Byzantine territory on condition that they serve in the army; at a later date (sixth century onward?) the term was used to refer to elite mounted troops, recruited mainly, but not always, from among the barbarians.

Gerokomeion (pl. *gerokomeia*): homes for care of the aged, frequently set up by the church or the state.

Glagolitic: alphabet for the Slavic languages, based on that developed by Constantine/Cyril for the mission to Moravia in the ninth century.

Greek Fire: the incendiary weapon supposedly invented by Kallinikos and used for the first time in the Arab siege of Constantinople in 678; its composition was a state secret which is still not known; it was shot through a tube and was difficult to extinguish.

Haradj: the tax paid by non-Muslims under Islamic states, especially the Ottoman Empire.

Hegoumenos/Egoumenos: the abbot of a monastery.

Hesychasm: the term *hesychia*, means "peace and quiet," and this was a goal of the ascetic tradition from an early date; as a movement, *Hesychasm* refers to the followers of Gregory Palamas in the fourteenth century.

Hyperpyron: (*nomisma hyperpyron*, lit. "highly refined"), the gold coin introduced by Alexios I in 1092, of 20.5 carat gold; this became the normal name for the gold coin thereafter.

Iconoclasts: those after 726 who were opposed to the veneration of ikons and who wished to remove them from public and private view.

Iconophiles: also Iconodules, those after 726 who wished to put an end to Iconoclasm and restore the public and private veneration of ikons.

Idiorrythmic monasticism: the monastic practice in which monks live essentially on their own, following their own ascetic practices but maintaining a connection with a monastery and frequently worshiping together with the other monks; this form of monasticism was known in early Byzantine times, but it was generally disfavored until it became common in Mount Athos in the fourteenth century.

Ikon: Greek "eikon," literally meaning "image," but usually used to refer to an image, most commonly painted on a wooden panel, depicting a religious subject and designed for veneration rather than for aesthetic purposes.

Imperator: the title originally given to successful military commanders in the Roman Republic; later it came to be one of the standard titles of the emperors, from which we get the English word "emperor." It continued to be used as part of the imperial nomenclature, on coins and inscriptions, through the early Byzantine period.

Kleisourai: literally "defile," administrative districts, usually smaller than a *theme*, mostly in frontier areas, especially in the East, from the end of the seventh century.

Kouropalates: an imperial dignity, given by the emperor normally to members of the imperial family, following in rank the titles of *caesar* and *nobilissimos*; on occasion the dignity was given to foreign princes.

Kritis: a judge, who was probably a subordinate official of the *strategos* of a *theme*, although he might have been an imperial tax collector; from the eleventh century onward, with the decline of the *themes*, the *kritis* assumed a greater role as a provincial governor.

Limes: Latin word normally translated as "border;" but in the early Byzantine period this was not normally a fortified border but a frontier area, often marked with a road running along its length, marking off the territory of the empire from the barbarian land beyond.

Logothete (Gr. *logothetes*): literally "accountant" or "secretary," in the early Byzantine period, the head of a department of state; from the seventh century onward the logothetes became independent and the most important civilian administrative officials.

Magister militum (pl. *magistri militum*): literally "master of the soldiers," the highest-ranking commander of the early Byzantine army.

Mesopotamia: the area of the Tigris and Euphrates valleys (mainly modern Iraq), contested between Byzantium and the Persian Empire until the seventh century; the center of the Abbasid caliphate from the mid-eighth century onward.

Monophysitism: literally "one-nature-ism," the belief that the person of Christ has only one nature (*physis*), the divine, and that he is, therefore, essentially God, to the diminution of his human aspect. Monophysitism was espoused by Dioskoros of Alexandria and condemned by the Council of Chalcedon (451), but it survived to be the dominant form of Christianity in Egypt (Coptic Christianity) and Syria (Jacobite Christianity), despite many attempts to heal the split between it and the Orthodox (Chalcedonian) church of Constantinople.

Moravia: region in ancient Pannonia, with its center probably in the modern states of the Czech Republic and Slovakia, the first Slavic state, from the ninth century onward a bone of contention among the competing powers of Byzantium, the papacy, and the German Empire.

Neoplatonism: a philosophical system based very loosely on the ideas of Plato, refined and broadened by Plotinus and Porphyry, it had a powerful influence on all of Byzantine thought, especially through the theological school of *Alexandria*.

Nobilissimus/nobelissimos: imperial title, generally ranking directly below the *Caesar*.

Nomisma: the Byzantine gold coin, the *solidus*, that from the time of Constantine I to Constantine IX was struck at a constant weight of 1/72nd of a pound of pure gold.

Orphanotropheion (pl. *orphanotropheia*): orphanage, frequently set up by the church or the state.

Orphanotrophos: literally, the director of an orphanage, commonly a monk, but in Constantinople the *orphanotrophoi* became secular state officials with fiscal responsibilities. In the eleventh century John the Orphanotrophos essentially controlled the affairs of state for a considerable period.

Parakoimomenos: literally, "the person by the bedside," the official, usually a eunuch, who was the chamberlain or personal attendant of the emperor; this office probably derived from that of the *praepositus sacri cubiculi* of the Later Roman Empire, but with this name it is first attested in the eighth century; in the tenth and eleventh centuries a number of powerful individuals held the post, which therefore had considerable significance.

Paroikoi: tenant farmers, especially in the context of the regime of large landholdings in the tenth century and afterwards. *Paroikoi* are sometimes called "Byzantine serfs," and the parallel is not entirely false since the *paroikos* was tied to the land which did not belong to him. The *paroikoi* are to be distinguished from the free peasants who held land in their own name; from the thirteenth century onward virtually all peasants seem to have been *paroikoi*.

Partitio Romaniae: literally, the "Division of the Roman Empire," an agreement drawn up by the Venetians and the Crusaders in the spring of 1204 as they besieged Constantinople, laying out the way in which the Byzantine Empire would be divided: the Latin Emperor was to receive one-quarter of the empire and the Venetians and the Crusaders three-eighths each.

Patriarch: the bishops of the five leading sees of the empire: Rome, Constantinople, Alexandria, Antioch, and Jerusalem; after the seventh century only the first two had real importance; in the late empire new patriarchs were recognized, as a mark of their independence from the patriarch of Constantinople: Bulgaria in the thirteenth and Serbia in the fourteenth century.

Pronoia: literally a gift or a grant, the system of grants of state-owned lands to individuals (usually large landowners in their own right) on condition that they provide military service; the *pronoia* system allowed the *pronoiar* to reap all the economic benefits from the land, but the sovereignty of the state over that land was not surrendered.

Protimesis: literally meaning "preference," the system, in the legislation of the tenth century and following, by which peasant land could be purchased, giving priority to family members, neighbors, etc.; the idea was to prevent large landowners from acquiring peasant land.

Ptochoi: the poor, especially in the context of the struggle over the alienation of peasant land in the tenth and eleventh centuries.

Razzia: Arabic, literally "raid," the type of attack by desert-dwellers on the settled agricultural land that preceded the rise of Islam and may have contributed to the rapid success of Arabic armies in the seventh century.

Scholai: a *schola* literally meant any "office" or body of officials, but it came to refer particularly to the *scholae palitinae*, the palace guard created by Diocletian or Constantine; by the fifth century they came to play a mainly ceremonial role and recruited primarily aristocratic youth; by the eighth century, however, they once again had an active military role as an important part of the *tagmata*.

Senate: the deliberative body of ancient Rome, whose members were in Byzantine times the wealthiest and most powerful members of society; the Senate in Rome lasted until the late fifth century, while that of Constantinople was created by Constantine I; it existed until the end of the empire, but its legal authority had ended by the ninth century.

Senators: members of the Senate of Rome and, later, of Constantinople, wealthy families who in the West were the backbone of the conservative (often pagan) landowning aristocracy, while in the East they were more normally aristocrats of service, whose position and wealth came directly from the emperor.

Sleepless Monks: the *akoimetoi*, a community of monks founded in Constantinople in the early fifth century whose members were dedicated to "ceaseless prayer," which they accomplished in eight-hour shifts. They tended to a strict maintenance of Chalcedonian orthodoxy and were outspoken opponents of Theopaschitism in the sixth century.

Solidus: see *nomisma*.

Strategos: "general," from the seventh or eighth century the commander of a *theme*, who held both civil and military power.

Stylites: ascetics, such as Symeon Stylites and Daniel the Stylite, beginning in the fifth century, who spent their careers at the top of a column.

Syriac: a Semitic language, spoken broadly in Syria and Mesopotamia in antiquity that became an important literary vehicle for the Christian culture of the third to seventh centuries, especially among the Jacobites (Monophysites) and Nestorians.

Tagmata: from the eighth century special professional regiments of troops under the direct control of the emperor (in distinction to the *themata*, which were controlled by the *strategoi* of the themes); a significant number of the *tagmata* were stationed in Constantinople.

Theme: (Greek *thema*), from the seventh or eighth century, the provinces into which the Byzantine Empire was divided, governed by a *strategos*.

Theurgy: the use of magic or special powers to force divine powers to do one's will, especially connected with the Neoplatonic school of Plotinus and his followers.

Traditores: Christians who betrayed their faith in order to save their lives by handing over the Scriptures or other Christian items to their enemies during the Great Persecution at the beginning of the fourth century.

Zealots: the term has two meanings: (1) Iconophile monks and their followers of the late eighth to tenth centuries, who demanded strict adherence to canon law, the punishment of Iconoclasts, and the prohibition of the appointment of laymen as bishops; (2) the political and social party that took over Thessaloniki in the mid-fourteenth century.

General Bibliography

Major parts of the records from the monasteries at Mount Athos have been published in *Archives de l'Athos* (Paris, 1937 onward), the records of the ecumenical councils of the church in *Acta Conciliorum Oecumenicorum* (Leipzig, 1922–74), and details of the historical geography of the empire in *Tabula Imperii Byzantini* (Vienna, 1976 onward). The illuminated manuscripts from Mount Athos have been published in S. M. Pelekanides et al., *The Treasures of Mt. Athos: Illuminated Manuscripts*, 3 vols. (Athens, 1973–9), many of the important Byzantine ivories by A. Goldschmidt and K. Weitzmann, *Die byzantinischen Elfenbeinskulpturen des X.–XIII. Jahrhnderts*, 2 vols. (Berlin, 1930–4, reprint 1979), an important collection of ikons by G. and M. Soteriou, *Eikones tis Monis Sinai*, 2 vols. (Athens, 1956–8). Byzantine coins have been published in the old (but still valuable) catalogue of the British Museum collection and more up-to-date catalogues of the collections of the Bibliothèque Nationale de France and Dumbarton Oaks.

In recent years some important and accessible collections of texts have appeared in English translation, and these may be of use to the student wishing to get a first-hand introduction to the written sources for Byzantine history. Among these are C. Mango, *The Art of the Byzantine Empire 312–1453* (Englewood Cliffs, NJ, 1972), on the written sources for Byzantine art, D. J. Geanakoplos, *Byzantium: Church, Society, and Civilization Seen through Contemporary Eyes* (Chicago, 1984), a good collection of sources arranged by topic; access to Byzantine saints' lives can be found in F. Halkin, *Bibliotheca Hagiographica Graeca*, 3 vols. (Brussels, 1957), and – perhaps most important – the sources collected and made available on the Internet by Paul Halsall in the Internet Medieval Sourcebook. The Internet is certain to have a powerful impact on the study of Byzantine civilization, as it allows resources in widely scattered places to be brought together for educational and scholarly purposes and – perhaps most important of all – to be drawn to the attention of students and the interested public.

GENERAL WORKS

Cavallo, Guglielmo, ed., *The Byzantines*. Chicago, 1997.

Haldon, John, *Byzantium. A History*. Charleston, SC, 2002.

Kazhdan, Alexander, ed., *The Oxford Dictionary of Byzantium*, 3 vols. New York, 1991.

Kazhdan, A., and G. Constable, *People and Power in Byzantium*. Washington, 1982.

Mango, C., *Byzantium. The Empire of New Rome*. London, 1980.

Mango, C., ed., *The Oxford History of Byzantium*. Oxford, 2002.

Ostrogorsky, George, *A History of the Byzantine State*, trans. J. Hussey. Oxford, 1968.

Treadgold, W. T., *A History of the Byzantine State and Society*. Stanford, CA, 1997.

THE EARLY BYZANTINE PERIOD (306–717)

Brown, Peter, *The World of Late Antiquity*. London, 1971.

Haldon, H. F., *Byzantium in the Seventh Century: The Transformation of a Culture*. Cambridge, 1990.

Jones, A. H. M., *The Later Roman Empire: A Social, Economic, and Administrative Survey*. 3 vols. Oxford, 1964.

Kaegi, W. E., Jr., *Heraclius, Emperor of Byzantium*. Cambridge, 2002.

Whittow, Mark, *The Making of Byzantium, 600–1025*. Berkeley, 1996.

THE MIDDLE BYZANTINE PERIOD (717–1204)

Angold, M., *The Byzantine Empire, 1025–1204. A Political History*, 2nd edn. London, 1997.

Brand, C. M., *Byzantium Confronts the West, 1180–1204*. Cambridge, MA, 1968.

Hill, B., *Imperial Women in Byzantium, 1025–1204. Power, Patronage and Ideology*. London, 1999.

Lilie, R.-J., *Die byzantinische Reaktion auf die Ausbreitung der Araber*. Munich, 1976.

Stephenson, P., *Byzantium's Balkan Frontier. A Political Study of the Northern Balkans, 900–1204*. Cambridge, 2000.

Stephenson, P., *The Legend of Basil the Bulgar-Slayer*. Cambridge, 2003.

THE LATE BYZANTINE PERIOD (1204–1453)

Angold, M., *A Byzantine Government in Exile: Government and Society under the Laskarids of Nicaea (1204–1261)*. Oxford, 1975.

Bartusis, M. C., *The Late Byzantine Army: Arms and Society, 1204–1453*. Philadelphia, 1992.

Lock, P., *The Franks in the Aegean, 1204–1500*. London, 1995.

Nicol, D. M., *The Last Centuries of Byzantium, 1261–1453*, 2nd edn. Cambridge: Cambridge University Press 1993.

Runciman, S., *The Fall of Constantinople 1453*. Cambridge, 1965.

SOCIETY AND ECONOMY

Brown, Peter, *The Body and Society: Men, Women and Sexual Renunciation in Early Christianity*. New York, 1988.

Dalby, A., *Flavours of Byzantium: The Cuisine of a Legendary Empire*. Totnes, 2003.

Harvey, A., *Economic Expansion in the Byzantine Empire, 900–1200*. Cambridge, 1989.

Hendy, M. F., *Studies in the Byzantine Monetary Economy c.300–1450*. Cambridge, 1985.

Laiou-Thomadakis, Angeliki, *Peasant Society in the Late Byzantine Empire: A Social and Demographic Study*. Princeton, NJ, 1977.

Lemerle, P., *The Agrarian History of Byzantium*. Galway, 1979.

Miller, T. S., *The Birth of the Hospital in the Byzantine Empire*. Baltimore, MD, 1985.

Miller, T. S., *The Orphans of Byzantium: Child Welfare in the Christian Empire*. Washington, 2003.

Ringrose, K. M., *The Perfect Servant: Eunuchs and the Social Construction of Gender in Byzantium*. Chicago, 2003.

BYZANTINE WOMEN

Elm, S., *Virgins of God: The Making of Asceticism in Late Antiquity*. Oxford, 1994.

Garland, L., *Byzantine Empresses: Women and Power in Byzantium AD 527–1204*. London, 1999.

Hill, B., *Imperial Women in Byzantium 1025–1204. Power, Patronage, and Ideology*. New York, 1999.

Holum, K. G., *Theodosian Empresses: Women and Imperial Domination in Late Antiquity*. Berkeley, CA, 1982.

McClanan, A., *Representations of Early Byzantine Empresses: Image and Empire*. New York, 2002.

Nicol, D. M., *The Byzantine Lady: Ten Portraits, 1250–1500*. Cambridge, 1994.

Talbot, A.-M., *Women and Religious Life in Byzantium*. Aldershot, 2001.

BALKANS: BYZANTIUM AND THE SLAVS

Fine, John V. A., *The Early Medieval Balkans: A Critical Survey from the Sixth to the Late Twelfth Century*. Ann Arbor, MI, 1983.

Fine, John V. A., *The Late Medieval Balkans. A Critical Survey from the Late Twelfth Century to the Ottoman Conquest*. Ann Arbor, MI, 1987.

Obolensky, Dimitri, *The Byzantine Commonwealth. Eastern Europe, 500–1453*. London, 1974.

Runciman, Steven, *A History of the First Bulgarian Empire*. London, 1930.

RELIGION, THEOLOGY, AND THE CHURCH

Constantelos, D. J., *Byzantine Philanthropy and Social Welfare*. New Brunswick, NJ, 1968.

Cutler, A., *The Aristocratic Psalters in Byzantium*. Paris, 1984.

Cutler, A., *The Hand of the Master: Craftsmanship, Ivory, and Society in Byzantium (9th–11th Centuries)*. Princeton, NJ, 1994.

Frend, W. H. C., *The Rise of the Monophysite Movement*. Cambridge, 1972.

Hussey, J. M., *The Orthodox Church in the Byzantine Empire*. Oxford, 1986.

Lossky, V., *The Mystical Theology of the Eastern Church*. Cambridge, 1957.

Meyendorff, J., *Byzantine Theology: Historical Trends and Doctrinal Themes*. New York, 1974.

Speake, Graham, *Mount Athos: Renewal in Paradise*. New Haven and London, 2002.

INTELLECTUAL HISTORY

Beck, H.-G., *Kirche und theologische Literatur im byzantinischen Reich*. Munich, 1959.

Beck, H.-G., *Geschichte der byzantinischen Volksliteratur*. Munich, 1971.

Cameron, Alan, *The Greek Anthology from Meleager to Planudes*. Oxford, 1993.

Dvornik, F., *Early Christian and Byzantine Political Philosophy*, 2 vols. Washington, 1966.

Kazhdan, A., and Λ. Epstein, *Change in Byzantine Culture in the Eleventh and Twelfth Centuries*. Berkeley, CA, 1985.

Lemerle, P., *Le premier humanisme byzantin*. Paris, 1971.

Treadgold, W., *The Byzantine Revival, 780–842*. Stanford, CA, 1988.

Wilson, N. G., *Scholars of Byzantium*. Baltimore, MD, 1983.

ART AND ARCHAEOLOGY

Cormack, R., ed., *The Byzantine Eye. Studies in Art and Patronage*. London, 1968.

Cormack, R., *Writing in Gold: Byzantine Society and its Icons*. Oxford, 1985.

Curcic, Slobodan, *Gracanica: King Milutin's Church and its Place in Late Byzantine Architecture*. University Park, PA, 1979.

Kitzinger, E., *Byzantine Art in the Making*. Cambridge, MA, 1977.

R. Krautheimer, *Early Christian and Byzantine Architecture*, 4th edn. Harmondsworth, 1986.

Maguire, H., *Art and Eloquence in Byzantium*. Princeton, NJ, 1981.

Maguire, H., *The Icons and their Bodies: Saints and their Images in Byzantium*. Princeton, NJ, 1996.

Mango, C., *Byzantine Architecture*. New York, 1970.

Mathews, T. F., *The Clash of Gods: A Reinterpretation of Early Christian Art*. Princeton, NJ, 1993.

Mathews, T. F., *The Early Churches of Constantinople: Architecture and Liturgy*. University Park, PA, 1971.

Ousterhout, R. G., ed., *The Blessings of Pilgrimage*. Urbana, IL, 1990.

Ousterhout, R. G., *Master Builders of Byzantium*. Princeton, NJ, 1999.

Parani, M. G., *Reconstructing the Reality of Images: Byzantine Material Culture and Religious Iconography (11th–15th centuries)*. Leiden, 2003.

Rodley, Lyn, *Cave Monasteries of Byzantine Cappadocia*. Cambridge, 1985.

Rodley, Lyn, *Byzantine Art and Architecture: An Introduction*. Cambridge, 1994.

A Selection of Primary Sources in English Translation

Note: This is only a very select list of the many translations of Byzantine sources. Many more can be found in collections such as the *Select Library of Nicene and Post-Nicene Fathers*, many translations of patristic texts, and increasingly online at sites such as the Internet Medieval Sourcebook and the New Advent site of the Catholic Encyclopedia. A useful, although increasingly outdated list of translated sources is Emily Albu Hanawalt, *An Annotated Bibliography of Byzantine Sources in English Translation*. Brookline, MA, 1988

Barbaro, Nicolò, *Diary of the Siege of Constantinople*, trans. J. R. Jones. New York, 1969.

Choniates, Niketas, *O City of Byzantium. Annals of Niketas Choniates*, trans. Harry J. Magoulias. Detroit, 1984.

Chronicon Paschale. *Chronicon Paschale 284–628 AD*, trans. M. and M. Whitby. Liverpool, 1989.

Constantine Porphyrogenitus, Treatises on Military Expeditions. *Constantine Porphyrogenitus. Three Treatises on Imperial Military Expeditions*, ed. J. F. Haldon. Vienna, 1990.

Digenes Akritas. *Digenes Akritas, trans. John Mavrogordato*. Oxford, 1956, reprint 1999; *Digenis Akritis. The Grottaferrata and Escorial Versions*, trans. Elizabeth Jeffries. Cambridge, 1998.

Doukas. *Decline and Fall of Byzantium to the Ottoman Turk*, trans. H. J. Magoulias. Detroit, 1975.

Evagrios Scholastikos. *The Ecclesiastical History of Evagrius Scholasticus*, trans. M. Whitby. Liverpool, 2000.

Eusebios, Ticennial Oration. H. A. Drake, *In Praise of Constantine: A Historical Study and New Translation of Eusebius' Tricennial Oration*. Berkeley, CA, 1976.

Farmer's Law. W. Ashburner, "The Farmer's Law," *Journal of Hellenic Studies* 30 (1910), 85–108.

John Lydus. A. C. Bandy, *Ioannes Lydus On Powers or the Magistracies of the Roman State*. Philadelphia, 1983.

Kinnamos, John, *Deeds of John and Manuel Comnenus*, trans. Charles M. Brand. Records of Civilization Sources and Studies 95. New York, 1976.

Komnena, Anna. *The Alexiad of the Princess Anna Comnena*, trans. E. A. S. Dawes. London, 1928.

Leo of Synada. *The Correspondence of Leo, Metropolitan of Synada and Syncellus.*, ed. and trans. M. P. Vinson. Washington, DC, 1985.

Liudprand of Cremona. *The Works of Liudprand of Cremona*, trans. F. A. Wright. London, 1930.

Malalas, John. *Chronicle of John Malalas*, trans. E. Jeffreys, M. Jeffreys, et al. Melbourne, 1986.

Mauropous, Ioannes. *The Letters of Ioannes Mauropous Metropolitan of Euchaita*, ed. and trans. A. Karpozilos. Thessaloniki, 1990.

Menander. *The History of Menander the Guardsman*, trans. G. Blockley. Liverpool, 1985.

Nikephoros, Patriarch of Constantinople. Cyril Mango, *Nikiphoros, Patriarch of Constantinople: Short History*. Washington, DC, 1990.

Palamas, Gregory. *Saint Gregory Palamas. The One Hundred and Fifty Chapters*, ed. R. E. Sinkewicz. Toronto, 1988.

Parastaseis Syntomoi Chronikai. Averil Cameron and J. Herrin, *Constantinople in the Early Eighth Century: The Parastaseis Syntomoi Chronikai*. Leiden, 1984.

Prokopios of Caesarea. *Procopius*, ed. and trans. Averil Cameron and H. B. Dewing. 7 vols. Cambridge, MA, 1968–79. (Many other translations available)

Psellos, Michael. E. R. A. Sewter, *Fourteen Byzantine Rulers: The Chronographia of Michael Psellus*. Harmondsworth, 1966.

Simokatta. M. and M. Whitby, *The History of Theophylact Simocatta*. Oxford, 1986.

Sphrantzes, George. *A Contemporary Greek Source for the Siege of Constantinople 1453: The Sphrantzes Chronicle*, trans. M. Carroll. Amsterdam, 1985; *The Fall of the Byzantine Empire: A Chronicle by George Sphrantzes, 1401–1477*, trans. M. Philippides. Amherst, MA, 1980.

Theophanes. *The Chronicle of Theophanes Confessor. Byzantine and Near Eastern History AD 284–810*, trans. C. Mango and R. Scott. Oxford, 1997.

Three Byzantine Saints. *Three Byzantine Saints*, trans. E. A. S. Dawes and N. H. Baynes. Oxford, 1948.

Timarion. Barry Baldwin, *Timarion*. Detroit, 1984.

BYZANTINE EMPERORS

467–472	Anthemius
472	Olybrius
473–474	Glycerius
474–475	Julius Nepos
475–476	Romulus "Augustulus"

395	PARTITION – EASTERN EMPIRE

Dynasty of Theodosios

395–408	Arcadius
408–450	Theodosios II
450–457	Marcian

Dynasty of Leo

457–474	Leo I
474	Leo II
474–491	Zeno
491–518	Anastasios

Dynasty of Justinian

518–527	Justin
527–565	Justinian I
565–578	Justin II
578–582	Tiberius II
582–602	Maurice
602–610	Phocas

Dynasty of Herakleios

610–641	Herakleios
641–668	Konstans II
668–685	Constantine IV
685–695	Justinian II (exiled)
695–698	Leontios
698–705	Tiberios III
705–711	Justinian II (restored)
(no dynasty)	
711–713	Philippikos
713–716	Anastasios II
716–717	Theodosios III

Isaurian Dynasty

717–741	Leo III the Isaurian
741–775	Constantine V Kopronymos
775–780	Leo IV
780–797	Constantine VI
797–802	Irene
802–811	Nikephoros I
811	Stavrakios
811–813	Michael I Rangabe
813–820	Leo V the Armenian

Amorian Dynasty
820–829   Michael II the Amorian
829–842   Theophilos
842–867   Michael III

Macedonian Dynasty
867–886   Basil I the Macedonian
886–912   Leo VI the Wise
912–913   Alexander
912–959   Constantine VII Porphyrogenitos
919–944   Romanus I Lekapenos
959–963   Romanus II
963–1025 Basil II Bulgaroktonos and Constantine VIII
963   Regency of Theophano (widow of Romanus II)
963–969   Nicephorus II Phocas
969–976   John I Tzimiskes
1025–1028 Constantine VIII
1028–1034 Romanus III Argyros
1034–1041 Michael IV the Paphlagonian
1041–1042 Michael V Kalaphates
1042   Zoe and Theodora
1042–1055 Constantine IX Monomachos
1055–1056 Theodora alone
1056–1057 Michael VI Stratiotikos

Prelude to Komnenoi
1057–1059 Isaac I Komnenos (abdicated)
1059–1067 Constantine X Doukas
1067–1071 Romanus IV Diogenes
1071–1078 Michael VII Doukas
1078–1081 Nicephorus III Votaniates

Dynasty of the Komnenoi
1081–1118 Alexios I Komnenos
1118–1143 John II Komenos
1143–1180 Manuel I Komnenos
1180–1183 Alexios II
1183–1185 Andronikos I

Dynasty of the Angeloi
1185–1195 Isaac II Angelos
1195–1203 Alexios III Angelos
1203–1204 Isaac II and Alexios IV
1204   Alexios IV
[LATIN EMPIRE from 1204 to 1261]

Empire of Nicaea
1204–1222 Theodore I Laskaris
1222–1254 John III Doukas Vatatzes

1254–1258   Theodore II Laskaris
1258–1261   John IV Laskaris

Dynasty of the Palaiologoi
1259–1282   Michael VIII Palaiologos
[1261, RECAPTURE OF CONSTANTINOPLE]
1282–1328   Andronikos II
1293–1320   Michael IX
[Period of anarchy]
1328–1341   Andronikos III
1341–1376   John V
1341–1354   John VI Kantakouzenos
1376–1379   Andronikos IV
1379–1391   John V (restored)
1390   John VII
1391–1425   Manuel II
1425–1448   John VIII
1449–1453   Constantine XI Dragatses Palaiologos
[1453, CAPTURE OF CONSTANTINOPLE BY MEHMED II]

Selected Foreign Rulers

Serbia
ca. 1166–1196   Stefan Nemanja
1196–ca. 1228   Stefan the First-Crowned
1243–1276   Stefan Uroš I
1276–1282   Stefan Dragutin
1282–1321   Stefan Uroš II Milutin
1321–1331   Stefan Uroš III Decamski
1331–1355   Stefan Uroš IV Dušan
1355–1371   Stefan Uroš V Nejaki

Ottoman Sultans
1288–1326   Osman
1326–1362   Orchan
1362–1389   Murad I
1389–1402   Beyezid I
1402–1421   Mehmed I
1421–1451   Murad II
1451–1481   Mehmed II

Index

Note: This index seeks to help the reader find the most important references for the most useful terms. The emperors are generally introduced in chronological order, and it is easy to find them by using the table of contents; therefore, only a few of the more important emperors appear in this index. Finally, there are no references to the terms listed in the glossary, since they are easy to locate. Individuals are commonly listed here by their first name, in part because their "last name" is frequently an epithet rather than a true family name; there are, however, some exceptions, when an individual seems more generally to be known by his or her family name.